Please remember that this is a library book,
and that it belongs only temporarily to each
person who uses it. Be considerate. Do
not write in this, or any, library book.

Social Change and Modernity

EDITED BY

Hans Haferkamp and Neil J. Smelser

UNIVERSITY OF CALIFORNIA PRESS

Berkeley   Los Angeles   Oxford

University of California Press
Berkeley and Los Angeles, California

University of California Press, Ltd.
Oxford, England

Library of Congress Cataloging-in-Publication Data

Social change and modernity / edited by Hans Haferkamp and Neil J. Smelser.
    p.   cm.
    Includes bibliographical references and index.
ISBN 0-520-06554-9 (alk. paper). — ISBN 0-520-06828-9 (pbk. : alk. paper)
1. Social change.   2. Social history—Modern, 1500– .   3. Civilization,
Modern.   I. Haferkamp, Hans, 1939– .   II. Smelser, Neil J.
HM101.S6915   1991
303.4—dc20

                                                           91-18642
                                                           CIP

Printed in the United States of America
9 8 7 6 5 4 3 2 1

CONTENTS

INTRODUCTION

Hans Haferkamp and Neil J. Smelser

1. SOCIAL CHANGE AND MODERNITY

Those who organized the conference on which this volume is based—including the editors—decided to use the terms "social change" and "modernity" as the organizing concepts for this project. Because these terms enjoy wide usage in contemporary sociology and are general and inclusive, they seem preferable to more specific terms such as "evolution," "progress," "differentiation," or even "development," many of which evoke more specific mechanisms, processes, and directions of change. Likewise, we have excluded historically specific terms such as "late capitalism" and "industrial society" even though these concepts figure prominently in many of the contributions to this volume. The conference strategy called for a general statement of a metaframework for the study of social change within which a variety of more specific theories could be identified.

2. THEORIES OF SOCIAL CHANGE

Change is such an evident feature of social reality that any social-scientific theory, whatever its conceptual starting point, must sooner or later address it. At the same time it is essential to note that the ways social change has been identified have varied greatly in the history of thought. Furthermore, conceptions of change appear to have mirrored the histori-

Haferkamp is grateful to Angelika Schade for her fruitful comments and her helpful assistance in editing this volume and to Geoff Hunter for translating the first German version of parts of the Introduction; Smelser has profited from the research assistance and critical analyses given by Christan Joppke.

1

cal realities of different epochs in large degree. In his essay for this volume Giesen shows that even though ideas of time existed and evolved over thousands of years—ranging from the identification of time as a period of action and a period of living to the differentiation of time according to hierarchical position (the gods are eternal; empires rise, prosper, and fall; humans have a finite lifespan), to the conception of time as progress—stability and order were the norm and changes were exceptional. But in more recent centuries the dominant conceptions of change itself have changed. Social change as a concept for comprehending a continual dynamic in social units became salient during the French Revolution and the industrial revolution in England, both periods of extraordinary dynamism. Comprehensive change became normal, and, accordingly, social philosophers and later sociologists gradually replaced the older ideas of natural constants and the contractual constructions of natural and rational order with conceptions of social change, even though precise formulations were slow to appear. For these thinkers social change was "a property of social order, known as change" (Luhmann 1984, 471). Moreover, in the midst of change observers began to look in retrospect to the dramatic changes that had occurred in earlier epochs, for example, in the development of the Egyptian Empire or the Western Roman Empire.

Contemporary theories of social change have become more generalized in order to explain far-reaching processes of change in past and present. In a review of contemporary theories of change Hermann Strasser and Susan C. Randall have identified the following attributes for these changes: "magnitude of change, time span, direction, rate of change, amount of violence involved" (1981, 16). In our view any theory of change must contain three main elements that must stand in definite relation to one another:

1. Structural determinants of social change, such as population changes, the dislocations occasioned by war, or strains and contradictions.
2. Processes and mechanisms of social change, including precipitating mechanisms, social movements, political conflict and accommodation, and entrepreneurial activity.
3. Directions of social change, including structural changes, effects, and consequences.

Graphically, these may be arranged as follows:

| Structural determinants | $\longrightarrow$ | Processes and mechanisms | $\longrightarrow$ | Directions and consequences |

Even this rendition of the metaframework for models of change is overly simple, for among the structural determinants of different processes of social change are the accumulated consequences of previous sequences of change.

Wiswede and Kutsch (1978, vii) argue that although "the analysis of social change represents the touchstone of sociology," it "obviously still appears to be underdeveloped today." The editors accept this judgment and advance two reasons for it. The first reason is that despite the evident fact that comprehensive social changes cannot be explained by monocausal theories, such theories still survive in one form or another: cultural emanationist theories, materialist theories, and more specific examples such as the explanation of social changes by the size and composition of the population of a society (Cipolla 1978) or by changes in key actors' attitudes (Opp 1976). Such theories generally break down when confronted with explaining unexpected changes or when they are used for predicting or forecasting. The second reason for the underdevelopment of the study of social change is that those who accept the necessity of multicausal explanations face a formidable task in arranging the great arsenal of determinants, mechanisms, processes, and consequences into sufficiently complex interactive and predictive models. Simple theories are easier to create but are more likely to be inadequate, whereas complex theories are more likely to be realistic but are more difficult to construct formally.

Another point of tension in the scientific study of social change is that between the striving for general theories and the carrying out of specialized studies dealing with certain societies and certain periods of time. Certainly the more comprehensive theories of the sociological masters still survive and inform the research of many scholars, even though the focus of these scholars has become more limited. Examples of the more focused study of changes in economic structure and stratification are found in the contributions of Goldthorpe, Haferkamp, and Münch to this volume; examinations of changes in political and social structures are found in the contributions of Touraine and Eyerman.

This volume strikes a kind of balance between comprehensiveness and specialization. Although the contributors and editors have kept in mind Wilbert E. Moore's cautionary words about "the myth of a singular theory of change" (Moore 1963, 23), we have nonetheless been able to organize the volume around some general themes in the contemporary study of social change. These themes are the persistence of evolutionary thought, structural differentiation and cultural change, theories of modernity, modernity and new forms of social movements, modernity and social inequality, and international and global themes. This introduction takes up these themes in the order listed.

2.1. Developments in the Paradigm of Evolutionary Theory

The lasting attractiveness of the paradigm of evolutionary theory in sociology is a remarkable phenomenon given the controversial history of this perspective in sociology. In very recent times, however, it has been less the evolutionary writings of Spencer (*The Study of Sociology* [1872], *Principles of Sociology* [1876–96]) than those of Darwin that have provided the models for sociologists (Giesen 1980, 10–11; Luhmann, this volume; Giesen, this volume). Recent evidence of the continuing vitality of the evolutionary perspective is found, among North American sociologists, in the works of Talcott Parsons (1961, 1966, 1967, 1971a, 1977), Neil J. Smelser (1959, 1976), and Gerhard Lenski (1970, 1976) and among West German sociologists, in the theories of Jürgen Habermas (1976, 1981) and Niklas Luhmann (1984). The work of Shmuel N. Eisenstadt (1970, 1976) shows a similar influence.

These evolutionary conceptions have not been without their critics. Parsons's emphasis on evolution as an increase of adaptability, that is, the capacity to control and gain greater independence from the environment, has come under attack from a variety of sources (Granovetter 1979; Schmid 1981, 1982; Luhmann 1984). This line of criticism stresses the apparent teleology of Parsons's formulation and his failure to explain the structural prerequisites that are presumably necessary for further evolution. West German neoevolutionary thought has also come in for its share of critical reactions (on Habermas, see Berger 1982; Schmid 1981; Honneth and Joas 1986. On Luhmann, see Haferkamp and Schmid 1987). One particular line of criticism of Habermas's work is that it is too normative and not sufficiently explanatory in its force: "He fails to give a plausible reason why a rise in the capability for moral reflection should in all cases cause a rise in the adaptability of a social formation" (Schmid 1981, 29). In this volume Goldthorpe, impatient with the generalities of both classical evolutionary theory and Marxist thought, echoes Popper's (1944–45, 1945) still-pertinent criticism.

Despite these critical responses, evolutionary theory—or at least selected aspects of it—continues to reappear. In this volume a number of authors (Luhmann, Eder, and Hondrich) take up evolutionary questions directly. Other authors, who are more closely identified with either systems theory or conflict theory (Giesen, Smelser, and Eisenstadt), also touch on evolutionary issues. Thus, Eder, although mainly looking at societal contradictions, also asks about the evolutionary functions of contradictions.

Looking at the contributions to this volume that take up evolutionary themes in terms of the metaframework sketched above, it is possible to identify the following elements: triggering mechanisms for change, sustaining mechanisms for change, the end state of change (directionality), and the change process considered as a whole.

1. Triggering mechanisms. In addition to the various internal mechanisms (such as technology, cultural lags, and contradictions), Smelser suggests that "intersocietal relations" be systematically included as triggering mechanisms. Eder focuses on contradictions and treats them as "mechanisms [that] initiate or continue communication." Communication, in turn, initiates sequences of change. In a related formulation Eisenstadt identifies "structural variety" in societies, which is a breeding ground for conflicts. And in the most unorthodox formulation Luhmann develops the notion of "improbability." In an earlier formulation Luhmann (1984) criticized Parsons's and other neoevolutionary theories on the basis that they did not specify a process but simply defined the requirements for structural development. By contrast, Luhmann argues that, when viewed retrospectively, all developments are improbable in that they could not have been explained by prior existing determinants (for example, the distribution of power or wealth). Changes are, rather, the product of what Luhmann calls autopoiesis, that is, the tendency for self-production in social systems. Luhmann thus departs from the traditional causal assumptions of evolutionary theory and builds a high degree of indeterminacy—summarized by the phrase "the improbability of the probable"—into his conception of change. Eder also introduces the notion of liberty and improbability into his perspective on change but not in such a central way.

2. Sustaining mechanisms. The contributors to this volume develop many such mechanisms by making reference to biological analogies. Hondrich considers differentiation and segmentation to be "two opposing yet collaborative principles of evolution, the former representing the dynamic, innovative, expanding and risky aspect of evolution, the latter standing for preservation, stability, and a reduction of risks." Eder works out an elaborate classification of mechanisms for his three stages (variation, selection, and stabilization), involving learning processes within groups, classification struggles, and conflicts between society and environment. Again striking a note of indeterminacy, Luhmann regards the sustaining mechanisms for change as autopoiesis, that is, as self-referential systems permanently producing themselves and heading into an open-ended future.

3. Directionality. The contributors range across the board with respect to the determinacy of the end states of change. Eder speaks of a telos

(of contradictions), the aim of which "is to reproduce communication. . . . This ongoing stream of communication constitutes social reality as being something in flux, as something always in change." On the level of moral ideas Eder works on the "assumption of an evolutionary change in moral consciousness which was evoked by the initial dissolution of the religious basis of morality in the sixteenth century" (1985, 10). At this level telos signifies the development of a morality based on the autonomy of the subject and is thus reminiscent of Piaget's and Kohlberg's conceptions of moral development. Hondrich, using a traditional biological analogy, finds directionality in the "interests of evolution," which are primarily those of survival. Luhmann appears to replace his earlier emphasis on the directionality found in "differentiation," "complexity," or even "progress" with a directionality that is more improbable. Smelser, who in an earlier (1959) formulation stressed both differentiation and complexity as lending directionality, is now more skeptical about very general statements concerning evolutionary goals or directions. Eisenstadt argues against positing any directionality toward modernization on the basis of prior structural properties—calling them merely "necessary conditions of modernization"—and argues that the fortuitous intervention of elites is necessary to create modern social structures. Finally, Giesen considers that the notion of directed development is wholly inappropriate.

4. Overall process. One of the features of contemporary evolutionary theory is that even though traditional models of development survive, there is also a preoccupation with pathology, paradox, decay, and dissolution as well as with growth (Elias 1985). Although Hondrich relies mainly on functionalist theories of differentiation and acknowledges the increases in size and efficiency accompanying differentiation, he also sees an increasing homogeneity in society and points to various threats posed to society by functional differentiation. Extreme differentiation, for example, is always accompanied by the development of a substratum of black markets, informal groups, and secret networks. Eder also points to pathologies in the evolutionary process that generally lead to a higher level of morality. Luhmann's stress on "backward developments" and Giesen's insistence that both emergence and decay are present in any social process also underscore the more pessimistic flavor of the most recent evolutionary models.

2.2. Patterns of Structural and Cultural Change

Among the most persistent themes that appear in the evolutionist and neoevolutionist literature are those of differentiation, integration, conflict, and, in particular, the relationship among these. The notion of differentiation (or specialization) was central in the work of Adam Smith, Karl Marx, Herbert Spencer, and Emile Durkheim. The same notion informs the work of a number of contemporary theorists, notably Parsons. Yet both the causes and consequences of social differentiation remain unclear; they are explored by many of the contributors to this volume.

One way of organizing existing thought on structural differentiation is to trace the ways in which this phenomenon has been related to both integration and conflict. In the theories of Adam Smith and Herbert Spencer differentiation was regarded as a fundamental principle of change, but the integration of specialized activities was not problematic in their theories because it was regarded as a result that emerged from the aggregation of voluntary exchanges in society. Differentiation (the division of labor) also played a central role in the theories of Karl Marx and Emile Durkheim. Marx posited contradictions, conflicts, and ultimate disintegration as arising from the differentiation of economic and social positions in economic systems. Durkheim stressed the need for positive integration in a differentiated society if anomie and conflict were not to become endemic. In his contribution to this volume, Alexander acknowledges the power of Durkheim's theory of differentiation but finds shortcomings in its naive evolutionary assumptions and its mechanistic quality.

One of the most comprehensive theories of differentiation is that of Parsons, who laid great stress on the adaptive upgrading that is attained through greater specialization of roles, organizations, and institutions. Yet this very focus on the functional consequences of differentiation, Alexander notes, perhaps diverted Parsons from a closer focus on "the actual processes by which that new and more differentiated institution actually came about." This lack of attention to mechanisms was the focus of earlier criticism of Parsons's efforts (Lockwood 1956; Dahrendorf 1955, 1958) and is at the center of Alexander's criticisms of both Durkheim's and Parsons's theories of differentiation. The stress on functionally positive consequences may harbor a certain apologetic note, even an "ideological patina." The works of Smelser (1959), Eisenstadt (1969), Bellah (1970), and Luhmann (1982) have constituted something of a corrective in that they have stressed mechanisms and processes more and positive functionalist aspects less. But the dynamics of structural differentiation are still not fully understood.

The focus on structural causes and mechanisms of differentiation is found in Alexander's contribution to this volume. He argues that to improve the theory of differentiation, it is "necessary [to have] . . . a more phase-specific model of general differentiation and of social process alike." Here Alexander focuses on the key role of war and conflict.

He argues that the theory of differentiation has as yet been unable to incorporate the notions of "political repression," "ferocious violence," "oppression," and "war." By distinguishing between polarization and differentiation on the one hand and various historical situations on the other, Alexander works toward a scheme that will more readily incorporate processes of change such as revolution, reform, and reaction. One advantage of his formulation is that it proposes a reciprocal relationship between conflict, conquest, and repression on the one hand and processes of differentiation on the other. Each set of variables plays a central causal role in the development of the others. In related formulations Eder regards conflict as a starting mechanism of social change through variation, and Eyerman's analysis begins with societal conflict.

This focus on conflict brings to mind the Marxist heritage of differentiation as the source of the contradictions that destabilize and ultimately destroy a society. Lockwood's and Dahrendorf's criticisms of Parsons's formulations of the positive relation between differentiation and integration pushed both of them somewhat in a Marxist direction in that they regarded conflict as the core consequence of differentiation, especially the differentiation of authority. Dahrendorf's current views of social change still echo this position: "Social change is defined in terms of direction and rhythm by that power of unrest for which it is so difficult to find a sufficiently general name, by incompatibility, discord, antagonism, contradiction and resistance, through conflict" (Dahrendorf 1987, 11). Finally, it should be noted that Eisenstadt's insistence on the centrality of group conflict in the development of civilizational change is in keeping with the general thrust noted: the effort to synthesize systematically the conceptions of conflict, differentiation, and integration.

To align these conceptions graphically, we refer the reader to Table 1. The only empty cell in the table is the one representing integration as one of the active causes of differentiation. Little attention has been given to this relationship in the literature on social change. But it is at least plausible to think that a highly integrated society with a legitimate and responsive state might tend to produce orderly structural innovation and differentiation as a response to internal group conflict, whereas a less-integrated system might produce chronic and unresolved group conflict and instability. It might also be supposed that a well-integrated society would be less likely to export its internal conflicts in the form of aggressive wars. Pirenne hinted at this relationship when he contrasted the North European "Hanse" with the Italian republics of Venice, Genoa, and Pisa:

> This confederation of German maritime towns, which forms such a striking contrast to the continual wars of the Italian towns of the Mediterra-

TABLE 1. Differentiation, Conflict, and Integration in Various Theories

		Differentiation
Conflict	causes ⟶	Alexander Eder Eyerman
	is caused by ⟵	(Dahrendorf) (Lockwood) Alexander Eisenstadt
Integration	causes ⟶	
	is caused by ⟵	(Parsons) Eisenstadt

nean, gave them a predominance on all the Northern waters, which they were to keep to the end of the Middle Ages. Thanks to their agreement, they succeeded in holding their own against the attacks launched against them by the kings of Denmark and in promoting their common interests abroad. (Pirenne 1937, 150)

In addition to a rebirth of interest in differentiation, which is a phenomenon primarily at the social-structural level, there has been a revitalization of interest in cultural change and the power of culture as an active determinant of institutional change. This tradition brings to mind above all the work of Max Weber, which established the dynamic power of culture, particularly religion, in social change. For a prolonged time debate raged mainly over whether material factors were fundamental or whether culture could in fact be regarded as having independent significance in change. In more recent times, however, there has been a rediscovery of culture as an independent variable. In West Germany this was epitomized by a special issue in 1979 of the *Kölner Zeitschrift für Soziologie und Sozialpsychologie* titled *Kultursoziologie* (Cultural sociology), which included the articles "Zum Neubeginn der Kultursoziologie" (A fresh start for cultural sociology) by Wolfgang Lipp and Friedrich H. Tenbruck (1979) and "Die Aufgaben der Kultursoziologie" (The tasks of cultural sociology) by Tenbruck (1979). In 1986 a second special issue of this journal was dedicated to the theme of *Culture and Society*. It focused on Jürgen Habermas's writings on the development of morality (1976, 1981) and on revised neo-Marxist approaches to culture. The interest in culture has been revitalized in England and the United States as well, particuarly by Raymond Williams and the Birmingham group, Clifford Geertz, Robert Bellah, and students of the mass media, especially Michael Schudson, Gaye Tuchman, and Todd Gitlin.

In considering cultural change we distinguish between the explanation of cultural change as such and the explanation of other processes of change that refer to culture as a determinant. Most contemporary theoreticians acknowledge that culture should be regarded as an analytically distinct aspect of social life to be analyzed on its own level. But the effort to pursue the study of culture, independently considered, is hampered by the difficulty of coming up with a proper definition of culture and a proper representation of its empirical manifestations. Culture seems to present the analyst with a kind of "elementary diffuseness" (Neidhardt 1986). How can we grasp culture's enormous variety of empirical manifestations and treat it as a totality? How do we deal with the complex and multiple cultures (high culture and folk culture, elite culture and street culture) that are present in all societies? Or should they be considered an unrelated patchwork? These are some of the methodological questions that have troubled students of culture.

Reviewing studies of culture in his contribution to this volume, Wuthnow concludes that the main approach to culture has been psychological, culture as "beliefs and outlooks, . . . moods and motivations." However, he regards this kind of conceptualization as unsatisfactory, particularly when it comes to studying cultural change. As an alternative Wuthnow suggests that culture be defined as "discourse" and other "symbolic acts," with attention being drawn to "speakers and audiences." This definition would be a more sociological one because it stresses the interactive and communicative aspects of culture. It would be one way of extracting common or social beliefs and knowledge (see Eder 1983, 1985; Haferkamp 1985; Miller 1986) and of working toward a conceptualization of mind (*Geist*) as developed in Lévi-Strauss's structuralism.

Wuthnow's approach also has empirical and methodological implications: it looks toward the analysis of "discursive texts, the rituals in which discourse is embedded." Although the study of symbolic acts of speakers and audiences has developed to a degree in the research on small-group discussions (Pollock 1955; Mangold 1962), Wuthnow emphasizes institutional contexts and longer periods of time in the study of texts, debates, rituals, and the discussions created by or taking place in political organizations, religious groups, and even "subversive" organizations and marginal groups (see Haferkamp 1975). Giesen's contribution to this volume adopts this strategy. He assesses texts from various periods in past centuries and draws from them evidence of long-term changes in the cultural modes of thinking about time and the notion of social change. Eisenstadt's conception of the "premises of societies" could be given empirical meaning by the study of similar kinds of texts and rituals that have held a central place in the histories of societies.

One tradition of sociological theory and research has treated cultural change as dependent on changes in the situation of classes, strata, carrier groups, etc. The most evident and perhaps most extreme thread in this tradition is found in the work of Marx and Engels. But it is also found in Durkheim in his view that changes in religion, morality, law, and cultural values such as individualism are rooted in the increasing complexity of society. Wuthnow divides this tradition into two large categories of "cultural adaptation theory" and "class legitimation theory," both of which view cultural change as a response to or result of other types of change. He finds both versions too one-dimensional and general and calls instead for "multifactoral . . . explanations of cultural change . . . considering the specific contexts, processes, and mechanisms that translate broad societal changes into concrete episodes of innovative cultural production."

To put this approach into the terms suggested by our metaframework, the broad conditions emphasized by these theorists can best be placed in the category of "structural determinants." These structural determinants, however, are somewhat nonspecific in character. It is not possible to derive from them the precise processes and mechanisms of cultural change, the patterns of cultural innovation, or the ultimate directions and consequences of cultural change. Such processes, patterns, and consequences result from partially independent dynamics that operate within the broad conditions established by the cultural dimensions. Examples of research that build on this multideterminative model are Cohen (1955), Luhmann (1985), and Chambliss and Seidman (1971). At a more abstract level the programs of Luhmann and Giesen, which stress indeterminacy, improbability, and looser models, underscore the point that patterns of cultural change cannot be derived from general structural preconditions.

Another tradition has treated cultural change itself as a determinant, one that serves as a constant source of pressure for change, a release mechanism for change, or a shaper of social reality. Max Weber is the exemplar of this type of analysis. However, his insistence on the "reciprocal relationship" between religious belief and economic action indicates that cultural changes themselves have social-structural factors among their determinants. Parsons's formulations of change also stress the active role of culture. He emphasizes that differentiation results in a more complex structure of society, which gives rise to new and more general value patterns that are important in guaranteeing stability in a more complex setting (Parsons 1971b, 14ff.). At the same time, however, he puts society's "cultural code" in a position at the top of the hierarchy of social control, "which, . . . is able to control processes of action on a lower level" (Schmid 1982, 185).

Eisenstadt's contribution in particular elaborates this notion of the reciprocal interaction between idea and institution. He stresses that in processes of social change, culture—and ideas in particular—plays an arbitrating role. As a concrete illustration, Eisenstadt takes the cultural ideas of hierarchy and equality and asks how they work out differently in different social settings. Starting from Sombart's question "Why is there no socialism in the United States?" (1976) and adding the question of why socialism has been relatively weak in Japan, he points out the different consequences of equality and hierarchy as values. In the United States the deep institutionalization of the value of equality of opportunity has historically diminished tendencies toward collective class consciousness and the mobilization of political parties on that basis, whereas in Japan the fundamental institutionalization of hierarchy and the relative absence of any notions of equality worked toward the same end. It might be added that it was mainly in the European countries, where the two ideas of hierarchy and equality have existed side by side in uneasy tension, that class-based political action has been more in evidence. Such is the power of fundamental "premises of society."

The editors believe that they see a kind of theoretical convergence, both in the contributions to this volume and in the larger trends in sociological analysis in both Europe and North America. This convergence involves an impatience with and desertion of one-sided models of cultural and social change, whatever their primary emphasis, and an active development of multicausal models that stress reciprocal effects and the cumulative effect of diverse processes of change that are partly independent of one another.

3. THEORIES OF MODERNITY

Among the most conspicuous theories of social change are those that go under the name of "modernity" or "modernization" and include other related terms, such as "development," as well. Yet within this family of theories there are significant differences about whether modernization involves continuity or discontinuity, whether the theorist is relatively optimistic or pessimistic, and whether the "modern" phase of social development has given way to some other era.

Two examples of scholars who have stressed the continuity of development are Weber and Parsons. Weber's description of Occidental rationalism is particularly emphatic on this point, stressing the organizational continuities between such apparently diverse systems as rational bourgeois capitalism and socialism. Parsons posited the constancy of certain values (especially universalistic achievement) in modernization and in a "relatively optimistic" moment forecast that modernity would continue to flourish for another one hundred to two hundred years (Parsons 1971, 141). Others regard the process as involving a somewhat more chaotic picture. In 1883 Charles Baudelaire characterized modernity as half "transitory, volatile, possible" and half "eternal and unchanging" (Baudelaire 1925, 168). Hanns-Georg Brose, following from this viewpoint and from the position of Habermas, has argued that the general characteristic of modernity is "the contradiction between innovation and decay, new and enduring, and also its conservation and treatment of time in the modern experience" (1985, 537).

Most nineteenth-century theories of modernity (although not given that name) were optimistic in character and based on ideas of progress. Although this kind of interpretation has been dampened, some contemporary treatments still retain elements of it. By and large, the theorists who focus on the specific characteristics of "advanced industrial societies" often implicitly assume that capitalism, democracy, the market economy, and a prosperous society will assert themselves and live on (Zapf 1983, 294). A similar optimism appears in Dieter Senghaas (1982). In Senghaas's work there is no trace of the autumn of modernity. Indeed, a feeling of elation persists, the kind that was typical of the European *grande bourgeoisie* in the nineteenth century, that was experienced in the United States during much of the twentieth century, and that has developed in contemporary Japan, whose business leaders are fond of the term "Eurosclerosis."

Some traces of the optimistic view are seen in Calhoun's essay in this volume. He has previously criticized theories of development because they do not offer convincing explanations of continued integration. In this volume he makes an effort to account for integration by referring to the circumstances that others hold responsible for disintegration and conflict, namely, increasingly indirect interpersonal relationships. These relationships are manifested in large-scale markets, corporations (as closely administered organizations), and information technology. They foster the much-discussed secondary relationships. Calhoun, however, goes beyond this to describe "tertiary" and "quaternary" relationships. Tertiary relationships are those in which actors are aware of the physical presence of others, as in the case of the relationship of a district representative to his political constituency. Quaternary relationships, however, "occur outside of the attention and generally of the awareness of at least one of the parties to them," as in communication through mass media. Calhoun regards this as "the extension of social integration to an ever larger scale, yet with greater internal intensity, through reliance on indirect social relationships." The specifc note of optimism is that these integrative tendencies operate as counterdeterminants to conflict and disintegration.

The theoretical literature shows a more pessimistic streak. Weber took a clearly ambivalent stance, recognizing the greater efficiency and rationality of modern capitalism, but also stressing the progressive disenchantment and the constraining influences of the "iron cage." Pessimistic countertendencies to modernity are seen even more clearly in the work of Marx and Engels (1848), who insisted that in the last analysis the destructive tendencies of modern capitalism will prevail. A variety of contemporary theorists, including analysts in the Frankfurt School, who focus on "late capitalism," also foresee the decay, decline, and ultimate fall of modern societies.

Bendix (1979) offers another variant of modernity that tempers Western European rationalism with realism. He notes the loss of the Western feeling of superiority, which had lasted for centuries, and argues that excesses in the developments that brought about modernity are responsible for that loss. With these excesses in mind, Bendix writes that "the harnessing of nuclear power marks the beginning of a scientific and technical development that for the first time in the consciousnesses of many people calls into question the 350-year-old equation that links knowledge with progress" (Bendix 1979, 13). This evaluation is consistent with Bendix's stress on the twofold nature of the value of modernity and his rejection of an exclusively optimistic or pessimistic interpretation.

Above and beyond these different assessments there is general agreement that modernity involves both rapid and all-encompassing change and that the origins of this process go back several centuries. There are, however, some differences in identifying the decisive turning points. Dahrendorf argues that the beginning of modernity can be seen in Erasmus of Rotterdam, whose era fell "between the autumn of the Middle Ages and the first traces of the Protestant ethic and the spirit of capitalism, that is, the turning point of the fifteenth and sixteenth centuries, the key period of the modern world" (1987, 12). Parsons also places the beginning of modernity in the Renaissance and Reformation, but in addition he stresses the salience of the industrial and democratic revolutions and the educational revolution that followed. In his contribution to this volume Eyerman dates the decisive origins of modernity much later. He stresses the impact "of industrialization, urbanization, and political democracy on essentially rural and autocratic societies." More specifically, he identifies the place and time as "Europe in the latter half of the nineteenth century." Bendix also describes modernization as emerging from the changes in the social structures in England and France that were associated with the industrial and political revolutions in these societies. Perhaps these differences in interpretation can be reconciled by indicating that those who identify earlier origins refer more to cultural origins and those who stress later developments emphasize the dramatic changes in social structure.

The issue of the end of modernity and the onset of postmodernity (if, indeed, there has been such an onset) is also a matter of disagreement. Fundamentally, the dispute is over the question of continuity versus discontinuity. Eyerman (this volume) categorizes contemporary Western societies as postmodern, noting that "postmodernity is at once more universalistic (concerned with humanity and nature, women's liberation, and world peace) and more parochial (concerned with local control and self-reliance)." Most of the contributors, however, characterize postmodernity as a process, a special type of social change that did not originate in earlier eras.

The elements of any theory of the process of modernization can usually be identified under the headings of structural determinants, processes and mechanisms, and outcomes. These elements indicate that theories of modernization belong in the category of theories of social change. In his contribution to this volume Berger asserts that modernity cannot be equated with capitalism because capitalism is only one type of modernity. He argues that modernization involves the liberation and increasing autonomy of associations of action in almost all societal areas. Associations have built up the economy, the state, religion, and communities. Then, linking Marx with Luhmann, Berger goes on to argue that the economy, once set free, develops into an autopoietic system. It reproduces itself from the elements it has already produced (capital, wage labor, profit, etc.). This liberated system, however, may devour the prerequisites for its further change by subordinating the environment to economic exploitation. Efforts at ecological preservation through social control and social planning constitute an effort to avert this result. At the same time capitalism is restricted from below by social movements that challenge its autonomous development and ultimate self-destruction. We now turn to these modern (or postmodern) social movements.

3.1. Modernity and New Social Movements

To give salience to social movements in connection with social change and modernity is to give salience to the notion of process. The term "movement" is so close conceptually to the notion of change that the following theoretical possibilities are suggested: either social movements constitute modernity, or they at least make a very large contribution to its appearance. Eyerman suggests the first possibility when he states, "Modernity connotes movement." Elsewhere Touraine has expressed a similar view: modern society is the first type of society to reproduce itself, and new social movements are the decisive force in this process (Touraine 1981).

To speak of "new" social movements is to imply a category of "old" social movements. Those who write in this tradition appear to conceive of old movements as those that were distinctively associated with the class system of industrial capitalism, for example, liberalism and the workers' movements. New movements are those that are less class-based, including the women's movement, various ethnic movements, the ecology movement, the peace movement, and the antistate movement. Conceptually, this distinction creates a few problems. Some of the "new" movements, for example, the women's movement and the peace movement, have very long histories. Also, it is possible to identify various kinds of movements, such as popular uprisings in Rome and religious movements in medieval times and the Reformation, that are older than those identified as "old." This suggests that the distinction between old and new as currently discussed is limited mainly to the distinction between classical industrial capitalism and contemporary industrial (or postindustrial) society.

Be that as it may, the old social movements are commonly seen as representing the struggle for power and control over the organization of living conditions; thus they are perceived as being essentially economic in character. These movements were commonly regarded as threats to the capitalist system. Tenbruck (1981) has argued, for example, that much of Durkheim's sociology reflects an anxiety about the consequences of these kinds of movements and is an effort to find various kinds of social arrangements that could incorporate them into a newly formed society. Although offshoots of these old movements can still be found in various advanced countries, writers making use of the new-social-movement framework consider the old type of social movement to be no longer threatening. Accordingly, as Berger noted in discussion at the conference, "the proletariat has lost its role as privileged actor and subject of historical change." Much of this loss of force (and threat) has been attributed to long periods of increased prosperity, the nullification of many of the impulses of the workers' movement by the policies of the welfare state, and the incorporation of these movements into political parties and the state.

For Touraine modernity means the development of a system of production and distribution of cultural goods that threatens the current cultural self-definition of many actors. These actors anticipate personal and social progress through an increased sense of their own subjectivity, but this subjectivity is threatened because culture is currently being industrially produced and distributed. Subjectivity manifests itself in two ways: as a force of opposition to domination and in the recognition of other individuals as unique people with whom personal relationships can be formed. Thus the new social movements are fighting for "cultural creativity and autonomy and the capacity to act on all aspects of human experience."

Eyerman, although in agreement with many of Touraine's views, does not give such a distinctively modern role to the search for subjectivity. In his estimation, "The development of a new sense of self, of subjectivity and individuality, which distinguishes the modern individual from the traditional one" has been the theme of prior social movements for more than a hundred years. Eyerman regards his own views as belonging to the theoretical tradition represented by Weber, Simmel, and Michels. These scholars studied the "effects of modernity on the individual and the new forms of organization that it entailed." For them modernity meant "new possibilities for the expression of human subjectivity."

In their contributions to this volume, Eyerman and Touraine are in agreement on yet another point: whereas the old social movements concentrate on industrial society and the work process, the new ones are associated with postindustrial society and events outside the work process. But Eyerman characterizes postindustrial society in a different way than Touraine: it involves the expansion of the state, the explosion of the knowledge industry, and the development of the new mass media (the latter being closely involved in Touraine's production of culture). The expansion of the state leads to the politicizing of new areas of social life. This in turn evokes reactions from both the political left and the political right and offers issues for activists in new social movements. The tension between the knowledge industry and corporate and state interests on the one hand and education and knowledge on the other hand produces an additional arena for conflicts and movements. The mass media are instrumental in creating the new social movements and to some degree become part of them.

Both Touraine and Eyerman hold that the new social movements have great potential for shaping the future of modern societies. In their estimation these movements are already proclaiming the characteristics of the social structure that will prevail in the future. In contrast, Eder's contribution regards these movements more critically and describes them as having a more specific class base. Many of the new social movements, he argues, are carried by the petty bourgeoisie who want to protect their life world: "These 'new' social movements try to formulate another way of controlling the professional regulation of society by referring to health, "green" nature, aesthetics, and in general, to the idea of the 'good life.' "

By way of contrast, Tiryakian believes that contemporary social movements are much more in conflict with modernity than do Touraine, Eyerman, and Eder. Youth movements, the counterculture, movements of religious fundamentalism, movements of value rationality (*Wertrationalität*), and movements that involve an ethic of absolute values (*Gesinnungsethik*) all unite in their opposition to modernity. In his contribution to this volume Tiryakian examines the romantic movement since the second half of the eighteenth century and argues that it emerged from the "rejection of one major side of modernity: the seemingly cold, drab, impersonal, anonymous, standardized, rationalized, 'lifeless,' 'technocratic,' industrial order." The romantics subscribed to the view that "seeks and finds, often in the imagination, the creative center of human energy, the potential for altering or conjuring a different order than the industrial one at hand." Tiryakian also regards witchcraft and exotism as expressions of the romantic impulse. These are movements of reenchantment, which in his view are an almost necessary reaction to the disenchantment that characterizes modernity. Tiryakian also examines several movements of dedifferentiation, such as those committed to a *Gesinnungsethik* (including the radical religious movements of the Reformation, the great nationalist movements, and the student movements of the 1960s). He employs the following chain of causality: Differentiation leads to a power hierarchy, which leads to the exclusion of some groups, which leads to dedifferentiation. Finally, like Hondrich, Tiryakian considers that movements of dedifferentiation are not only inhibitors of development but also forces that encourage regeneration and rejuvenation.

3.2. Modernity and Social Inequality

A number of the contributions to this volume take up the reciprocal relations among structured inequality, group contradictions and the conflicts that arise from them, and modernity. These relations are evidently complex. Inequality plays a large role in shaping modernity because it generates class and group conflicts, which become the basis of the institutional invention and innovation that come to constitute the structures of modernity. The increasing proliferation of roles and institutional structures, however, provides an ever-increasing number of structural bases for inequality. Indeed, some have identified distinctive patterns of inequality (such as class, gender, and race) as the fundamental characteristic of modernity. The chapters by Goldthorpe, Haferkamp, and Münch explore these issues.

Goldthorpe's essay is a theoretical and methodological critique. In particular he is impatient with both the historicist and the evolutionary models. His criticisms are common: that these models are often evoked for normative and political purposes and that they continually founder when held to the test of explaining empirical patterns of change. This is not to say that evolutionary concepts such as variation and selection are not fruitful but that they become so only when they can be tested against historical materials. Goldthorpe regards history as a profusion of material, a particularly long sequence of events containing shorter or longer periods that can be evoked and studied to confirm or disconfirm theories of varying levels of generality. The complexity of the theory is related to the historical scope considered.

This approach is consistent with Goldthorpe's focus on a relatively limited set of issues and a limited historical scope: the changes in class structure in modern Western societies since the end of the Second World War. He believes that it is possible to make precise and confirmable statements for this period. Goldthorpe's account finds both the Marxist and liberal generalizations—the one foreseeing the degradation of the working class and an increase in social inequality, the other foreseeing an upgrading of the working class and an equalizing tendency—to be incorrect. His main point is that these and other evolutionist writings (including some in this volume) are too historicist. His methodological focus is on those periods of time, actors, and actions to which the instruments of empirical social research have access. In their chapters Münch and Haferkamp also focus on relatively short periods of time and on a small number of societies. Münch examines developments from the American Revolution up to the present day, Haferkamp from the French Revolution to the present, each examining empirical tendencies in relation to general theories of inequality and modernity.

With respect to the overall diagnosis of patterns of inequality in the contemporary West, we find three general points of view.

1. One group of authors, most of them Marxist-oriented, sees increasing inequality, although they are not in agreement about its structural bases. Braverman (1974), focusing on the labor process in monopoly industry, argues that in the wake of Taylorization labor power (even white-collar labor) is increasingly deskilled and that this process has produced greater proletarianization. Gorz (1982) takes a different line, stressing that the working class is divided between a well-organized core in primary labor markets (characterized by high wages, employment security, and moderate unionism) and a fragmented, nonorganized lumpenproletariat at the periphery of the laboring society which, in the form of "new" social movements, attacks the growth- and security-oriented alliance between labor and capital. It should be noted that the authors in this group look almost exclusively at the labor process.
2. A second group of authors sees enduring or unchanging social inequality. These authors refer to current levels of social inequality as "stable" (Hradil 1983, 192) or even "ultrastable" (Beck 1983, 35). Their claims are based on the fact that the distribution of property and income has not changed more than a few percentage points in the past fifty to a hundred years. Among the contributors to this volume Goldthorpe seems closest to this position when he argues

that neither the Marxist theory of increasing inequality nor the liberal position of a leveling process appears to be substantiated by empirical trends. Although the conditions of the working class in the West have on balance been upgraded more than degraded since the Second World War (with many consequences for income, wealth, and life-style), mass unemployment has persisted since the mid-1970s, if not worsened. As a result equalizing trends have abated.

3. Yet another group of authors observes a tendency toward a reduction in inequality. These voices have been heard for some time: Alexis de Tocqueville, Theodor Geiger, Helmut Schelsky, Talcott Parsons, Norbert Elias, Reinhard Bendix, Otis Dudley Duncan, and Karl Otto Hondrich are among them. Recent empirical studies (for example, Schade 1987) have produced results that are consistent with this position. This argument appears to be most viable when other dimensions of inequality are taken into account, especially political inequality, educational inequality, and the leveling of life-styles. The chapters by Münch and Haferkamp in this volume appear to stress these other dimensions. Münch develops a general model to explain changing levels of equality and inequality. His model is based on Parsons's perspective, in which many different processes of change proceed simultaneously, some working toward equality and some toward inequality. On balance, Münch finds the forces pressing for equality in the United States to be stronger. At the same time, he points out the double tendency in this country, by which both equality and inequality are legitimized: "The conflict between these two positions has been a major factor in hindering the establishment of a societal community properly embracing society as a whole, as opposed to a society breaking apart into different societal groups." Haferkamp stresses leveling tendencies as well. He argues that the masses have increased resources at their disposal and that this improves their potential for achievement. He also identifies a strengthening of the value of equality as an important factor in the leveling process. But above all he stresses the process of negotiation among significant economic and political groups (business, labor, agriculture, and the professions), a process that typically results in leveling compromises, and the continuing access to the centers of political power on the part of these groups.

Many of the apparent confusions and contradictions among these diagnoses of inequality probably stem from the problem of confounding apples and oranges. Different answers will emerge depending on which aspect of inequality—the labor process, the distribution of property and income, social mobility and status attainment, or access to education, power, and prestige—is chosen for focus. In any event, rather than treating the subject of inequality as a unified whole it seems essential to disaggregate the notion into its various dimensions in order to identify the different patterns of inequality and the different mechanisms that determine the character of each.

The metaframework laid out at the beginning of this introduction is applicable to the study of inequality and its changes. With respect to structural conditions and mechanisms, the two great traditions in sociology are the functionalist and the conflict approaches. The functionalist approach stresses cultural (value) determinants and allocative mechanisms; the conflict approach stresses structures of domination and processes of conflict. None of the three chapters on inequality in this volume falls conveniently under either of these headings. Münch lists twelve factors—half working toward greater inequality, half toward greater equality—but these cannot be regarded as "factors" in the strong causal sense. Rather they are parts of complex networks of facilitating and discouraging forces. Haferkamp's approach is rooted more explicitly in the theory of action. It begins with the actors—elites and masses in particular—and views these actors as producing resources and values, both intentionally and unintentionally. These resources and values become the starting-points that define the production and distribution of services and power. Goldthorpe's theoretical approach is least explicit, but it appears to be more nearly structural (stressing unemployment, the welfare state, etc.), giving little attention to the cultural factors that inform the contributions of both Münch and Haferkamp. But all three contributors appear to be in fundamental agreement on two related assumptions: First, the determinants of inequality are multiple and must be combined in complex, interactive explanatory models. Second, the interplay between structural conditions and carriers (elites, interest groups, etc.) in the processes that produce stability or changes in social inequality is complex.

With respect to directions and effects, we refer the reader to the previous discussion of the three groups of thought about the directions of change in social inequality as well as the discussion of the new social movements, which have arisen out of the distinctive patterns of inequality associated with postindustrialism or postmodernity.

3.3. International and Global Themes

Modernity is characterized by more than new values, new institutional structures, new patterns of inequality, and new social movements. Because the societies of the world are growing increasingly interdependent along economic, political, and cultural lines, modernity is also characterized by increasing globalization and internationalization. Of course this process is variable. Some societies (Hondrich's "niche societies") are relatively isolated from external influences, but others, whose fortunes are tied to other societies by trade, economic penetration, and international conflict, are deeply enmeshed in the international system. Different groups in society are differentially involved in the international world. For example, the worlds of some bankers, politicians, scientists, scholars, and sports celebrities are mainly international in character.

Although world–national society relationships have become increasingly salient over the past two centuries, social scientists have been relatively slow in explicitly incorporating these relationships into their analyses in systematic ways. Of course the names of Adam Smith, Karl Marx, Vladimir Lenin, Franz Boas, and Max Weber come to mind as exceptions to this generalization. But up to around 1950 mainstream sociology focused almost exclusively on national societies and their institutional and group life.

After 1950, however, interest in global society and the international system increased. The voices of Stein Rokkan and Niklas Luhmann in Europe and Talcott Parsons in the United States should be mentioned in this regard. In the late 1960s and early 1970s dependency theory (Cardoso 1969) and world-system theory (Wallerstein 1974) further crystallized and advanced this perspective. In 1987 Norbert Elias stated that sociology today is now possible only as a sociology of world society. In his other work (1956, 1985) Elias joins many political scientists in focusing on the relations among the United States, the Soviet Union, and the societies dependent on them. In a complex, multidimensional analysis Elias argues that the world scope of battles among dominant power groups has become larger and that by now virtually the whole world is enmeshed in the extended struggle between the superpowers. Given these developments it should come as no surprise that four of the contributors to this volume (Robertson, Eisenstadt, Smelser, and Hondrich) stress the themes of globalism and internationalization.

One way of organizing the discussion of these articles is to note that each involves explicit criticisms of the dominant, if not exclusive, role given to international economic factors by scholars such as Wallerstein. This "economic program in the sociology of world society" has been attacked forcefully by Bendix (1978), who identifies numerous other lines of international influence. Intellectuals, scientists, and journalists, for example, are conduits through which influences of one country are carried to another. The mechanism by which this occurs is that these actors identify institutions in other societies that they regard as superior to their own and become the spearhead of reforms and social change in their own societies. These institutions, moreover, may be of the most diverse kinds: French parliamentary democracy, the German penal and civil law, the British factory system, and the computer technologies of different countries.

In his contribution Robertson also acknowledges the importance of economic factors, but places a "cultural-sociological explanatory program" alongside the economic program. Much of Robertson's analysis hangs on the notion of "world images," a formulation that clearly owes much to Max Weber (1920). Robertson argues that it is necessary to go beyond societo-centric approaches and consider the world as an entirety. Societies, particularly their elites, shape the world according to their definitions of the world and their images of world order. Memories of world-historical events and processes are especially important, as the post–World War II generation's rejection of the politics of appeasement and the 1960s generation's rejection of some of the more aggressive postures of Cold War politics demonstrate. The notion of world images touches sociology and the other social sciences because they are in the business, as it were, of generating images of the world society. These images come to influence the thinking of bankers, politicians, and others responsible for shaping world events, sometimes through the educational process and sometimes through more direct avenues. Friedrich H. Tenbruck (1984) has assembled evidence on how American and, later, West German sociologists took part in the process of spreading certain world images in the West after 1945.

Eisenstadt's contribution also contains an explicit critique of the economic program in sociology. In addition to relations of domination that follow economic lines, Eisenstadt focuses on independent global and imperial tendencies on the part of societal elites. As the cultural premises of these elites are "exported" through colonization and other processes, they meet a combination of receptiveness and resistance on the part of "importing" societies and are molded in a series of fusions and compromises. His argument here is not unlike that of Gusfield (1967). One of Eisenstadt's most important observations is that modernity itself (as it crystallized historically in Western Europe and North America) can be regarded as a culture and that this culture has become a world culture in its diffusion in the twentieth century. But again this is not simply a question of domination. Rather it is a matter of domination, diffusion, combination with traditional values, and continuous reshaping. Furthermore, this process of diffusion has been characterized (Tiryakian 1985) by changing centers of modernity: first Western Europe, later the United States, and now a complex mix in which Japan and other Asian societies play a key role, China lurks in the background, and the Soviet Union remains a major question mark.

TABLE 2. Evolutionary Approaches

Criteria of comparison Theoretical approach	Reference theory	Unit of analysis	Starting mechanism	Follow-up mechanism	Directedness to aims	Process models	Application
Luhmann	post-Darwinian	social systems that organize their elements themselves	self-production of systems in situations of improbability (autopoiesis)	continuation of the autopoiesis of social systems	improbability as openness and multifariousness of chances	autopoietic construction, continuance and decomposition of social systems	self-description of modern societies
Giesen	neo-Darwinian	society	self-production of systems in situations of improbability		nondirectedness	many simultaneously proceeding evolutionary processes with phase shifting (e.g., start of system 1, decomposition of system 2, continuance of system 3)	cultural interpretational patterns of time
Smelser		society	besides internal effects, external effects, esp. intersocietal effects	e.g., routinization, equalizing, transformation, rationalization	slight progress	upgrading	

Hondrich	societies	blind variation and segmentation	differentiation and segmentation	interests of evolution: survival, evolutionary success, heterogeneity and homogeneity	variation, selection, stabilization, paradoxes and extraordinary development in relation to the master trend	all modern nation-societies of the contemporary world, esp. supersocieties and niche societies
Eder	1. groups 2. inter-group societies 3. society, environment	contradictions, conflicts	variation, selection and stabilization in and among groups and between society and environment	morality at the highest level; ongoing stream of communications	higher development in morality and pathological developments	moral representations
Eisenstadt	societies, civilizations with leading elites	structural variety, existence of a distribution of resources, elites, conflict	acceptance by social movements or masses	nondirectedness, uncertainty of the outcome of evolutionary processes	success or failure of change	spread of modernity from Europe over the world

TABLE 3. Theories of Modern Social Movements

Criteria of comparison / Theoretical approach	Concept of modernity	Causes of social movements	Stabilization of new social movements	Effects and consequences of new social movements	Relation of modernity to social movements	Differences between old and new movements	Process model
Touraine	modernity = self-producing society	industrial production and distribution of cultural goods = threat to subjectivity	permanent self-production	subjectification, which destroys individualization; restriction of state power	new social movements advance modernity	old social movements: striving for power and autonomy; new social movements: striving for subjectivity	actors produce social change and are influenced by it
Eyerman	postmodernity = 1. structured according to universalistic principles 2. parochial principles appear anew	1. state expansion 2. development of a knowledge industry 3. mass media	continuance and intensified meaning of the three reasons and causes	postmodernity	modernity = movement	old social movements: related to the industrial working process; new social movements: related to postindustrial processes outside work	postmodernity produces new social movements; these produce postmodernity

Tiryakian	modernity = disenchanted, rationalized and differentiated societies	extreme disenchantment, rationalization, and differentiation exclude some groups	permanent pressure toward counterdevelopments—reenchantment and dedifferentiation—is produced by the enhancement of disenchantment, rationalization, and differentiation	comprehensive modernity: disenchanted and enchanted, rational and irrational, differentiated and dedifferentiated	social movements like Romanticism and exotism take part in constituting modernity; they are also functional	distinction between old and new social movements doesn't matter	disenchantment (rationalization [differentiation]) leads to modernity, which leads to reenchantment (derationalization [dedifferentiation])

TABLE 4. Theories of Modernity and Social Inequality

Criteria of comparison / *Theoretical approach*	Unit of analysis and period of analysis	Dimensions of social inequality	Diagnosis	Causes of social inequality in modernity	Carriers and basis of change of social inequality in modernity	Effects and consequences of social inequality in modernity
Goldthorpe	"the West" since end of World War II	class positions	persistence of marked social inequality	trends in the economic system: distinct upgrading is strongly countered by enduring unemployment	actors, actions	
Haferkamp	United States and West German societies since French Revolution	resources achievements, power	greater reduction of inequality of resources, achievements, and power in West Germany than in the USA	single actors and masses, their mobilization of resources, values, and negotiations	actors, actions, and structures	conflicts, which constantly lead to reversible leveling-out processes
Münch	United States society since American Revolution	communal, political, economic, cultural subsystems	reduction of social inequality in the USA but a fairly strong markedness of inequality remains	six reasons/causes promoting equality and six reasons/causes promoting inequality within the traditionally given system of equality/inequality	actors, intentions, structures (unintentional)	US society breaking apart into different societal groups

Smelser's contribution reminds us that at this time in world history it is necessary "to rethink the fundamental assumption, long established in our disciplines, that the primary unit of analysis is the nation, the society, or the culture." The basis for this recommendation lies in the increasing salience of external factors in the internal dynamics of nations. By systematically examining a number of theories that have appeared during the past century Smelser distills four dimensions of intersocietal influence, dimensions that constitute a program for systematic research: economy, polity, culture, and societal community. The dynamics of international influence differ for each dimension, but all must be taken into account to gain a comprehensive picture of the international influences on the fate of nations.

4. NOTE ON TABLES

Taken together, the contributions to the theory of social change in this volume are multifaceted, extensive, and complex. As an aid to the systematically minded reader we append a tabular summary of both the introduction and the main points of the contributions themselves. We classify the contributions, with some acknowledged arbitrariness, under the three headings of "Evolutionary Approaches" (Table 2), "Theories of Modern Social Movements" (Table 3), and "Theories of Modernity and Social Inequality" (Table 4). In each case we list on the horizontal axis some general categories that can be identified as elements in theories of social change, and on the vertical axis we list the names of the contributors. The cells of each table contain brief specifications of the formulation that each contributor has made with respect to each element. We hope this presentation is helpful, that it involves little distortion, and that it adds a degree of systematization to the materials presented here.

REFERENCES

Baier, Horst. 1977. Herrschaft im Sozialstaat. *Kölner Zeitschrift für Soziologie und Sozialpsychologie* 19 (special issue, *Soziologie und Sozialpolitik*):128–42.

Baudelaire, Charles. 1925. *Ausgewählte Werke*. Vol. 3, *Kritische und nachgelassene Schriften*. Munich: Müller.

Beck, Ulrich. 1983. Jenseits von Stand und Klasse? *Soziale Welt* 2 (special issue, *Soziale Ungleichheiten*):35–74.

Bellah, Robert. 1970. *Beyond belief*. New York: Harper and Row.

Bendix, Reinhard. 1978. *Kings or people: Power and the mandate to rule*. Berkeley: University of California Press.

———. 1979. Westeuropa als Gegenstand und Quelle sozialwissenschaftlicher Forschung. In *Sozialer Wandel in Westeuropa: Verhandlungen des 19. Deutschen Soziologentages in Berlin, 1979*, ed. Joachim Matthes, 11–24. Frankfurt: Campus.

Berger, Johannes. 1982. Die Versprachlichung des Sakralen und die Entsprachlichung der Ökonomie. *Zeitschrift für Soziologie* 11:353–65.

Braverman, Harry. 1974. *Labor and monopoly capital.* New York: Monthly Review Press.

Brose, Hanns-Georg. 1985. Die Modernisierung der Zeit und die Zeit nach der Moderne. In *Soziologie und gesellschaftliche Entwicklung: Verhandlungen des 22. Deutschen Soziologentages in Dortmund, 1984*, ed. Burkhart Lutz, 537–42. Frankfurt: Campus.

Cardoso, Fernando Henrique. 1969. *Mudancas sociais na America Latina.* Sâo Paulo: Difusao Europeia do Livro.

Chambliss, William J., and Robert B. Seidman. 1971. *Law, order, and power.* Reading, Mass.: Addison-Wesley.

Cipolla, Carlo Maria. 1978. *The economic history of world population.* Harmondsworth, Eng.: Penguin.

Cohen, Albert K. 1955. *Delinquent boys.* Glencoe, Ill.: Free Press.

Dahrendorf, Ralf. 1955. Struktur und Funktion. *Kölner Zeitschrift für Soziologie und Sozialpsychologie* 7:491–519.

———. 1958. Out of utopia: Toward a reorientation of sociological analysis. *American Journal of Sociology* 64:115–27.

———. 1987. Soziale Klassen und Klassenkonflikt: Ein erledigtes Theoriestück? In *Soziologie der sozialen Ungleichheit*, ed. Bernhard Giesen and Hans Haferkamp, 10–30. Opladen, W. Ger.: Westdeutscher Verlag.

Eder, Klaus. 1983. Was ist neu an den neuen sozialen Bewegungen? In *Krise der Arbeitsgesellschaft? Verhandlungen des 21. Deutschen Soziologentages in Bamberg, 1982*, ed. Joachim Matthes, 401–11. Frankfurt: Campus.

———. 1985. *Geschichte als Lernprozess? Zur Pathogenese politischer Modernität in Deutschland.* Frankfurt: Suhrkamp.

Eisenstadt, Shmuel N. 1969. *The political systems of empires.* New York: Free Press.

———. 1970. Social change and development. In *Readings in social evolution and development*, ed. Shmuel N. Eisenstadt, 3–33. Oxford: Pergamon Press.

———. 1976. *Tradition, change, and modernity.* New York: Wiley-Interscience.

Elias, Norbert. 1956. Problems of involvement and detachment. *British Journal of Sociology* 7:226–52.

———. 1985. *Humana conditio: Beobachtungen zur Entwicklung der Menschheit am 40. Jahrestag eines Kriegsendes (8 Mai 1985).* Frankfurt: Suhrkamp.

———. 1987. Technik und Zivilisation. Paper presented at 23d Biannual Meeting of the German Sociological Association (Soziologentag), September 29– October 2, 1986, at Hamburg, West Germany.

Giesen, Bernhard. 1980. *Makrosoziologie eine evolutionstheoretische Einführung.* Hamburg: Hoffmann and Campe.

Gorz, André. 1982. *Farewell to the working class.* Boston: South End Press.

Granovetter, Mark. 1979. The idea of "advancement" in theories of social evolution and development. *American Journal of Sociology* 85:489–515.

Gusfield, Joseph R. 1967. Tradition and modernity: Misplaced polarities in the study of social change. *American Journal of Sociology* 72:351–62.

Habermas, Jürgen. 1976. *Zur Rekonstruktion des Historischen Materialismus.* Frankfurt: Suhrkamp.

———. 1981. *Theorie des kommunikativen Handelns.* 2 vols. Frankfurt: Suhrkamp. (See English translation: 1985. *The theory of communicative behavior.* Translated by Thomas McCarthy. 2 vols. Boston: Beacon Press.)

Haferkamp, Hans. 1975. *Kriminelle Karrieren: Handlungstheorie, Teilnehmende Beobachtung und Soziologie krimineller Prozesse.* Reinbek bei Hamburg: Rowohlt.

———. 1985. Mead und das Problem des gemeinsamen Wissens. *Zeitschrift für Soziologie* 14:175–87.

Haferkamp, Hans, and Michael Schmid, eds. 1987. *Sinn, Kommunikation und soziale Differenzierung: Beiträge zu Luhmanns Theorie sozialer Systeme.* Frankfurt: Suhrkamp.

Honneth, Axel, and Hans Joas, eds. 1986. *Kommunikatives Handeln: Beiträge zu Jürgen Habermas' "Theorie des kommunikativen Handelns."* Frankfurt: Suhrkamp.

Hradil, Stefan. 1983. Entwicklungstendenzen der Schicht- und Klassenstruktur in der Bundesrepublik. In *Krise der Arbeitsgesellschaft? Verhandlungen des 21. Deutschen Soziologentages in Bamberg, 1982,* ed. Joachim Matthes, 189–205. Frankfurt: Campus.

Lenski, Gerhard. 1970. *Human societies.* New York: McGraw-Hill.

———. 1976. Social structure in evolutionary perspective. In *Approaches to the study of social structure,* ed. Peter M. Blau, 135–53. London: Open Books.

Lipp, Wolfgang, and Friedrich H. Tenbruck. 1979. Zum Neubeginn der Kultursoziologie. *Kölner Zeitschrift für Soziologie und Sozialpsychologie* 31:393–98.

Lockwood, David. 1956. Some remarks on "the social system." *British Journal of Sociology* 7:134–46.

Luhmann, Niklas. 1982. *The differentiation of society.* New York: Columbia University Press.

———. 1984. *Soziale Systeme: Grundriss einer allgemeinen Theorie.* Frankfurt: Suhrkamp.

———. 1985. *A sociological theory of law.* New York: Methuen.

Mangold, Werner. 1962. Gruppendiskussionen. In *Handbuch der empirischen Sozialforschung,* ed. René König, 209–25. Stuttgart: Enke.

Marx, Karl, and Friedrich Engels. [1848] 1976. *Manifesto of the Communist party.* In *Collected Works,* vol. 6. London: Lawrence and Wishart.

Miller, Max. 1986. *Kollektive Lernprozesse: Studien zur Grundlegung einer soziologischen Lerntheorie.* Frankfurt: Suhrkamp.

Moore, Wilbert E. 1963. *Social change.* Englewood Cliffs, N.J.: Prentice-Hall.

Neidhardt, Friedhelm. 1986. "Kultur und Gesellschaft": Einige Anmerkungen zum Sonderheft. *Kölner Zeitschrift für Soziologie und Sozialpsychologie* 27 (special issue, *Kultur und Gesellschaft*):10–18.

Opp, Karl-Dieter. 1976. Der verhaltenstheoretische Ansatz. In *Zwischenbilanz der Soziologie: Verhandlungen des 17. Deutschen Soziologentages in Stuttgart, 1975,* ed. M. Rainer Lepsius, 60–69. Stuttgart: Enke.

Parsons, Talcott. 1961. Some considerations on the theory of social change. *Rural Sociology* 26:219–39.

———. 1966. *Societies: Evolutionary and comparative perspectives.* Englewood Cliffs, N.J.: Prentice-Hall.

———. 1967. Christianity and modern industrial society. In *Sociological theory and modern society,* by Talcott Parsons, 383–425. New York: Free Press.

———. 1971a. Comparative studies and evolutionary change. In *Comparative methods in sociology: Essays on trends and application,* ed. Ivan Vallier, 97–139. Chicago: University of Chicago Press.

———. 1971b. *The system of modern societies.* Englewood Cliffs, N.J.: Prentice-Hall.

———. 1977. *Social systems and the evolution of action theory.* New York: Free Press.

Pirenne, Henri. 1937. *Economic and social history of medieval Europe.* London: Kegan Paul, Trench, Trubner.

Pollock, Friedrich. 1955. *Gruppenexperiment: Ein Studienbericht.* Frankfurt: Europäische Verlagsanstalt.

Popper, Karl R. 1944–45. The poverty of historicism. *Economica* 11:86–103, 119–42; 12:69–89.

———. 1945. *The open society and its enemies.* London: Routledge and Kegan Paul.

Schade, Angelika. 1987. *Der Weg zur Gleichheit: Thesen und Daten zum Abbau sozialer Ungleichheiten.* Frankfurt: Peter Lang.

Schmid, Michael. 1981. Struktur und Selektion: Emile Durkheim und Max Weber als Theoretiker struktureller Selektion. *Zeitschrift für Soziologie* 10:17–37.

———. 1982. *Theorie sozialen Wandels.* Opladen, W. Ger.: Westdeutscher Verlag.

Senghaas, Dieter. 1982. *Von Europa lernen: Entwicklungsgeschichtliche Betrachtungen.* Frankfurt: Suhrkamp. (See English translation: 1985. *The European experience. A historical critique of development theory.* Translated by K.H. Kimmig. Leamington Spa, England: Berg.)

Smelser, Neil J. 1959. *Social change in the industrial revolution.* Chicago: University of Chicago Press.

———. 1976. *Comparative methods in the social sciences.* Englewood Cliffs, N.J.: Prentice-Hall.

Sombart, Werner. 1976. *Why is there no socialism in the United States?* New York: International Art and Sciences Press.

Strasser, Hermann, and Susan C. Randall, eds. 1981. *An introduction to theories of social change.* London: Routledge and Kegan Paul.

Tenbruck, Friedrich H. 1979. Die Aufgaben der Kultursoziologie. *Kölner Zeitschrift für Soziologie und Sozialpsychologie* 31:399–421.

———. 1981. Emile Durkheim oder die Geburt der Gesellschaft aus dem Geist der Soziologie. *Zeitschrift für Soziologie* 10:333–50.

———. 1984. *Die unbewältigten Sozialwissenschaften oder Die Abschaffung des Menschen.* Graz, Austria: Styria.

Tiryakian, Edward A. 1985. The changing centers of modernity. In *Comparative social dynamics,* ed. Erik Cohen, Moshe Lissak, and Uri Almagor, 131–47. Boulder, Colo.: Westview Press.

Touraine, Alain. 1981. *The voice and the eye: An analysis of social movements.* Cambridge: Cambridge University Press.

Wallerstein, Immanuel. 1974. *The modern world system*. New York: Academic Press.

Weber, Max. 1920. *Gesammelte Aufsätze zur Religionssoziologie*. Vol. 1. Tübingen: J. C. B. Mohr (Siebeck).

Wiswede, Günter, and Thomas Kutsch. 1978. *Sozialer Wandel*. Darmstadt: Wissenschaftliche Buchgesellschaft.

Zapf, Wolfgang. 1983. Entwicklungsdilemmas und Innovationspotentiale in modernen Gesellschaften. In *Krise der Arbeitsgesellschaft? Verhandlungen des 21. Deutschen Soziologentages in Bamberg, 1982*, ed. Joachim Matthes, 293–308. Frankfurt: Campus.

PART ONE

Modernity and Social Movements

Modernity and Social Movements

Ron Eyerman

In this essay I discuss the concept of modernity as it has been inherited from the classical thought of Weber, Simmel, and Michels and as it is interpreted in contemporary sociology. My concern is not to give a comprehensive account of the development of the concept of modernity in sociology but rather to focus on one area: social conflict and social movements. In this connection my prime concern is the effect of modernity on both the development and the sociological understanding of social movements. In other words, I am not concerned merely with the history of a concept but rather with the relationship between concepts of understanding and historical reality.

1. MODERNITY

As used in classical sociological theory, the concept of modernity has its roots in the attempt to come to grips with the meaning and significance of the social changes occurring in Europe in the latter half of the nineteenth century, namely, the effects of industrialization, urbanization, and political democracy on essentially rural and autocratic societies. The term "modernity" was coined to capture these changes in progress by contrasting the "modern" with the "traditional." The theme, if not the concept, of modernity pervades sociology and the work of its founding fathers, Marx, Weber, and Durkheim. In their work modernity was meant to be more than a heuristic concept. It carried connotations of a new experience of the world. Modernity referred to a world constructed anew through the active and conscious intervention of actors and the new sense of self that such active intervention and responsibility entailed. In modern society the world is experienced as a human construction, an experience that gives rise both to an exhilarating sense of freedom and possibility and to a basic anxiety about the openness of the future.

This is how modernity was understood in classical sociology. One theme that stands out in this account of social change and its effect on human experience is the development of a new sense of self, of subjectivity and individuality. This idea distinguishes the modern individual from the traditional one. The sociological account of this difference is based on changes in the understanding of the relationship between man and the supernatural, changes in property relations, and the demographic changes that accompanied industrialization. In this chapter I focus on the latter changes. Industrialization involved more than the development of a new means of producing the necessities of life; it involved the centralization and coordination of the production, distribution, and consumption of goods. It drew masses of laboring individuals from rural communities and farm labor to centralized urban workplaces. This uprooting of relatively stable populations was interpreted both positively and negatively—as liberating, alienating, or both—by sociologists and the people whose experience the sociologists sought to capture.

Liberation and alienation, however they were interpreted and experienced, involved both a physical and a mental break with the rural, family-based community. They meant that the traditional social networks that formed the basis of social identity no longer had direct control over the migrating individual. Alienation from the traditional community and its forms of identity and control meant that the alienated individual was open to new influences. The social changes associated with modernity thus made possible the formation of new social networks and political identities, for example, the rise of "voluntary associations" (which stood in contrast to those traditional associations into which one was born and that one took largely for granted). Such voluntary associations, which provided the basis for new social and political identities for the recently uprooted individual, could be work-related, such as trade unions, or neighborhood-based, such as community and religious groups. Often these voluntary organizations overlapped and competed for the attention of individuals in their attempt to refocus political and social orientations.

The break with tradition and the rural community meant the break with established identity-giving authority. The new individuals, freed from the traditional collective, were free to reorient themselves and to reconstruct their world: to "make history," as Marx put it, "but not under conditions of [their] own choosing." The social changes associated with modernity, industrialization, and especially urbanization were neither chosen nor directed by the individuals involved in these demographic changes. They were its victims, not its instigators. Once in motion, however, these shifts opened new possibilities. The social movement that began "behind the backs" of actors could be transformed into a positive social force, into a social-political movement for Marx or into new forms of social solidarity for Durkheim.

Marx concerned himself with the new forms of political identity created by modernity and the possibility of forming a collective will, but Weber and his associates, such as Simmel and Michels, turned their attention to the effects of modernity on the individual and the new forms of organization that this entailed. For Weber and Simmel modern society is constituted *of* as well as *by* individuals; it is a product of their interactions rather than a traditional form of social organization. Thus modernity entails new possibilities for the expression of human subjectivity in forms of social interaction that are not entirely a product of tradition. Of course Weber and Michels also studied the new forms through which human action could be institutionalized and guided by systems of rules that could be just as effective as traditional forms in constraining human freedom even though they were not traditional in the sense of being based on longstanding cultural patterns. Weber's studies of bureaucracy, together with his ambiguous interpretation of its "rationality," and Michels's study of political parties provide examples of modern forms that constrain individual freedom of expression and action. Both, however, interpreted modernity as a break with the traditional bonds of rural society that entailed the possibility of a new freedom of action and expression for the individual and thus a new relationship between the individual and the collective.

This new sense of freedom associated with modernity included an awareness and an experience of time. For the modern individual time involves process and duration; it also involves a sense of dynamic change that turns attention to the future rather than to the past. The modern individual is aware of himself or herself not only as an individual, that is, as a creator of self and society, but also as an individual with a future. This experience, together with its ideological expression in sociological theories and political tracts, varies according to social class.

This new sense of time and future orientation applies as much to the arts as to social and political relations. In fact, the concept of modernity used in social theory and the concept of modernism used to describe movements in the arts and literature have a common basis. Both focus on the new sense of individuality, future orientation, and creative possibility and identify these attributes with both the individual and collective movements. Like the modernist painter or writer, social theorists of modernity—I think primarily of Simmel in this connection—attempted to capture the dynamism of the modern experience in the very form of their writing. Simmel's vivid descriptions of the city and the new-found relationship between the individual and the group in modern society remind one of the attempts by expressionist painters and by authors such as Joyce to capture the dynamism of the modern experience in forms that match its content.

This attempt to match modern content with modern form permeates the classical sociological interpretation of modernity. Modern sociology, like modern society itself, faces the problem of organizing the dynamism of modernity in efficient ways. The modern concept of efficiency means getting the most out of energy expended and harnessing forces already in motion. Again, one can point to Weber's study of bureaucracy as an example of an attempt to come to grips with how best to organize modernity. Marx's and Durkheim's studies of the division of labor can be understood in the same way.

This problem of organizing the forces of modernity is directly political in its interest and its implications. This is true not only for the conflict that still defines modern political theory—the conflict between individual freedom and collective responsibility or, as expressed in the notion of modernity itself, between freedom and alienation—but also in the reorganization of social and individual identity that the processes of modernity make necessary. Cut loose from the relatively secure and stable networks of the rural community, the modern individual is forced to reconstitute a sense of self that includes new ways of acting politically and defining the political community. How and in which direction this redefinition of the political community occurs is a matter of great theoretical and practical concern. The Marxist theorists Luxemburg and Lenin had competing ideas about the role of organization in harnessing the energies of modernity and developing the political consciousness of the modern individual. In their well-known debate about the nature of political organization in relation to the spontaneity of mass movements and the role of the party and the professional politician in the development of political consciousness, these two Marxists differed in their interpretation of the type of organization and the amount of guidance necessary to attain the goal they held in common: the creation of a modern society based on a new balance between the individual and the collective. Both took for granted that modern politics was a matter of harnessing newly freed energies and directing mass movements, but they disagreed about what form the harnessing and directing was to take. Lenin stressed the role of a tightly knit organization and a politically conscious intellectual leadership, whereas Luxemburg stressed the necessity of participation in collective struggles. She held that a mass movement was itself a form of political socialization in which individuals gain a new sense of self and a new awareness of the political nature of modern society.

More to the center of the modern political theory, Weber was concerned about how the dynamic forces of modernity would form themselves politically. That modern politics would be class politics was accepted by Weber as much as it was by the Marxists. In political terms modernity meant class conflict and interests defined through class-related political parties. Weber also concerned himself with the significance of social movements in modern politics and the role of leadership and organization in these movements. More like Hegel than Marx, Weber viewed mass movements with trepidation rather than expectation. It was politically important to him (as well as to Durkheim) that the development of "the masses" be a transitory and temporary phenomenon and that the reconstitution of individual and collective political identity take place as quickly as possible. Without this reconstitution he feared that modern democracy might not survive. Thus political parties and other voluntary organizations were important in mediating between the individual and the collective and in transcending the formation of mass movements. Weber thought that mass movements were dangerous because the individual who participated in them lost that independence of thought and action that constituted the great positive potential of modernity, becoming instead subject to irrational impulses and charismatic leaders. This could easily lead to a restoration of premodern forms of authority and organization.

Although Weber saw mass movements as necessary to the transition from traditional to modern society, he believed that these movements were a stage to be transcended as quickly as possible. Transcendence took the form of reconstituting the relationship between the individual and the collective in modern organizations and institutions. Modern organizations were those that could balance the newly won freedom of the individual with a sense of collective responsibility. Mediating voluntary organizations, such as political parties, that could reconstitute individual political identity in progressive forms were the means to this end. The modern nation-state in which these political parties were organized formed the framework and the object of this new, modern political identity. The state was another term for the reorganization of political life. It constituted a new balance between individual freedom and collective responsibility and was the ultimate object of individual and collective political identity. Recognizing oneself as a member of a nation and having a sense of national identity was the highest form of political identity for Weber and thus an important aspect of modern political socialization. The question of how to reconstitute the political identity of the modern individual into a national identity was central to Weber's sociological and political theory.

The same can be said for Michels. Although his classic *Political Parties* (1959) claims to be an empirical study of the German Social Democratic party (SPD), it is really a treatise in modern political theory. The central issue is the reorganization of modern political identity and the formation of political interests in modern society. Michels begins with the claim that modern politics demands organization and that organization, although necessary, eventually undermines its democratic ideals. This is his famous "iron law of oligarchy." One can immediately see, however, that it is mass movements and the alienation of the modern individual that make this reorganization necessary. In other words, Michels takes Weber's discussion of the meaning of modernity as the starting point of his analysis: the newly freed individual and the new masses require organization. Thus, for Weber and Michels "democracy" essentially means mass rule. The dangers inherent in mass rule have already been mentioned; these dangers also make the reorganization of the masses necessary. Michels's point is that organization can never be democratic because it is the antithesis of the mass movement and mass rule.

Before turning to the issue of social movements and their relationship to modernity and modern politics, one further theme connected to modernity needs to be mentioned: social mobility. If modernity means the physical mobility of masses of individuals, it also connotes the possibility of upward social mobility. In contrast to tradition, which is usually characterized as having a fixed and static social structure, modernity, at least at the outset, is characterized as being more fluid and open. Mass demographic movement implies fluidity and the possibility of moving up as well as out; at least this is how it is usually portrayed. Much sociological analysis has gone into investigating this claim associated with modernity. It is not my intention to review this literature but merely to point out that social mobility is part of the ethos of modernity, both for sociologists and for everyday actors.

This aspect of modernity also has direct political implications, both in its social-science formulations and in its political theory and practice. For many contemporary Marxists social mobility is a form of false consciousness and thus a hindrance to the formation of a collective political will. For liberal theorists social mobility, both individual and collective, is a central assumption and aim of politics and political theory. Liberals connect mobility with individual freedom, thus making it a cornerstone of the promise of modernity and their interpretation of it. For conservatives social mobility and modernity are equally threatening and are identified with one another as a threat to freedom, which is associated with the stability that hierarchy is said to provide.

To summarize, modernity refers to the constitution of subjectivity, the social construction of the modern self, and the political and cultural expressions of these phenomena at both the individual and the collective level.

2. SOCIAL MOVEMENTS

Social movements are central to modernity. They are central both be-cause modernity connotes movement and because modernity involves new political alliances and allegiances in which mass movements play a significant role. But social movements are more than the spontaneous gathering of masses of individuals. They are a distinct form of collective behavior. They are purposive and relatively structured forms of collec-tive behavior. Crowds, even traffic jams, are made up of masses of indi-viduals, but they are not modern movements. Unlike crowds, social move-ments are composed of groups of individuals gathered with the common purpose of expressing subjectively felt discontent in a public way and changing the perceived social and political bases of that discontent. What makes social movements modern is not their collective but their distinctly political character.

The idea of legitimacy is central to the modern understanding of poli-tics. Political action requires minimally "that an actor or actors make some explicit claim that the *means* of action can be recognized as legitimate *and* the *ends* of action become binding for the wider community" (Offe 1985, 826–27, italics in original).[1] Thus it is possible to make a distinction be-tween sociocultural and sociopolitical movements. Sociocultural move-ments, for example, religious sects or countercultures, make use of legiti-mate and accepted forms of collective action—public demonstrations, recruitment, bloc voting, and so on—in their attempts to increase their numbers and secure the right to practice their beliefs. Yet they usually do not intend by these actions to make these beliefs or practices binding on the entire political community. When they do, as in the case of many contemporary Islamic movements, they are no longer sects or socio-cultural movements but full-fledged sociopolitical movements.

So far I have distinguished sociopolitical movements from socio-cultural movements and other, more spontaneous, forms of collective behavior. To differentiate sociopolitical movements from ad hoc protest groups, I further require that sociopolitical movements have a more or less generally accepted set of shared beliefs. Such a set of beliefs provides for a common understanding and definition of a conflict situation and allows continuity from one specific situation to the next. Sociopolitical movements must also possess some form of organization and means of communication to give them stability and continuity.

' Sociopolitical movements, then, are more than masses of people gath-ered in protest; they require forms of organization and communication

---

1. This distinction between the means and ends of action can also be found in Merton 1949. The argument here can be found in extended form in Eyerman and Jamison 1991.

that allow continuity over time and space. The forms these movements take differ in modern societies depending on the specific political culture, but the existence of such organizations and networks of communication is a characteristic of modernity and modern politics. Sociopolitical movements, in other words, are a defining characteristic of modern politics and modern society.[2]

In pointing out that modern social movements require a degree of organization and networks of communication in order to ensure their continuity over time, it is necessary to distinguish sociopolitical movements from more highly structured organs such as political parties, which are themselves characteristic of modernity and modern politics. Although they are more structured than crowds and mass mobilizations, sociopolitical movements are less structured than political parties. They expand and contract, continually taking in and losing participants. They are more flexible in organization and tolerant in beliefs than political parties because their purpose is less a practical and instrumental one than an expressive one. However, the line between parties and movements cannot be drawn too firmly. Sociopolitical movements may produce their own political parties or work with and within other parties as tactics for achieving some of their ends. Not all who participate in the movement need join or even accept the idea of a more formal political party as part of the movement itself. For many participants, in most cases for even the majority, the movement may be only a vaguely defined or experienced set of beliefs and emotions through which one may discover and express dissatisfaction without necessarily feeling loyalty to any organization or political program.

To maintain a sense of continuity, sociopolitical movements require both the fluidity of ideas and emotions, as expressed in public demonstrations, pamphlets, and newsletters, and the stability provided by more formal organization and leadership. The leadership stands for and speaks for the movement at times when no mass public is visible, something that seems necessary and yet that creates problems of its own.

When defined as more-or-less organized forms of collective action aimed at social change, social movements are a distinctly modern phenomenon. They depend on and express our modern political culture, which permits and recognizes mass discontent as part of the repertoire of political action and which is based on the awareness that fundamental change is indeed possible. Modernity and modern politics rest on the

2. See Barnes and Kaase 1979. Social movements are not aberrations. Rather they are continuous with modern political culture. Social theorists like Alain Touraine and Amitai Etzioni define modern and postmodern societies by their responsiveness to social movements and social conflicts. Touraine makes social movements the constitutive element of modern and postmodern societies. See Touraine 1977, 1981; Etzioni 1968.

assumption that society and policy are made by people, not gods or kings. The absence of such awareness, that is, the lack of a political content to mass discontent, distinguishes modern social movements from more traditional forms of popular discontent and rebellion.[3]

It is common today to distinguish "old" social movements from "new" ones (Melucci 1980, 1981). Such a distinction rests on two sets of criteria. The first, associated with Alain Touraine, builds on the theory of the historical transition from an old industrial society to a new postindustrial society (Touraine 1981). From this point of view the labor movement is an old social movement because it expresses the conflicts of industrial society and industrialization, that is, the conflicts between labor and capital. New social movements, such as the women's movement, express conflicts representative of the new postindustrial society. A second set of criteria differentiating between new and old social movements stems from the issues they raise and the locus of the changes they wish to bring about. In this case the labor movement not only reflects the old struggle between labor and capital but also is rooted in and concerned with the labor process itself in its demands for change and its vision of the future. New social movements, however, express concerns that according to established ways of thinking are outside the labor process. These concerns are primarily noneconomic issues, such as gender relations and the meaning of war and peace. The new social movements express concerns that are more cultural than economic. They aim at changing norms and values rather than productive and distributive relations.

These distinctions between old and new social movements provide a convenient way of categorizing various contemporary political conflicts and social movements. For one thing, classes and related class interests, which provided the prime source of collective identity and motivation for collective action in the past (at least in Europe), seem less a factor today, at least for explaining social movements. Contemporary social movements seem motivated by concerns other than those directly associated with income and economic security. In addition, rather than focusing on the labor process the realm of concern has shifted to what has been called the "life-world," which involves issues of personal identity, personal life, neighborhood, sexuality, and life-style.[4] Finally, the types of demands put forward by the new social movements lie, to some extent, outside the realm of traditional compromise politics, whether that be labor-market politics or representative democracy as it currently exists. Unlike working-class movements, which can offer and withdraw

3. Examples of this distinction between traditional and modern forms of rebellion can be found in Hobsbawm 1959.

4. On the use of the phenomenological concept of life-world see Habermas 1981 and Peterson 1984.

their labor power in exchange for concessions from capital, the new social movements have little to offer in exchange. Their demands tend to be made in nonnegotiable terms and are usually expressed negatively: antiwar, antinuclear, and so on. Whether this approach represents tactics or is an early stage of movement development remains to be seen. The literature on social movements includes a long-standing discussion concerning the strategies and tactics of social movements (see Jenkins 1981). In any case the distinction between old and new social movements seems worthwhile to make from an analytical point of view. From the actor's point of view its validity seems beyond question.[5]

3. MODERNITY AND SOCIAL MOVEMENTS

Thus far I have discussed the sociological understanding of modernity and modern social movements. In this section my task is to take up the question of how modernity itself has affected the development of modern social movements. In the preceding section I drew an analytical distinction between old and new social movements. My task here is to connect this discussion with the changes in economic and social structure that may be referred to as "postmodern." I argue that what I call "new" social movements are the expression of postmodernity.

Three societal dynamics underlie the development of postmodernity: the expansion of the state, the explosion of the knowledge industry, and the development of the new mass media. These three dynamics of social change have both influenced social movements and been influenced by them. The old social movements were at once the product of modernity and an essential element in its dynamism. The working class movement, for example, was the product of industrialization and urbanization, but modern democracy was a force in its development in specific directions. Similarly, new social movements are both the product of modernity and a reaction to it. It is important, however, to distinguish the postmodern critique of modernity from the premodern critique. The premodern, or Romantic, critique of modernity focused on modernization as such and based itself on an idyllic past, usually with right-wing political overtones. In contrast, the postmodern critique of modernity, although sharing some of the features of Romanticism—which are especially evident in the environmental movement—represents a "progressive" transcendence of modernity rather than its outright rejection.

At this point I would like to discuss three of the changes underlying the postmodern condition. First, since the end of World War II Western

---

5. Witness the "new" left and the conflicts within the Greens in Germany and elsewhere between the new and the old politics and forms of political identity.

societies have undergone an exceptional transformation in economic and social structure. To a great extent the root of this transformation lies in the expansion and intervention of the state into areas that previously were the domain of civil society, including private economic activity regulated by a market and social activity, such as child-care, regulated by tradition. This shifting ground between state and civil society, between public and private areas of action and responsibility, is part of the field of ambiguity and potential conflict from which new social movements emerge. State expansion and intervention have politicized private domains and provoked a reaction from both the political left and the political right.

Second, in the postwar period Western societies have also experienced a shift toward knowledge-based, capital-intensive production, which requires more highly educated workers. The state-supported transformation of the employment structure has been underpinned by a revolution in education in which the links between education and production have become more pronounced and rationalized through various forms of manpower planning. What I call the new social movements are to a great extent peopled by the highly educated and the content of their critique of modern society builds on both their educational experience and their occupational expectations.[6]

A related development important to the understanding of the new social movements is the expanded employment opportunities for women—especially married women—made possible by the knowledge industry and the general expansion of the public sector. The expansion of service, administrative, and care-giving occupations, which coincided with the growth of the state and its intervention into what previously were private services, has opened up many new paid employment opportunities for women. New opportunities for work and education helped establish the condition in which the social values and norms that defined a proper "woman's place" could be challenged. Here the interplay between the beliefs of a sociopolitical movement (the women's movement) and a shifting economic and social structure of opportunity becomes clear. Structural possibilities and social conflicts grew together, opening fields of contention from which sociopolitical movements would emerge.

Third, the changes in representative democracy that occurred as part

6. Some, primarily Marxists, have interpreted these new social movements as the protests of the privileged, that is, as expressions of a new class or at least the new strata of an educated elite seeking to protect or to better its social standing against opponents in the old society, including both capital and labor. Alvin Gouldner's new class theory is a variation on this theme, as are the more traditional Marxist accounts of "proletarianization," "new working class theory," and the various attempts at structuralist class analysis, from Poulantzas to E. Wright.

of modernity have laid the grounds for postmodernity. During the
course of their development the old social movements became participatory movements. Whatever their original intentions or ideologies, they
came more and more to be concerned with getting a piece of the modern
pie and participating in modern politics as equal partners with capital
and other powerful political and economic actors.[7] These movements—
and here I think primarily of the labor movements of Western Europe—
developed into organizations that became part of the institutionalized
power and decision-making structures of modern society. Such movements developed into centralized organizations and associated with political parties, slowly gaining power and influence but losing the dynamism
and the mass engagement with which they began. Perhaps this development was both necessary and successful, for no one can deny the actual
power labor movements enjoy today in Western Europe. Except for
ceremonial occasions, however, hardly anyone would deny that the
"movement" aspect has disappeared.[8] Political power and participation
were bought at the price of accepting a certain definition of modern
politics, that of administration and redistribution through the centralized state, and of the loss of a social movement. In the dialectic between
movement and organization, the movement got lost. This development
is also important in understanding new social movements and their rejection of modernity. For the new movements modernity is associated with a
particular type of politics. The new social movements are expressions of
the rejection of the politics of administration and its representatives in
both labor and capital. In this sense they are postmodern because they
reject the identities of class and the ideology of political modernism.

With this rather cursory discussion of the social and economic background to postmodernity I now turn to the effects of modernity on the
new social movements. I discuss three dynamics in this connection: state
intervention, the knowledge industry, and the mass media.

3.1. State Intervention

I have mentioned some of the ways that state intervention in social and
economic spheres has influenced the development of social movements

7. Let me be clear that this does not mean, except of course from a particular theoretical and political point of view, that they thus lost their mission or suffered *embourgeoisment*
and the like. How one interprets this alteration, if it really was that, is a matter of preference, which I have discussed elsewhere (Eyerman 1981).

8. Again, interpreting this development is a matter of preference and there are differences of opinion. Walter Korpi (1979), for example, sees this development as an expression
of increased power and maturity. From a more radical Marxist point of view the opposite
would be the case.

in recent times. State expansion and intervention into labor market planning, education, family life, and child-rearing, both passively through taxation and other forms of economic redistribution and actively through the reorganization of services traditionally performed privately, have had the effect of politicizing new spheres of social life. This politicization has generated reactions on both the political left and the political right and has provided issues for activists in new social movements. Although the creation of the nation-state and the resulting political identity was central to what classical social theory meant by modernity, postmodernity is at once more universalistic (concerned with humanity and nature, women's liberation, and world peace) and more parochial (concerned with local control and self-reliance). And in contrast with modernist political movements, which had a class character and drew political identity from material concerns, such as labor and capital, postmodernist movements are more idealistic and diffuse in their participants and interests.

In addition to its expanded role as employer and redistributor of funds, the state has become the arena as well as the focus of political action. All these factors have influenced the development of social movements in the recent past, and go a long way in explaining their emergence, the types of issues raised, and the particular activists who populate them. But there is another side to state intervention: the state as activist and political agent.

I can perhaps best show what I mean with examples from my own research concerning the development of European environmentalist movements.[9] The Swedish state has played a very active role in defining environmental issues and deciding environmental policy since the early 1970s. Sweden was one of the first countries to create a governmental agency concerned with environmental protection, and this early activism on the part of the state, an activism in favor of environmental protection, has played a significant role in the way the Swedish environmentalist movement has developed. For one thing, this positive attitude toward regulation and control took many issues and potential mobilizing forces away from the environmentalist movement. For another, state intervention has had the effect of turning environmental protection into a series of legal and technical issues. As a result the environmentalist movement has been forced to accept the state's definition of the situation and to shape its reaction along lines and according to rules it has had no part in framing. Thus the movement developed more as a movement of experts who could

9. This research, which is funded by the Swedish Humanities and Social Science Research Council (HSFR), compares the development of environmentalist movements in Sweden, Holland, and Denmark. For an example of another issue related to this discussion, see Cramer, Eyerman, and Jamison 1987.

participate in environmental debates by virtue of being conversant in the legal and technical language of the field and who were recruited as a counterweight to government and industry experts. The movement became more and more professionalized, which shaped the type of issues taken up, the type of activist attracted to the movement, and the type of organization used. Professionalization created a potential rift between a knowledgeable leadership and a less knowledgeable, and thus less powerful, rank and file. Furthermore, the government has been able to recruit many of the movement-produced experts into its own administration of the environment. Other contemporary social movements have had analogous experiences. The women's movement, for example, has to an almost equal extent been "legalized" and administered through state definition and intervention into the "women's problem."

Although too much can be made of this trend—as in the claims either that social movements are functional to societal adaptation or, more cynically, that they are forms of "artificial negativity" that help "one-dimensional" societies rationalize their forms of domination—new social movements share with old ones a tendency toward institutionalization and, from another point of view, incorporation. However, as resource mobilization theorists have shown, the threat of incorporation, that is, "selling out" to the establishment, is often a stimulus that gives life to social movements. The threat of incorporation is often met with protest and the formation of new, rebellious groups within the movement. This internal conflict is common to all social movements, both old and new. What is significantly different, however, is the forms through which this incorporation can take place. Old social movements in the West fought against a hostile state and a well-entrenched ruling elite and for the most part sought recognition as legitimate combatants in the struggle for political and economic rights, a struggle carried out in the name of democracy. They could be called modernizers insofar as democracy is measured by inclusion and participation on an equal basis with other combatants. New social movements, however, have emerged from within this structure of modernity and have done so partly as a reaction against it. For the old social movements the prime areas of conflict and identity as well as the means of incorporation were work and the state. Participation in the established institutions on an equal basis with other powers is not the goal of the new social movments, nor is the state the means to attaining their goals. They cannot be called modernizers. The new social movements fear having their ideas and identities included and redefined in the ideologies and the platforms of the older political parties and thus incorporated into the bureaucratic world of state regulation and control. What was the prime goal of the old social movements is anathema to the new.

3.2. The Knowledge Industry

The expansion of education and the closer links between the production of knowledge and the practical interests of the state and private economic sectors in increased productivity and profits have provided much fuel for contemporary conflict and the emergence of new social movements. Many participants in the new social movements are the products of this transformation, at once the beneficiaries of higher education and detractors of its shifting aims. The argument that higher education is manipulated by technocratic interests, which grew out of the student movements of the 1960s, has been extended into new areas by recent sociopolitical movements. Activists in the environmentalist movement use this critique of the relationship between education, science, and state-corporate interests (and the view of nature that underlies it) as a platform from which to criticize Western society in general. Many activists in the peace movement share this general criticism. They describe science, knowledge, and technology as arms of common state and corporate interests and identify the military-industrial complex as central to the modern mode of production. Thus, the knowledge industry and the links between education, knowledge, and corporate and state interests provide a common focus for new social movements and in this way have influenced their development. At the same time, because many activists in these movements are highly educated professionals employed in the very institutions they criticize, the movements have influenced the production of knowledge.

To take another example from my ongoing research, the environmentalist movement in Europe has developed in particular ways in part because of the interaction between professional scientists—both as activists and as the representatives of government or private interests—and the movement itself. The environmentalist movement has helped shape the course and content of knowledge production in part because of this interaction. Many scientists, and not just ecologists and biologists, have been influenced in the type of research they do and the broader theoretical frameworks they apply by their own or their colleagues' participation or interest in environmentalist organizations. New scientific frameworks have been developed or greatly modified in conjuction with the rise of environmentalism—the science of ecology is but one obvious example— and research programs have been instituted and funded for the same reasons.

The same may be said about the more applied areas of technological development. The concept and development of "alternative technology" arose within the environmentalist critique of modern production and consumption practices. Both the development of new scientific frameworks and the formulation of alternative technologies have focused on the modernist orientations of the knowledge industry. This modernism is identified in the productivist orientations that are thought to underpin contemporary knowledge production, which view nature as an object of human intervention and redirection. Because of the universalistic, rational-scientific orientation of much of modern environmentalism, which stems from the background of its activists and the political-cultural context in which it has developed, the environmentalist movement in Europe has contributed to the postmodern critique of modernity. This has the somewhat paradoxical effect of opening rational alternatives to modernity to modern rationality. Some of these alternatives (not all of course) contain the seeds of a new form of knowledge production, based on a new cosmological orientation and a new view of the relationship between humanity and nature (see Cramer, Eyerman, and Jamison 1987).

3.3. Mass Media

Like the state and the knowledge industry, the new mass media have helped "create" the new social movements. Coverage in the mass media and the instant attention gained through modern communication technologies have helped build these movements into significant social and political forces and have influenced their internal strategies, organization, and leadership. As Todd Gitlin has documented in his brilliant account of the influence of the mass media on the development of the student movement in the United States, the media in many senses became the movement (Gitlin 1980). New social movements are shaped by the mass media in several ways. Activists are conscious of media attention. They are also aware of their own importance in making and shaping "events" and in catching the public eye. To be noticed by the media is to gain legitimacy and significance and the ability to influence policy as well as the public at large. Modern movements must learn to use the media; otherwise the media will use and abuse them.

Modern politics is played out before the public. The mass media are the producers as well as important interpreters of this drama. The mass media, either because of their form or because of the values they embody, are attracted to the spectacular and the flamboyant. This has the effect of making the media event and the colorful movement leader a significant factor in the development of modern social movements. Would such an organization as Greenpeace, one of the fastest-growing organizations in the environmentalist movement, be possible without the mass media and modern techniques of communication and administration? I think not.

Other movement organizations are also influenced by the modern media. Gitlin demonstrates that the American student organization Students for a Democratic Society (SDS), a rather small group of well-brought-up students, was given celebrity status through media attention, which transformed not only the organization and its leadership, giving precedence to the colorful and the violent, but also its aims and its ideology, giving precedence to "radical" ideas and positions even though such views had previously only had marginal status within the movement. Philip Lowe and David Morrison show how the media and media attention have significantly affected the tactics and the aims of British environmentalist organizations (Lowe and Morrison 1984). Unlike the SDS, environmentalist groups have for the most part received favorable coverage in the media, especially as long as environmental issues remain free from partisan politics. This explains why environmental activists have been at pains to steer free of political parties. Lowe and Morrison go so far as to suggest that modern environmentalism, as opposed to the earlier conservation movement, would never have achieved its influence without its creative use of the media.

No modern movement can hope to gain influence without taking into account the centralized state and its forms of discourse and organization, and no modern movement can afford to ignore the mass media. And just as taking the state into account entails paying the price of becoming organized and centralized, media attention has its own price. In this way modern social movements are shaped by various key aspects of modernity at the same time that they play a significant role in the development of modernity.

4. CONCLUSION

I have attempted to show how the development of modernity has created the grounds for the emergence of modern social movements and how, in turn, these social movements have been influenced by modernity. I have also tried to show how social movements are a central part of what we mean by modernity and how they have influenced our understanding of modernity.

REFERENCES

Barnes, S., and M. Kaase, eds. 1979. *Political action: Mass participation in five Western democracies.* London: Sage.

Cramer, J., R. Eyerman, and A. Jamison. 1987. The knowledge interests of the environmental movement and the potential for influencing the development of science. In *Sociology of the sciences yearbook, 1987,* ed. S. Blume, J. Bunders, L. Leydesdorff, and R. Whitley, 89–115. Dordrecht, Netherlands: Reidel.

Etzioni, A. 1968. *The active society.* New York: Free Press.

Eyerman, R. 1981. *False consciousness and ideology in Marxist theory.* Stockholm: Almqvist and Wiksell and Humanities Press.

Eyerman, R., and A. Jamison. 1991. *Social movements: A cognitive approach.* Oxford: Polity Press.

Gitlin, T. 1980. *The whole world is watching: Mass media in the making and the unmaking of the new left.* Berkeley: University of California Press.

Habermas, J. 1981. *Theorie des Kommunikativen Handelns.* Vol. 2. Frankfurt: Suhrkamp.

Hobsbawm, E. 1959. *Primitive rebels.* Manchester: Manchester University Press.

Jenkins, J. Craig. 1981. Sociopolitical movements. In *Handbook of political behavior,* 4:81–153. New York and London: Plenum Press.

Korpi, Walter. 1979. *The working class in welfare capitalism.* London: Routledge and Kegan Paul.

Lowe, P., and D. Morrison. 1984. Bad news or good news: Environmental politics and the media. *The Sociological Review* 32:75–90.

Melucci, A. 1980. The new social movements: A theoretical approach. Part 2. *Social Science Information* 19:199–226.

———. 1981. Ten hypotheses for the analysis of new movements. In *Contemporary Italian sociology,* ed. D. Pinto, 173–94. Cambridge: Cambridge University Press.

Merton, R. 1949. *Social theory and social structure.* New York: Free Press.

Michels, R. 1959. *Political parties.* New York: Dover.

Offe, C. 1985. New social movements: Changing the boundaries of institutional politics. *Social Research* 52:817–68.

Peterson, A. 1984. The sex-gender dimension in Swedish politics. *Acta Sociologica* 27:3–18.

Touraine, A. 1977. *The self-production of society.* Chicago: University of Chicago Press.

———. 1981. *The voice and the eye: An analysis of social movements.* Cambridge: Cambridge University Press.

Two Interpretations of Contemporary Social Change

Alain Touraine

1. DECLINE OR TRANSFORMATION OF SOCIAL MOVEMENTS?

Social movements cannot be identified with campaigns for institutional reforms. But they can be understood as countercultural or "alternative" forms of collective action or as protest movements, directed against forms of social organization more than against cultural values. These two types of collective action—more "cultural" or more "social"—are present in the seventies and eighties. Both the future and the very nature of what I referred to some ten years ago as the "new social movements" appear to be uncertain. Those who study social movements have taken two views about the future of these movements. The first view sees the end of social movements inasmuch as they are defined as organized collective actions aimed at transforming the social order. According to these observers, our era is characterized by movements that defend or try to expand individual freedom and that oppose the state's power. The social and political space, in German, the "Öffentlichkeit," is becoming a no-man's-land between a more and more individualistic private life that expects society to be permissive and international relations that are dominated by the confrontation between the two nuclear superpowers and by the resistance of Islam and other communitarian movements to Westernization. Social movements, especially the most important one, the labor movement, are melting down because our democratic regimes are able to answer social demands with institutional reforms and because these social movements have often been transformed into instruments of power and repression rather than of protest.

The second view holds that we are living in a period of transition between the decline of the labor movement and the formation of new social movements that belong to postindustrial society. In this society,

55

industrialized production and the diffusion of symbolic and cultural goods take the central role that belongs to "productive forces" in industrial society. This period of transition is in many ways similar to the first half of the nineteenth century when social problems, such as poverty and proletarianization, were more visible than were the still fragmentary and repressed social movements.

These two interpretations appear to be entirely opposed to each other; they are not, however, mutually exclusive. Here again, a comparison with the nineteenth century is useful. For liberals, reason and interest were going to displace tradition and privilege. They believed that an open economy and a liberal society would permit a better use of material and human resources and enhance freedom of expression and the circulation of ideas. Such opinions were not rejected by those who identified industrialization with the development of a new economic domination and the class struggle. Marx spoke of the revolutionary action of the bourgeoisie, and most socialist thinkers believed as much in progress as they did in class struggle; they expected the development of productive forces to overcome, both naturally and through purposeful action, the domination of private interests.

These two analyses of social movements are challenged by the liberal-conservative view of a completely open, constantly changing society that no longer has any nature, essence, or center, a society that is nothing but a number of loosely connected changes. Critical sociologists, however, discover conflicts not only in production but in all aspects of social life and see new social movements that challenge social organization as a whole and propose alternative forms of social, economic, and cultural life.

These two images may seem to be so opposed as to be mutually exclusive. The social sciences are confronted with the opposition of these two interpretations of contemporary social change. The optimistic liberal interpretation seems to be prevailing today or at least is more relevant in a period of new technological developments, milder economic difficulties, and the absence of a major crisis involving the two superpowers. For this reason, I consider the optimistic view first before examining the idea of new social movements because the existence of such movements has always been defended only by a minority and attacked on one side by liberals and on the other by Marxist structuralists, who discern nothing but the logic of domination and the reproduction of social inequalities in social processes.

2. THE END OF SOCIETY

The main impact of the idea of modernization, in both its positivist and its liberal versions, came from its assumption that all social structures and systems of social control are crumbling. Modern societies can no longer be defined by principles, values, and norms but instead are defined by change, the triumph of instrumental rationality, and the destruction of all absolute principles. Positivists believed that these evolutionary changes would lead to a scientific society governed by political engineers. Liberals predicted that society would be transformed into a market in which all goods and services would be priced according to their utility.

But this confidence in reason and change could not exclude a deep-seated anxiety: how would it be possible to introduce order into change, that is, to maintain the unity of society, the continuity of law, and the possibility of education in a society that would be like a stream in whose waters one cannot step twice?

Beyond the diversity of its thinkers and schools, sociology is a general interpretation of modern society: its central purpose is to understand the interdependence of order and movement. We must be clear on what classical sociological thought was if we want to understand the importance and the novelty of neomodernist thought, which challenges the solutions that were elaborated by classical sociology during the period of Western industrialization. What we call classical sociology was actually a limited moment in the history of social thought, a moment from which we are probably departing, that was built around the central notion of society.

Modernity can be defined as a process of growing differentiation of economic, political, and cultural subsystems. But the concept of society gained a central importance during the long period that corresponded to a limited development of modernity, when economy, politics, and culture were still closely interrelated. In merchant societies, the state was intervening into economic life to protect roads and ports, to check weights and measures, and to ensure the reliability of currencies. European national states eliminated the power of feudal landlords, private wars, and all obstacles to the circulation of people and goods. They imposed the realm of law over their territories. Of course the state was not only a maker of laws and a judge. It was an absolute power and a maker of wars as well. But the idea of the national state and a direct correspondence between a nation and the state gained ground, first in England and France, then in Sweden. Finally, it triumphed with the American and French revolutions and the Rousseauian ideal of the people's sovereignty.

Before the Renaissance, social thought was the comparative history of civilizations, that is, religions. From the sixteenth to the nineteenth centuries it became political philosophy. Society meant the polity for Hobbes, Locke, Montesquieu, and Rousseau. Tocqueville was more the last of these great political philosophers than the first sociologist. These political philosophers opposed the social to the nonsocial as order to chaos.

The idea of the national state as a unifying principle was then, at a

higher level of modernization, replaced by the idea of capitalism, because the central agent of social change was no longer the national state
but the bourgeoisie. The concept of capitalism is not a purely economic
one because it identifies the economic structure with the process of
global change. This identification supposes the existence of strong links
between "civil society" and the state, between economy and politics. The
idea of society finally appeared as a combination of the national state and
capitalism. Thus the idea of society, like the earlier idea of the national
state, is an effort to link what the process of modernization tends to
separate: economic activity, political and military power, and cultural
values.

Durkheim among the great classical sociologists has the most an-
guished awareness of the decomposition of social order and of the necessity to give the idea of society a central role, both in sociological analysis
and in the reconstruction of social order. Parsons, in contrast, was more
optimistic and gave us a triumphal image of society. He identified society
with rationality without sharing Weber's and Durkeim's preoccupation
with the consequences of modernization.

The idea of society is to a large extent a myth. It tries to overcome the
growing separation of the main elements of social life by introducing a
central principle of social organization. This sociologism is criticized by
those who observe that modern societies are built on power, exploitation,
and war as much as on rationality, law, and science. I am not, however,
directly interested in these well-known criticisms. My central preoccupation is with the consequences of contemporary hypermodernization, a
development that appears to destroy all unifying myths that try to bring
together individualistic culture, constantly changing economic activities,
and a state that is more and more directly defined by its political, military, and economic competition with other states. The importance of the
idea of society is that contemporary hypermodernization appears to destroy it, and it is doing so as rapidly as industrialization destroyed the
idea of the national state and led to the notion of society.

The main characteristic of contemporary modern society is the extreme separation between the state and social life, a separation that can
no longer be overcome by another unifying myth. This separation is felt
very intensely in Europe, the continent where the first national states
were created. The economies and cultures of European nations have
become transnational; their citizens use a higher and higher proportion
of foreign products and, even more important, they are subordinated to
the nuclear superpowers. The separation between the state and social
life was felt less intensely in the United States during the years immediately after World War II, which explains the broad influence of Parsons's
sociology. But from the 1960s on, American citizens became conscious of

the separation between state and society. But unlike European countries, their own state had acquired imperial influence, had become a nuclear superpower, and thus could no longer be reduced to a political institution like congress or municipal bodies.

At the same time that military power and international strategy are separating themselves more and more from internal policies, mass consumption is overcoming the barriers of social and economic stratification. Although some sociologists maintain old-fashioned ideas in this area, socioeconomic status clearly has decreasing predictive power in explaining consumption patterns and political choices. Often it is more useful to to consider upwardly or downwardly mobile groups or ethnic subcultures than socioeconomic strata in explaining social behavior.

These observations are sufficient to describe the analysis of those who believe in the waning of social movements. Their central idea is that social movements have existed only inasmuch as they were at the same time political movements. They believe that only action against state power gives unity and a central importance to protest movements, which otherwise tend to be diverse and limited. Peasant movements in seventeenth-century France became important only because they opposed state taxes in addition to the domination of the landlords. If it had not been unified by political action, especially by that of the socialist parties, whose main purpose was not to transform working conditions but to conquer political power, what we call the labor movement would have been only a series of limited protest movements. The predominant role of political action in the labor movement is demonstrated by the fact that socialist parties have played their most important role in countries where unions were relatively weak and where purely political problems were more central than social problems, for example, the Austro-Hungarian Empire and France. The idea of socialism as a global social movement has been more actively developed in these countries than in Great Britain or the United States. This observation leads many to conclude that a social movement is actually a mixture of social protest and political action. This mixture often leads to contradictions, as demonstrated in the Soviet Union during the first years after the revolution.

Following the logic of this analysis, if political action and social protest now tend to be more and more separated, social movements must disappear. Liberals, when they go beyond a superficial apology for technological progress and abundance, defend an idea that is as powerful as the ideas of progress and rationalization that were introduced by their predecessors. This idea is the triumph of individualism, that is, the separation between individual needs and aims and state problems. Individualism destroys not only the public space, from institutions to socialization agencies, but also the very possibility of social movements. On one side, liberals say, we see the presence of individuals, with their sexuality and violence as well as their need for security and their efforts to climb up the social ladder. On the other side is the state, which is first of all a military power and which is often able to absorb social life and manipulate it, as in communist countries, or to identify itself with nationalist and religious forces, as in many Third World countries. Protest movements appear against the state. They range from the dissidents and the refuseniks in the Soviet Union to the mass movement in the United States opposing the Vietnam war and include movements opposing the permanent threat of nuclear war. But these antistate movements cannot be identified as social movements.

This hyperliberal view is highly original and creative. It has been reinforced by the necessity to find a way out of structuralist pessimism. If social domination is complete, if the whole of social organization functions as a system of social control that maintains inequality, privileges, and power, if social movements are impossible and social actors illusory, and if nothing exists but integration, manipulation, expulsion, and stigmatization, then the only possible exit is individualism. This was Barthe's and Foucault's answer at the end of their lives and it is also the "California" answer. It is an aesthetism, the search for pleasure, friendship, and voluntary groups, and it is directly inspired by ancient Greece. According to this view, the real objective of the new social movements is to get rid of society, not to transform it. The new social movements are very far from the social movements that struggled for political freedom and social justice, that is, the social ideas corresponding to the unifying myth of the past. The new social movements recognize as their central value the autonomy of individuals and groups. They try to express this autonomy by withdrawal, sectarian behavior, or terrorism. No longer do social movements seek to control the main cultural resources and models of society through conflicts in which enemies are defined by a process of social domination. This liberal criticism of the so-called new social movements is much more interesting than the vague analysis that lumps various currents of opinion, revolts, social demands, innovations, and antistate campaigns together under this name.

The hyperliberal view is far removed from both nineteenth-century optimism and the ideology of classical sociology. This latter body of thought believed in the progressive triumph of civil society over the state and the churches and the parallel development of social and economic integration with social and political movements. This ideology has been particularly strong in the United States, where it is another version of the American dream: the effort to build a society that is at the same time economically dynamic, politically democratic, and socially open to organizational demands and protests. This is why classical sociology was more influential in the United States than in Europe, especially between the two world wars and during the 1950s.

Before I consider the issue of the existence of new social movements, we must recognize as a partial conclusion that the image of a civil society in which opposite and complementary social movements conflict with each other while sharing the same confidence in the idea of progress is an illusion. This illusion, however, is still alive. It was directly present in Italian unionism between 1969 and 1975 and in the ideology of self-management that culminated in the LIP strike in France during this same period. These unionists sought to free their movement from the control of political parties and to create a society dominated by face-to-face conflicts and negotiations between management and workers. But we know today—and we should never have forgotten—that the state never can be reduced to the political expression of civil society and cultural demands cannot be identified with programs of social transformation.

Culture, society, and state power are more and more separated from each other. The consequence is that no social movement can bear in itself a model of an ideal society. Their actions are limited. Either the cultural and political unity of the national society is strong, which limits social conflicts and movements, as has generally been the case in the past, or this unity is weak or absent and nothing can integrate cultural demands, which are more and more individualized. The history of modernization is not the victory of the market and economic actors over states and churches but the decomposition of community, the growing separation of state economic activity, and personality problems. At the end of the decomposition of "society," defined as interrelated economic, cultural, and political systems that are integrated by institutions and socialization processes, it seems logical to announce the end of social movements, which are destroyed by the double triumph of individualism and state power and can no longer transform a society that has disappeared.

If we consider not only the most industrialized countries but also the rest of the world, the most important collective movements today are not social movements, such as socialism, communism, or unionism, which have been largely transformed into the ideological bases of state power, but rather the Islamic movement and, more broadly, the movements calling for identity, specificity and community that link cultural demands and state power and suppress, generally in a violent way, public space and social movements. The world appears divided into two parts: Western countries that are dynamic, individualistic, anomic, and deprived or freed from collective action, and Third World countries that are dominated by cultural or even religious nationalism. In between these two parts the communist world crushes both individual demands and collec-

tive action; its use of the vocabulary of the labor movement only emphasizes communism's destruction.

In such a situation, is it not logical to consider that social movements
take place only in historical settings in which principles of social integration and open social conflicts coexist? Without a principle of social integration based on a legitimate state, no central social movement can be
created; without open social conflicts and a recognized plurality of interests, social movements are reduced to rebellions. Social movements were,
according to this view, directly linked with societies integrated by unifying myths—of the national state or society—as well as with autonomous
economic relations. We now observe their decomposition in countries
that have lost their principles of unity and integration as well as in
countries where an absolute state tolerates no diversity and imposes its
rule in the name of a communitarian destiny.

3. POSTSOCIAL MOVEMENTS?

The decline of modern societies, together with the consequent decline of
the particular stage of social thought we call sociology, leads us to a
representation of social life as a flow of continuous changes. It means the
triumph of modernization but at the same time the end of the idea of
society. Large parts of what we call sociology, if this field of knowledge
can be redefined as the study of social life instead of the study of society,
corresponds to this purely dynamic view of social life. The modern
theory of organizations, which is dominated by H. Simon's concept of
limited rationality, is the most elaborate form of such neorationalism.
According to this theory, actors do not behave according to their status in
the system but according to their position in the process of change. In
this approach, a word that has long been marginal in sociology all of a
sudden takes on a central importance: that word is "strategy." Individual
and collective actors do not act according to values and norms. Rather,
like states, they act in strategic ways, trying to get the best possible results
in a given process of change that is never completely controlled by a
central authority. In a parallel way, Goffman or the ethnomethodologists
represent social actors as states who use diplomacy and war in their
dealings with other actors, and those other actors are more strangers
than partners in a system of roles and role expectations. Social movements cannot appear in such a "Cold War" environment. Strategy does
not require either affective mobilization or collective consciousness. It
only requires the rational search for optimal solutions, and in particular
the minimization of risks and uncertainty.

The importance of strategy does not recall the nineteenth century,
whose political life was dominated by mass movements, but the eigh-

teenth century, because not ordinary people but powerful elites elaborate strategies. The members of these elites are highly individualistic and value their own pleasure. Such an individualism can go very far in criticizing the established order, social conventions, and moral rules, as far as the Marquis de Sade and the legendary figure of Don Juan went. In our time, as in the eighteenth century, love affairs and perspectives on war appear to be more important than social problems and collective protests, which are still loosely organized and which do not represent any major threat to the institutional order. The social scene looks empty in comparison with the overfull theater of the nineteenth century, which was agitated by democratic campaigns, labor movements, and national movements. The contemporary period criticizes principles and methods of social integration and mechanisms of social control more actively than it organizes social conflicts and social movements. Traditions are more directly attacked than domination, and confidence in the future and its opportunities is stronger than criticism of power elites. The idea of postmodernity correctly describes this situation.

We are living in a period dominated by rapid social changes, a deep crisis of established values, and the initiatives of elite groups, who are able to elaborate complex strategies. Our time is also dominated by international problems: the permanent risk of a major crisis involving the two nuclear superpowers and the difficult birth of new national states, especially in the Middle East. Only an empty space exists between Freud and Khomeini. This space used to be occupied by Marx and the social and political thinkers who spoke for the labor and other social movements, both reformist and revolutionary. Social life seems to have lost all principles of unity. Is it still possible to define democracy in such a social situation? It seems more appropriate to speak, on the one hand, of the permissiveness of mass society and, on the other hand, of a constant mobilization of the state in dangerous international crises. The state is no longer at the center of society but on its frontier. The unity of social life is limited to mass consumption. It is deprived of any capacity to impose obligations or sanctions but leaves individuals a free space for isolation, withdrawal, or exit. These images correspond especially to the European present because in Europe the deep crisis of the national states limits nations to the role of members of a more-or-less common market and to an economic and cultural space in which extreme individualism and mass culture easily combine and cooperate in eliminating all kinds of active social and political participation. Intermediary bodies—parties, unions, churches—are weakened. In the gap between planetary and individual problems, it seems impossible to organize collective action. The concept of a good or fair society cannot be defined because the idea of society itself is disappearing. We seldom refer to social systems, institutions, and power structures, but we very often refer to processes of change, their risks, and their positive aspects.

Let us accept once more the conclusion of the decline of the idea of society and its direct consequence: the decomposition of collective action aimed at the transformation of social, economic, and political organization. But are we allowed to conclude from this waning of a long period of direct correspondence between the national state, socioeconomic organization, and cultural demands that no central principle of social organization can any longer exist and that no social movement, that is, collective action that aims at controlling central cultural resources and models, can be organized? This is the core problem. The notion of social movement is not important if it is used to name a heterogeneous set of protest actions and conflicts that try to modify particular aspects of social and political organization. However, the concept has a central place in sociological analysis if it introduces the hypothesis that there exists in a given society a central conflict—for example, for political liberties or workers' rights—and that this conflict is associated with the defense of central, social, and cultural values, for example, internal peace or economic development. For these reasons, the analysis of social movements cannot be separated from the question of the unity of the social situation in which they appear. In the past we defined this unity as a culture, then as a civilization, then as a political regime, then as the social relations of production, and finally as a socioeconomic system. Does this unity take a new form in contemporary industrialized societies or does it disappear, as I just discussed, to be replaced by boundless and loosely related changes? And what could this principle of unity be if it is no longer the community's rules of exchange, a civilization's collective creeds, the modern national state, or the capitalist system? In the past, modern societies have always provided an answer to this question, introducing a new principle of unity at the same time they were destroying an old principle. But perhaps the moment has come when there is only a nihilist answer to these questions. Is not present-day sociology smothered by the ruins of the idea of society and its concrete expression, the functionalist school?

The answer cannot be a novel one; it must come from the heart of the Western cultural tradition because it necessarily appeared along with the process of modernization itself. I earlier observed that when religion and the political principles of social integration were decaying, the concept of individual subject, that is, the production of individualization, took on an increasing importance. The subject, which Western tradition also refers to as the conscience, is not the expression of an absolute, a transcendence, or an individual existence. It is consciousness of the human capacity to create and transform its environment and culture. During the sixteenth century, modernization not only produced a new rationalism and a rapid development of the natural sciences; it also created, through the Reformation, a new moral individualism. With the development of bourgeois society, emphasis is put on personal feelings, morality and intimacy. Today, the subject is defined by its capacity and right to oppose political or cultural processes and to defend its freedom. The more we move away from religion and what Comte called the metaphysical era, the more the subject stops being transcendent and transforms itself into a principle of protest against the social and political order.

The idea of subject is both linked and opposed to the idea of individual. It is linked because it presupposes the loosening of communitarian bonds and even of social roles; it is opposed because utilitarianism leads to a deterministic view of human behavior, which is supposed to be led by self-interest. On the contrary, the defense of personal freedom and, more especially, of the capacity for each individual to choose and control his individual life creates a constant tension between the logic of social integration and the reference to human rights.

The individual subject can be the principle of collective action only when two conditions are met. The first is that the defense of the subject must not be just a call for identity; rather, it should be a force of opposition to the dominations exerted on the person's language, tastes, values, and projects. Such a defense becomes much more important today than it was in the past because the industrialized production and diffusion of cultural goods are growing rapidly in importance. The second condition is that the individual cannot represent himself as a subject if he does not recognize other individuals as subjects. This idea has assumed a more and more central place in our culture; we call it "love." The individual becomes a subject through love and ceases to be a subject when he or she denies other individuals the right or the possibility to be subjects, as Levinas repeatedly pointed out.

The contrast with industrial society is striking. The liberation of individuals and societies was identified with the development of "production forces," and freedom was identified with modernization. In a postindustrial society—defined by the central role of "cultural" industries—freedom of the individual subject must be defended against mass production and mass consumption. The image of our society is dominated by this bipolar view, rationalization on one side, "subjectivation, that is, the recognition of the rights of persons and groups," on the other, instead of the unified "progressive" view of modernity, which is so visible in theories of modernization. This transformation is probably more acutely felt in Europe than in North America because of the memory of the totalitarian regimes that destroyed European nineteenth-century optimism. Social movements no longer pretend to control and reorient the process of modernization; they oppose moral principles to "total" powers. These new movements not only assert principles and aims; they also define themselves by their opposition to the social and cultural forces that dominate the production of symbolic goods. These movements consider such a conflict to be central to the new postindustrial society, which is organized around the production of symbolic or cultural services, such as the mass media, which shape our images of the world, medical care, which determines our perceptions of life, birth, reproduction, illness, and death, and to a certain extent science and education.

Once again, let us compare the two opposite images of social life. What we have described on the one side is the image of diverse and continuous change that eliminates all principles of unity and integration of the social system and completely separates individual actors. These actors follow utilitarian strategies in states that are more and more the makers of war and less and less the makers of law. On the other side is the image of a social system organized around the production and diffusion of cultural goods and structured by conflicts between those who rule this production and those who resist the domination that is exerted on them not as citizens or workers but as persons.

These two images are not contradictory: they are both complementary and opposed. Democracy cannot exist if there is no exit from a central social conflict and if there is no external element that can mediate between conflicting interests. The liberal reference to social change and to the creation of new opportunities is the classical way of finding compromises between opposing class interests. An open geographical, technological, and economic frontier allows a society to negotiate the results of growth instead of being stifled by a paralyzing conflict. But if social conflicts must be complemented by an open political system, such a system, to be representative and democratic, needs to be based on social conflicts.

Although complementary in some ways, these two images are nevertheless opposed to each other. The strategic approach to social life corresponds better to the interest of powerful categories, the conflict-oriented approach attracts those who feel dominated, and the idea of subject appeals more directly to intellectuals. But this apparent opposition is a limited one. First, the idea of subject is not a purely abstract one in a society where the main social conflicts are organized around it. Second, utilitarianism is not to be found only among rich and powerful people in a mass-consumption society. Finally, social conflicts and the subject are concepts that cannot be separated from each other: the central social conflicts concern conflicting views about subject-building. Liberal utilitarianism, social movements, and the idea of the subject are as interrelated as opposed teams and the field on which they compete.

It is more useful to recognize that each of these three main themes can take a relatively different importance according to the historical situation. Here we can use the Greek differentiation between periods and epochs, that is, between types of societies and processes of transition. Periods are historical ensembles organized around particular cultural orientations and social conflicts. Epochs are moments of rupture and transformation. During an epoch of transition, such as the Renaissance, individualism, the rejection of traditional rules, stronger competition, and the risk of war gain ground. Do we live today in a new historical period or are we still in an epoch of rupture and transition? I believe that we are leaving such an epoch. What have been called new social movements during the 1970s and the early 1980s expressed in many cases this crisis of industrial values, the push toward a more permissive society, and a deep preoccupation with the risks of war. During the last decade the desocialization of society has been highly visible. This situation recalls the end of the nineteenth century when Durkheim was acutely sensitive to the decomposition of traditional forms of social control, and when Weber, going beyond his misgivings about the effects of modernization, was fascinated by the value-orientations of a modernized society.

There is another way of contrasting historical situations. Sometimes the subject becomes self-aware through achievement and "engagement." Other times, however, the subject becomes self-aware through struggling against reification, that is, disengaging, and freeing himself or herself from the world of objects. Thus an epic image of the subject is criticized by a romantic image of its process of self-production. The subject is never located in the middle of social life, as is the image of the prince or symbols of national unity; it is the common reference of conflicting social actors, both in their positive projects and in their attacks against what they consider to be dangerous for the subject. No particular actor can identify himself or herself with the subject.

I conclude that the hypermodernity of our society, because it destroys the possibility of a permanent order and the very idea of society, makes the formation of "proper" social movements impossible. But collective movements have not always been social; often, before developing in a political or economic arena, they had been religious. Conflicting social interests and cultural innovations expressed themselves in religious forms from the time of ancient societies to the European sixteenth century. In the same way, what we call social movements are becoming less specifically social. Their main objective is no longer to create an ideal society but to defend the freedom and creativity of the subject in a universe that appears to be dominated by money and pleasure, technology and war. Perhaps we are already living in a new historical period, in a postindustrial society. One of the arguments in favor of such a hypothe-

sis is the necessity to distinguish between two kinds of collective actions
that are different from the social movements characteristic of industrial
society: on one side are a new progress of individualism and a new fear
of war and catastrophes; on the other side are the new social movements
that challenge the control of cultural goods.

4. SOCIAL MOVEMENTS AND HISTORICAL MOVEMENTS

In the preceding section I concluded that there has been neither the
triumph of social movements in a society that has become entirely civil, as
the nineteenth- and twentieth-century progressives hoped, nor their disappearance. Rather we see a growing separation between the two axes of
collective action on which social actors may be situated: synchronic and
diachronic. The synchronic axis situates actors by their roles in a social
system that is defined by the level of "historicity" (that is, the capacity of
self-production). The diachronic axis situates actors by their participation
in the process of change and by the strategies that orient this process.
When speaking of social movements we refer almost exclusively to dominated and powerless actors. Earlier I observed that strategies of change or
development are more easily elaborated by powerful elite groups. It is a
mistake, however, to identify each of these main orientations of collective
behavior with a specific social category. Instead, we must offer a more
complete view of the actors in social life and the historical process by
defining both the dominant and the dominated actors in structural conflicts and processes of historical change. The term social movement
should not be used to characterize only opposition forces or low-status
groups. On the contrary, the term identifies the main actors—both dominant and dominated—of central social conflicts through which the main
cultural resources and values are transformed into forms of political and
social organization. Social movements are those movements that deal with
structural problems in a given society. Historical movements are those that
aim at control of the process of historical development. The separation
between the two categories of problems and actors is more extreme in our
societies, which have achieved a high level of historicity, than it was during
the industrial period. Although British and American social thought was
more influenced by liberalism and emphasized processes of change, German and French social thinkers, especially the Marxists, emphasized structural conflicts.

   Having recognized the strength and influence of the hyperliberal ideas
that identify social problems with processes of social change and modernization, let us begin the effort to give a more complete view of collective
actors in our society by considering the historical movement that opposes
the process of change and the elite that controls this process.

The antinuclear and ecological movements oppose a hyperindustri-alization that destroys natural equilibriums and reinforces militarism. They attack not only the social elite but also the belief in economic growth and new technology, which they consider illusory, dangerous, and self-destructive and which they believe create unbearable tensions and con-flicts in the world that can lead to an apocalyptic war. These criticisms are generally directed against technocrats, but often they have an anti-capitalist component that maintains a certain continuity with the labor movement. The continuity from revolutionary socialism to new social movements was enhanced by the central role of radical leftists in the protest campaigns that gained momentum after 1968. This radicalism expressed itself through a post-Marxist structuralism that denounced all aspects of social life as representing the logic of domination, manipula-tion, and exclusion in favor of the ruling groups. This radical criticism is directed against what Althusser called the state's ideological apparatuses. This expression makes clear that the enemy is no longer a social class or even a power elite but the state itself as a system of total control. This is a clear demonstration that this radicalism is not a social movement but a historical movement, and that it is more antimodern or antistate than anticapitalist. Its main preoccupation is to fight the identification of the totalitarian state with modernization and growth.

This absence of concern with defining relevant social actors and the global character of its attacks differentiate these "critical" intellectuals from social movements, which are always organized around a social con-flict between clearly defined actors. Historical movements constantly swing from a countercultural global critique to a series of loosely con-nected campaigns because the absence of a clear definition of the parties to a social conflict deprives it of any principle of stabilization. Neverthe-less, historical movements like political ecology are not just counter-cultural; they combine a critique of the process of economic change with attacks against a power that is defined more in political than in social terms. When this conflict-oriented dimension disappears, a historical movement can be transformed into a sect that marginalizes itself by rejecting society's cultural orientations and forms of social organization.

If we define a social movement as the confrontation of opposed groups for the control and use of the main cultural resources and values, in knowledge and ethics as much as in economic life, antinuclear and ecological actions are not social movements. Rather they are "alternative" movements that try to globally transform cultural orientations, social organization, and political power. Their antimilitarist and antimodernist actions are directly opposed to the individualism and strategies of the ruling group, which values any social change it can use for its own interest. The ruling group's historical optimism values utility and pleasure; the pessimism of alternative movements opposes policies and programs it considers to be carried forward by impulses of power and death.

These two movements have one thing in common: they are both more political than social, that is, they question processes of change rather than forms of social organization. Their common strength is to define themselves at the state level and to intervene directly at the center of public life.

The new social movements that protest the power that controls the production of cultural goods are different and in many ways opposed to these historical, "alternative" movements. Debates and conflicts about the effects of the mass media or biological and medical technologies are not political discussions. Rather they question a sociocultural domination while accepting a positive judgment about modern technology in general. Today, as at the beginning of industrial society, social movements and historical movements are both mixed and separated, but a great distance always exists between social movements that attack civil powers and historical movements that oppose the state. This distance is now even larger than was the gap that separated labor unions from communist or socialist groups at the beginning of the nineteenth century.

Feminist movements are more complex. It is necessary to distinguish in them at least two different orientations. On one side exists a feminist liberalism, which is an emancipatory movement following the tradition of British and American nineteenth-century reform movements. This movement rejects the identification of women with private life and fights for an equal participation of women in all aspects of public life and in all occupations, law and politics in particular. Simone de Beauvoir was the central figure of this progressive liberalism, which occasionally becomes radical by linking itself to socialist ideas but is most influential among women who enter into social and occupational elites. The women's liberation movement is quite different from this liberal or radical feminism. It emphasizes the particular features of feminine sexuality and fights directly against male domination. This movement has been especially active in the United States and its links with psychoanalysis have been emphasized both by American writers and by A. Fouque, head of the most militant group in France. The liberal wing of the women's liberation movement is a historical movement, and its optimism is similar to the orientations of dominʾnt groups. The radical wing of the women's liberation movement is a social movement of opposition. It is fragile because it emphasizes women's sexuality and the differences between men and women. The difficulty of building equal heterosexual relations runs the risk of isolating militant women in a homosexual rupture that could result in the creation of a marginal culture that ceases to be a social movement. This fragility, which contrasts with the efficiency of liberal feminism, should not prevent us from recognizing the deep and lasting effect of a movement that transforms the man-woman relationship.

The experience of industrial society clearly indicates the two main obstacles that hinder the development of social movements. On the one hand, such movements, because they are not political but purely social, are likely to dissolve into a plurality of campaigns and protest movements. On the other hand, if they are tightly linked with political action—as was unionism, which was generally subordinated to socialist parties—this action imposes its rules on the social movements and can even lay the groundwork for a new "popular" political power that suppresses social movements and public liberties.

Contemporary antinuclear movements are far from serving an authoritarian state, but their main strength comes from an antistate orientation. This orientation is especially evident in Germany, a country that is still dominated by the horrors of the Nazi regime. This antinationalism represents, as much as nationalism, a predominance of political over social orientations.

The idea of a growing separation between social and historical movements will not be accepted easily. On the contrary, many people think that the distance between these two kinds of collective action is shrinking and even disappearing. This idea was one of the main assumptions of *gauchisme* and I consider it to be one of the main obstacles to the formation of social movements in Western countries. If we consider Soviet society, it is true that the global, national and cultural protest of Solzhenitsyn or Bukovskii was stronger, at least during the Brezhnev period, than the social criticism elaborated by Plioucht or Sakharov. But when we consider Western countries it is false and almost preposterous to say that all aspects of social life are subordinated to the interventions of a repressive and military state power.

It is too early to know how new social movements will grow, but it seems reasonable to expect that the social movements that question cultural domination will be more distant from political action than was the labor movement in industrial society, and will be even more distant than the movements of peasants and craftsmen that characterized preindustrial societies. In many countries, especially in Germany and France, we observed the separation of two types of protest. In France, two opposite movements came from May 1968: one attacked the state and used a vocabulary that came from the revolutionary tradition; the other gave life to grassroots movements, in particular to women's liberation and campaigns on behalf of immigrant workers. In other countries the same duality is visible. For example, in the United States during the 1960s the student movement at Berkeley was quite different from the radical political orientation of student protest on campuses like Columbia or Cornell.

These new social movements, like their predecessors, have both a defensive and an offensive face. The defensive face is the more visible: the defense of identity and, sometimes, of community against the domination of new technologies and new power. The stronger this defensive action, the more likely the social movement or the historical movement is to fight against the state because when a social actor feels unable to make headway he rejects society, power, and modernity in a global way. An offensive action tends to identify itself in an optimistic way with the new cultural orientations it seeks to control and to reject its enemies as obstacles to progress. The risk here for social movements is to become incorporated too early and too easily into the institutional system and to be absorbed by political forces. Offensive action reveals more clearly the problems and orientations of a postindustrial society. In particular, it substitutes the idea of system for the old idea of evolution, and it acts on behalf of a cultural rather than an economic concern.

The liberal critique of social movements has rightly shown that new social movements must leave the political field, strictly speaking, because they defend individuals who feel threatened—but at the same time excited—by the new cultural productions. Private life does not replace public life, as is too often contended; rather it becomes the core of public life. Culture becomes political in much the same way that the economy became political in the eighteenth and nineteenth centuries when workers and craftsmen fought as producers and as agents of a practical reason that opposed itself to the irrationality of profit.

Today individuals are dominated in their perceptions and emotions. They cannot resist this domination but oppose it with the whole of their personalities, their imaginations, their primary groups, and their personal projects. This view of the individual corresponds to the new global definition of the social field, which is no longer a collective activity that transforms nature but a system whose elements are interdependent and whose modernity is defined by its level of complexity and its capacity for internal and external communication. A society of communication replaces a society of production in the same way that a Cartesian "soul" is replaced by an existentialist image of the subject.

To round out this definition of the main social and historical actors of our time, let us not forget the social movement created by those who control the production and diffusion of cultural goods. The leaders of these industries, like all dominant groups, are not just looking for more profit or more power; they seek to create a social movement that organizes the main cultural resources and models of our society in a way that corresponds to their interests. This new elite speaks of creativity, complexity, and freedom of choice. It links these values to the development of a centralized system of cultural production and to the diffusion of new needs and new values of success and seduction. In particular, it favors the search for pleasure, commercial eroticism, and the discovery of cultures that are historically or geographically different from ours. These are important elements of the elite's ideology. Social movements of opposition criticize its emphasis on acquisitiveness and on symbols of social status, as well as its commercialization of interpersonal and cultural experiences.

5. FROM OLD TO NEW SOCIAL MOVEMENTS

The protest movements, opinion campaigns, and social conflicts that are lumped under the vague name of social movements and that attracted the interest of an unusually large number of sociologists during the 1970s are a very heterogeneous set of collective actions. Here I seek to disentangle the phenomena that have been mixed together in a situation of economic and cultural crisis. Let us sum up the results of our analysis. Three main types of collective behavior may be distinguished.

The first type includes those that manifest the crisis and decline of industrial society. After a long period of growth and the predominance of the ideology of modernization, protest movements reject the very idea of development. The Club of Rome was one of the first groups to criticize the myth of endless growth and to recognize the limits of growth. Many people today are convinced that we should end development and enter into a new equilibrium. They defend the idea of a self-sustaining equilibrium against the idea of self-sustained growth. The fascination with oriental cultures stems from this idea. Although only superficially known, these cultures are used as expressions of opposition to aggressive rationalism.

The second type of collective behavior focuses on the hypermodernist ideas in which systems and structures are replaced by processes of change. The more optimistic groups have developed strategic views of these changes to use them on behalf of their own interests. The more pessimistic groups are preoccupied with a possible loss of individual cultural identity and the uprootedness of a society that is more and more similar to a market in which nothing prevents the stronger from dominating the weaker.

The convergence of the critique of industrial society, sometimes inherited from socialist ideas, and antidevelopmentalism led to the success of a *gauchisme* that took new forms by fighting cultural as well as economic domination. But this *gauchisme* was far from being a class-conscious movement like the labor movement. It was not even specifically anticapitalist. Rather it rejected all aspects of the process of modernization and cultural change. It did not believe in the existence of collective actors or the possibility of new liberation movements. It limited itself to opposing a complete and closed system of domination. Its pessimism came in part from its tendency to maintain itself within the limits of industrial capitalism, Marxism, and the labor movement and in part from the fact that it was highly conscious of the failure and crimes of the regimes that pretended to come out of the labor movement and to be socialist. That explains its view of society as a coherent system of signs and instruments of domination. Its image of social life can be called semiological because it considers all social phenomena as signs of an omnipresent logic of domination and exclusion. This extreme view attained a predominant influence in sociology during the 1970s after the collapse of the optimistic view of social development shared by both functionalists and Marxists. It penetrated sociological thought in the United States later than in Europe but maintained itself later in the United States than in France, where it almost entirely disappeared at the end of the 1970s. Only in Germany did it rest on a solid intellectual tradition.

The third type of collective behavior involves the control and use of the main cultural resources. On one side, a dominant ideology emphasizes the individualism of consumers and proudly creates a society that is ever richer in information and capacities for communication. On the other side, opposition movements defend identity and community but imagine at the same time a society more favorable to initiative, personal development, and interpersonal communications.

Sociological analysis, which separates the various meanings of collective behavior, can never be identified with historical analysis because historical analysis gives a synthetic view of the various analytical meanings entwined in complex phenomena. What sociological analysis considers to be most important is not in general what has the deepest and most lasting effects from the point of view of historical analysis. Protest movements depend for their historical successes or failures on external factors even more than on their intrinsic importance. The relative historical importance of crisis behavior, reactions to change, and social movements depends first of all on the capacity of a collectivity to pass from one societal form to another. When dynamism and creativity are at a low level, crisis behavior and critiques of modernization are strong. When the construction of a new type of society and culture is active, positive and negative reactions to social change gain ground. Finally, when a new type of society has already been built and when the rupture with interests and values of the old society is complete, new social movements gain a central place and define new problems and values.

In a schematic way, crisis behaviors are still stronger in Europe, especially in the oldest industrial countries, and positive and negative reactions to social change are predominant in the United States. Thus new social movements are formed in different contexts on the two sides of the Atlantic. In some European countries, especially Germany, critical social thought is stronger because it is more directly based on antistate attitudes. In the United States, the creation of new cultural orientations is more active because new social movements are linked, as in Germany, with antistate attitudes but, unlike Germany, the attacks are more directed against an "imperialist" state than against the destruction of society by state power. For this reason new social movements are more influential in the United States but critical action and radical ideas are more important in Germany. France is the unexpected case of a country where a period of active cultural and social innovation (around 1968) was followed by a successful effort to revive old models of social and political action and by a strong distrust of all social movements, a result of the protracted influence of the Communist party on the French intelligentsia. These factors reinforce the traditional subordination in France of social movements to political forces that express the growing political influence of the new middle classes, which were republican in the nineteenth century and are socialist in the twentieth century.

But, on the whole, more optimistic conclusions can be reached. Western countries are emerging from a long period of crisis. At first they were dominated by a pessimistic version of social ideas that corresponded to industrial society and by a structural Marxism that eliminated social actors and movements from its analysis. Then at the end of the 1970s came a short period when private issues completely dominated public life. Soon new economic and technological developments and the success of liberal ideas favored either a conservative nationalism or, in a deeper sense, the interpretation of a new cultural situation by dominant groups. New movements of opposition are organizing themselves in the face of this dominant ideology. As at the beginning of industrialization in the nineteenth century, these movements are now going through a phase of utopian communism and infantilism. Their new demands are too early and too easily institutionalized in our open political system. These two factors make it difficult to form new social movements, but it would be a mistake not to perceive that the social scene has already been transformed. The first observers who spoke, fifteen years ago, of a postindustrial society have been accused with some reason of not having distinguished clearly enough postindustrial from industrial society. Today it is easier to see that technological transformations represent only a new stage of industrialism and that new cultural and social demands appear—in the cultural sphere—far from the economic and occupational area and constitute the main basis of postindustrial society.

These transformations of social practices call for a new representation of social life. We need new sociological models or a new kind of social thought. This thought should be as different from classical sociology as that body of thought was from the political philosophy of the sixteenth or eighteenth centuries. The central question of the new type of social analysis is the following: when all absolute principles of social organization have disappeared and when a more and more complex civil society has separated itself completely from the state and no longer derives any principle of unity from it, should we abandon the very idea of social system? Or put another way, should we only conceive of social life as a flow of changes in which social actors elaborate rational strategies or resist a flow that is dominated by a state that is no longer a political institution and is more and more a maker of war?

Although developing a critique of the idea of society, my analysis affirms that social life has a unity. It is a system that is defined and constituted by the conflicting relationships between dominant and dominated groups for the control of what I call historicity, that is, the main cultural models through which a collectivity shapes its relationships with its environment. Our "society" no longer has any institutional or moral unity, sovereignty, or central principle of legitimacy. It does, however, have the unity of a drama.

Many people have thought that the decline of all forms of transcendence would lead to the triumph of the rational pursuit of interest and the transformation of society into a marketplace. This is the dominant assumption of present-day historical movements, including both those in favor of such an evolution and those opposed to it. But the best social thinkers have always recognized, in addition to interests, the existence of convictions. When the process of secularization triumphs, the world of religious and political passions does not disappear; it becomes social. Gods were replaced by reason and reason by history; now history is replaced by the subject. Social life can never be reduced to rationality and conflicts of interests. On the contrary, economic behavior is integrated into social movements that fight for the social control of cultural values, that is, for the transformation of convictions into forms of social organization.

From industrial to postindustrial society, collective action stops being explained by social or economic situation. Classes, as defined by a situation, are being replaced by social movements and by the action of social categories that are defined by both relations of domination and cultural orientations. This eliminates the notions of human nature and natural law but it also eliminates the ideas of the laws of historical evolution and economic structure. All aspects of social organization result from the conflictual process of the self-production of social life.

In the present intellectual situation the most urgent task is to reintroduce the ideas of modernity and development that have been so strongly attacked during the last twenty years. The analysis of social movements is linked with the idea that the level of self-production of social life tends to rise and to create new opportunities and new conflicts. The idea, so fashionable today, of postmodernity is useful only if it frees us from the exhausted industrial image of modernity. Postmodernity corresponds to a moment in which the consciousness of historicity is lost, in which "mannerism" is triumphant in art, and in which intellectuals no longer appear to be able to express and represent collective and personal experiences. Postmodernity corresponds to decreased creativity and a crisis of collective action.

It is urgent to analyze new forms of cultural creation, social domination, and social movements. It is also urgent to overcome the strange pessimism that foresees the decline of our democracy even as we observe a rapid extension and diversification of public opinion and the public space, an evolution at least as important as the new threats appearing against our liberties. Social thought has been dominated too long by the crises of industrial society, the labor movement, and the ideologies, optimistic or pessimistic that were linked with them. Today we lack a general analysis of social change and the new forms of cultural and social life that are rapidly spreading around us. Sociological analysis cannot rise as late as Minerva's bird. It is rather at dawn, when a new day begins and new images and new people appear on the social scene, that sociologists must understand the new drama that is being performed.

Dialectics of Modernity

Reenchantment and Dedifferentiation as Counterprocesses

Edward A. Tiryakian

A generation ago the sociology of development featured a vast literature having modernization as leitmotif. Owing to a variety of factors, some intellectual and others ideological, adepts of modernization analysis (with some notable exceptions, such as Inkeles [1983]) have left center stage in macrosociology. The intention of this chapter is neither to recall them for a belated encore nor to drive unnecessary nails into the coffin of a superannuated theory. I would, however, like to make some extended reflections on that fundamental social state necessarily presumed by the term "modernization": namely, "modernity" itself. The concept of modernity was never really given its theoretical due in the heyday of modernization analysis but, by a quirk of fate, it is in a period of global socioeconomic crisis (Amin 1982; Brandt Commission 1983; Tiryakian 1984) that the theme of modernity has become a fruitful heuristic vein of sociological analysis. The concept has, however, been shorn of the optimistic and evolutionist biases of the modernization paradigm, biases that tacitly equated the end point of modernization with a Camelot-like United States and by extension with pax Americana.

If American sociologists were the major contributors to comparative modernization analysis (Black 1976), the recent major writings on the theme of modernity have had as many inputs from one side of the Atlantic as from the other (for example, Balandier 1985; Bell 1985; Berger 1973, 1977; Bernstein 1985; Eisenstadt 1973; Featherstone 1985; Habermas 1981, [1981] 1984; Nelson 1981; Tiryakian 1985a; Touraine 1984). Thus modernity is a choice topic for an exchange of theoretical perspectives such as the present volume. Having examined the burgeoning literature on modernity I propose that the single major background figure who is the common denominator to the various approaches on the problematics of modernity is Max Weber. Weber left us an important patrimony by indicating the complexities of the broad sociohistorical processes that underlay the development of Western modern society. He saw societal, even civilizational, change as real (that is, as having objective social consequences) but not as teleological. And it is the very ambiguity of the modern situation, so accurately and poignantly presented by Weber, that gives him wide appeal today.[1] I propose to take two important facets of modernity that stem from Weber that seem to be accepted as "givens" by various writers and argue that a comprehensive analysis of large-scale change requires these two facets to be related to counter-processes of change.

Weber's legacy is multilayered and multitiered, but there are two central and interrelated Weberian themes commonly accepted by scholars of different ideological leanings (for example, Luhmann 1982; Tilly 1984; Habermas [1981] 1985) as being the master processes of Western social change: differentiation and rationalization. If these are the processes of social change that have generated the modern Western capitalist industrial social order (including its bureaucratic forms of social organization), the competitive civilizational advantage of the West, for Weber, has also required an ancillary sociopsychological process of no less significance in the formation of Western modernity. That process involves emptying the world of magic (*Entzauberung*), a process stemming from the interrelated cognitive shift to this world as the locus of salvific activities (hence a devaluation of the sacraments as ingress to otherworldly salvation), *and* the replacement of magic by rational calculation. This process is exemplified by the way that the scientific method has become the accepted mode of mastering the world.

The heart of Weber's perspective is expressed in two passages in his famous address, "Science as a Vocation." In the first Weber links scientific progress today to a broader Western process of "intellectualization" or "intellectualist rationalization," which

> means that principally there are no mysterious incalculable forces that come into play, but rather that one can, in principle, master all things by calculation. *This means that the world is disenchanted.* One need no longer have recourse to magical means in order to master or implore the spir-

1. The ambiguity of our modern condition resides in this: On the one hand scientific and technological advances have become rationalized and institutionalized as an integral part of the modern order. On the other hand the meaning of that order for its actors, which is also an integral feature of the motivational dispositions of human beings in seeking and pursuing socially approved goals, is no longer assured, not even by scientific knowledge. At best the scientist replaces John Bunyan's "Christian" (in *Pilgrim's Progress*) as the modern pilgrim. At worst the scientist, in the never-ending quest for empirical certitude as a substitute for the certitude of faith, continually undoes the meaning of the world.

its. . . . Technical means and calculations perform the service. This above all is what intellectualization means. (Weber 1958, 138, emphasis mine)

The second passage is Weber's pithy summarization of the present age:

The fate of our times is characterized by rationalization and intellectualization and, above all, by the "disenchantment of the world." Precisely the ultimate and most sublime values have retreated from public life either into the transcendental realm of mystic life or into the brotherliness of direct and personal human relations. (Weber 1958, 155)

The major contemporary social theorist Habermas acknowledges the legacy of Weber's interpretation. He observes:

Weber's investigations can be used to substantiate the view that all the paths of rationalization branching through civilizations . . . point in the same direction, that of a disenchanted understanding of the world purified of magical ideas. ([1981] 1985, 196)

Weber judges the rationalization of worldviews by the extent to which magical thinking is overcome. In the dimension of ethical rationalization, he observes disenchantment primarily in the interaction between the believer and God. . . . In the cognitive dimension, disenchantment of the manipulation of things and events goes along with a demythologization of the knowledge of what is. . . . With this the fixation on the surface of concrete phenomena that is anchored in myth can be superseded in favor of a disinterested orientation to general laws underlying the phenomena. ([1981] 1985, 212–13)

Although Weber's famous thesis concerning the religious grounds of Western modernity continues to be contested (Marshall 1982), including even his interpretation of the Puritan doctrine of predestination (Roth 1986), his pronouncements on rationalization, differentiation, and disenchantment as the key factors of Western modernity have become an integral part of the sociological canon. Indeed, several features of late-twentieth-century society may be thought of as further accentuating the key aspects of modernity advanced by Weber so many years ago.

For the sake of brevity let me choose just a few illustrations. In four decades the computer revolution has brought about changes as momentous as those of the industrial revolution two hundred years ago. Of course this still-unfolding revolution is a radical extension of the process of rationalization and mastering the world through exact calculations. Computer technology is enabling us to systematically explore both microscopic and macroscopic worlds, from cells and genes to planets and galaxies, with the result that the boundaries of the life-world are rapidly changing. Also, the continuous progress of the life sciences and biotechnological developments is redrawing the frontiers of knowledge about the biochemical bases of life and death. In the process the disenchantment of the world has taken a new turn as human beings increase their empirical knowledge and ability to control the processes of reproduction. The ability to control and limit reproduction, which is conducive to changes in morality, and the ability to gain advance information concerning the fetus are contributing to the further disenchantment of the world by taking away the allure, mystery, and charm of sexuality and gender. This, perhaps, has been the ultimate domain of enchantment. It has also been a primitive domain because fertility rites have universally been used by religious cults in harnessing magical forces.

For good measure we might propose one further domain that has become increasingly disenchanted in the present century: the domain of authority. The disenchantment of authority is part of the process of secularization, and one can point to the Reformation and the disenchantment of papal authority as the beginning of this trend. The disenchantment of monarchical authority began in England in the seventeenth century with the regicide of Charles I. This event ended the view of the monarch as a divine representative who was the incarnation of magical powers. The Enlightenment and the industrial revolution further diminished the sacred aura of the monarch, leading in the nineteenth century to either republican regimes or constitutional monarchies as the typical bases of the Western polity. Monarchical and imperial authority were even more impaled during World War I, in Europe (the demise of Austria-Hungary and Wilhelmine Germany) and elsewhere (the Ottoman Empire, China, etc.). World War II and its aftermath not only witnessed the demise of some remnant monarchies (for example, in the Balkan countries) but, more important, the demise of colonial authority and the total disenchantment of the colonial premise of "assimilation." In our recent past political authority in Western democracies has been further disenchanted, both because of Watergate and because of the broader aspects of political delegitimation involved in this "twilight of authority" (Nisbet 1975).[2]

Weber's basic perspective on modernity may be termed a post- or late-Enlightenment view of the significant underlying processes of Western social change: it lacks the optimism and some of the presuppositions of the *philosophes* but still contains the core belief that human endeavors— scientific, political, and economic—can lead in the not-too-distant future to the regeneration of the human condition without recourse to the transcendental. Thus Weber's thought shares the general liberal orienta-

2. I refer here not simply to political institutions but to various other institutions in which political authority has lost its diffuse aura, including the nuclear family and educational institutions.

tion of modern social science toward modernity (Seidman 1983; Ezrahi 1990).

To be sure, the tumultuous events of the past twenty years or so, coming on top of the global wars and totalitarian regimes that severely pockmarked the West, have greatly shaken and modified the liberal perspective. Youth movements of the counterculture (Yinger 1982; Leventman 1982), autonomist movements against the nation-state (Tiryakian and Rogowski 1985), and movements of religious fundamentalism have suggested to several scholars that the "revolt against modernity" (an identical title used by Lipset [1980] in the context of political movements and by Bell [1985] with respect to cultural movements) has deep roots and merits attention even though the secular trends still point to the fulfillment of the promises of the Enlightenment. Here again, let me invoke Habermas as illustrative of the late-twentieth-century heirs of the Enlightenment-Weberian perspective. To cite Bernstein:

> One might epitomize Habermas' entire intellectual project and his fundamental stance as writing a new *Dialectic of Enlightenment*—one which does full justice to the dark side of the Enlightenment legacy . . . but nevertheless redeems and justifies the hope of freedom, justice, and happiness. The project of modernity, the hope of Enlightenment thinkers, is not a bitter illusion . . . but a practical task which has not yet been realized and which can still orient our actions. (1985, 31)

Perhaps we might best speak of the current sociological evaluation of modernity as pluralistic.[3] The public arena is not as bereft or disenchanted of magical or mystical (or, very broadly, *irrational*) currents and movements as Weber's image of modernity seemed to suggest. These movements and orientations, which might be taken as a subclass of Weber's *Wertrationalität* (Weber 1978, 1:24–26), are seen by some not just as aberrations of modernity but as providing new vehicles of meaning to modernity in a period that is characterized by disenchantment with progress but enchantment with scientific and technological advances (Swatos 1983; Balandier 1985, 149–52). In other words, the values of liberalism and their institutionalization in the public and cultural agencies of modern Western societies have become acknowledged as no longer sufficient to define the situation of modernity; at the same time the countervalues and counterprocesses that have surfaced in the past twenty years are not themselves taken as the parameters of a new order of modernity.

The recent rethinking of modernity has provided an important, albeit perhaps painful, corrective evaluation of our present situation and the

---

3. Benjamin Nelson was very sensitive to this heterogeneity. His sensitivity is aptly conveyed in the title of his posthumous volume, *On the <u>Roads</u> to Modernity* (1981) (emphasis mine).

processes of social change that have formed it in the immediate past. However, in my judgment there is a need both to broaden the theoretical refinement of the master processes of change in the West and to question the assumption that the fate of modernity and the fate of the West are so inextricably bound as to be for all practical purposes one and the same. The theoretical position I advance is that Western sociology—and here we include the Marxist as well as the liberal traditions together as one general macrofamily—is correct in viewing Western civilization as dynamic and as having exerted a mighty influence vis-à-vis other regions of the globe for two or more centuries. But the very dynamics of change of Western modernity have contained not only the processes of differentiation and disenchantment but also the processes of dedifferentiation and reenchantment. These two latter processes should be seen neither as aberrations in the major evolutionary trajectory of modernity nor as nugatory and epiphenomenal but rather as fundamental to the dialectics of change. They may be termed "counterprocesses" of modernity, akin to Boulding's notion of "anti–tropic processes" that offset the exhaustion of a system's potential in the production process (Boulding 1985, 16).

1. REENCHANTMENT

The intellectual view that magic and enchantment were driven out of the dominant sphere of Western culture has two major periods of modernity in mind. The first is that of Reformation Europe when Protestantism (especially among the Puritan and the radical sects) stripped the world of the magical mystification associated with the Catholic Church (the sacramental system, the cult of saints, belief in miracles, and the other features of the popular religion). The second period, which may be thought of as a "mop-up" phase of secularization, is that of the nineteenth century, when empirical science replaced religious versions of world reality with its own accounts.

I contend here that this view grossly simplifies the relationship of enchantment to Western modernity in that it essentially conceives of enchantment and modernity as incompatible and that advances of modernity necessarily require cognitive and cultural disenchantment. In fact, from the Enlightenment on the cultural sphere has had a variety of new ways of viewing the world as magical and enchanted. This is what I mean by "reenchantment." I further contend that advances of modernity in the West evince components of reenchantment, particularly but not exclusively in the cultural sphere.

A neglected feature of "the secularization of the European mind," to borrow Chadwick's phrase (1979), is the "alteration of consciousness" in the Western mentality. I shall sketch the major aspects of this process and

its manifestations in the recent modern period and defer for another
occasion a more detailed treatment with documentation.

Weber's crucial insight concerning the shift in the focus of salvific
activities to this world is highly pregnant but calls for additional theoretical analysis. The shift entails secularization, but only if we understand by
this term that what previously was seen as "mundane" came (not immediately, of course, but over the course of time) to be viewed as having
religious significance in its own right. The Protestant deemphasis of the
church's sacraments and sacred images, all of which pointed to the mar-
vels of the "other world," went hand in hand with the sacralization of
formerly "mundane" human spheres: work (which of course received
paramount attention by Weber), predication (the reemphasis of the
"word" of God rather than the images of God), and—particularly in the
nineteenth century, although it began with Luther—the domesticity and
the sacredness of the conjugal unit.

This shift of sacredness from the transcendental or otherworldly
sphere, where human agency has very little efficacy or power, to this
world, where human agency has much greater rein, is one of the most
important features of Western modernity. It involves a rejection of the
fatalistic attitude that what happens in this world is predetermined, inherent, or follows inexorable laws.[4] Once the Western mentality came to
the awareness that human agency was decisive in this world and free of
otherworldly supervision, it also, ironically, became free to see anew that
this world was differentiated between what was marvelous, enchanted,
and magical and what was not. In this transformation otherworldly beings, space, etc., came to be viewed in terms of this world. This secularization of magical consciousness has several ramifications that are integral
to an appreciation of the process of reenchantment as a major aspect of
Western modernity.

Perhaps the most important Western cultural movement of the modern period has been the romantic movement. It began somewhere in the
second half of the eighteenth century and, depending on what we take as
its central characteristics, we can either take a conservative approach and
say that it came to a close somewhere in the middle of the nineteenth
century, or take a bolder stance and propose that romanticism has re-

4. Paulo Freire has broadly designated this orientation as the "magical level of consciousness" (Freire 1973, 44). The phrase is suggestive, but in terms of this analysis it is better to
think of a "premodern"and a "modern" magical consciousness. The premodern magical
consciousness conceives the forces that alter the operations of the world as being ultimately
beyond human control, albeit capable of being invoked by special human agents or by some
rituals some of the time. The modern magical consciousness denies a transcendent reality
but accepts that the world can be transformed (even radically, as in the case of millenarian
and revolutiontary movements) from its natural appearances and operations solely by
human means.

mained a powerful cultural current since its emergence. In this latter view romanticism was most recently manifested in the countercultural and youth movements of the late 1960s in which the dominant themes were the emancipation of the self from an oppressive society, the return to nature and rejection of industrial society, the primacy of one's feelings, the donning of bohemian appearance, and at the same time the search for a new harmony among human beings. An earlier major renewal of romanticism was the surrealist movement, which was the most broad-based cultural movement of this century, certainly in painting, poetry, and the cinema (from Buñuel to Monty Python), and which had an important political spillover (Gershman 1969; Benjamin 1978). Whatever its specific time frame, romanticism has had a major impact not only in the arts but also in other cultural spheres such as philosophy, religion, and, as Shalin (1986) has cogently argued, sociology itself.

I have suggested that a basic orientation of romanticism in its various forms is a rejection of one major side of modernity: the seemingly cold, drab, impersonal, anonymous, standardized, rationalized, lifeless, technocratic industrial order. But it is more than a rejection; it is also an orientation that seeks and finds, often in the imagination, the creative center of human energy, the potential for altering or conjuring a different order than the industrial one at hand. Romanticism typically places great emphasis on emotions, violence, and mood, the covert and the esoteric in opposition to the overt and exoteric. The properties of space and time—as well as the properties of objects *in* space and time—may be taken as different from the objective time-space matrix of the scientific-industrial order. Romanticism assumes that the scientific-industrial order can be transformed, perhaps by bringing together the past and the future so as to produce a new present. Of course, these observations are meant to be suggestive traits, and, given the great diversity of manifestations, no specification of this general *Weltanschauung* is possible in just a few lines. The point I wish to make is that romanticism is one of the most powerful instances of reenchantment as a feature of modernity.

A reflection of this reenchantment is the infusion and profusion throughout the nineteenth century and into the present age of themes of the fantastic, the imaginary, the grotesque, the mythic, and a particular fascination with the demonic and "darkness." Because much of this cultural elaboration was imputed to earlier ages (particularly the medieval period), we have tended to think of premodern Westerners and Western society as riddled with magical consciousness and modern consciousness as emancipated of this mythic, illusory cognitive mapping of reality. However, a brief consideration will suffice to indicate how much the culture of modernity has been stamped by the lure of the magical and enchanting. In classical music, from late Mozart (the operas *The Magic Flute, Don*

Giovanni) through Wagner (*Lohengrin, Tristan and Isolde,* the *Ring* cycle) and Mahler (*The Youth's Magic Horn*), including the great classics of ballet (*Swan Lake, Les Sylphides*), there is a tremendous number of enchanted and magical themes—and even satanic themes (*Faust,* "Mephistopheles' Waltz")—that provide the human setting for artistic creativity. The same is true in poetry and novels, from Blake and Walter Scott to Lautreamont. In the nineteenth century, side by side with this artistic stimulus of the enchanted, also emerges the study of the fabulous and the enchanted as these have been conceived by "folks" who live on the margin of the industrial urban scene. The collection of folklore and fairy tales, pioneered by Jacob and Wilhelm Grimm in the first half of the century and modernized by William J. Thoms and later by Paul Sebillot, became an important endeavor having a widespread appeal that continues today and had a bearing on the development of cultural anthropology and the study of popular culture (Dorson 1978).

Reenchantment in the form of witchcraft, it may be said in passing, even attaches itself to the very capitalist society that has generated a cultural opposite such as romanticism. I refer here to various aspects of cultural nationalism in nineteenth-century Europe that evoked mythical periods of national identity. But I also draw attention to the instance of socialism, including that of Marx,[5] who used current romantic metaphors not only in the *Manifesto*'s opening dramatic "A spectre is haunting Europe. . . . All the Powers of old Europe have entered into a holy alliance to exorcise this spectre" but even in the later *Grundrisse* and in *Capital* in his discussion of the reification of commodity production: "This enchanted and perverted world. . . . It is an enchanted, perverted, topsy-turvy world. . . . The crude materialism of the economists . . . mystifies social relations" (Bottomore 1983, 411–12). And in recent months the American stock market, the center of capitalism and the industrial order, has been subject to a phenomenon known as the "triple witching hour"!

This does not exhaust the theme of reenchantment as a major counterprocess of modernity. Related to, but distinct from, romanticism is another major thread, which I would term *exotism.* Strictly speaking, if we understand by exotism the appeal or the enchantment of the unfamiliar, perhaps even to the point of seeking to travel to the unfamiliar or to bring the unfamiliar home, exotism has a very long history in the West. It is closely intertwined with many of the myths, legends, and epics of Western culture. However, exotism bears, as Weber (or Goethe before him) might say, an "elective affinity" with Western modernity. Modern

5. The long-neglected studies of Seillière (1907, 1908, 1911, 1918) on mystical and neoromantic currents in the ideologies of imperialism, pan-Germanism, and Marxist socialism merit reconsideration in the present context.

exotism, beginning with the romantic fascination with "primitive" nature
and its indigenous population living in a state of goodness, has had
crucial psychological and political functions in the dynamics of change in
Western society.

Psychologically, the enchantment of the exotic has had at least two
major consequences for the Western mentality. First, it has provided an
important compensation for the landscape that has been transformed by
the industrial revolution into a vast sea of grays and blacks as a result of
the exhaust of industrial fumes. Industrialization brought about an objective "graying" of the West, particularly in the heartland of Northern
Europe. One major feature of exotism is the emphasis on bright colors,
"colorful" scenes, and "local color." Southern Europe, on the periphery
of industrial Europe, was an early favorite setting for depictions of the
exotic (as was North America and its Indians). The setting of the exotic
rapidly crossed the Mediterranean, so that still early in the nineteenth
century, North Africa and the Islamic world became major vehicles of
Western exotic depiction. From there the exotic imagination spread to
other settings: sub-Saharan Africa, the Pacific islands, and the continent
of Asia. In particular nineteenth century exotism found "the tropics"
(that is, the area between the Tropic of Cancer and the Tropic of Capri-
corn) as its locale par excellence. The more industrialization rationalized
space and nature in the West, the more exotism provided Westerners
with a complementary setting: nature and populations "in the raw."

Second, exotism also provided the Western mentality with an important psychological outlet for an affective life that was becoming increasingly sublimated and inhibited with the advance of "the Victorian ethos":
an ethos of sobriety and somber clothing that made public references to
bodily functions, particularly sexuality, taboo. Exotic places and their
natives, who were seen as living under very different rules of the game
(as were the lower social strata, particularly those of a different ethnicity
from that of the elites and the new middle classes), became vehicles
outside the pale of civilization through which the erotic could be displayed. The linkage of the exotic and the erotic is vividly marked in
depictions (paintings, novels, operas) of "native women" whose bare bodies and passionate nature could be vicariously (or otherwise) enjoyed in
safety. Another illustration of this linkage is colonial stamps (for example, those issued by the Third Republic right up to World War II), which
featured bare-breasted "Black Eves."

Exotism not only had those two psychological functions; it also had
economic and political functions. Economically, Europe in the middle of
the nineteenth century developed a craving for exotic products that
contributed to the formation of a consumer society. Baudelaire attracted
attention in 1848 by advocating "peppers, English powders and saffrons,

colonial stuff, exotic asparagus, all that would have pleased them, even musk and incense," and in 1850 Ferdinand Hediard introduced the Parisian middle class to exotic fruits in his *Comptoir d'Epice et des Colonies:*

> Hediard was first to bring tropical fruits and vegetables with strange names, such as guavas, mangoes, loquats and papaws. . . . Oranges, tangerines, and grapefruits, then a luxury, began to appear on middle-class French tables. The French expansion into Tunisia, the Congo and Indochina helped Hediard. By 1889, exoticism was all the rage in Paris. (Dorsey 1986)

To bring the exotic to the West is one side of the economic coin; to take Westerners to the exotic is the other. I have in mind here the development of the tourist industry. It began in the nineteenth century, first in the European periphery (Scotland, Spain, Italy, even southern France), and subsequently spread to all parts of the world, particularly those subject to exotic themes that represented the opposite of the locale of the industrial setting, themes such as "colorful natives," "balmy skies," and "unspoiled nature." In the process, "touristization" often involved making a setting conform to the expectations of the exotic by staging events (dances, festivals, even sexual activities) that supposedly typify the setting for the benefit of the tourists. As a result, tourists tend to be shielded from the actual everyday life of the indigenous population.

Equally significant is the political dimension of exoticism. The lure and enchantment of exotic lands was instrumental in the exploration and subsequent colonization of overseas territories from early in the nineteenth century right up to World War I. Even after World War I the colonial empires were given important legitimation and justification because of their exotic appeal, which was periodically displayed to Western publics by means of "colonial expositions." Exotic imagery not only emphasized the appeal of strange, foreign, and "colorful" lands and peoples but also, tacitly, emphasized the need for these to be coupled (read annexed, given in perpetual trust, etc.) to Western societies that had acceded to a civilization of progress. Such imagery on occasion suggested the need to seek and rescue "lost" Westerners, such as the mythic Prester John or the not-so-mythic David Livingstone in the case of Africa, and in the course of searching the territory being explored came under the political sphere of influence of the West. Once under Western suzerainty, the exotic aura that overlay the colonies, or more broadly, the non-West, functioned to legitimate Western dominance and to keep "exotic" non-Westerners from being taken seriously. The important study of Said (1978) provides ample documentation of the widespread functions of "orientalism" as a Western categorization and cultural agent of domination of the Middle East and Asia. Curtin's earlier study (1964) provides complementary materials on Sub–Saharan Africa.

If, as I contend, reenchantment is a dialectical aspect of Western modernity, are there manifestations of the exotic today after the decolonization of former empires? I would propose that this is indeed the case but that there has been a shift in the locale of the exotic. Instead of foreign parts of the globe inhabited by strange creatures (who are thought to be a mixture of goodness and barbarism), today outer space and extraterrestrial beings are the focus of the exotic. Even as decolonization involved a certain "disenchantment" of the world (in the sense that it stripped away the veils the West had placed on the colonies), reenchantment has been renewed in the popular culture of science fiction, which has commanded a large appeal from the time of Jules Verne and H. G. Wells down to "Star Trek", *E.T.*, and the like. (For a sociological overview of science fiction, see Bainbridge 1986.) As I noted for an earlier wave of exotism, the exotism of outer space not only has psychological and economic functions (for example, generating important objects of consumption in a consumer society) but also may have similar political functions of legitimating enormous expenditures for space exploration, colonization, and military defense (as in the case of the Strategic Defense Initiative, in which the fiction of an impenetrable defense shield has already cost billions of dollars). In any event, modern science fiction illustrates that advancements in science and technology, so much part of the rationalization process, *and* advancements in the sphere of the imaginary are dialectically related.

Although this does not complete the account of forms of reenchantment in modern society (for example, a more comprehensive treatment would have to look at the economic and political consequences of cultural nostalgia, particularly as the enchantment of the past attaches itself to successive decades), it is time to consider the second major counterprocess of modernity.

2. DEDIFFERENTIATION

The discussion of the counterprocess of dedifferentiation is briefer than that of disenchantment, not because of their relative importance but because I have recently dealt at some length with the former (1985b). Because dedifferentiation has been treated residually or negatively, I illustrate the importance of this process through a general consideration of Western modernity.

Obviously the legal-rational authority structures of modernity and its industrial technological order are characterized by a high level of functional differentiation. As an implicit normative standard of modernity, this was contained in one of Parsons's "pattern variables," namely "specificity versus diffuseness" (with specificity representing the pole of modernity). By extension dedifferentiation has tended to be viewed as a pathological aspect of social evolution, a regressive process that has as its consequence the undoing of rationalization and differentiation. This, for example, was the tenor of Parsons's discussion of social movements committed to a *Gesinnungsethik,* movements as diverse as the religious radical movements of the Reformation or the student movements of the 1960s (Tiryakian 1985b).

For a more balanced perspective on the relationship between dedifferentiation and modernity, it is crucial to keep in mind, as Rueschemeyer has emphasized (1986), that any division of labor involves a distribution of power. Ideally, the evolution of the structural differentiation of a social system allows it to have greater adaptation to its environment and increased efficiency as its components work interactively. But social systems do not operate in a power vacuum. Therefore, unless Plato's conception of a meritocracy, as outlined in *The Republic,* has been implemented in the form of a universal testing system designed to rationally allocate persons to differentiated slots, then the process of differentiation will tend to have an increasing hierarchical character, with more differentiated subunits having less responsibility and less control. This means that unit members at lower echelons will have less identification with and commitment to the goals of the system and greater passivity and apathy may ensue, even if the system's officials resort to Platonic myths and rituals. Thus the process of differentiation can generate pathologies (which Durkheim analyzed in part in *The Division of Labor in Society*), and by itself is not the guarantor of integration.

To be sure, a hierarchic, differentiated social system can show growth, integration, and economic efficiency, which might be taken as standards of success. But insofar as major groups of actors are excluded de facto or de jure from responsible action, the system will tend to operate at less than optimal levels of efficiency. Moreover, a change in the environment may provide the social system in question with a challenge that it cannot respond to given its present modes of stratification and differentiation.

Dedifferentiation as a counterprocess involves the restoration of the potentiality of a unit to an earlier phase of development that was characterized by a greater homogeneity of the member units. It is a process of regeneration and rejuvenation of structures; it is also a process by which the member units renew their commitment to and involvement with the system as a whole. This process tends to be more condensed and intense than differentiation.

Rueschemeyer (1986, 141–69) has indicated that several features of dedifferentiation in modern societies are worthy of note: its bundle of rights and duties underlying moral individualism, its tension with role fragmentation and routinization, its contribution to the integration of complex institutional patterns, and so forth. The point is not that dedifferentiation is an atavism of modernity but more that it is a necessary complement of differentiation, in part because it provides for the social mobilization of actors. Insofar as the democratic impulse is one major thrust of Western modernity, the quest for the autonomy and the enhancement of life for all the people, within and among societies, will periodically be expressed in forms of dedifferentiation that are dialectically opposed to the tendencies of differentiation.

Historically, I would point to the major social revolutions of the modern period, from the French Revolution to the sexual revolution, as exemplifying dedifferentiation. The same applies to the great nationalist movements of the nineteenth and twentieth centuries. In these and other instances the actors and groups of actors seeking to emancipate themselves from a differentiated system call on the modern values of egalitarianism, freedom, and autonomy. Because differentiation often rests on the basis of ethnic segmentation, those who wield power in the division of labor are seen as either too alien or too distant. Dedifferentiation involves a dedifferentiation of social roles and social space, whereas differentiation tends to allocate some persons to some roles and to put and keep them in a given confine of social space. This general confinement (which from the perspective of the elites of a differentiated system is a rational allocation of resources) is in acute tension with modern values that stress the freedom of movement and the self-development of human beings (either as individuals or as groups).

3. CONCLUSION

This chapter discussed modernity in terms of two significant processes that have had a variety of manifestations in the course of Western social change. Reenchantment and dedifferentiation run counter to rationalization as the master process of Western modernity, but they are analytically and empirically necessary to understand modernity "in all its states," to borrow a phrase from Balandier (1985). I argue that modernity must be approached dialectically, not unidimensionally, and that it is necessary to bring the counterprocesses into focus for a more adequate theoretical understanding of the dynamism of modernity.[6]

The consideration of counterprocesses is also necessary for a more

6. In terms of Parsonian system analysis (Parsons 1978, 352–433) the process of dedifferentiation, I would suggest, is one that reemphasizes or redirects attention to the I (Integration) and L (Latency) cells, whereas differentiation has a predominant emphasis on A (Adaptation) and G (Goal-directed) cells of action systems.

general interpretation of the modern "human condition" (Parsons 1978). If rationalization, differentiation, and secularization are interrelated features of the dynamics of change, they are not simply features that have provided many of the benefits implicit in the "promise of the Enlightenment," that is, the promise of the general emancipation of the human condition by human praxis. They have also led to new forms of hierarchical control, depersonalization, and the homogenization of the physical and social environment. These features, without a counterbalance, could take modernity into the stasis envisioned by Weber's apt metaphor of "the iron cage," or, even more drastic, that envisioned by Orwell. In fact, however, reenchantment and dedifferentiation, in their diverse manifestations, have served to renew and regenerate the Western societal system, whether by social movements that challenge existing patterns of structural differentiation or by movements of the imagination that challenge the finitude of material reality and have thereby contributed to its ongoing reconstruction.

REFERENCES

Amin, Samir, Giovanni Arrighi, Andre Gunder Frank, and Immanuel Wallerstein. 1982. *Dynamics of global crisis*. New York: Monthly Review Press.

Bainbridge, William Sims. 1986. *Dimensions of science fiction*. Cambridge: Harvard University Press.

Balandier, Georges. 1985. *Le détour: Pouvoir et modernité*. Paris: Fayard.

Bell, Daniel. 1985. The revolt against modernity. *The Public Interest* 81 (Fall):42–63.

Benjamin, Walter. 1978. On surrealism. *New Left Review* 108 (March–April):47–56.

Berger, Peter L. 1973. *The homeless mind: Modernization and consciousness*. New York: Random House

———. 1977. *Facing up to modernity*. New York: Basic Books.

Bernstein, Richard J., ed. 1985. *Habermas and modernity*. Cambridge: MIT Press.

Black, Cyril E., ed. 1976. *Comparative modernization*. New York: Free Press.

Bottomore, Tom, ed. 1983. *A dictionary of Marxist thought*. Cambridge: Harvard University Press.

Boulding, Kenneth. 1985. *The world as a total system*. London: Sage.

Brandt Commission. 1983. *Common crisis: North-South cooperation for world recovery*. Cambridge: MIT Press.

Chadwick, Owen. 1979. *The secularization of the European mind in the nineteenth century*. Cambridge: Cambridge University Press.

Curtin, Philip D. 1964. *The image of Africa: British ideas and action, 1780–1850*. Madison: University of Wisconsin Press.

Dorsey, Hebe. 1986. In the heart of Paris, shrines to fine food. *New York Times*, travel section, 3 Aug., 19.

Dorson, Richard M., ed. 1978. *Folklore in the modern world*. The Hague: Mouton.

Eisenstadt, S. N. 1973. *Tradition, change, and modernity*. New York: Wiley.

Ezrahi, Yaron. 1990. *The Descent of Icarus: Science and the Transformation of Contemporary Democracy.* Cambridge: Harvard University Press.

Featherstone, Mike, ed. 1985. *Theory Culture & Society* 2, no. 3 (special issue, *The fate of modernity*).

Freire, Paulo. 1973. *Education for critical consciousness.* New York: Seabury.

Gershman, Herbert S. 1969. *The surrealist revolution in France.* Ann Arbor: University of Michigan Press.

Habermas, Jürgen. 1981. "Modernity vs. postmodernity." *New German Critique* 22 (Winter):3–14.

———. [1981] 1985. *The theory of communicative action.* Vol. 1, *Reason and the rationalization of society.* Boston: Beacon Press.

Inkeles, Alex. 1983. *Exploring individual modernity.* New York: Columbia University Press.

Leventman, Seymour, ed. 1982. *Counterculture and social transformation.* Springfield, Ill.: Charles C. Thomas.

Lipset, Seymour Martin. 1980. The revolt against modernity. Paper presented at conference, Modernization vs. Traditional Values, 22–24 Oct., Carnegie Center for Transnational Studies, Cold Spring Harbor, N.Y. Revised version published as "The new fundamentalism." *Society* 20 (November–December 1982):40–58.

Luhmann, Niklas. 1982. *The differentiation of society.* New York: Columbia University Press.

Marshall, Gordon. 1982. *In search of the spirit of capitalism.* New York: Columbia University Press.

Nelson, Benjamin. 1981. *On the roads to modernity: Conscience, science, and civilizations.* Ed. Toby E. Huff. Totowa, N.J.: Rowman and Littlefield.

Nisbet, Robert. 1975. *Twilight of authority.* New York: Oxford.

Parsons, Talcott. 1978. *Action theory and the human condition.* New York: Free Press.

Roth, Guenther. 1986. Review of *The heavenly contract: Ideology and organization in pre-revolutionary puritanism,* by David Zaret. *Contemporary Sociology* 15 (July):550–53.

Rueschemeyer, Dietrich. 1986. *Power and the division of labour.* Stanford: Stanford University Press.

Said, Edward W. 1978. *Orientalism.* New York: Pantheon.

Seidman, Steven. 1983. "Modernity, meaning, and cultural pessimism in Max Weber." *Sociological Analysis* 44 (Winter):267–78.

Seillière, Ernest. 1907. *L'Impérialisme démocratique.* Paris: Plon.

———. 1908. *Le mal romantique: Essai sur l'impérialisme irrationnel.* Paris: Plon.

———. 1911. *Les mystiques du néo-romantisme.* Paris: Plon.

———. 1918. *Le péril mystique dans l'inspiration des démocraties contemporaines.* Paris: La Renaissance du Livre.

Shalin, Dmitri N. 1986. Romanticism and the rise of sociological hermeneutics. *Social Research* 53 (Spring):77–123.

Swatos, William H., Jr. 1983. Enchantment and disenchantment in modernity: The significance of "religion" as a sociological category. *Sociological Analysis* 44 (Winter):321–38.

Tilly, Charles. 1984. *Big structures, large processes, huge comparisons.* New York: Russell Sage Foundation.

Tiryakian, Edward A., ed. 1984. *The global crisis: Sociological analyses and responses.* Leiden: E. J. Brill.

———. 1985a. "The changing centers of modernity." In *Comparative social dynamics: Essays in honor of S. N. Eisenstadt,* ed. E. Cohen, M. Lissak, and U. Almagor, 131–47. Boulder, Colo.: Westview Press.

———. 1985b. "On the significance of de-differentiation." In *Macro sociological theory: Perspectives on sociological theory,* ed. S. N. Eisenstadt and H. J. Helle, 1:118–34. Beverly Hills, Calif.: Sage.

Tiryakian, Edward A., and Ronald Rogowski, eds. 1985. *New nationalisms of the developed West.* London: Allen and Unwin.

Touraine, Alain. 1984. *Le retour de l'acteur.* Paris: Fayard.

Weber, Max. 1958. "Science as a vocation." In *From Max Weber: Essays in sociology,* ed. Hans Gerth and C. W. Mills, 129–56. New York: Oxford University Press, Galaxy Books.

———. 1978. *Economy and society.* 2 vols. Ed. Guenther Roth and Claus Wittich. Berkeley: University of California Press.

Yinger, J. Milton. 1982. *Countercultures: The promise and peril of a world turned upside down.* New York: Free Press.

PART TWO

Modernity and Inequality

Modernity and Ascription

Hans Haferkamp

1. PATTERNS OF DEVELOPMENT IN MODERNITY

Reflection on the character of modern society suggests that there are two starting points that are not especially viable. The first is Weber's description of Occidental rationalism (Weber 1920); the second is Parsons's "relatively optimistic" description of modern society ([1971] 1972, 179) in which he forecast that this society would flourish for another century or two. The modern societies of Northwest Europe, the United States, Canada, and Japan are not characterized by maturing processes alone; they also give evidence of counterdevelopments (foreseen by Marx) and developmental excesses that cloud the picture of continuing upward progress.

These observations are not new. Antinomies and instances of hypertrophy have always occupied a central place among sociology's major topics. Yet insistence on the particular structural features of "advanced industrial societies"—features that include the upward march of capitalism, democracy, the market economy, and prosperity—tends to live on (see Zapf 1983, 294). One example of this tendency is Dieter Senghaas (1982), who does not discuss the autumn of modernity or the beginnings of postmodernity; rather his analysis is characteristic of the optimism of the European *grande bourgeoisie* around the turn of the century, the United States since midcentury, and contemporary Japan.

Why has this affirmative view of modern social change persisted? As modern theory has moved away from philosophy and become more empirical in character, theorists tend to stick to positive "givens," concluding that a comparison of data from past and present indicates continuing progress. This type of analysis underscores the optimistic diagnosis. But this approach is in one sense odd because a comparison of past and present should also reveal instances of hypertrophy and counterdevelopments worthy of note. In fact, establishing the counterdevelopments and developmental excesses has been left to social scientists with a philosophical bent (from Marx and Engels [1848] 1964), to novelists like Baudelaire (1925), and, occasionally, to sociologists like Weber, who sang the praises of rational capitalism but also saw counterdevelopments. Today some theorists, specifically representatives of the Frankfurt school and social thinkers like Arnold Gehlen, see decline and fall everywhere and emphasize the decay of civilization in modern societies. Yet these negative characterizations also have a way of losing any sense of proportion.

Bendix (1971) has brought out the problems of Western European rationalism from a realistic stance. He identifies the loss of the feeling of Western superiority, which had lasted for decades. He also notes that "the harnessing of nuclear power marks the beginning of a scientific and technical development calling into question the 350-year-old equation of knowledge with progress for the first time in the consciousness of many people" (1979, 13). Following Bendix's approach, we find development, excess development, and counterdevelopment unfolding as follows:

1. The development of various resources used to secure survival and a better life has a counterdevelopmental side that is especially evident in the widespread environmental damage that accompanies it. In addition, counterdevelopments are making themselves felt with the underutilization of potential resources (for example, the labor of youths, women, older people, and foreigners). One of the questions that arises in connection with the deployment of resources is the pattern of social distribution of resources and rewards. The evidence in modern societies indicates that these resources and rewards tend to be evening out. For example, educational resources are being concentrated to a greater extent in the lower social strata.

2. All modern societies show a rising level of production measured in terms of goods and services. At the same time, however, counterdevelopments are evident. The continuing application of technology gives rise to new hazards to health and new forms of oppression. These kinds of developments have raised questions about the meaning and purpose of societal development.

3. Modern societies also show growth in power and authority relationships. Both increasing numbers of decision makers and increased political participation are evident (Baudelaire 1925). The involvement of the lower and middle strata in Western European societies ranges from strong interest in politics and high polling rates in

elections to civil protest. These kinds of movements often result in the abandonment of government proposals, and there has been a kind of diffusion of power in the realm of decisions about the deployment of atomic energy and destructive weapons.

4. Remuneration has increased, as suggested by the terms "super-abundance" and "the affluent society." Rewards are distributed so as to provide a high level of welfare for almost all actors, and there are minimum standards of economic provision for all phases of the life cycle. Although welfare measures also tend to distribute wealth downward, there remains a residual of poverty in all modern societies (Lockwood 1985).

5. Knowledge of one's own society has been enhanced, often at the expense of traditional religious interpretations. However, it is often impossible to apply this knowledge to the planning process because national planning efforts are subverted by international developments over which planners have little or no control.

6. A further hallmark of modern societies is the high degree of individualism and the desire for self-realization on the part of their citizens. The citizens resent control from above or from any other part of the political spectrum. Increased individualism may, however, spill over into the legitimization of deviance and crime, result in an increasing suicide rate, and give rise to anxieties about future prospects for life. Individualism is accompanied by a loss of community commitment and a loneliness on the part of the masses.

Some of the developments, developmental excesses, and counter-developments mentioned here come about very rapidly, others very slowly. Modernity is synonymous with the continual entry, at different rates, of new elements that are in conflict with established arrangements.

Significant distinctions can be drawn between modern and other societies on the basis of six dimensions: (1) increasing mobilization of resources, (2) increasing levels of positive effort, (3) power relationships, (4) increasing levels of consumer welfare, (5) increasing dissemination of self-reflection, and (6) increasing levels of individualism. Also, the increasing downward distribution of each of these dimensions distinguishes modern societies from others. And of course it is also possible to see differences among modern societies with respect to these six dimensions. But let us confine our comparison to the United States and the German Federal Republic. We can make the following observations:

1. The mobilization of resources is well advanced in both societies. However, important resources lie fallow, both in the potential pool of labor and in the field of education and training. Although West Germany exhibits high levels of achievement and educa-

tional standing, the proportion of willing actors unable to produce effort is higher than in the United States, as is evident in statistics on unemployment and rejected students. Also, lower-class social groups in West Germany are still underrepresented at universities and other institutions of higher education compared with the United States.

2. The level of positive effort is high in both societies but its downward distribution is more pronounced in West Germany—as typified by the image of the "hard-working German"—than it is the United States. A phenomenon that is particularly advanced in West Germany is that achievement problems are identified at the highest level. An increasing number of West German actors now reject the old equation, "level of achievement equals level of welfare" (see Ronge 1975; Kitschelt 1985).

3. Power is becoming increasingly diffuse in both societies. However, the downward distribution of power is more pronounced in West Germany. A higher degree of political participation has been achieved there, and changes in power have occurred whenever the workers' party has attained a mandate to govern. In the United States the existing ruling authority has more effectively defended itself against influences from below.

4. In West Germany remuneration is more evenly spread, and the distribution of goods is less skewed than in the United States.

5. The ability to indulge in self-reflection and to self-steer relationships is downwardly distributed to a more marked extent in the United States than in West Germany.

6. Likewise, individualization is stronger in the United States and the trend is accelerating. North American permissiveness is not yet evident in West Germany.

This mixed picture shows that it is impossible to identify either one of these nations as clearly *the* more modernized.

2. CHANGE THROUGH ACTION

How can developments in modern society be explained? Why is change so rapid and intense on the one hand and so slow on the other? How can developments of different magnitudes be related to one another?

If these questions are to be answered properly, it is necessary to have some kind of conceptualization of permanent change, and not to simply attempt to explain current arrangements as an extension of past trends. Everything is in permanent flux.

The conceptualization of social change must also take into account that different structures do not simply exert influence independently of one another; they also exert influence *on* one another. Thus, inequality in the distribution of resources and power in the economic sphere is neutralized by political institutions, such as universal suffrage, social guarantee systems, and public services, in such a way that civic society and capitalism mutually encourage one another (Marshall [1949] 1977).

Furthermore, learning effects also occur in the process of social change. Rapid developments in one society serve as models for change in other societies. This statement applies both to positive developments and to instances of pathology such as refusals to work and protest movements.

Thus change means that altered or even new actions or modes of behavior generate a whole series of ramifications, not simply repetitions of the past.

Both microsocial and macrosocial changes occur. Microsocial change is the altering of action or the initiating of new action on the part of a small number of actors who are aware of one another. Macrosocial change encompasses the alterations in action or the emergence of new interrelationships of action that involve many actors who are not aware of one another. Often changes on the macrosocial level can be traced back to changes on the microsocial level: a new or altered action or behavior is always generated or discovered in elementary interrelationships of action and developed as a habit by individual actors in small groups (Relationship 1 of Model 1). The actors attempt to transfer the action or behavior to other groups, or these groups follow suit (Relationship 2 of Model 1).

For example, a new attitude to family size, a new sexual behavior, or a new medical discovery may be adopted initially by a small number of actors before being exhibited to others as a model or gradually becoming appreciated by others and then deliberately imitated. Social change can also be given impetus when new personalities take over macroactor roles, for example, new party leaders and presidents, innovative entrepreneurs and labor union leaders with initiative, church leaders who convey a "message," productive scientists and academics, or imaginative legislators. Individuals and elites with an innovative orientation tend to rise to the top and usher in societal change especially at times of crisis (Nisbet and Perrin 1970, 320).

Change is introduced by either personalities, significant actors, or very small groups who exploit elements of the current social and material situation. If change is to be set in motion by significant actors, it needs to be taken up by many others and introduced into everyday action and behavior. It must be able to be transferred and must allow the

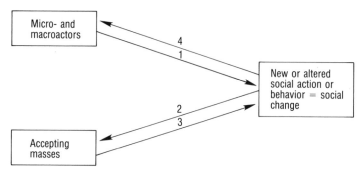

Model 1. Actors and Social Change

possibility of others adjusting to it. Hence the following distinctions among actors may be drawn:

1. Microactors who introduce alterations but act or behave in isolation and do not succeed in transferring the alterations to others or who do not set any processes of adjustment into action.
2. Microactors who interact with others among the masses and who generate alterations or adjustments.
3. Macroactors who address themselves to large masses, or whose behavior is relevant to them, but whose actions are not adopted or whose behavior has no effect.
4. Macroactors who assert themselves in processes of transfer and adjustment.

Action or behavior carried out on a mass scale—or its rejection—(Relationship 3 of Model 1) affects the position of the micro- and macroactors producing the innovations (Relationship 4 of Model 1). Mass acceptance of new actions and modes of behavior strengthens the innovators' positions in the first instance. The initial effect is one of creating prestige. Soon, however, the actors thus singled out become relatively weaker as the accepting masses improve their living situations by adopting the new action or mode of behavior. Nothing much has changed for the original innovators. They had already been able to put these actions and behavior modes into practice, and in the long run they are unable to derive advantage from the gratitude of the accepting masses. These interrelationships are laid out in Model 1.

Parsons's differentiation between change *within* the system and change *of* the system (1951, 480) is no more than a relative distinction. The mass of microactors within an interrelationship of action are able to bring about as much change as can successful macroactors from without: the end result in either case is the emergence of a new relationship of action. The classic illustration of the first case is the American Revolution. At the outset none of the macroactors, nor any small group, had any notion of the action interrelationship that was later to arise in North America. Yet step by step the actors and groups moved away from the status of being a British colony: "I never had heard of any Conversation from any Person, drunk or sober, the least Expression of a wish for separation, or Hint that such a Thing would be advantageous to America" (Benjamin Franklin, cited in Rossiter 1956, 41).

In modern societies, as elsewhere, the chief concern is with a secure and better life, which first means survival, then living the good life. This, however, can only be achieved if in each case a certain new level of resource mobilization can be attained. Anyone wishing to survive or to raise his or her living standards has need of the assistance and coopera-tion of other actors. These other actors, as carriers of resources, can be activated (Relationships 1 and 2 in Model 2) to generate additional posi-tive achievement if they are promised rewards or threatened with punish-ment. Because rewards provide a stronger motivation to produce the desired positive effort than punishment, elites substitute rewards for punishment as the production of goods and services grows (Haferkamp 1983).

To refer to Model 2, raising the resource potential (Relationship 3) has the unintended consequence that those in possession of the new re-sources become more important in relation to the owners of the old resources (Relationship 4). This means that the new resource holders are able to generate more positive effort in comparison with other important micro- and macroactors (Relationships 5–7) and that the relative weights of positive effort are altered (Relationships 8–9). But now some power needs to be conceded to the new carriers of achievement, so that power is ultimately shared with them. This sharing of power affects the distribu-tion of rewards (Relationships 15–19) and the possibility of self-steering (Relationships 20–24) and individualization (Relationships 25–29).

The trends toward growth and downward distribution are the unfore-seen consequences of the mobilization of resources that occurs in all stratified societies. If this path is not taken and resources at the lower levels of society are left unutilized, societies remain below their potential level of performance. If no drive is made to raise the level of achieve-ment among the masses, less power is generated than is possible. And if power is not shared and the interrelationships of action are controlled not by increasing rewards but by the use of punishment, then the forces at the top ruin the very interrelationships of action they wish to profit from. The historical examples of the fall of the pharaonic empires (see Wittfogel 1938) and the major problems faced by socialist societies in the present day come to mind in this regard (see Senghaas 1982, 277).

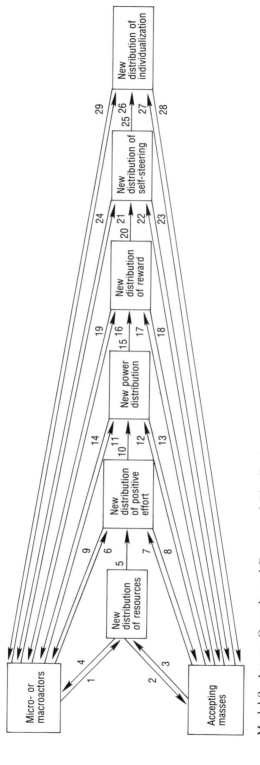

Model 2. Actors, Growth, and Downward Distribution

The arguments formulated thus far serve to explain many different developments. Resources are exploited to a much greater extent in modern societies than elsewhere. This has had many consequences, the most immediate of which is the greater part entrepreneurs have played. It is possible to continue in this vein and explain many differences between modern societies and nonmodern ones. But let us turn to the end of the chain of influences, to extreme individualization. It is particularly advanced in the United States and least developed in Japan; Western Europe, including West Germany, lies in between. Evidently, however, the degree of individualization is not correlated with resource mobilization, for in this respect there are no telling differences between the United States and the German Federal Republic, and Japan is remarkable for its particularly high degree of mobilization.

Even among the intermediate links in the causal chains of Model 2, the combinations are not maintained as we would expect. Can it be said, for example, that in the United States, with so many subcultures, we also encounter the highest measure of political participation in general? Or that in West Germany, with its pronounced leveling of authority, we find the work performance at the lower levels that would be appropriate to such conditions? And how can the incidence of counterdevelopments and pathologies be explained? Do we find that the production of toxins and pollution is at its highest level where the most resources have been mobilized? Do minorities have a particularly strong blocking power where the spreading out of achievement-orientation is especially advanced? Why do resources for achievement remain unused? Why do monopolies of power exist that are not based on appropriate achievement? Something more than just resource mobilization and its consequences needs to be added to our model of actors and interaction efforts if we are to understand and interpret the development of modernity. I believe that two other additional factors are essential:

1. Contractual action, which makes everything, including ascription, the object of negotiation.
2. Radical values of equality.

Both factors are typical of modern societies, albeit in different ways from one society to another, and they are the most significant elements of action in these societies. The influence exerted by these two factors on the change toward individualistic modern society is presented in Model 3. This model shows the complex relationship between the fundamental processes of change and the hallmarks of modernity. Macroactors, together with microactors endowed with initiative, assign others to a place in the status hierarchy (Relationship 3 in Model 3), and their ascriptions are either accepted or rejected (Relationship 31). When significant actors

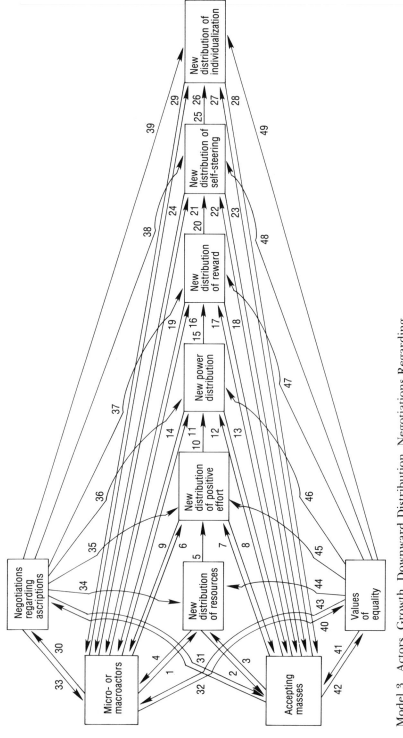

Model 3. Actors, Growth, Downward Distribution, Negotiations Regarding Ascriptions, and Values of Equality

interact with the accepting masses, recognized ascriptions emerge (Relationships 32–33). These ascriptions then have effects on the various types of distribution (Relationships 34–39). Actors also create new values (Relationship 40), which are either internalized or rejected by the masses (Relationship 41). This interaction leads in turn to a recognized system of values (Relationships 42–43), which also exerts its influence on all the distributions (Relationships 44–49).

In the following section I concentrate on contractual action regarding the ascription of positive effort, how this trend became widespread, and how it influences the processes of social change that lead to modern societies (Relationships 30–39).

3. CONTRACTUAL ACTION AND ASCRIPTION

The two most important processes involved in the "transition from simple/primitive societal organization to complex/differentiated [organization are] . . . (1) increasing differentiation and specialization of social functions, and (2) the replacement of ascriptive principles by achievement principles for societal organizations" (Strasser and Randall 1981, 74). I assume in Model 3 that the first process exists, as shown by the chain of relationships leading from resource mobilization to individualism. I have not, however, found that the second process is actually taking place and thus I omit it from my models.

By a change from ascription to achievement principles, sociologists generally mean that there are few characteristics that are solely ascribed to particular actors. Status in particular is no longer simply accorded to a person or a group but is acquired by virtue of abilities and measurable success in specific activities. One important consequence is that status in the family system, or any other ascribed status, now plays an ever-smaller part in comparison with status acquired by objective achievement, which is usually based on occupation.

I question this dichotomy and make the following alternative assertion. Modernizing societies emphasize greater achievement, and more positive effort is actually accomplished. Thus achievement is truly an important part of modern societies. Yet more ascription also occurs in modern societies. The paradoxical result is that both more achievement *and* more ascription arise and that achievement is to a considerable extent ascribed.

Achievement, or making positive effort, means solving problems in life, whether one's own or someone else's, or at least making a contribution to their solution. Not only is such achievement or effort ascribed, but it is also generally measurable. The following observations can therefore be made to avoid constructing a mistakenly one-sided theory of ascription. Actions carried out by actors can be distinguished according to whether or not these actions make a contribution to solving fundamental life problems, such as whether people are dead or alive, sick or healthy, hungry or well-fed, imprisoned or free. These straightforward differentiations are fundamental life problems that, in modern societies as anywhere else, constantly cry out for solution (see Haferkamp 1991, 311). Although further life problems can be defined and needs shaped and manipulated (Hondrich 1973, 60), these activities cannot be undertaken until the basic problems have been solved. Even holders of power are not able to define all life problems or needs in such a way that they gain greater advantage for themselves by labeling basic life problems as the problems of others that they happen to be able to solve themselves.

Interactions, groups, and interrelationships of action in modern societies not only may live on or develop further, but also may decay or self-destruct. Achieving, or generating positive effort, therefore has as its opposite the causing of damage, which occurs whenever solving life problems is prevented or impaired. Damage, like achievement, is objectively measurable and subjectively ascribable. Instances of achievement or damage can be identified by actors in everyday life through observation, even in modern societies. Analysts are able to recapture such processes, which could involve, in the case of achievement, an entrepreneur's success in the marketplace, the output produced by an employee, the trouble-free handling of administrative procedures, or the discovery of new knowledge by an academic (Bolte 1979, 22). All of these are achievements that are measurable in objective terms.

When achievements are generated by several actors, measuring the level of achievement becomes a more complicated matter. Even in these cases, however, it is possible to make objective observations. Insurance companies are constantly refining their schemes for assessing the risks of the actions of organizations and corporations. Banks develop guidelines on credit, making judgments about the ability of borrowers to perform and grow in major interrelationships of action. These examples involve estimates of likely achievement. And at a higher level analysts make measurements of economic growth and progress for entire societies (Senghaas 1982, 136–37). To complete the picture, it is also possible to ascertain the extent of damage and destruction. Measurements may range from the assessment of bodily damage by medical experts to measures of the decline and fall of whole societies (see Wittfogel 1938).

These observations by no means rule out alterations in the values measured. Such alterations are especially evident in the changing view of nuclear power in modern societies in the mid-1980s. Something that had long been treated as an outstanding achievement is now—as the risks become more evident—being scaled down accordingly. Also, measurement and objective assessment are not rendered impossible by the fact that a long period of time sometimes elapses before actors realize that something either preserves or destroys life.

These remarks on the possibility of identifying achievements are necessary to avoid creating the impression in the arguments that follow that the evolution of instances of achievement or damage are based solely on ascription.

Achievement and damage may be objectively measured and subjectively ascribed at one and the same time, for actors treat achievement and damage no differently than they do other elements of their lifeworlds. Not only are these elements represented by actors within their consciousnesses—with greater or lesser degrees of success—but also they are defined from the outset, just as every situation of every actor is defined.

Ascription means that an actor assigns certain characteristics to other actors irrespective of whether these other actors have these characteristics in reality. In other words actors deal out labels to other actors. A vivid illustration of this is the ascribed ability to perform witchcraft or to obtain divine action. These are extreme cases in which either damage leading to infirmity or death or achievement leading to healing is attributed to individual human beings in the absence of any objective evidence. Ascriptions, however, can be investigated to determine whether or not the ascription is based on achievement.

Of course, false ascriptions may arise—a false accusation of murder (see Becker 1963, 20), or a false paternity charge—but they are the exception, not the rule. It is wrong to take exceptions from everyday life or oversubtleties raised by analysts and elevate them to the level of general rules. Since its beginnings science has been driven by the intention of being able to describe and explain reality more fully and more correctly than can actors in their life-worlds. To dispute that science does this is tantamount to lagging behind Comte and, even more so, behind the sociologists who followed him. Durkheim, Weber, Simmel, and Mead would have little sympathy with the skepticism so widespread in sociology today about the possibility of making statements that reach beyond the knowledge of the life-world.

Certainly one is bound to admit that there are many cases that lack such straightforward reference points as life and death, health and sickness. On the contrary, social relations are complex, and it is absolutely impossible to provide a totally correct, faithful image of this complexity. It is possible, however, to carry out objective measurements of individual or partial achievements. Yet aggregating these measurements is a difficult and at times extraordinarily complex process. Moreover, levels of complexity are rapidly attained that no human consciousness is able to picture, even in aggregate terms. Actors circumvent this difficulty when they reduce complexity by using ascriptions. Matters are then selected and simplified. Some aspects are singled out for particular attention, others are generalized, and this mixture is understood as a judgment about reality (see Schutz 1964–67). Even these ascriptions, however, maintain a link with reality, for the aspects subjected to representation, selection, overemphasis, or generalization are indeed characteristics of reality in the first instance.

In the majority of cases ascriptions take place unintentionally. However, one can also consciously put forward a distorted ascription. Actors knowingly exaggerate their own achievement and deliberately understate that of their adversaries. Ascriptions in this sense have always existed. Establishing their existence is a sociological banality. More difficult questions, however, concern the alterations involved in processes of ascription and their effect both on social change and on developments leading toward, and taking place within, modernity.

Reduction of complexity is the usual underlying motive for ascription. Since the advent of large-scale productive organizations, expanded bureaucracies, economies organized on the basis of a division of labor, and stratified authority groupings the generators of achievement are complex in themselves. The output produced by many workers on one payroll, and even the achievements of a single entrepreneur or politician with a large supporting staff at his or her disposal, is mainly ascribed to a group, and most of all to a large group, such as the work force, the party membership, the management, or the government (Offe 1970). Such ascriptions occur even though objective measurements of achievement and aggregation are possible. The "structuring practices of agents" can be seen in operation and "summary representations" can be asserted by the analyst. The best example of this is econometrics (Knorr-Cetina 1981, 34). Another example is the presentation of the "state of the union."

Below this level in modern societies the ascription of achievements occurs with regard to actions and the results of actions in diverse occupations and related positions. Within any one occupation ascriptions are founded on the ascribed quality of typical occupational activities as well as on the quantitative aspects of work produced. In other words we find ascriptions of important and less important positions. Moreover, the ascription of the ability to cause damage in modern societies is also bound up with large groupings of nations and occupational and related groups. This observation becomes obvious when talks take place between management and striking workers. Both sides ascribe damage-causing action to the other. Similarly, harmful actions are ascribed to terrorists, professional criminals, a foreign power's military leaders, and the leaders of sects.

Increasing complexity leads to increasing differentiation. The result is that there is no guarantee that ascriptions made by an ever-greater variety of actors will in any way become uniform. In principle one would expect each actor to develop his or her own ascriptions based on his or her individual social and biographical situation. Empirically, however, the actor frequently encounters a closed and rigid system of ascription. Such systems arise in homogenous, closed societies as well as in traditional societies, and they are always present under conditions of oppressive authority. This is quite natural, for uniform ascriptions ensure that interactions will be predictable, which is typical for these types of societies. Once an action or actor is evaluated in the public eye as worthy in terms of achievement, then what that actor can lay claim to is also established. This process occurs against the background of force in societies with a strong ruling authority. In such cases ascriptive power is monopolized, with the result that that which is produced in the upper levels is recognized as achievement. Thus whoever possesses power generally has ready and more direct access to ascriptive power.

Wherever societies have become more complex and are internally differentiated (through occupational groupings, political groupings, including those of minorities, or immigration) and wherever there have been a large number of external contacts, existing ascriptions become problematic and discussions, conflicts, and struggles over ascription ensue. Such discussions and conflicts are typical of modernity. The ascriptions of the majority stand opposed to those of the minority. Discussions and conflicts surrounding ascriptions also arise when the circumstances of power are loosened, especially as a result of the differentiation of functions and functional systems (Luhmann 1984, 186). These debates focus on the following questions: What constitutes achievement? Who has accomplished it? Which achievements are more important than others? Whose actions cause damages? What brings more damage than benefit?

Conflicts over ascription are aggravated when conceptions of equality become established but inequality continues to exist. Equality carries with it a suggestion of ascription: all achieve to an equal extent. For this reason the inequalities that exist need to be justified. Disadvantages and liabilities are also regarded in the population at large as equally distributed. This raises the problem that a disproportionate amount of blame for such action (for example, criminal action) is placed on particular strata, especially minorities. Equality, however, no longer needs to be justified or provided with a basis because it is accepted as the natural state. Inequalities with regard to power, reward, and negative sanctions are best explained and justified in terms of differences in achievement and the causing of damage. It is for this reason that ascription conflicts focus on these kinds of inequalities.

To gain outside recognition of their own positions, inferior new groups or actors build up self-definitions and ascriptions concerning not only their own achievements but also their share of power and resources in society. In addition, they formulate images of society that explain the existing reality that they believe to be unjust. They construct images of a future society and ascribe to themselves a more important position within it. Their social self-confidence, their sense of social identity, develops, providing a basis on which it is easier to perform actions. For such a self-assessment to be maintained, an internal organization that nurtures self-ascription is necessary.

But self-ascriptions do not remain stable. The various actors try, within achievement relations, to enforce their definitions of their own and others' resources and achievements. Thus there are negotiations about resources and achievements and about a new, more just distribution of power and privileges. Concepts such as "status management" and "stratification policy" are a reflection of these processes. Negotiations mean that actors, groups, or parties attempt to reach agreements about ascriptions and the recognition of ascriptions in their future relations.

Negotiations encourage the tendency toward more equality, for negotiations always imply that communication takes place between the parties involved and the willingness to communicate confers a sense of legitimacy on the other party. Thus either party may oppose a particular proposition or set certain conditions. This process of negotiation can progress to the point where elites themselves accept conceptions of equality and only ascribe achievements of equal value to themselves, as has been true of members of the nobility in many bourgeois and proletarian revolutions.

The crucial point is that modern ascriptions are not necessarily correct just because they emerged from a process of negotiation. Some evidence suggests that definitions of the situation are more adequate if large numbers of actors from various positions participate in shaping them, but there is no guarantee of the correctness of mass ascriptions. The persecution of witches and of the Jews, each of which was supported by large majorities, makes this point clear.

Finally, in modernity ascriptions are of a less lasting character. One may observe a permanent state of change. Groups are continually appearing on the scene with new demands that repeatedly lead to ascription struggles.

4. AN EXPLANATION FOR DIFFERENTIAL RATES OF ACHIEVEMENT IN TWO MODERN SOCIETIES

There are many developmental processes that can be explained using the frame of reference described above, and negotiations about the ascription of achievement and damage play a central part in them. Negotiations are conducted in a similar way with regard to resources and power, rewards, rights, abilities to engage in self-steering, and individualization. Moreover, the road to modernity is a trend away from the monopolization of the power of definition by elites in favor of the downward distribution of this power. I demonstrate this trend by examining changes in achievement ratios in the United States and the Federal Republic of Germany. This empirical analysis also includes references to Britain and France because these societies strongly influenced developments in both the United States and Germany.

The initial determining factor for the development of modern societies is the mobilization of increasing amounts of resources. The most important stages in this process for modern societies have been the modernization of agriculture, the industrial revolution, the modernization of commerce and transportation, and the educational revolution. These phases of resource mobilization bring about alterations in the relations pertaining to achievement and other factors. Europe in general and Britain in particular long played the leading part in continuously mobilizing new resources. Today resource mobilization in the United States and Western Europe is much more similar. If we examine the differences in the downward distribution of achievement in the United States and West Germany, it is clear that observable differences in the mobilization of labor and power and in education are insufficient to explain the contrasts in achievement. Nor is there any essential distinction between the United States and West Germany with regard to the ascription of significance to resources. Factors other than the mobilization and distribution of resources must therefore be responsible for differentials in the distribution of achievement in these two societies.

Similarly, there are no significant differences in the overall levels of achievement in the United States and West Germany. For example, performance ability in the two societies—measured in terms of the growth of gross national product per head—is moderate in both cases (World Bank 1985, 175). An examination of who, according to objective criteria, accomplished achievements shows sharp increases in the levels of achievement in the lower strata in both societies. These increases can be traced back over more than a hundred years.

The industrial revolution, in particular, brought substantial change in potentials for achievement. Entrepreneurs, and indeed the urban middle class in general, were able to offer their new approach to economic and other activities. They gave many microactors the opportunity to achieve. Using new machines, industrial workers produced a huge new range of commodities. To do this they had to demonstrate orderliness, discipline, willingness to work, and physical application, none of which were by any means achievements to be taken for granted. At an early stage supplementary large groups of highly qualified workers were sought (Geiger 1949, 87–88). The larger leap forward in achievement, however, was accomplished by the dependent masses and no longer, as in the period preceding and following the French Revolution, by the bourgeoisie. The bourgeoisie had already attained a high level of achievement at the time of the great political revolutions and could not improve much more on that level. The masses, however, did not emerge from the shadows of economic developments until the industrial revolution.

From around 1860 until the present day the increase in the achievement of the masses in productivity terms has been impressive. This increase has been particularly evident in Sweden and other Scandinavian countries but increases in achievement in Germany and in the United States have also been significant (Kuznets 1966, 64–65, 73). Economic growth in both Europe and the United States during this period can be attributed to a great extent to increased efficiency in the labor force (Kuznets 1966, 72–81, 494). Even in recent times major increases in the productivity of labor as a factor of production are still being accomplished. Annual increases in this statistic in Federal Germany fluctuated between 1.5 percent and 11.3 percent during the period 1960–84 (Statistisches Taschenbuch 1985, Table 3.3). Productivity per employee-hour increased during the period 1960–84 at annual rates ranging from 1.3 to 6.5 percent (Statistisches Taschenbuch 1985, Table 1.7). Very recent investigations confirm the gain in significance for human labor power (Kern and Schumann 1984). Angelika Schade has concluded that all data "support the contention that there has been a consistent, long-term increase in the efficiency of the masses" (Schade 1986, 75).

At the same time that the efficiency of the masses has been increasing, evidence in several spheres indicates declining achievement among elites. First, economic growth in both the United States and Germany is attributable less to the propagation and deployment of capital than to the raising of labor productivity (Kuznets 1966, 72–81). Second, the elite in Germany has proved to be a political failure several times in succession. Instances include the failure to moderate the policies of Kaiser Wilhelm II, the lack of identification with the Weimar Republic, and the failure to resist national socialism (Mayer 1980, 167). In contrast to these failures, in the years since World War II the German elite has made many significant achievements including guaranteeing authority and undertaking democratic, economic, and sociopolitical reconstruction. However, in comparison with earlier historical periods the tasks undertaken and fulfilled have been narrower in scope (Baier, 1977). In the economic sphere entrepreneurs have functioned poorly in the modern period, particularly beginning in the mid-1960s. They are too strongly oriented to the short term (Vondran 1985, 42) and are one-sided in the emphasis they give to technical developments (Mayer 1980). Hence bankruptcies, crises, and mismanagement among big-name corporations are not unusual (Wurm 1978, 184). This situation is not substantially different from that in the United States where elites have failed, the race problem providing a case in point. In recent decades in particular U.S. leaders have had to live with significant political and military defeats; and the rates of economic development are not significantly different from those in West Germany.

The lack of differences between the United States and West Germany in the objective achievements of the upper and the lower reaches of society does not explain the achievement ratios discussed in the introduction to this chapter: namely, that German elites tend to be less capable and American elites more capable of achieving, whereas German working people are more efficient than their American counterparts. To explain this difference one must take into account an ascriptive effect that arose before the industrial revolution and still affects the situation today.

By the fifteenth century (at the latest) economic action interrelationships began to emerge in a differentiated form. Their potentials for creating either achievement or damage were measurable in terms of protecting against external threats and offering monarchs and nobility possibilities for using force domestically. These interrelationships gave rise to what marks the beginning of modernity: the first significant conflict over ascription. A new group—the bourgeoisie—was accomplishing important achievements, and it was ascribing these achievements to itself in a process of self-definition. This process culminated in the description of society as a whole as "civil society," a definition first successfully asserted with the bourgeoisie's ascriptive victory in the United States. Before the American Revolution Americans ascribed the achievement of solving all basic societal problems solely to themselves. From this point of view the British sovereign was solely interested in collecting taxes. The First Congress made an appeal to the people in England: Did we not add all the strength of this large country to the power that chased away our common foe? And did we not leave our native land and face sickness and death to further the fortune of the British crown in faraway lands? Will you not reward us for our zeal? (Adams and Adams 1976, 105–6). The small number of representatives of the British crown had nothing of equal value they could set against these self-ascriptions by American macroactors.

The situation in Germany was very different. There, the bourgeoisie attempted to import the outcome of the French Revolution. The ascriptive victory that the French bourgeoisie won can be explained by the greater weight of its achievement. Already before the revolution the bourgeoisie, because of its successes in craft trades, technical achievement, industry, and commerce, had attained a far greater importance than the king, with his absolute power, and the nobility, which had some share in his ruling authority (Claessens 1968, 132). At the same time the Third Estate had the more able agitators among its own ranks. Whenever Louis XVI's spokesmen faced the advocates Saint Just and Robespierre, they invariably got the worst of the situation (Jonas 1982). Other important and like-minded actors who intervened in the ascription battles were radical philosophers and apostate priests, who could do nothing other than ascribe. Abbé Sieyès is known to have posed the rhetorical question "What is the Third Estate?" and then immediately answered, "Everything." A handbill distributed at the time shows a person from the Third Estate carrying the king, nobility, and clergy on his shoulders. Despite the bourgeoisie's ability to achieve, this image was an exaggeration; yet this incredible overestimation of itself was common throughout the Third Estate (Jonas 1982).

Third Estate agitators even succeeded in enforcing the bourgeoisie's self-ascription on other groups as well: the nobility itself propounded ideas of equality, and the priests who remained in office were no longer convinced of their special status (Jonas 1982). This situation provided the basis for the forced dissemination of notions of equality. Thus the ascription struggle between the very top and the very bottom had been decided before the French Revolution actually occurred: "Whoever heard the theories propounded at [in the late eighteenth century], and the fundamental principles tacitly but almost universally recognized . . . could not have avoided coming to the conclusion that France as it then existed . . . was already the most democratic nation in Europe" (Tocqueville 1967, 130). The conflict culminated in the French Revolution and a convincing ascriptive victory for the bourgeoisie. This victory ensured that this stratum's superiority in achievement found recognition and that it was established for posterity.

Ascriptions, once established, can endure for long periods. Thus even today the French elite—the bourgeoisie—is still able to claim entitlement to a particularly large portion of the national income (World Bank 1985, 229).

In Germany the situation was different. The Prussian bourgeoisie in 1848 had neither the accomplishments nor the self-confidence of its

French and American counterparts. The leading positions of state in Germany were occupied by actors who were strong achievers and who successfully asserted their right to fulfill important tasks, speaking of themselves as the first servants of the state. Even allowing for the effects of the ideology of equality and the bourgeoisie's ascriptive activities, the bourgeoisie could not hope to win ascription conflicts with the ruling class. Thus, after a short period of insecurity among the rulers as to what role they should play, the course of events in Prussia led to reaction.

To this day the bourgeoisie in the Federal Republic of Germany does not have recourse to any enforced recognition of achievement, as do the bourgeois strata of France and the United States. Hence the different levels of ascriptive success of the business bourgeoisie in Germany and the United States play an essential part in determining the differences in recognized achievement ratios. The recognized achievement of the elite is less in West Germany than it is in the United States. The masses in West Germany, however, proved particularly able to ascribe special achievements to themselves.

Although workers in Britain, Switzerland, and Belgium (the three European societies then more industrialized than Germany) had an awareness that they had an important but disputed position in society, they were not able to combine this awareness with a sufficient number of actors who could organize themselves, go on the offensive, and assert this self-ascription. The first attempts at enforcing this self-definition were the foundings of trade-union umbrella organizations in 1868 in Germany (about twenty years after the commencement of industrialization) and in Britain (about one hundred years after the take-off period). Other nations did not follow suit until very much later. More significant than the foundings of trade-union umbrella organizations was the formation of workers' parties. These parties not only put worker self-ascriptions into effect in labor disputes and negotiations but also involved workers in all aspects of the public negotiating processes in which political parties normally express their positions. Not until after 1885 did workers' parties come into being in Britain, Switzerland, and Belgium, whereas actors in Germany created the *Allgemeiner Deutscher Arbeiterverein* (the General German Workers' party) as early as 1863 under Lassalle in Leipzig, followed in 1869 by the *Sozialdemokratische Arbeiterpartei* (Social Democratic Workers' party) or SDAP under Liebknecht and Bebel in Eisenach. The macroactors Lassalle, Liebknecht, and Bebel formulated self-ascriptions for industrial workers that could not have been clearer. The self-ascriptions are not surprising if one bears in mind that two of Marx's major works appeared in the years 1848 and 1867. The fact that Marx's first works were published in German was undoubtedly a major reason why worker self-ascription was first put forward by German industrial workers and their leaders. This new self-awareness is evident in the *Allgemeiner Deutscher Arbeiterverein*'s federation anthem:

> Mann der Arbeit, aufgewacht
> Und erkenne Deine Macht!
> All Rader stehen still,
> Wenn Dein starker Arm es will!
>
> Man of labor, now arise!
> What power is yours, if you have eyes.
> All the wheels grind to a stand,
> If this be the wish of your strong hand.

Like the French bourgeoisie, the self-image of the German workers tended to exaggerate their own importance. But Marx and the labor movement's leaders succeeded—in what, given the prevailing perception of the role and significance of employers, was basically a hopeless situation—in providing industrial workers and their organizers with a strong self-assurance using this self-definition.

As we know, not only does no workers' party exist in the United States to this day, but the level of union organization there is one of the lowest in the world. At the outset of unionization in the United States moderation was already prevailing. Faced with that situation, the leader of the American Federation of Labor (AFL), Samuel Gompers, deemed it advisable to be invulnerable to attack. After the turn of the century he proclaimed that the demands of the AFL had nothing in common with those of foreign revolutionaries and with ideologies advocating a change of the system. He asserted that American workers only wanted more money and reduced hours (Merkl and Raabe 1977, 17). Clearly, given prior conditions, actors in the lower echelons have scored significantly more impressive successes in Western Europe than they have in the United States.

If we compare the bourgeoisie's ascriptive success or failure in political revolutions, that is, success in the United States and France and failure in Germany, and these differences are related to the strength or weakness of the working people's self-definition, strong in Germany and weaker in the United States, then the answer to the question of why the recognized achievement ratio is more favorable to the masses in Germany than it is in the United States lies close at hand. The great turnaround as German elites declined at the beginning of the modern period and the specific "lead in achievement" accomplished by the dependent masses in West Germany cannot be attributed solely to an objective rise in the value of the bourgeois strata's achievements in the United States and France, in the first case, and in those of the proletarian strata at a later stage in Germany, in the second case. For, quite apart from the actual achievement values, there were also changes in the subjective assessments of these values. These changes were the result, on the one hand, of the successes of macroactors who appeared on the scene and interacted with the many microactors below and, on the other hand, of the influence brought to bear by egalitarian and democratic norms and values.

REFERENCES

Adams, Willi Paul, and Angela Meurer Adams, eds. 1976. *Die Amerikanische Revolution in Augenzeugenberichten.* Munich: Deutscher Taschenbuch Verlag.

Baier, Horst. 1977. Herrschaft im Sozialstaat. *Kölner Zeitschrift für Soziologie und Sozialpolitik* 19 (special issue, *Soziologie und Sozialpolitik*):128–42.

Baudelaire, Charles. 1925. *Augewählte Werke.* Vol. 3, *Kritische und nachgelassene Schriften.* Munich: Müller.

Becker, Howard S. 1963. *Outsiders: Studies in the sociology of deviance.* New York: Free Press.

Bendix, Reinhard. 1971. Sociology and the distrust of reason. In *Scholarship and partisanship: Essays on Max Weber,* by Reinhard Bendix and Guenther Roth, 84–105. Berkeley: University of California Press.

Bolte, Karl Martin. 1979. *Leistung und Leistungsprinzip.* Opladen, W. Ger.: Leske and Budrich.

Claessens, Dieter. 1968. *Rolle und Macht.* Munich: Juventa.

Ferguson, Adam. [1767] 1969. *Essays on the history of civil society.* Farnborough, Eng.: Gregg.

Geiger, Theodor. 1949. *Die Klassengesellschaft im Schmelztiegel.* Cologne: Kiepenheuer.

Haferkamp, Hans. 1983. *Soziologie der Herrschaft. Analyse von Struktur, Entwicklung und Zustand von Herrschaftszusammenhängen.* Opladen, W. Ger.: Westdeutscher Verlag.

———. 1991. *Soziales Handeln: Theorie sozialen Verhaltens und sinnhaften Handelns, geplanter Handlungszusammenhänge und sozialer Structuren.* Opladen: West-deutcher Verlag.

Hondrich, Karl Otto. 1973. *Theorie der Herrschaft.* Frankfurt: Suhrkamp.

Jonas, Friedrich. 1982. *Soziologische Betrachtungen zur Französischen Revolution.* Ed. Manfred Hennen and Walter G. Rödel. Stuttgart: Enke.

Kern, Horst, and Michael Schumann. 1984. *Das Ende der Arbeitsteilung? Rationalisierung in der industriellen Produktion: Bestandsaufnahme, Trendbestimmung.* Munich: Beck.

Kitschelt, Herbert. 1985. Materiale Politisierung der Produktion. Gesellschaftliche Herausforderung und institutionelle Innovationen in fortgeschrittenen kapitalistischen Demokratien. *Zeitschrift für Soziologie* 14:188–208.

Knorr-Cetina, Karin D. 1981. The micro-sociological challenge of macro-sociology: Towards a reconstruction of social theory and methodology. In *Advances in social theory and methodology: Toward an integration of micro- and macro-sociologies,* ed. K. D. Knorr-Cetina and A. V. Cicourel, 1–47. Boston: Routledge and Kegan Paul.

Kuznets, Simon. 1966. *Modern economic growth: Rate, structure, and spread.* New Haven: Yale University Press.

Levy, Marion J. 1967. Social patterns and problems of modernization. In *Readings on social change,* ed. Wilbert E. Moore and R. Cook, 189–208. Englewood Cliffs, N.J.: Prentice-Hall.

Lockwood, David. 1985. Civic stratification, 1985. Paper presented at conference, Sociological Theories and Inequality. Organized by the Sociological Theory section of the German Sociological Association, 10–11 Oct., Bremen, 1985.

Luhmann, Niklas. 1984. *Soziale Systeme: Grundrisse einer allgemeinen Theorie.* Frankfurt: Suhrkamp.

Marshall, Thomas Humphrey. [1949] 1977. Citizenship and social class. In *Class, citizenship, and social development,* by T. H. Marshall, 71–134. Chicago: The University of Chicago Press.

Marx, Karl, and Friedrich Engels. [1848] 1964. *Manifest der Kommunistischen Partei.* In *Karl Marx, Die Frühschriften,* ed. Siegfried Landshut, 525–60. Stuttgart: Kröner.

Mayer, Karl-Ulrich. 1980. Struktur und Wandel der politischen Eliten. In *Deutschland-Frankreich: Baustein zum Systemvergleich,* ed. Robert Bosch Stiftung Gmbh, 1:165–95. Gerlingen, W. Ger.: Bleicher.

Merkl, Peter H., and Dieter Raabe. 1977. *Politische Soziologie der USA.* Wiesbaden: Akademische Verlagsanstalt.

Nisbet, Robert A., and Robert G. Perrin. 1970. *The social bond: An introduction to the study of society.* 2d ed. New York: Knopf.

Offe, Claus. 1970. *Leistungsprinzip und industrielle Arbeit. Mechanismen der Statusverteilung in Arbeitsorganisationen der industriellen Arbeitsgesellschaft.* Frankfurt: Europäische Verlagsanstalt.

Parsons, Talcott. 1951. *The social system.* Glencoe, Ill.: Free Press.

———. [1971] 1972. *Das System moderner Gesellschaften.* Munich: Juventa. (First published in English: 1971. *The system of modern societies.* Englewood Cliffs, N.J.: Prentice Hall.

Ronge, Volker. 1975. Entpolitisierung der Forschungspolitik. *Leviathan* 3:307–37.

Rossiter, Clinton. 1956. *The first American revolution.* New York: Harbrace.

Schade, Angelika. 1986. *Prozesse der Angleichung: Theoretische Ansätze und empirische Überprüfung.* Master's thesis, Department of Sociology, University of Bremen.

Schutz, Alfred. 1964–67. *Collected papers.* Vols. 1–3. The Hague: Nijhoff.

Senghaas, Dieter. 1982. *Von Europa lernen. Entwicklungsgeschichtliche Betrachtungen.* Frankfurt: Suhrkamp. (See English translation: 1985. *The European experience.* Leamington Spa, Eng.: Berg.)

Simmel, Georg. [1908] 1968. *Soziologie: Untersuchungen über die Form der Vergesellschaftung.* Berlin: Duncker and Humblot.

Statistisches Jahrbuch für die Bundesrepublik Deutschland. Wiesbaden: Statistisches Bundesamt Wiesbaden.

Statistisches Taschenbuch. Arbeits- und Sozialstatistik. 1985. Bonn: Bundesminister für Arbeit und Sozialordnung.

Strasser, Hermann, and Susan C. Randall. 1981. *An introduction to theories of social change.* London: Routledge and Kegan Paul.

Strauss, Anselm. 1978. *Negotiations, varieties, contexts, processes, and social order.* San Francisco: Jossey-Bass.

Tocqueville, Alexis de. 1967. *Die gesellschaftlichen und politischen Zustände in Frankreich vor und nach 1789.* In *Alexis de Tocqueville.* 2d ed., ed. Siegfried Landshut, 117–40. Cologne: Westdeutscher Verlag.

UNESCO. *Statistical Yearbook.* Paris: United Nations Educational, Scientific, and Cultural Organization.

Vondran, Ruprecht. 1985. Gemeinsamkeiten und Unterschiede im Management. In *Die Arbeitswelt in Japan und in der Bundesrepublik Deutschland: ein Vergleich,* ed., Peter Hanau, Saburo Kimoto, Heinz Markmann, and Kazuaki Tezuka, 9–46. Neuwied: Luchterhand.

Weber, Max. 1920. *Gesammelte Aufsätze zur Religionssoziologie.* Vol. 1. Tübingen: J. C. B. Mohr (Siebeck).

Wiswede, Günter, and Thomas Kutsch. 1978. *Sozialer Wandel.* Darmstadt: Wissenschaftliche Buchgesellschaft.

Wittfogel, Karl A. 1938. Die Theorie der orientalischen Gesellschaft. *Zeitschrift für Sozialforschung* 7:90–122.

World Bank. 1985. *World development report.* Washington, D.C.

Wurm, Franz F. 1978. *Leistung und Gesellschaft.* Opladen, W. Ger.: Leske and Budrich.

Zapf, Wolfgang. 1983. Entwicklungsdilemmas und Innovationspotentiale in modernen Gesellschaften. In *Krise der Arbeitsgesellschaft? Verhandlungen des 21. Deutschen Soziologentages in Bamberg, 1982,* ed. Joachim Matthes, 293–308. Frankfurt: Campus.

Employment, Class, and Mobility

A Critique of Liberal and Marxist Theories of Long-term Change

John H. Goldthorpe

1. THEORIES OF CHANGE IN CLASS STRATIFICATION

In this chapter my concern is with theories of long-term change in the class stratification of advanced Western societies. Such theories fall into two main types on which I shall concentrate: (i) those that form part of more general liberal theories of the development of industrialism or "postindustrialism"; and (ii) those that form part of more general Marxist theories of the development of capitalism or "late-capitalism." In this first section of the chapter, I review these theories in sufficient detail to bring out the wide differences that exist between them. In the following section, I examine how well they fare in the light of recent research. I focus my attention here—without apology—on research that has produced *quantitative* results, since, as will be seen, most of the issues that arise in comparing the two types of theory are ones of an inescapably quantitative kind.[1]

---

1. It will also be apparent that, contrary to the mood ("argument" would be too strong a word) of much recent "methodological" writing in sociology, I adhere to the—essentially Popperian—view that if theories are to have any informational and hence explanatory value, they must be open, either directly or through propositions derivable from them, to criticism and to possible refutation in the light of empirical inquiry. I am aware of the philosophical difficulties that arise from a naive—or even with a sophisticated—"falsificationist" position, most notably, the possibility that the empirical results that apparently disconfirm a proposition may themselves be called into question via the concepts and theories that guided and conditioned their production. However, it seems to me that in the actual practice of any kind of scientific endeavor such difficulties can be largely circumvented, for example, by the proponents of a theory being themselves prepared to state what empirical results, produced in what way, would lead them to regard their theory as no longer valid. I believe that most of the authors whose work I discuss in this paper do, at least in practice, take a view of the relationship between theory and research that is broadly compatible with my own, and none

The main conclusion that I reach is that neither liberal nor Marxist theories stand up at all well to empirical testing, and that the claims of both must now in fact be seen as in major respects invalid. Consequently, in the final section of the chapter, I am led to ask whether anything of a general kind can be said about why these theories should have proved to be so unsuccessful and, if so, what lessons may be learned from their failure.

The trends of change proposed by the theories that I wish to examine can be usefully treated as occurring (i) in the division of labor or, more precisely perhaps, in the structure of employment; (ii) in the class structure; and (iii) in rates and patterns of social mobility within the class structure. Some amount of variation is of course to be found among both liberal and Marxist theories, and I cannot pretend here to do full justice to this. Rather, I shall concentrate on those features of liberal theories on the one hand and of Marxist theories on the other that would appear to be central to the genre. On the liberal side, I draw most heavily on Kerr et al. ([1960] 1973) and also Kerr (1983), Bell (1967, 1973), and Blau and Duncan (1967); on the Marxist side, I draw on Braverman (1974), Carchedi (1977), Wright (1978, 1985), and Wright and Singelmann (1982). These sources will not be further cited except where direct quotations are made from them.

1.1. Changes in the Structure of Employment

It is a central claim of liberal theories that in the course of the development of industrial and postindustrial societies the structure of employment is, in net terms, progressively "upgraded." The proportion of the total labor force engaged in work that requires minimal skills and expertise—and in turn minimal training and education—tends steadily to decline, while a corresponding expansion occurs in the types of employment that call for various new skills and often for expertise grounded in theoretical knowledge, and that may moreover entail the exercise of authority and responsibility. Two major sources of this upgrading are identified. First, the continuing advance of technology in all forms of production tends to eliminate merely "laboring" or highly routinized jobs, while creating others that must be filled by technically and scientifically qualified personnel. Second, the tendency, analyzed by economists such as Clark (1957), Kuznets (1966), and Fuchs (1968), for labor within a growing economy to shift intersectorally—initially from agriculture and extractive industries to manufacturing but then from manufacturing to services—also generates an increased demand for high-level skills, both technical and "social." Furthermore, the organiza-

---

explicitly adopts a position that would render his or her theoretical arguments immune to empirically based criticism.

tion of services, public and private, tends to multiply administrative and managerial as well as professional positions.

In direct contrast—indeed, in more or less explicit opposition—to this thesis of the progressive upgrading of employment, Marxist authors claim that the long-term trend of change in Western societies is in fact for employment to be systematically degraded. Within the context of the prevailing methods of industrial organization, as informed by modern "scientific management," the consequence of technological advance is that one type of work after another, in all sectors of the economy alike, is effectively "deskilled," and this tendency far outweighs any increase that may occur in professional or managerial positions. Thus, Marxists argue that a large part of the growth of nonmanual or white-collar employment that has so impressed liberal authors is made up of jobs that are already degraded and that, in terms of skill levels and autonomy as well as pay and conditions, are in no way superior to the manual jobs they have replaced.

This systematic degrading (or, more emotively, "degradation") of labor results ultimately, in the Marxist view, from the fact that capitalist production entails the exploitation of workers by their employers. This means that, under capitalism, the labor process must be organized in such a way as to meet not only the requirements of productive efficiency but also the requirements of the social control of labor. And in this latter respect, the possibility of using new technology and managerial methods in order to remove skill—and thus autonomy and discretion—from the mass of employees and to concentrate them in the hands of management is one that employers will seek always to realize. In sum, while liberals view change in the structure of employment as essentially an adaptive response to technological and economic progress, Marxists would rather see it as reflecting the outcome of an abiding class struggle.

1.2. Changes in Class Structure

As regards change in the class structures of Western societies, liberal theorists stress two main developments, both of which they would regard as following directly from the net upgrading of employment. They point, on the one hand, to the contraction of the working class, in the sense of the body of manual wage-earners and, on the other, to the emergence of what has most often been labeled the "new middle class" of nonmanual, salaried employees—as distinct from the "old middle class" of proprietors and "independents," whose social significance diminishes as large-scale enterprises increasingly dominate the economy. The class structure of industrial societies is in fact seen as coming increasingly to reflect the social hierarchy of the modern corporation, although at the same time across all classes a reduction occurs in the more evident inequalities—for example, in incomes and in standards and styles of living. Indeed, for some authors (for example, Duncan 1968), the very concept of a class structure is inappropriate to the gradational complexity found under advanced industrialism and is better replaced by that of a continuum of "socioeconomic" status.

Again, the position taken up by Marxist theorists is a quite contrary one, deriving as it does from their emphasis on the degrading rather than the upgrading of the job structure. Instead of a decline in the size of the working class, what they see in train is a process of widening "proletarianization" that will maintain the working class in a position of at least numerical, if not sociopolitical, preponderance.[2] In classical Marxism, the idea of proletarianization was applied specifically to the "driving down" of elements of the petty bourgeoisie into the ranks of wage labor; but in more recent analyses its meaning has been extended so that it has in effect become synonymous with those changes in the content of work and in working conditions that are claimed by the "degradation of labor" thesis—and especially as this thesis is applied to work of a nonmanual kind. Marxist authors would then reject the view that the long-run tendency is for the class structures of Western, late-capitalist societies to display increasing gradational complexity. While the growth of the professional, administrative, and managerial salariat may be acknowledged as having created some problems of both theory and practice (the problems of "middle layers," "dual functions," "contradictory class locations," etc.), such problems tend to be regarded as transient ones that are in fact finding their solution as the simplifying logic of proletarianization continues to work itself out. As Braverman puts it:

> The problem of the so-called employee or white-collar worker which so bothered earlier generations of Marxists, and which was hailed by anti-Marxists as proof of the falsity of the "proletarianization" thesis, has thus been unambiguously clarified by the polarization of office employment and the growth at one pole of an immense mass of *wage-workers*. The apparent trend to a large nonproletarian "middle class" has resolved itself into the creation of a large proletariat in a new form. (1974, 355, emphasis in original)

2. Poulantzas (1974) represents what must be regarded as a deviant Marxist view in this respect. His conceptualization of modern class structures would apparently require him to recognize, along with liberal theorists, a numerically declining working class, together with what he would regard as an expanding "new petty bourgeoisie." It is difficult to resist the conclusion that criticism by other Marxists of the position adopted by Poulantzas has been as much inspired by the uncongenial nature of its political implications as by preexisting theoretical disagreements. Thus, for example, Wright complains (1976, 23) "It is hard to imagine a viable socialist movement developing in an advanced capitalist society in which less than one in five people are workers." For an incisive critique of recent Marxist debates on class structure and action, see Lockwood (1981).

1.3. Changes in Social Mobility

For liberal theorists, industrial societies are highly mobile societies. The general assumption is that economic development and social mobility are positively associated: the more economically developed a society, the higher the rates of social mobility that it will display. Explanations of how this association comes about take somewhat different forms (Goldthorpe 1985a), but two processes are clearly given major emphasis (Treiman 1970). First, it is observed that the transformation of the structure of employment, which, as already described, is seen as following from technological and economic advances, must in itself generate high levels of occupational and class mobility. Moreover, because a net upgrading of employment takes place, the pattern of mobility will in turn show a net upward bias. In particular, the expansion of the professional, administrative, and managerial occupations of the new middle class is too great to be met entirely by self-recruitment and mobility from the old middle class, and in fact greatly enlarges the opportunities for the social ascent of individuals of working-class origins.

Second, it is argued that, quite apart from the effects of such structural change, mobility is also increased as a result of changes in the criteria and processes of social selection. The functioning of a modern industrial society entails a progressive shift away from "ascription" and toward "achievement" as the leading principle of selection, and this principle becomes embodied in the procedures of educational institutions and employing organizations. In turn, the operation of such "meritocratic" selection promotes greater openness and equality of opportunity in the sense that individuals' levels of educational and occupational attainment become less closely correlated with the attributes of their families or communities of origin. Because of the prevailing high levels of mobility, the potential for class formation and class conflict in modern societies is seen as steadily declining. The more readily that lines of class division are crossed, the less likely class is to provide the basis on which collective identities and collective action will develop. Mobility performs important legitimizing and stabilizing functions. To quote Blau and Duncan (1967, 440), "Inasmuch as high chances of mobility make men less dissatisfied with the system of social differentiation in their society and less inclined to organise in opposition to it, they help to perpetuate this stratification system, and they simultaneously stabilise the political institutions that support it."

Marxist theorists do not, in the case of mobility trends, provide a matching set of counterarguments to those that are advanced by liberal authors. Rather, major disagreement is apparent over the importance of mobility per se. Thus, where Marxists do not ignore the question of mobility altogether, they either attempt to dismiss it as one prompted more by ideological than by social-scientific concerns (see, e.g., Poulantzas 1974, 37) or they treat it as being one of no great consequence on the grounds that mobility between different class locations in fact occurs to only a very limited extent. Thus, for example, Carchedi (1977, 173) asserts that "generally speaking, a member of the working class remains a member of the working class" and that "the same applies to both the middle classes and to the capitalist class." The only way of any real significance in which individuals may change their class location is collectively and "through changes in the inner nature" of the positions they occupy. That is to say, individuals move not so much *between* classes as *with* classes. And the major instance of mobility in this sense evident within contemporary capitalism is one involving clearly downward movement, namely, "the case of the proletarianization of the new middle class" through the "devaluation" of its labor power. For Marxist authors, then, there is nothing in the dynamics of the class stratification of modern societies that tends in itself to undermine the possibilities for class-based action—even though this action may be inhibited by other "ideological" or "conjunctural" factors. On the contrary, as the degradation of work and the proletarianization of workers continue inexorably, class differences widen and class interests come into still sharper opposition.

2. REVIEW OF THE EVIDENCE

In coming now to assess the claims made by liberal and Marxist theories in the light of research findings, I proceed under the same headings as in the previous section. Apart from being convenient, to move through this same sequence of topics—from the evolution of the structure of employment via changes in class structure to trends in class mobility—should help bring out a certain coherence in the empirical results on which I draw.

2.1. Changes in the Structure of Employment

The Marxist thesis of the degradation of labor was developed as an explicit critique of liberal claims of a progressive upgrading of employment. It would, however, seem fair to say that in this respect it is Marxists rather than liberals who have been forced onto the defensive whenever the issue between them has been treated on an empirical basis. The major difficulty for the Marxist position has come from trends displayed in the official employment statistics of the more advanced industrial nations. These show—with considerable regularity—that the greatest increases in nonmanual employment over recent decades have occurred not in relatively low-level clerical, sales, and personal service grades but rather in professional, administrative, and managerial occupations. Furthermore, the major decreases in manual employment have been in the less-skilled rather than the more-skilled categories. Such statistics create in themselves a strong prima facie case against the degrading thesis and have thus forced Marxists into attempting counterarguments. These have taken two main lines.

First, some Marxists point out (see especially Wright and Singelmann 1982) that the discrepancy between the claims of the degrading thesis and the trends apparent in employment statistics could arise through changes taking place in occupational distributions at the societal level that are independent of changes in the organization of production within particular enterprises. Such changes could result simply from shifts in the division of total employment among different industries and sectors that themselves possess different occupational structures. In other words, it is possible that the increase in professionals, administrators, and managers is the consequence largely—or entirely—of the growth of the services sector, within which such occupations have always been more prominent than within, say, the heavy industries, which are now typically in decline. But, it may then be maintained, the effects of degrading are in this way only masked by countervailing tendencies that cannot continue indefinitely; and, as the "service economy" reaches its full development and shift effects on the structure of employment fall off, the reality of degrading will be made increasingly apparent.

However, while this line of argument is analytically sound, it does not of course follow that it is empirically valid, and in fact evidence has of late mounted strongly against it. Although Wright and Singelmann (1982) were able to produce some supportive results for the United States in the 1960s (Singelmann and Browning 1980), later analyses for the United States in the 1970s reported by Singelmann and Tienda (1985) and analyses for a number of European nations (Gershuny 1983) have all yielded results that run in a clearly contrary direction. What is here shown is that the major trends evident in national employment statistics persist even when all interindustry shifts are allowed for. That is to say, net upgrading tendencies must be seen as resulting not only from such shifts but further from technological, organizational, and other changes determining the actual occupational mix at the level of production units.

The second way in which exponents of the degrading thesis have sought to overcome the problem posed by the data on occupational distributions is to claim that the thesis relates not simply to shifts of workers among occupations but further to changes occurring within occupations themselves—that is, to changes in their specific technical and social content. This argument is difficult to either confirm or refute in any direct way. Detailed investigation of work-tasks and roles of the kind that is called for is scarcely feasible on an economywide basis and has in fact been limited to case studies—the results of which, not surprisingly perhaps, have proved quite inconclusive.[3] However, one unique data set has afforded the opportunity for an indirect test of the degrading thesis, understood in the way in question and in the context of a national society. In each of the three "rounds" of the Swedish Level of Living Survey, carried out in 1968, 1974, and 1981, a sample of the Swedish population was asked a range of questions on their work and working conditions. These results have recently been analyzed in the light of expectations derived from the degrading thesis (Åberg 1984a, 1984b). Little or no support emerges for the idea that the Swedish labor force experienced degrading over the period covered. For example, levels of work-related training and education generally increased, fewer employees reported a boring routine or a serious lack of autonomy in their jobs, and more found their work mentally (but not physically) demanding.

Efforts to reconcile the degrading thesis with the dominant trends apparent in employment statistics are thus scarcely convincing, and it is notable that some former adherents of the thesis now appear ready to abandon it (see Singelmann and Tienda 1985). It is not of course in question that at any one time in a technologically and economically dynamic society some kinds of work will be in the process of deskilling or degrading in some sense (even if not necessarily for reasons that Marxists would advance). But neither would there seem grounds for questioning the thesis that as old skills, autonomies, and responsibilities disappear, they are replaced—and indeed more than replaced—by new ones, as liberal theorists would maintain.

Does it then follow that in rejecting the degrading thesis, one is at the same time required by the empirical evidence to accept the liberal argument that labor forces are being progressively upgraded? Much depends

---

3. This point could scarcely be better demonstrated than by the very extensive literature generated by British industrial sociologists under the affliction of "Bravermania." See, purely for purposes of illustration of the generally prevailing incoherence of theory and evidence, the recent contributions of Crompton and Jones (1984) and Penn and Scattergood (1985) and the earlier debates to which these authors refer. It must, moreover, be recognized, as argued elsewhere, that

> even quite indisputable evidence of degrading *derived from particular case-studies* can be of little value in defending the degrading thesis against the upgrading thesis *in so far as the argument is about class structures.* Supporters of the latter thesis do not seek to deny that deskilling or other forms of degrading occur (although they might wish to see these as integral to the development of industrial, rather than of specifically capitalist, societies); but they would still maintain that the *net* result of technological and organisational change *over the economy as a whole* is an increase in skill levels *and in the proportion of the work-force in salaried or bureaucratic conditions of employment.* In other words, macro-sociological arguments can only be adequately discussed on the basis of macro-sociological data. (Goldthorpe and Payne 1986, 23)

on what exactly this argument is taken to imply. The decline of manual wageworkers and the expansion of the professional, administrative, and managerial salariat could plausibly be regarded as generic processes of advanced industrial societies. But other developments have of late become apparent in such societies that do not accord well with the more optimistic liberal scenarios that developed in the postwar years of the "long boom," which saw upgrading in effect at all levels of the occupational structure and as leading toward the eventual "professionalization of everyone." Most obviously, one may point to the return since the mid-1970s of large-scale and long-term unemployment to most (though not all) Western societies. This means that even though the balance of change may be in favor of upgrading among jobs that exist, job loss is for many communities, families, and individuals now the central economic reality.[4] The fact that unemployment remains, as in the past, heavily concentrated among those who were previously wageworkers brings out the persisting differentiation in economic life-chances between this group and those employees who enjoy the much greater security typically afforded by the "conditions of service" of bureaucratic personnel (Goldthorpe 1985b; Goldthorpe and Payne 1986).

Moreover, alongside increased unemployment, tendencies have appeared in most Western societies—though in widely varying form and degree—toward what is aptly described by a term arising from the French experience: *la précarisation du travail* (see Michon 1981). A growth has occurred of diverse forms of employment of a "nonstandard" kind— part-time work, temporary work, home-work, labor-only subcontracting, etc.—that creates a "secondary" labor force that is highly exposed to both market fluctuations and managerial authority. One could say that this is a labor force that is highly flexible and *disponible,* chiefly because its members lack the protection that "primary" workers possess, whether through organization, legislation, or mere custom and practice (Berger and Piore 1980; Goldthorpe 1984). Recognition of an emerging dualism in this sense need not entail an acceptance of current theories—Marxist or otherwise—of dual or segmented labor markets that are systematically differentiated by levels of skill, pay, or mobility. But it does underline the error of supposing that at the stage of advanced industrialism upgrading proceeds uniformly in all aspects of employment alike.

2.2. Changes in Class Structure

As was previously shown, a close connection exists for both liberal and Marxist theorists between the course of long-term change in the struc-

4. It is remarkable that in Bell's *The Coming of Post-Industrial Society*—subtitled *A Venture in Social Forecasting* and published in 1973—the index contains only three references to unemployment, and each of these turns out to be quite trivial.

ture of employment in Western societies and the development of their class structures. Thus, it might be expected that insofar as the accounts offered of changes in the structure of employment are called into question, analyses made at the level of class structure will also be undermined. However, while the structure of employment relations—together with the structure of property relations—can be regarded as forming, so to speak, the matrix of the class structure, the actual derivation of class structure is a good deal less straightforward than seems often to be supposed.

To start with the Marxist case, it has already been observed that to reject the idea of a comprehensive and progressive degrading of labor necessitated by the logic of capitalism is not to deny that the degrading of specific types of work, over specific periods, is a feature of modern economies. Thus, there would appear ample evidence to support the arguments advanced by Marxists (and others) that a wide range of nonmanual—especially clerical, sales, and personal service—occupations are now little differentiated in their associated employment relations and conditions from rank-and-file manual occupations. But what has then to be challenged in the Marxist position is the further claim—or simple assumption—that this degrading of nonmanual work can be equated with a process of proletarianization through which the numerical strength of the present-day working class is maintained, if not indeed enlarged.

What is most obviously neglected here is the question of the appropriate unit of class structure and thus of class analysis. In the tradition of such analysis, Marxist and non-Marxist, the appropriate unit has been seen as the family rather than the individual (see Goldthorpe 1983). And it must then be pointed out that for so long as this view is maintained, the implications for class structure of recent changes in the character of nonmanual employment cannot be reckoned as in any way so dramatic as Marxist theorists would make out. In all modern societies the expansion of lower-level nonmanual occupations has largely occurred via the increased employment of women, and women now predominate in these occupations. But where the significance of these changes for class structure has been considered by the authors in question, they have concentrated on the fact that growing numbers of women in nonmanual occupations are married to men who are manual workers and have taken this as further evidence of the consolidation of the working class as the differentiation between nonmanual and manual employment steadily weakens. As Braverman puts it (1974, 353), not only are clerical workers and factory workers increasingly recruited from similar social origins but increasingly "they are merged within the same living family." However, what is thus missed is the significance of the further fact that while many women in lower-level nonmanual work are married to manual workers, generally more would appear to be married to men in higher-level nonmanual positions, and that it is these latter women who create major difficulties for claims of proletarianization.[5] Why, one may ask, should women who perform deskilled nonmanual work but who are married to professionals, administrators, or managers, and thus share substantially in their standards and styles of living, be regarded as proletarian in the same way as women in similar jobs who are married to manual workers?[6]

It can of course be contended that in the case of societies where most married women at some time enter paid employment, the family should no longer be taken as the unit of class analysis, and that rather than the class position of married women being derived from that of their husbands, it should be seen as following from their own employment. This argument has found much favor with radical feminists who are concerned to demonstrate the inherent sexism of the conventional view (e.g., Delphy 1981; Stanworth 1984). But what its exponents have so far failed to show is that any analytical or explanatory advantage is to be gained from adopting it: that is, that when married women are systematically attributed class locations by reference to their own employment, this makes more intelligible their own class identifications or, say, their life-styles and patterns of sociability or their political involvements. Indeed, insofar as the question of married women's class identity has been seriously investigated, the results would suggest that wives themselves (and not just "sexist" sociologists) do derive their class positions from their husbands' employment rather than from their own (Jackman and Jackman 1983, 140–52; Hernes and Knudsen 1985). Instead, then, of the expansion of degraded, and largely feminized, nonmanual work leading to mass proletarianization and thus, presumably, to an increased potential for radical sociopolitical action, it would seem that the performance of such work by many married women who, however, still take

5. Thus, for example, data relating to married women aged 20–64 living in England and Wales (taken from the sample of the British general election study in 1983) reveal that of all such women whose present or last employment was in routine clerical and associated work (N = 301), 45 percent were married to men in professional, administrative, and managerial positions, as against only 27 percent married to manual wageworkers. The husbands of the remaining 28 percent were either themselves in routine nonmanual work or otherwise small proprietors, self-employed artisans, foremen and supervisors, or technicians.

6. Braverman appears (1974, 130) to sense the weakness in his argument here in citing Crozier's (1971) observation that "the proletarianization of white-collar employees does not have the same meaning at all if it is women, and not heads of family, who constitute the majority of the group." But rather than offering any serious response, he merely embarks on a diversionary attack on Crozier for being "pleased to use women as that category of the labor force for which any job is good enough."

their class identity from husbands in superior positions could be a major stabilizing influence within modern class structures.[7]

Furthermore, the simple equation of the degrading of nonmanual work with proletarianization again runs into difficulties—even if attention is concentrated on men—through the neglect of another, quite different issue: the differentiation of apparently similar jobs according to the characteristics of the individuals who occupy them. Although the distinction between "positions" and "persons" is crucial to class analysis, it need not prevent one from recognizing that employing organizations can, and do, channel different kinds of employees into essentially similar work-tasks and roles—but in the context of what are, or are envisaged as being, quite different work histories. Studies of clerical work in particular have shown that while women workers are overwhelmingly expected to remain in low-grade employment, men who are at any one time found in clerical jobs can be divided into two categories: those who, usually rather late in their working lives, have moved into such jobs from manual ones and have few further prospects, and those— generally younger and better educated—who are spending some time in clerical jobs early in careers that they, and their employers, see as leading eventually to administrative or managerial positions (Goldthorpe 1980; Stewart, Prandy, and Blackburn 1980). Even if men in both categories are engaged in deskilled, routinized work, it still does not follow that either case exemplifies mass proletarianization: these men either were rank-and-file wageworkers previously or are, for the most part, passing through jobs that, for them, are staging-posts on the way to the higher levels of bureaucratic structures.

In sum, one could say, claims of extensive proletarianization fail because workers in the widening range of degraded or low-grade nonmanual occupations are precisely not "an immense mass," as Braverman would have it. On the contrary, they constitute a workforce that is highly differentiated—by sex, age, and qualifications—in ways that clearly delimit the influence of the growth of this workforce on the shape of the class structure.

7. Support is lent to this suggestion by the finding in a recent British study that the association between a married woman's political partisanship and her class position, as assessed by reference to her own employment, is less strong than that between her partisanship and her *husband's* class position, and that once the latter variable is controlled for, introducing a woman's own class into the analysis does not in fact make any further significant contribution to accounting for her partisanship (Marshall, et al. 1988, chap. 5). It is of course always possible that a larger sample would be able to show a significant—if slight—effect, but such an effect might again be eliminated if a woman's education were also considered. The results reported by both Jackman and Jackman and Hernes and Knudsen would suggest that education has a far greater influence than employment on a woman's sociopolitical orientations.

In turning, then, to the position of liberal theorists, an awareness that the structure of employment does not "map" in any direct way onto the class structure must lead one to the question of how serious for their understanding of class structural change is their failure to recognize the widespread deterioration of labor market conditions within Western capitalism after the ending of the "long boom." It might in fact be maintained that their disregard of rising levels of unemployment is not in this respect of major consequence since the unemployed do not themselves form a class; or again, that the growth of a secondary labor force of men and women in nonstandard jobs will have little effect on the class structure insofar as women at least are themselves secondary earners within families and households and have other sources of economic support—and of social identity—than those provided by their work. Such arguments are not without force, and it must be said that whatever weaknesses may exist in the liberal account, the tendency that it emphasizes for the working class to contract and the salariat to expand remains rather more in accord with available evidence than the largely contrary tendencies that Marxist theories envisage. Nonetheless, radically changed circumstances in labor markets still reveal several ways in which liberal conceptions of the emerging class structure are gravely inadequate.

For example, although the unemployed may not constitute a class, it is increasingly apparent that a substantial increase in the numbers of long-term unemployed—as can be found, say, in the United Kingdom—results in a polarization of the working class in terms of incomes, life-chances, and life-styles.[8] Thus, contrary to liberal expectations, the overall range of economic and social inequality has significantly widened rather than narrowed. Moreover, while workers in nonstandard jobs are often secondary earners, attracted into the labor market in part by the availability of such jobs (married women working part-time, juveniles or semiretired persons in temporary work, etc.), this is by no means always the case. Most obviously, in depressed labor markets nonstandard jobs may be taken simply because nothing better is available. To the extent, then, that such employment represents the main source of families' economic support, the formation of an "underclass" is further promoted.

Finally, it should be noted that the more difficult economic conditions that have followed the long boom may be associated with a growth in the numbers of the self-employed and small employers. The processes at work here are various and complex: self-employment may represent an attempt to escape unemployment, some nonstandard jobs

8. The theme of working-class polarization has emerged independently from several British studies in recent years. See, for example, Hamnett 1984; Pahl 1984; Halfpenny, Laite, and Noble 1985; Goldthorpe and Payne 1986.

in effect impose self-employment on those taking them, small employers often play key roles in organizing the secondary labor force as, say, in subcontracting, and so on. However, what is clear is that liberal—and also, of course, Marxist—expectations that the importance of such "independents" would steadily diminish within modern economies have not been borne out, and the very idea that the petty bourgeoisie is a declining or transitional class now itself appears anachronistic in many Western societies (Berger and Piore 1980; Bechhofer and Elliot 1981; Scase 1982).[9]

2.3. Changes in Social Mobility

As regards class mobility, it was earlier remarked that liberal and Marxist theorists differ fundamentally on its nature and extent. For liberals, the mobility of individuals between different class positions is a process central to the "social metabolism" of industrial nations; for Marxists, mobility occurs to only a negligible degree, except in the form of the collective—and downward—movement associated with the degrading of labor and proletarianization. As thus posed, the issue is not difficult to decide: there is an overwhelming body of evidence that is consistent with the liberal view but renders the Marxist position untenable.

For example, Carchedi's claim that "generally speaking, a member of the working class remains a member of the working class" is clearly falsified by findings from mobility research, which show that within the populations of advanced Western industrial societies some 20–30 percent of the sons of manual wage earners are regularly found in quite different (that is, salaried professional, administrative, and managerial or self-employed) class positions—and that this proportion has been steadily rising. Mobility research also shows that about 20 percent of men of such origins who started their own working lives as manual wage earners are subsequently able to move out of such employment.[10] It may furthermore be observed that the idea of the mass proletarianization of lower-level nonmanual workers is also undermined by the tendency,

9. As Berger and Piore's work well brings out, the Italian case is a particularly important one in this respect. See also, for example, Brusco 1982; Bagnasco and Trigilia 1984.

10. I draw here on the results of work currently being undertaken, in collaboration with Robert Erikson, as part of the CASMIN (Comparative Analysis of Social Mobility in Industrial Nations) project, based at the Institut für Sozialwissenschaften of the University of Mannheim and supported by the Stiftung Volkswagenwerk. The data from national inquiries conducted in the early and mid-1970s have been systematically recoded in order to produce information of a generally high standard of comparability on rates and patterns of class mobility across a range of industrial societies. Reference in this paper is chiefly to findings for France, the Federal Republic of Germany, Great Britain, Sweden, and the United States. (For more detailed accounts, see Erikson and Goldthorpe, 1985a, 1985b, 1987).

previously referred to, for younger males to be promoted from routine clerical and sales jobs as part of a more-or-less planned career path. In addition, there is also considerable upward mobility from this kind of work that is of a more contingent kind—associated, say, with changes of employer. It may be estimated that in present-day Western societies men who begin their working lives in routine clerical and sales occupations have better than a one-in-three chance of being promoted to professional, administrative, or managerial positions; and this probability rises to around one-in-two for men who are of nonmanual class origins. The relevance of a point I have made elsewhere is thus brought home: "It is *work* that is degraded, and *individuals* who are proletarianized; and where high mobility prevails, the former process in no way entails the latter" (Goldthorpe 1985b, 189 [my translation], emphasis in original; cf. Gagliani 1981).

However, while there is no shortage of evidence to support the liberal claim that in industrial societies the amount of class mobility is substantial, this is not to say that liberal accounts of either mobility patterns or trends—or of the sources of change in these—need be accepted as they stand. Indeed, by reference again to the findings of mobility research, one can show that these accounts are seriously mistaken. The basic flaw is that liberal theorists have taken the clear evidence of increasing rates of upward mobility, which—as they themselves have emphasized—must be expected to follow from the expansion of the higher levels of the class structure, and have then interpreted this evidence as being indicative also of the increasing openness or social fluidity that they see as required by the logic of industrialism and that they believe is created through an emphasis on achievement rather than ascription in social selection. They have, moreover, felt supported in such an interpretation by further evidence of a "tightening bond" between educational and occupational attainment—or, in other words, by what might be regarded as evidence of the increasing sway of the meritocratic principle. However, what is here neglected is the possibility that rising rates of upward social mobility are not merely favored by the changing shape of the class structure but are attributable almost entirely to such structural shifts, and that little if any change need therefore be supposed in openness or fluidity. In fact, it is this latter interpretation, rather than the one advanced by liberal authors, that the research findings bear out. Contrary to liberal expectations that advancing industrialism should cause the association between individuals' class origins and their eventual class destinations to weaken steadily, this association has proved to be patterned in a remarkably stable way—once the effects of structural shifts are allowed for—both over time and cross-nationally. That is to say, while actually observed mobility rates vary quite widely within the experience of industrial nations, this variation is to a predominant extent structurally conditioned, and a large commonality would seem to prevail in underlying "mobility regimes" or "patterns of social fluidity" (Featherman, Lancaster Jones, and Hauser 1975; Grusky and Hauser 1984; Erikson and Goldthorpe 1985b, 1987). Some instances can be cited of fluidity showing an increase over time but, rather than exemplifying any inherent tendency of industrialism, these appear to be better interpreted as episodes arising out of the specific historical circumstances of particular nations (Simkus 1981; Goldthorpe and Portocarero 1981; Erikson 1983; Erikson, Goldthorpe, and Portocarero 1983).

Once, then, the idea of a general movement toward greater openness is rejected, other aspects of the liberal account of class mobility within industrial societies also come into question. If the observed increases in mobility are overwhelmingly the result of structural change, there seems no longer any good reason for believing that societies either have in the past or will in the future become more mobile pari passu with their economic development. For while economic development is of course associated with structural changes of a kind that will clearly affect class mobility, the historical record would suggest that this association is complex and is far more likely to produce fluctuations in mobility rates rather than any unidirectional change (Goldthorpe 1985a).

Again, it must follow that, in the absence of greater fluidity, the increase in intergenerational upward mobility into the expanding higher levels of the class structure that liberals have especially stressed will be accompanied by a decrease in downward mobility from these levels. And indeed the empirical findings show that what I have elsewhere referred to as the "service class" of modern industrial societies, that is, the class of salaried professionals, administrators, and managers (Goldthorpe 1982; see also Renner 1953; Dahrendorf 1964), is not only growing steadily but is also increasing in the intergenerational stability of its constituent families.[11] Moreover, declining downward mobility also implies less diversity in the social origins of those found at the lower levels of the class structure, and this trend—along with the declining outflow from the agricultural sector—has affected the composition of the working classes of modern industrial societies in a way quite overlooked in liberal scenarios: that is to say, they have become increasingly self-recruiting.[12] At the same

11. Results from the CASMIN project would indicate that for men born into service-class families in the first two decades of the twentieth century, there was typically around a three-in-five probability that they would themselves "succeed" to service-class positions, while for men born into such families over the next two decades, this probability increased to around two-in-three.

12. CASMIN results show that by the mid-1970s the proportion of the industrial working class—understood as manual wageworkers—who were at least "second-generation"

time, the tightening bond between education and occupation—the sup-posed consequence of meritocracy—means that decisive mobility away from the working class is now being more often achieved before entry into employment rather than in the course of the individual's working life. And from these two developments together, then, it may be ex-pected that the collectivity that actually occupies working-class positions at any one point in time will comprise a substantial, and growing, core of those who are in fact both "hereditary" and prospective "lifetime" mem-bers (Goldthorpe 1980, 1985b).

Finally, the idea that the greater importance of education in determin-ing employment chances is indicative of the prevalence of meritocratic social selection is itself thrown into doubt if no evidence of an accompany-ing increase in fluidity can be produced. In this case, the alternative hypothesis is suggested that education is simply substituting for the previ-ous determinants of processes of mobility or immobility without leading to any significant change in outcomes, so that, as one commentator has put it, these processes become in effect ones "in which ascriptive forces find ways of expressing themselves as 'achievement' " (Halsey 1977, 184; see also Parkin 1974; Halsey, Heath, and Ridge 1980).

In sum, then, while trends in rates and patterns of class mobility in modern industrial societies may well have had a stabilizing effect, as liberals have argued, their account of how this effect has been produced can only be accepted to a very limited extent: that is, insofar as it points to increased opportunities for upward movement as a consequence of class structural change. There is no evidence that modern societies have become generally more fluid, whether through the application of more meritocratic criteria of social selection or otherwise, or that these soci-eties have experienced progressive class decomposition. Recruitment to expanding service classes has been necessarily broad-based, but these classes are now in the process of consolidation; and working classes, although contracting, are becoming increasingly homogeneous at least in terms of their members' social origins.

Therefore, even if a secular decline can be traced in the propensity for collective identities and collective action to develop on a class basis (which might be disputed; see Bottomore 1982; Korpi 1983; Heath, Jowell, and Curtice 1985), there is little reason to attribute this decline, in the manner of Blau and Duncan, to class formation being inhibited by the increasing openness of Western industrial societies. If an expla-nation in structural terms is to be given—rather than, say, one primar-

---

was as high as 75 percent in Great Britain, around 65 percent in the Federal Republic of Germany, and 50 percent in France, Sweden, and the United States. It was in these last three nations, however, that the proportion of second-generation workers had most rap-idly increased in the recent past.

ily in terms of the organization and strategies of working-class movements (Esping-Andersen 1985; Przeworski 1985)—it would far more plausibly refer to the divisions created within contemporary working classes by developments that, as earlier noted, liberal scenarios conspicuously overlook: the growth of nonstandard forms of employment, the dualizing of labor markets, and the return of unemployment on a mass scale.

3. SOCIAL THEORIES, HISTORICISM, AND THE HISTORICAL RECORD

Why, then, should it be that when reviewed against the findings of systematic empirical research, liberal and Marxist theories alike appear so inadequate as a basis for understanding long-term trends of change in the class stratification of Western societies? The answer I would give at the most general level is the following: that these theories fail to do justice to the social processes that they address because in their conception and application there is a persisting historicist strain. They are theories that stem from an ultimate ambition of achieving some cognitive grasp on the course of historical development—which can then be used for normative and political purposes: that is to say, to show that certain political beliefs, values, and commitments have an "objective" superiority in being those that the movement of history favors, and that others can be "correctly" dismissed as historically outmoded.

The grave logical—and also moral—defects of such historicist endeavors have been evident enough at least from the time of Popper's devastating attacks on them (1944–45, 1945), which focused on the claims of classical Marxism and social-evolutionary theory. Since then historicism has to some extent been forced underground; but, as I have sought to show elsewhere (Goldthorpe 1971, 1979; see also Goldthorpe 1972), it has retained a powerful appeal for many social scientists—especially for those who would aspire to the more elevated status of "intellectual" and, moreover, within the liberal camp just as much as within the Marxist camp.

Thus, not only may one find Carchedi (1977, 17) speaking in more or less orthodox Marxist fashion of "dialectical determination" as "the mechanism connecting one stage of the development of capitalism to another" but, likewise, Kerr and his associates ([1960] 1973, chaps. 1 and 2) explicitly taking Marx's quest for the "laws of motion" of capitalist society as their model in their attempts to establish a developmental "logic of industrialism" (see also Kerr 1983, chap. 1). Other theorists have expressed themselves more guardedly—but chiefly, it would seem, in order to try to obtain the political advantages of a historicist position while protecting themselves against the more obvious objections to such a stance. For example, Wright (1985, 114–18) disavows the idea of "iron laws of history" and sees stages of class relations as no more than a sequence of "historical possibilities," yet still wishes to claim—without any attempt at explaining why this should be so—that "the overall trajectory of historical development" is of an inherently "progressive" kind. Or again, Blau and Duncan, while in large part pursuing purely descriptive and analytical goals, still base their ultimate interpretation and evaluation of long-term changes in the process of stratification on the central tenet of the "neoevolutionism" of Talcott Parsons, namely, that "a fundamental trend toward expanding universalism characterizes industrial society" (Blau and Duncan 1967, 429; see also Parsons 1951, 480–535; Parsons 1964, 1966).

Following Popper, it could be argued that theories of a historicist cast must in the end always disappoint when matched against the historical record since they are flawed by a basic misconception: that is, their exponents fail to recognize that, in any science, propositions can be either theoretical or historical but not both at the same time. Thus, their hope of "theorizing" the movement of history is vain in principle. However, for present purposes it may still be instructive to consider those deficiences that would appear in a more immediate way to undermine the analyses of social change that are conducted from essentially historicist positions.

To begin with, one cannot overlook the prevalence of what is in fact rather blatant wishful thinking. Marxists clearly want to be able to show progressive proletarianization, or liberals a steadily increasing equality of opportunity, so that they may thus fortify the faithful, confound their political enemies, and sustain their own beliefs and values. Logically, within a historicist program, political commitment should follow from a correct appreciation of the course on which historical development is set; but, psychologically, commitment seems often to dictate what view of history it is that must be represented as correct. Such an outlook is obviously then not one conducive to the recognition—and still less to the searching out—of evidence contrary to the developmental scenarios that are favored. For much more is at stake than an intellectual construction: historicism makes it difficult to accept Popper's advice that we should be ready to let our ideas die for us.

Further, though, there are also deficiencies to be noted that derive directly from the structure of historicist argument itself. Most serious here is the inadequate attention that is given to what might be called microsociological foundations, that is, to the way in which it is envisaged that the large-scale and long-term trends of change that are postulated actually come about at the level of social action (Nisbet 1969, 233). It is characteristic of historicist theories of social change—and indeed essential to their authors' project of "theorizing" history—that they should concentrate on identifying one central source of dynamism that is, so to speak, "built into" the overall process of historical development and drives it along from stage to stage. In Marxist theories this dynamism is usually seen as resulting from the contradictions that recurrently arise between the forces and the relations of production; in liberal theories this dynamism stems from the ever-renewed and reshaped requirements of technological change and economic rationality. In other words, the focus of interest is on what are taken to be successive "system exigencies" to which determinate responses must follow; and the way in which these exigencies are then experienced and accommodated by social actors can be of no more than minor concern. For if a historicist theory is taken as valid, then the patterns of social action that are involved in its realization are mere epiphenomena. If the analysis moves to the level of social action at all, it need do so only for illustrative and, perhaps, political purposes. Thus, for Marxists, the progressive degrading of jobs by employers and their managers is a necessary response as technological advance proceeds within the constraints of the capitalist mode of production—and serves to reveal its inhuman character; for liberals, the emergence of more meritocratic procedures of social selection is dictated by the universalist logic of modern industrial society—and shows how this offers ever-wider opportunities for the expression of talent.

However, the difficulty here is of course that if the theory is not valid, then there is no reason whatever for highlighting the patterns of action and the underlying values and motivations that are its supposed vehicles. They may not in fact be those that prevail in the determination of social change; if they are present at all, they may be opposed, cross-cut, or overwhelmed by a host of other factors of which the theory takes no account. Thus, while economic constraints may lead some employers to degrade jobs, other employers may survive by linking technological innovation to either the reduction or the upgrading of their work forces, or by opting for strategies that aim more at reshaping employment relations than job content—and that carry quite different implications for the composition of the work force and the class structure. Likewise, while in modern societies pressures may indeed exist for selection for education and employment to be based increasingly on achievement, the interests and factors favoring ascription are not thereby annulled, and the emergence of a more open and fluid society is in no way guaranteed. In sum, in the pursuit of the key dynamic inherent in the movement of history—which one may regard as not merely elusive but illusory—theorists who yield to historicist temptations become captive to remarkably limited and oversimplified views of the processes of social change, and, in turn, they seek to sustain what are at best one-sided and at worst wildly misleading accounts of its actual patterns.[13]

If, then, we are to move toward a more satisfactory theoretical treatment of social change—in class stratification or any other aspect of social structure or process—I would maintain that a prerequisite is to accept, once and for all, that historical and theoretical propositions should not be confounded. This would mean two things. First, we should, as social scientists, treat the historical record with respect. We should recognize it as being independent of our theories of social change, and not suppose that these theories can in any way transcend it. There is no empirical realm to which they can refer other than this record, and without having established it, as best we can, in an area of interest to us, we do not know what it is that we would wish our theories to account for. As Nisbet has argued, "Between the study of *change* . . . and *history* there is quite evidently an unbreakable relationship, when we come down from the empyrean heights of abstractions, wholes and universals. . . . Whatever the demands of a social theory, the first demands to be served are those of the social reality we find alone in the historical record" (1969, 303–4).

Second, though, we must recognize that simply by "tracing the path" followed by historical development we can explain nothing; there is no theory immanent in the course of history that we can discover and then, so to speak, apply back to history. Whether taken as comprising a series of events or empirical regularities *à la longue durée*, the historical record is, from the point of view of the social scientist, an *explanandum*—or rather a vast source of *explananda*—but not an *explanans* (see Gellner 1964, 20). This means, therefore, that the theories through which we may seek to gain an understanding of social change will not be in themselves historical (or evolutionary or developmental) theories; more specifically, one could say that they will not be theories that embody propositions about historical—as opposed to analytical—time. In the end, I would suggest, they will have to be, like theories addressed to questions of social order and stability, ones that are couched in terms of human action, individual and collective, and its intended and unintended consequences.[14] In other

13. From this point of view, a welcome recent development is the growing interest in providing macrosociology with better "micro" foundations through the revival of rational choice theory. Especially encouraging is the fact that such an approach must begin from an acceptance of methodological individualism, which is in itself a powerful prophylactic against lapses into historicism, and that this approach has been taken up both by theorists with evident liberal commitments (for example, Boudon 1977; Olson 1982; Hechter 1983) and by others who would still apparently wish to be regarded as *marxisant* at least (for example, Elster 1982, 1985; Przeworski 1985).

14. In this respect (as in others) sociologists interested in problems of long-term social change could, I believe, find useful guidance in the work of the "new" economic historians, whom they appear so far to have largely neglected.

words, we must learn to take seriously the idea that "men make their own history." This does not of course prevent us from recognizing that they do not make it "just as they please"; but what is precluded is any idea, overt or covert, that in the last analysis history is made "behind men's backs" in accordance with some immanent plan or ultimate goal.

REFERENCES

Åberg, Rune. 1984. Arbetsförhallanden. In *Välfärd i förändring*, ed. Robert Erikson and Rune Aberg, 102–15. Stockholm: Prisma.

———. 1984b. Teoriarna om arbets degradering och arbetsmarknadens dualisering: ett försök till empirisk prövning. *Sociologisk Forskning* 2.

Bagnasco, Arnaldo, and Carlo Trigilia. 1984. *Società e politica nelle Aree di Piccola Impresa*. Dorsoduro, Italy: Arsenale Editrice.

Bechhofer, Frank, and Brian Elliot, eds. 1981. *The petite bourgeoisie*. London: Macmillan.

Bell, Daniel. 1967. Notes on the post-industrial society. *The Public Interest* 6:24–35.

———. 1973. *The coming of post-industrial society*. New York: Basic Books.

Berger, Suzanne, and Michael Piore. 1980. *Dualism and discontinuity in industrial societies*. Cambridge: Cambridge University Press.

Blau, P. M., and O. D. Duncan. 1967. *The American occupational structure*. New York: Wiley.

Bottomore, Tom. 1982. The political role of the working class in Western Europe. In *Social class and the division of labor*, ed. Anthony Giddens and Gavin Mackenzie, 265–75. Cambridge: Cambridge University Press.

Boudon, Raymond. 1977. *Effets pervers et ordre social*. Paris: Presses Universitaires de France.

Braverman, Harry. 1974. *Labor and monopoly capitalism*. New York: Monthly Review Press.

Brusco, Sebastiano. 1982. The Emilian model: Productive decentralisation and social integration. *Cambridge Journal of Economics* 6:167–84.

Carchedi, G. 1977. *On the economic identification of classes*. London: Routledge.

Clark, Colin. 1957. *The conditions of economic progress*. 3d ed. London: Macmillan.

Crompton, Rosemary, and Gareth Jones. 1984. *White-collar proletariat*. London: Macmillan.

Crozier, Michel. 1971. *The world of the office worker*. Chicago: University of Chicago Press.

Dahrendorf, Ralf. 1964. Recent changes in the class structure of European societies. *Daedalus* Winter: 225–70.

Delphy, Christine. 1981. Women in stratification studies. In *Doing feminist research*, ed. Helen Roberts, 114–28. London: Routledge.

Duncan, O. D. 1968. Social stratification and mobility. In *Indicators of social change*, ed. Eleanor B. Sheldon and Wilbert E. Moore, 675–719. New York: Russell Sage.

Elster, Jon. 1982. Marxism, functionalism and game theory. *Theory and Society* 11:453–82.

———. 1985. *Making sense of Marx*. Cambridge: Cambridge University Press.

Erikson, Robert. 1983. Changes in social mobility in industrial nations: The case of Sweden. *Research in Social Stratification and Mobility* 2:165–95.

Erikson, Robert, and John H. Goldthorpe. 1985a. Are American rates of social mobility exceptionally high? *European Sociological Review* 1:1–22.

———. 1985b. Commonality and variation in social fluidity in industrial nations: Some preliminary results. CASMIN Working Paper 4.1, University of Mannheim.

———. 1987. Commonality and variation in social fluidity in industrial nations. *European Sociological Review* 3:54–77, 145–66.

Erikson, Robert, John H. Goldthorpe, and Lucienne Portocarero. 1983. Intergenerational class mobility and the convergence thesis. *British Journal of Sociology* 34:303–43.

Esping-Andersen, Gøsta. 1985. *Politics against markets*. Princeton: Princeton University Press.

Featherman, David L., F. Lancaster Jones, and Robert M. Hauser. 1975. Assumptions of social mobility research in the U.S.: The case of occupational status. *Social Science Research* 4:329–60.

Fuchs, Victor. 1968. *The service economy*. New York: National Bureau of Economic Research.

Gagliani, Giorgio. 1981. How many working classes? *American Journal of Sociology* 87:259–85.

Gellner, Ernest. 1964. *Thought and change*. London: Weidenfeld and Nicolson.

Gershuny, Jay. 1983. *Social innovation and the division of Labour*. Oxford: Oxford University Press.

Giddens, Anthony, and Gavin Mackenzie, eds. 1982. *Social class and the division of labour*. Cambridge: Cambridge University Press.

Goldthorpe, John H. 1971. Theories of industrial society. *Archives européennes de sociologie* 12:263–88.

———. 1972. Class, status and party in modern Britain. *Archives européennes de sociologie* 13:342–72.

———. 1979. Intellectuals and the working class in modern Britain. Fuller Bequest Lecture, University of Essex.

———. 1980. *Social mobility and class structure in modern Britain*. Oxford: Clarendon Press.

———. 1982. On the service class: Its formation and future. In *Social class and the division of labour*, ed. Anthony Giddens and Gavin Mackenzie, 162–85. Cambridge: Cambridge University Press.

———. 1983. Women and class analysis: In defence of the conventional view. *Sociology* 17:465–88.

———. 1984. The end of convergence: Corporatist and dualist tendencies in modern Western societies. In *Order and conflict in contemporary capitalism*, ed. John H. Goldthorpe, 315–43. Oxford: Clarendon Press.

———. 1985a. On economic development and social mobility. *British Journal of Sociology* 36:549–73.

———. 1985b. Soziale Mobilität und Klassenbildung: Zur Erneuerung einer Tradition soziologischer Forschung. In *Die Analyse Sozialer Ungleichheit*, ed.

Hermann Strasser and John H. Goldthorpe, 174–204. Opladen, W. Ger.: Westdeutscher Verlag.

Goldthorpe, John H., and Clive Payne. 1986. Trends in intergenerational class mobility in England and Wales, 1972–1983. *Sociology* 20:1–24.

Goldthorpe, John H., and Lucienne Portocarero. 1981. La mobilité sociale en France, 1953–1970: Nouvel examen. *Revue française de sociologie* 22:151–66.

Grusky, David B., and Robert M. Hauser. 1984. Comparative social mobility revisited: Models of convergence and divergence in 16 countries. *American Sociological Review* 49:19–38.

Halfpenny, P. J., A. J. Laite, and I. Noble. 1985. *The Blackburn and Darwen labour market*. Manchester: University of Manchester, Centre for Applied Social Research.

Halsey, A. H. 1977. Towards meritocracy? The case of Britain. In *Power and ideology in education*, ed. Jerome Karabel and A. H. Halsey, 173–86. New York: Oxford University Press.

Halsey, A. H., Anthony Heath, and J. M. Ridge. 1980. *Origins and destinations*. Oxford: Clarendon Press.

Hamnett, C. 1984. Housing the two nations: Socio-tenurial polarisation in England and Wales, 1961–81. *Urban Studies* 43:389–405.

Heath, Anthony, Roger Jowell, and John Curtice. 1985. *How Britain votes*. Oxford: Pergamon Press.

Hechter, Michael, ed. 1983. *The microfoundations of macrosociology*. Philadelphia: Temple University Press.

Hernes, Gudmund, and Knud Knudsen. 1985. Gender and class identification in Norway. Paper presented to the Social Stratification and Mobility Research Committee of the International Sociological Association, Harvard University, Cambridge, Mass.

Jackman, Mary R., and Robert W. Jackman. 1983. *Class awareness in the United States*. Berkeley: University of California Press.

Kerr, Clark. 1983. *The future of industrial societies*. Cambridge: Harvard University Press.

Kerr, Clark, John T. Dunlop, Frederick H. Harbison, and Charles A. Myers. [1960] 1973. *Industrialism and industrial man*. Rev. ed. Cambridge: Harvard University Press.

Korpi, Walter. 1983. *The democratic class struggle*. London: Routledge.

Kuznets, Simon. 1966. *Modern economic growth*. New Haven: Yale University Press.

Lockwood, David. 1981. The weakest link in the chain? Some comments on the Marxist theory of action. *Research in the Sociology of Work* 1:435–81.

Marshall, Gordon, Howard Newby, David Rose, and Carolyn Vogler. 1988. *Social Class in Modern Britain*. London: Hutchinson.

Michon, François. 1981. Dualism and the French labour market: Business strategy, non-standard job forms, and secondary jobs. In *The dynamics of labour market segmentation*, ed. Frank Wilkinson, 81–97. London: Academic Press.

Nisbet, Robert. 1969. *Social change and history*. New York: Oxford University Press.

Olson, Mancur. 1982. *The rise and decline of nations.* New Haven: Yale University Press.

Pahl, Ray. 1984. *Divisions of labour.* Oxford: Blackwells.

Parkin, Frank, ed. 1974. *The social analysis of class structure.* London: Tavistock.

Parsons, Talcott. 1951. *The social system.* Glencoe, Ill.: Free Press.

———. 1964. Evolutionary universals in society. *American Sociological Review* 29:339–57.

———. 1966. *Societies: Evolutionary and comparative perspectives.* Englewood Cliffs, N.J.: Prentice-Hall.

Penn, Roger, and Hilda Scattergood. 1985. Deskilling or enskilling: An empirical investigation of recent theories of the labour process. *British Journal of Sociology* 36:611–26.

Popper, Karl. 1944–45. The poverty of historicism. *Economica* 11:86–103, 119–37, 12:69–89.

———. 1945. *The open society and its enemies.* London: Routledge.

Poulantzas, Nicos. 1974. *Les classes sociales dans le capitalisme aujourd'hui.* Paris: Seuil.

Przeworski, Adam. 1985. *Capitalism and social democracy.* Cambridge: Cambridge University Press.

Renner, Karl. 1953. *Wandlungen der Modernen Gesellschaft: Zwei Abhandlungen über die Probleme der Nachkriegszeit.* Vienna: Wiener Volksbuchhandlung.

Scase, Richard. 1982. The petty bourgeoisie and modern capitalism. In *Social class and the division of labour,* ed. Anthony Giddens and Gavin Mackenzie, 148–61. Cambridge: Cambridge University Press.

Simkus, Albert A. 1981. Changes in occupational inheritance under socialism: Hungary, 1930–1973. *Research in Social Stratification and Mobility* 1:171–203.

Singelmann, Joachim, and H. L. Browning. 1980. Industrial transformation and occupational change in the U.S., 1960–70. *Social Forces* 59:246–64.

Singelmann, Joachim, and Marta Tienda. 1985. The process of occupational change in a service society: The case of the United States, 1960–1980. In *New approaches to economic life,* ed. Bryan Roberts, Ruth Finnegan, and Duncan Gallie, 48–67. Manchester: Manchester University Press.

Stanworth, Michelle. 1984. Women and class analysis: A reply to John Goldthorpe. *Sociology* 18:159–70.

Stewart, A., K. Prandy, and R. M. Blackburn. 1980. *Social stratification and occupations.* London: Macmillan.

Treiman, Donald J. 1970. Industrialisation and social stratification. In *Social stratification: Research and theory for the 1970s,* ed. E. O. Laumann, 207–34. Indianapolis: Bobbs Merrill.

Wright, Erik Olin. 1976. Class boundaries in advanced capitalist societies. *New Left Review* 98:3–42.

———. 1978. *Class, crisis and the state.* London: New Left Books.

———. 1985. *Classes.* London: Verso.

Wright, Erik Olin, and Joachim Singelmann. 1982. Proletarianisation in the changing American class structure. *American Journal of Sociology* 88 (supplement):176–209.

Social Change in the United States
The System of Equality and Inequality

Richard Münch

1. INTRODUCTION: A THEORETICAL MODEL OF CHANGE

In this chapter I analyze the development of the social systems of equality and inequality in America in terms of Parsonian action theory. I start with the assumption that every system of equality or inequality in communal, political, economic, and cultural realms—inasmuch as it is stable and has a binding, normative quality on the members of society—is rooted in the traditional relationships of equality or inequality among individuals and groups in society. It is also rooted in the traditional right of membership in society (rights of citizenship), the traditional everyday associations of individuals and groups, and the traditional beliefs in the natural equality or inequality of people.

In my first section on the systems of equality and inequality in America I give a description of the system of equality of relationships, associations, rights, and beliefs among the settlers in New England. But I also show that from the beginning the South established a different traditional and normatively binding model, a model of inequality in economic, political, cultural, and communal terms. Thus, the United States is based on two conflicting traditions, one favoring equality (conceived in terms of equal opportunity), the other favoring inequality. The conflict between these two traditions has been a major factor hindering the establishment of a societal community that embraces society as a whole. It also explains why American society has often broken apart into different societal groups.

My second assumption is that the traditional system of equality of the New England colonies (and later, states) was counteracted by factors

I am grateful to Neil Johnson for translating the original German version of this chapter.

arising from societal growth: Economic growth leads to economic differentiation and inequality, political growth leads to the differentiation of access to political decision making, cultural growth leads to cultural diversity and the unequal evaluation of cultural ways of life, and associational growth leads to the differentiation of society into different social groups and minorities. A decisive factor in changing the traditional New England system of equality to a system of inequality has been the continuous process of the immigration of new ethnic, racial, religious, and national groups to the United States. This process resulted in a society of unequals amid a cultural system in which belief in the equality of opportunity remained, even though that belief changed from the notion of absolute equality to an ideology that legitimized the oppression of the unsuccessful minorities by the successful majority. The Southern model of inequality was sustained by the growing inequality in society, which reached a point at which the Southern culture began to dominate the national culture. The victory of the Northern states in the Civil War laid the foundations for the Northern idea of the equality of opportunity to successfully assert itself as society developed, but this idea is in constant conflict with the Southern culture, which is increasingly important because of the present-day movement to the sunbelt.

My third assumption is that "unintended" factors in a society can moderate inequality. Among these factors are economic abundance, opportunities for political participation in local affairs, uniform formal education, and social inclusion. The way these factors work in America is demonstrated in the third section.

My fourth assumption is that there are intentional actions in society that are motivated by the tension between the cultural idea of the equality of opportunity and the social reality of inequality. The logic of cultural discourse leads some to take the idea of equality to its logical extreme and to claim that every existing inequality is illegitimate and evil. However, inasmuch as other ideas, such as the idea of individualism, are involved in this discourse, there are limits to how far the idea of equality can be carried. In the United States the idea of equality becomes limited to the idea of equal opportunity.

In this context I discuss the Supreme Court's role in interpreting basic cultural ideas and its role in the change from racial segregation to desegregation. I examine how the discourse on cultural ideas has shaped the social system of equal/unequal relationships. Insofar as cultural discourse becomes involved in political decision making, it will be controversial and needs the support of dynamic forces, that is, social movements. Here the role of the civil rights movement is of primary interest. But policies aiming at the equality of opportunity also require economic resources, such as programs of affirmative action. Nothing will change in everyday life, however, if people do not accept that change and are not prepared to associate communally with formerly excluded groups. Therefore, inclusion is also needed. School busing can be interpreted as forced inclusion. The level of communal association is the level where change is the slowest. But when it changes toward more equality the new system achieves the character of a normatively binding system. The day-to-day association of the younger generations in the educational system is a factor that can bring about a new belief in equality amid the tremendous cultural diversity that characterizes the present-day United States. The New England model of the association of homogeneous equals may be replaced by the association of heterogeneous equals.

2. THE PRINCIPLE OF EQUAL OPPORTUNITY

The 1776 Declaration of Independence states that all men are created equal and are vested with certain inalienable rights by the Creator, including the right to life, liberty, and the pursuit of happiness. In America this idea of human equality was never developed into the idea of socialism or communism. It has always been embraced together with the idea of freedom and individualism. The communist ideal "from each according to his ability, to each according to his needs," as formulated by Marx, was never able to gain a foothold on American soil (Marx 1962:21).

The idea that everyone should receive equal rewards—income, power, prestige—regardless of his or her own individual performance is anathema to Americans. The primary American conviction is that people are the architects of their own fortunes. Equal distribution of society's riches without reference to individual performance is an idea that is irreconcilable with such a conviction. It deprives the individual of the right to take control over his or her own fate. The Declaration of Independence speaks not of the equal distribution of happiness but of the equal right to seek one's happiness (Ginsberg 1967; Eidelberg 1976; Murray 1964; Becker 1958). If the individual's happiness is something imparted by society or the state, then the individual has lost the right to personally seek that happiness and to achieve it in greater measure the more assiduously he or she seeks it.

Equal rights in this sense means that no one may be hindered from autonomously striving for happiness. Initially, this simply meant that no laws were permitted that excluded individuals or particular groups from the ability to make that quest. This signified above all that no one should be denied access to the market as a result of privileges granted to others by the state. Accordingly, equality of market opportunities came to be seen more in terms of the state refraining from intervention in economic competition than in terms of the state involving itself by granting privileges to certain persons or groups. The quest for happiness was chiefly understood as a quest for wealth. As a rule, therefore, Americans spoke of three basic rights: to life, freedom, and property.

The meaning of equality in relationship to liberty is that everyone possesses the same rights to freedom, and each in turn can make either more or less extensive use of this right. Every individual is entitled to freedom of expression. All do not, however, participate in public discussion in the same way, and every opinion is not treated as being equally correct. The same is true of the freedom of communal association. No one may, de jure, be denied access at the outset from communities, which might be clubs or associations, religious communities, academic communities, or political constituencies. This does not, however, imply that everyone, de facto, really becomes a member of these communal groupings. The requirement is simply that membership should be attached to qualifications that anyone can gain. Everyone also has an equal right to engage in political activity even though not everyone actually takes part in the political decision-making process and not everyone carries the same amount of influence. Individuals or groups simply may not be excluded from such processes a priori.

Similarly, the equality of the right to life does not mean categorically that no one may lose his or her life. The Fifth Amendment to the Constitution guarantees that no one may be made to forfeit life, freedom, or property without due process of law. The "equal guarantee of life" accordingly signifies that the death penalty, for example, may not be imposed on individuals arbitrarily and without equal due process and also that it should be reserved for the most serious crimes. A further aspect of the equal right to life is that it includes everyone's right to the same police protection against crime and the guarantee that all will be treated equally in the procedure for drafting people into the armed forces. How safe, within this broad framework, the individual chooses to make his or her own life, whether to ensure a greater amount of protection against sickness or accident or be content with less, remains a matter for him or her to decide. Both life and freedom, then, are only guaranteed each individual to the same degree that everyone has the right to preserve his or her life and to strive for freedom. No a priori measures taken or laws passed by the state should create any inequalities with respect to the pursuit of these goals.

Equality, therefore, is interpreted as equal opportunity with regard to life, freedom, property, and happiness but not as actual equality in the distribution of property, happiness, longevity, and freedom to do as one pleases (Laslett and Lipset 1974; Lipset 1974). The state is expected not to stand in the individual's way as he or she strives for these goods and not to grant privileges to certain people at the expense of others. And the state is not expected to distribute goods equally. Such involvement by the state would be tantamount to the withdrawal of the right to individual striving for life, freedom, property, and happiness. State involvement would violate the principle of the equality of opportunity because an equal distribution of the goods of life among all people regardless of their effort and performance would rob the individual of the opportunity to perform better and hence acquire more of these goods that bring happiness. Individual effort and performance would be unequally rewarded. Those producing more effort and performance would be at a disadvantage relative to those producing less.

When considering this radically individualistic conception of the equality of opportunity, one must of course take into account the image of society that served as its basis. This was an image of society as a union of independent property owners who have no fundamental differences of opportunity among themselves when they compete with each other to expand their property (Berthoff 1971). No one was exceedingly rich or exceedingly poor. Differences in income and wealth were sufficiently limited that there were no conflicting classes of the privileged and the disadvantaged. Some were naturally more successful than others, but success or lack of it was purely a matter of individual fate and was never a collective experience of separately delimited estates, classes, or strata.

Those who were either unable or not permitted to take part in the competition to achieve success were cared for within the family: women, children, the aged, the sick, the infirm, and of course the slaves. The entire philosophy of the equality of opportunity applied solely to economically independent, male enfranchised citizens. Although the fact that slaves were excluded from civil rights was a thorn in the flesh of the new society—and was also the focus of both criticism and bad conscience on the part of liberals such as Jefferson and Madison—it nevertheless did not disturb the image of the equality of opportunity as it applied in general because slaves, like women, children, the aged, and the sick, were also under guardianship of a head of the family who would be able to hold his own amid the competition.

In this context a conception of the equality of opportunity was born in which the state was only involved in a negative sense. The state was not permitted to intervene by granting privileges in the competition between full citizens who, for all intents and purposes, were equal. Had it done so, then this would have created inequality between those who otherwise were equal. The equality of opportunity was ensured by way of the male full citizens' equal rights to participate in societal competition. Under such circumstances few could even conceive that the state should actively intervene to assist those who had to compete with a more limited endowment of means and abilities.

To this day this "ultraliberal" philosophy of the equality of opportunity has remained an essential element of American thinking. It is at the core of the tough conservative opposition to measures taken by the state designed to actively establish the equality of opportunity. Although today's liberals propound such an activist state policy, particularly in the area of education policy, conservatives see in this the danger that individual freedom, self-responsibility, and initiative will be destroyed by state tutelage and surveillance. Conservatives take this position even though the conditions of the equality of opportunity have changed fundamentally from those that originally prevailed during the course of societal development.

In the course of these changes, there has also been a concomitant transformation in the way that Americans assess the state's role in establishing equality of opportunity. More and more Americans have come to see the state as having the task of actively creating equality of opportunity (Berthoff 1971). This is a basic liberal conviction today, and even conservatives do not fundamentally reject state intervention, although they would like to see it restricted to a low level. However, this transformation in the role of the state by no means signifies a complete turnaround in favor of the collective establishment of equality. In the prevailing public opinion even industrialization and the increased pluralism of racial, ethnic, and religious groups have not made success or failure into a uniform collective experience. As always, success and failure are interpreted as the fate of individuals. And whatever degree of acceptance state programs aimed at creating equality of opportunity now have, these programs are understood primarily as support for individuals, not as a means to even out the distribution of goods.

Although there is now agreement about the state taking an active role in establishing equality of opportunity, the role the state is expected to take is predominantly restricted to establishing a balance in the starting conditions for the race to achieve success. This state role applies in equal fashion whether the guarantee of equality concerned is in the communal, economic, political, or cultural spheres.

Communal equality means that anyone can associate communally with anyone else and can enter into social relations with anyone else on an equal basis. No exclusive communities exist to which only the few, perhaps by virtue of their birth, are admitted, and there is no hierarchy of estates with differing rights. When understood in terms of equality of opportunity, equality in this sphere means that no one should be refused admission de jure to communal associations. But it does not mean that everyone is also able de facto to take up communal relations everywhere and with all others. That there is openness in social relations and in the membership of associational groupings does not mean that those without prior qualification may join. It does, however, imply that the criteria for qualification have to be defined such that no one is excluded through birth. Not everyone is able to become a member of the society of attorneys but everyone who has attained the necessary occupational qualification should be able to. More specifically, equality of social opportunity implies that equal opportunities are available to associate with others, to take up everyday social relations, to develop a style of life, and to meet in public places such as restaurants, shopping centers, sporting events, or the theater.

Economic equality means that all have a share in society's material wealth and no one is excluded from economic opportunity. Applying the notion of equality of opportunity, the key matter is to ensure that everyone is able to join the race for economic success and that no one is prohibited de jure from participating. Above all else, state guarantees of economic privileges are prohibited. What is not covered by this concept of economic equality of opportunity is the actual equal distribution of material goods. Anyone can take part in market competition but the success achieved need not be the same in each case. Specific aspects of economic equality of opportunity are equal rewards for equal achievement, equal opportunities to gain access to occupations and acquire occupational qualifications, and the provision of compensation for disadvantages via insurance and social welfare payments.

Political equality must be seen as equality in the selection and application of collective decisions. No one is excluded from the process and no one is granted privileges. When conceived of as equality of opportunity, the concern here is that the political process should be open to all who seek to put themselves in a position where they can exert political authority but not that the distribution of political decision-making competence should actually be equal. Specifically, political equality of opportunity encompasses equal opportunity to participate in the political decision-making process and to be given a hearing when political matters are under discussion, a body of law that is equal for all and is applied in the same way for all, and equal treatment for all by administrative bodies and the police.

Cultural equality should be interpreted as equality to participate in society's cultural discourses. In this context equality of opportunity means that all have the same chance to say their own piece in cultural discourse but not that every argument is equally valid. Some individual aspects inherent in the cultural equality of opportunity include the equal chance to intervene in intellectual discussions, to have access to educational institutions, to attain an education, and to carry out professional roles.

In all these dimensions of equality America has undergone a far-reaching process of development. Initially, social equality in New England coexisted with major inequalities in the Southern states. Industrialization, discrimination against blacks and other minorities, and the immigration of different groups produced a society harboring substantial inequalities, one that was a contradiction to the idea of equality. Present-day liberalism is aimed at addressing the increasing rift between the idea of equality and the reality of inequality. The negative definition of the equality of opportunity, in which the state refrains from involvement in the process of free competition, is making way for an approach in which the state is attributed an active role in creating equality of opportunity.

3. THE IDEA OF EQUALITY AND SOCIETAL INEQUALITY IN AMERICA

From the beginning the New England states had the strongest air of social equality, even if it only applied to religiously qualified, male full citizens. Especially in the early period in Massachusetts, a sharp line of distinction was drawn between those with and those without the right religious credentials. In time, however, the distinction was increasingly abandoned. In Connecticut and Rhode Island all adult males were taken into both the religious and the political communities. The full citizens in this society were farmers, merchants, lawyers, doctors, and preachers, all of whom were independent and possessed relatively ample means (Berthoff 1971). This society of equally ranking citizens with equal rights was fundamentally different from the European societies of the time, which were still divided into estates, classes, and strata, each with quite different rights and each with its own consciousness as a community that shared a collective fate. This social equality was one of the first characteristics Tocqueville noticed when he visited the New England states:

> But all the immigrants who came to settle on the shores of New England belonged to the well-to-do classes at home. From the start, when they came together on American soil, they presented the unusual phenomenon of a society in which there were no great lords, no common people, and, one may almost say, no rich or poor. (Tocqueville [1835–40] 1966)

The members of this society were Puritans. The religious bond between them and the common awareness that they were living for the idea of a religiously ordered society strengthened their sense of social equality in quite a special way.

Later, at the time of the founding of the United States, Thomas Jefferson also regarded basic equality as an essential prerequisite for the proper functioning of the Constitution. He believed that the individual enjoyment of equal rights was best preserved in a society of independent farmers. Initially, he took a dim view of the development of large-scale manufacturing because it creates a class of dependent wage-earning laborers unable to lay claim autonomously to their own rights. Later, however, he was forced to admit that, in the interests of its economic strength, the United States could not do without the development of industry.

The immigrants to the Southern colonies were different in character and came to America for different reasons than the Northern immigrants. Although some settlers had religious motives, even in Virginia, settlement was undertaken primarily for economic reasons. The introduction of slavery in 1620 and the development of large-scale plantation operations created a different society in the South. Equality only applied within a relatively small governing stratum of large plantation owners, who were attempting to imitate aristocratic conditions. A clear differentiation between a higher and a lower stratum soon crystallized in the South, making inequality both an omnipresent hallmark of the society and a collectively experienced phenomenon. Thus, social relations were fundamentally equal in the North but paternalistic and authoritarian in the South (Tocqueville [1835–40] 1966; Berthoff 1971; Dollard [1937] 1957; Graven 1949; Gray 1958; Morgan 1975; Ratner, Soltow, and Sylla 1979; McGill 1963).

The contrast between North and South in the structuring of social relations is visible to this day and can be observed in all spheres, whether between farm owners or industrialists and their employees, politicians and their electorate, or teachers and their pupils. This disparity, in combination with the differences of interest between industry in the North and plantations in the South, was the basis on which the Civil War was fought between 1861 and 1865. Even today it represents a fundamental antithesis, as has been evident in the wake of the desegregation policy pursued since the end of the 1950s by the Supreme Court and Congress. The conflict has been carried to such an extent that some Southern state governors, such as George Wallace of Alabama, have openly resisted Supreme Court decisions on desegregation (Wilson 1980).

Today in the South blacks remain socially excluded wherever there is a chance, even in opposition to the policies of federal government and the federal courts, and are treated, through informal channels at least, as second-class citizens. Immigrants from Latin America, especially from Mexico, whose numbers grow by the day, are treated in a similar fashion.

Social equality, then, is still primarily an ideal held in the Northern part of the country. Inequality is far more in evidence in the South, where the prevailing public opinion among those in privileged positions is to attempt to maintain that inequality. The Democratic party had to push through its entire civil rights policy, as well as all the welfare policies of the 1960s and 1970s, not so much against the Republican party as against the dogged resistance of their own representatives in the South, who voted against these policies as a matter of principle (Wilson 1980). Hence the disparity between North and South remains a constant danger to the cohesion of the societal community.

Developments in the North also brought fundamental changes to the original society of equal-ranking property owners. By the time the United States was founded differences existed between the farmers and the owners of capital, that is, the merchants and the bankers. Nevertheless it is an exaggeration to derive, as Charles A. Beard attempted, the shape and content of the American Constitution from these differing interests that were not equal in all respects, and to see in the Constitution the dominance of the capitalists' interests (Beard [1913] 1968). This hypothesis is not backed up by fact and certainly finds no confirmation in the interests of the founders of the Constitution (Brown 1956; Wilson 1980).

Far-reaching changes occurred with the development of industrial capitalism and its corporations, and with the continuing revolutionary changes in technology, communications, and services. Another decisive factor producing major changes was the immigration of totally different racial, ethnic, and religious groups. The stream of immigrants reached its highest levels in the first decades of the twentieth century but ebbed after annual immigration quotas for specific groups were set in 1924. Since then the inflow of Latin American and Southeast Asian immigrants has increased dramatically especially in the South and West.

The present-day United States comprises a multitude of different racial, ethnic, religious, and socioeconomic groups. This heterogeneity is the precise opposite of the original social homogeneity found in the New England colonies. In Manhattan today, the East Side and the West Side, indeed, the Upper and the Lower East Side, Harlem, Little Italy, and Chinatown are all different worlds. The Puerto Rican neighborhoods and those where more recent Southeast Asian and Latin American immigrants have settled might also be mentioned (although the latter are not represented in the numbers that they are in the South and West). Los Angeles now threatens to burst at the seams under the pressure of the wide variety of racial, ethnic, religious, and socioeconomic strata among the immigrants (Glazer and Moynihan [1963] 1970; Gordon 1964; Mindel and Habenstein 1976; Turner 1984; Turner, Singleton, and Musick 1984).

Under conditions such as these, what is the meaning of social equality? It certainly no longer means that all live in similar circumstances and that anyone can associate with anyone else. Only in Latin America can such a crass distinction be found as that between Harlem and the neighboring upper-class district of the Upper East Side. To all intents and purposes, the different groups live within their own neighborhoods as they would in a ghetto. Is there, then, still such a thing as communal association among equally ranking citizens? Certainly there is not. The closest approximation today is that everyone eats their hamburgers at McDonald's, Burger King, or Howard Johnson's. This, however, is not convivial dining but simply the result of the conversion of eating into mass consumption. Conviviality is still nurtured over dinner at French, Chinese, Italian, Greek, and German restaurants, but in such situations one is among one's own friends.

Has the American melting pot given rise to a qualitatively new societal community with an identity of its own? Have the new immigrant groups conformed to the dominant values of the Anglo-Americans? Or does society consist of a multitude of relatively separate racial, ethnic, religious, and socioeconomic groups living alongside one another? (See Bannister 1972.) The answer, at least in its general tendency, is the third alternative of the pluralism of coexisting but unequal groups. Together with blacks (Rainwater 1970; Pettigrew 1975; McCord, Howard, Friedberg, and Harwood 1969), the groups that have most recently immigrated have always made up the lowest strata in an economic sense: first the Irish Catholics, then other Catholics from Southern or Eastern Europe (mainly Italians and Poles), then the Asians and Puerto Ricans, and finally the Mexicans and other Latin American groups.

The Germans and some of the Jews (not the relatively poor Jews of New York, living in their ghetto) represented exceptions to this hierarchy of immigration. Through economic success and by virtue of their education, they were able to assimilate themselves. The Jews, especially, have a disproportionately high representation among the most educated strata. In their case inclusion into the societal community was facilitated by the adoption of fundamental American values and most of all by the success flowing from their keenness to succeed.

Among the other groups, the Irish Catholics were best able to find their way into the dominant Anglo-American societal community. To some extent this also applies to another major Catholic group, the Italians, but so far not to the Hispanics (Navarro 1971). There is a vast difference between the Catholic Church in the North and its position in the South. In the North it has actually achieved a position of some respect within society, and well-regarded families such as the Kennedys serve as representatives of Catholicism in the North. In the South, however, the state of the church corresponds to the underprivileged position of the Hispanic groups it represents.

Under these conditions social inequality is a collective experience. This experience, however, has discontinuities. There is a marked socio-

economic stratification within ethnic and religious groups and it is more
pronounced in proportion to the number of generations of immigrants
that make up the group. Given the burgeoning growth of immigration
from Latin America and the regional concentration of this immigration
in the South and West, Hispanics are the most clearly delineated and
homogeneous underprivileged section of society today (Wagenheim and
Wagenheim 1973; Grebler, Moore, and Guzin 1970; Steiner 1970). They
have not yet had time to send their second and third generations to
schools and colleges. In a society where there is no large-scale collective
welfare system to redress social imbalances and where competition for
economic success means everything, the Hispanics and other groups like
them inevitably constitute an army of the poor, frequently living below
subsistence level. America today is a society of inequality. In this respect
it is radically and diametrically opposed to its origins in New England
(Myrdal 1944; Kahl [1953] 1967; Coleman 1966; Blau and Duncan
1967; Jencks et al. 1972; Collins 1979; Zeitlin [1970] 1977).

The difference between the highest and lowest income levels is
greater in the United States than in other industrial nations. The lowest-
income groups and lowest-paid occupations are predominantly made up
of the particularly disadvantaged minorities, namely blacks, Puerto Ricans, Mexicans, and other Hispanic groups. Within the same occupation
minorities earn less on average than their white colleagues (Kaufmann
1983; Reimers 1984). And despite the unified educational system, occupational qualifications differ widely by race. The most immediate reason
for this is that there is a very unequal distribution in the quality of
education given, with the disadvantaged minorities winding up with the
lowest quality education. In addition, the social welfare net is relatively
undeveloped. Anyone who falls ill, loses the ability to be gainfully employed, is otherwise unemployed, or leaves the work force owing to old
age becomes among society's poorest. Here, too, the disadvantaged minorities are hardest hit.

In the field of politics the inequality that exists is no less striking.
Political participation is more a matter of individual initiative and free
association and less one of caring for needs via large organized parties.
Accordingly, the variations in the degree of qualification to participate
that stem from different levels of education and income are especially
important. Political participation rests in the hands of the educated strata
(Almond and Verba 1963; Verba and Nie 1972). Similarly, the discussion
of political subjects in the mass media is clearly dominated by the educated Anglo-American strata. It is not infrequent, especially in the
South, that formal equality before the law is undermined by informal
inequalities in the assessment of legal cases and criminal acts and in the
meting out of penalties. The same tension between formal equality and

informal inequality is evident in the way public authorities and the police treat minorities. Blacks, Puerto Ricans, and Hispanics who have dealings with the police are more likely to encounter mistrust and unfriendliness than their white counterparts (Mayhew 1968; Cicourel 1968; Cohen and Kluegel 1978; Terry 1967; Thornberry 1973, 1979).

In the cultural sphere inequality is apparent in the Anglo-American domination of matters of religion, moral theory, the arts, and the academic world. The other racial and ethnic groups occupy an extremely marginal position here. Under such conditions there is no sign of a cultural melting pot. For a long period entry into institutions of higher education was extremely unequally distributed. There are also substantial differences in the quality of the education obtained. The low-level groups and strata show a disproportionately high rate of attendance at the poorer-quality high schools, colleges, and universities. The professions have long been dominated by Anglo-Americans, and to the extent that members of the disadvantaged minorities have actually gained entry into the professions they tend to occupy its lower echelons. One apparent exception to this trend is that Asian groups have recently been particularly successful in entering the professions. They have also achieved top performances in schools and universities well out of proportion to their numbers (Collins 1979).

In terms of communal association, a pronounced vertical differentiation of social prestige has developed in the United States as of the 1960s. The Puerto Ricans, Mexicans, other Hispanic minorities, and blacks form the lowest groups in the ranking. Above them are the Asians and Eastern Europeans, especially the Poles, then the Italians; the Anglo-Americans are paramount in the scale of prestige. There are sharply outlined social barriers between these groups. People marry within their own groups and only develop new acquaintances and friendships within the same confines. Clubs, associations, and religious communities are also largely ethnically homogeneous in their composition. And when it comes to their place of residence, different groups stick together in their own neighborhoods. For a Harlem black Manhattan's neighboring Upper East Side is further away in a communal sense than the moon. And in the South racial segregation prevailed in public places right into the 1960s. Although racial segregation is no longer official policy, racial and ethnic groups communally distribute themselves quite clearly among different public places: different residential neighborhoods, hotels, restaurants, theaters, and cinemas.

Great differences are apparent in the life-styles of racial and ethnic groups, from living conditions and eating habits to family circumstances. There is a huge discrepancy between the life-style of a well-off Anglo-American family and the grim living conditions of the lowest groups.

They belong to two different worlds. A social relationship between them on a common basis is inconceivable (Coleman and Rainwater 1979).

However, it would be pharisaical if a European were to take a moralizing tone in pointing out the gross contrast between the wealth enjoyed by a majority and the poverty faced by a minority and how this contradicts the great idea of equality in American society. No European country has ever had to cope with a comparable influx of heterogeneous immigrant groups. At present over a million people immigrate into the United States each year (Anderson 1983). And apart from this, the situation is further aggravated by the fact that the majority of immigrants come from the poorest countries and enter the lowest strata, thus contributing to the continuation of inequality.

4. IN SEARCH OF GREATER EQUALITY

Even under the difficult conditions discussed above one should neither overlook the countervailing forces that work in favor of realizing social equality of opportunity nor underestimate the amount of effort that is made in this direction. The economic prosperity that prevailed for so long and the common striving for success have to be seen as countervailing forces. So, too, are the egalitarian ways of dealing with others in everyday communication and the uniformity of the educational system, at least on a formal basis.

Most of the inequalities in the economic wealth of the United States do not take the form of a rich minority and a poor majority (for example, the contrast between rich capitalists and poor workers). Rather they take the form of a well-off majority and a poor minority (Potter 1954). This reality is fundamentally at variance with the usual theories of class inequality. Within the ranks of the well-off majority the general prosperity functions as a great leveler, as expressed in equal participation in mass consumption. Striving for success is the commonly shared philosophy and the conversion of that success via consumption the commonly shared practice.

Most of the families in this majority category have a detached house in the suburbs, two cars, color TV, dishwasher, and freezer. The family members deck themselves out generously in the latest fashions, wear blue jeans, eat hamburgers at McDonald's, Burger King, and Howard Johnson's, watch "E.T." and "Dallas," and take vacations in places like Florida every year. A leveling in life-styles has occurred in the United States via mass consumption. Such a leveling has not been reached in Europe. A family in which both the husband and the wife work has sufficient income to be able to satisfy most conceivable middle-class wishes. To a fair extent both the university professor and the newspaper vendor on the corner share this style of life, and in this respect they are much more equal than their European counterparts.

In everyday communication Americans do not stress the differences between higher and lower social echelons. Top-level professionals, once outside their occupational spheres, are treated as ordinary citizens. This can be seen in typical day-to-day interactions. Newspaper vendors, for example, do not take a reverent stance in their dealings with professors, particularly if they make more money than the professors. Within the occupational sphere differences of rank are not automatically reflected in forms of address. The sales assistant's approach to the sales manager is not one of subordination, just as the latter does not take an authoritarian stance in relation to the assistant. This equality in everyday dealings is highlighted by the normal practice of keeping communications through-out all levels of rank on first-name terms (Collins 1979). In the occasional awkward situation where the lower-ranking person feels the difference is too great, he or she tends not to address the other directly in order to avoid embarrassment. A student, for example, might avoid direct ad-dress rather than call the professor "Professor Smith."

The most important factor in social leveling, however, is the breadth of the educational system, which gives a vast majority of Americans the opportunity for twelve years of education before they complete high school and allows half of those graduating each year to attend college for a further two to four years. Accordingly, educational differences are less of a social barrier than they are in Europe. Nevertheless, the uniformity of the educational system cannot be taken altogether literally. There are likely to be greater differences of quality between high schools in Harlem and the Upper East Side than there are between the secondary modern (*Hauptschule*) and the grammar school (*Gymnasium*) in the same suburb of Cologne. In addition, the high dropout rate in the United States is a major problem. There are also huge differences in the quality of colleges and universities. An Anglo-American graduate of the Harvard Law School will not mix with his or her Mexican-American counterpart from a less highly regarded law school in Texas by dint of having the same formal qualification alone. Because informal vertical differentiation ex-ists, the formal uniformity in the educational system cannot, in and of itself, level out social differences. The children belonging to the lower groups and strata also attend the poorer schools, colleges, and universi-ties in most cases.

The decentralization of the political system in the United States, espe-cially the autonomy of municipalities, counteracts the tendencies toward a political differentiation into a ruling elite and a mass of ruled subjects. By European standards there are more varied possibilities for participat-ing in political life. Although this does not make political involvement something that is shared by all groups, it does at least make it a matter where a far greater number of citizens are active, and where they develop a common awareness of being active citizens with equal rights (Dahl 1967).

Most important in establishing equality in the United States is the belief that the unequal distribution of opportunity is illegitimate. This belief has led, first and foremost, to an active state policy of establishing equality of opportunity, which has been driven forward by the liberals. Although the conservatives can put a damper on this policy, they cannot eliminate it (Burkey 1978; Slawson 1979). Today the vast majority of the population supports measures securing equality of opportunity in all areas when these measures are explicitly intended to improve an individual's qualifications in the competitive job market. The majority does not, however, offer such support for efforts to redistribute income in a way that bears no relation to individual performance (Wilson 1980).

American individualism, which blocks income redistribution that bears no relation to individual performance and which resists state-administered care in the place of individual responsibility, provides the explanation on the ideological level for the fact that it was not until 1935 that the first comprehensive and effective social legislation was introduced in the United States. In response to the Great Depression, Franklin D. Roosevelt took the lead with his New Deal (Leiby 1978). The Social Security Act of 1935 incorporated two programs. One was an insurance scheme to provide pensions and unemployment pay, under which the insured were required to pay contributions; the other was state support, not based on contribution payments, for the aged and the blind (later also for other invalids) and for needy families with dependent children (Piven and Cloward 1971). This social legislation was expanded on in 1964 and 1965 by Lyndon B. Johnson and the liberal majority in Congress. The intent of the 1964 Economic Opportunity Act was to bolster the fight against poverty. State assistance was granted to training programs aimed at improving levels of occupational qualification. The following programs were supported: training schemes for unemployed youth, English lessons for adults having no command of the language, neighborhood programs intended to give work experience to the young, corporate-student programs enabling college students from needy families to take part-time work, and community action programs allowing residents of poor neighborhoods to participate in the planning and provision of services for their own benefit (Sundquist 1969; Plotnik and Skidmore 1975; Slawson 1979). The Medicare Act, another piece of major social legislation, was passed in 1965. It provided for health care among the aged and the poor, to be paid for from the federal budget. The growth in social welfare payments has made a marked impact on the federal budget over the years. Between 1950 and 1976 expenditures in this sphere rose from $10.5 billion to $198.3 billion, their share of federal expenditures increased from 26.2 percent to 56 percent, and their share of the national product rose from 4 percent to 12.3 percent (Wilson 1980; U.S. Bureau of the Census 1978).

Despite this tremendous increase in social expenditures, there is no doubt that even today, the United States still lags well behind the European countries, which in this respect lead the world (Thurow 1969; Beeghley 1983). The prevailing public opinion continues to favor direct support designed to establish equality of opportunity, but opposes the collective redistribution of income. In an opinion poll carried out in 1976, although 94 percent believed no one should be allowed to starve for want of government aid, 89 percent believed there were too many welfare recipients who actually were able to work, and 64 percent expressed the view that the criteria for welfare payments were not strict enough (Wilson 1980).

A further indication of the American resistance to the collective establishment of social equality is given by the limited place socialism has had in the political arena. Any moves to initiate socialist parties have quickly run into the quicksand of American individualism. Insofar as socialist ideas have been formulated, they have never seriously demanded that there be a collective leveling of the distribution of goods. Rather they simply demand that the state give active support to those beginning the race for success with more limited chances and that true equality of opportunity be actively created (Lipset 1974; DeLeon 1978; Gilbert 1977).

The same applies to the policies of the trade unions. Although the American labor unions have never fought to have the economic system remodeled along socialist lines, they are among the toughest in the world when it comes to asserting the interests of their own members. These interests, however, are not conceived of as the collective equalization of the distribution of income, but as obtaining the best possible wages for relatively limited groups of workers with homogeneous interests. Unions are very strongly differentiated according to different industries and job specializations, and their duties are to the interests of the particular groups concerned and not to those of working people as a whole. Thus unions are no more than instruments workers use to more effectively promote their own positions in the competition for better wages, and the individual worker does not expect any more than this from his or her union. Far from producing an increasing equality in wage levels, trade-union policy actually gives rise to increasing differentiation. The unions improve the positions of particular groups of workers, not only in opposition to the corporations but also in the face of competition from other groups of workers (Lipset [1963] 1979).

5. THE ROAD TOWARD GREATER EQUALITY

Since the 1950s the main thrust against social inequality in the United States has been in the area of civil rights policy. The civil rights movement has forced the pace of progress, using both Supreme Court decisions and civil rights legislation in Congress. Although various social groups and minorities have experienced oppression in the course of American history, the paradigmatic case, which so far has been the chief object of civil rights policy, is that of the blacks. Former slaves were not made citizens of the United States until the Fourteenth Amendment was added to the Constitution in 1868. And in 1870 the Fifteenth Amendment prohibited denial of the right to vote on the grounds of race, color, or previous status as a slave. Of course these amendments did not end racial segregation and discrimination in practice. Nevertheless, the Fourteenth Amendment in particular was to play a key role in future Supreme Court civil rights decisions. Although it created a framework for the implementation of equal rights for all citizens, it was not until the 1950s that decisive steps were taken in this direction (Shapiro and Hobbs 1978; Pritchett 1979; Gunther and Dowling 1970; Berger 1967; Wilson 1980). The question at this time was what precisely should be subsumed under the Fourteenth Amendment's privileges and immunities and its provision for individual equality before the law.

For a long period the terms of the Fourteenth Amendment were given a very restrictive definition, which led to a number of Supreme Court decisions accepting what was known as jim crow legislation on racial segregation and discrimination. In the *Slaughterhouse* cases of 1873 (16 Wallace 1873), in which black rights were not the point at issue, the "privileges and immunities" clause was interpreted so narrowly as to be effectively nullified (Gunther and Dowling 1970). In the civil rights cases that came before it ten years later, the Supreme Court declared unconstitutional a Congressional law forbidding racial discrimination in public facilities, such as hotels and transport, on the grounds that the Fourteenth Amendment was only applicable to governmental bodies and not to privately run organizations (Gunther and Dowling 1970). In *Plessy v. Ferguson* in 1896 the Supreme Court judged that segregated but equivalent public facilities—in this case separate railroad cars for blacks and whites—were in compliance with the Constitution. Three years later in *Cumming v. Richmond County Board of Education* the Court held not only that segregated schools were compatible with the Constitution but also that it was permissible for a school district to only provide a high school for white children, ignoring the needs of black children. The Court reminded blacks of their ability to make use of private schools.

In 1909, following an antiblack riot, a small group of blacks and whites together founded the National Association for the Advancement of Colored People (NAACP). The association's publication, *The Crisis*, which was edited by W. E. B. DuBois, drew attention to the oppression of blacks. The organization endeavored to work as a lobby in Congress but its primary effort was to cause change by filing lawsuits. Its first successes were achieved in the mid-1930s. In *Missouri ex re. Gaines v. Canada*, decided by the Supreme Court in 1938, Lloyd Gaines, who had graduated from all-black Lincoln University in Missouri in 1935, sought admission to law school. There was no law school for blacks in Missouri, so he applied for entry to the University of Missouri's white law school only to have the application rejected with the provision that the extra costs Gaines would incur by attending a school located in another state were to be reimbursed to him. The federal Supreme Court compelled the University of Missouri to admit Gaines on the basis of the "separate but equal" ruling, which held that separate schools for blacks and whites were permissible but that they also had to be equally accessible. In a similar case ten years later the University of Oklahoma set up a special law department with three professors for a single black student as a result of the decision in *Sipuel v. Board of Regents of the University of Oklahoma*. Subsequently, in *Sweatt v. Painter* (1950) and *McLaurin v. Oklahoma State Regents for Higher Education* (1950) the Supreme Court prohibited this practice, arguing that such minidepartments did not guarantee equal academic standards.

During the 1950s the liberal Warren Court ushered in a new phase of civil rights decisions. The case that proved decisive was *Brown v. Board of Education of Topeka* (Kluger 1975). In that case Oliver Brown, a black, wanted to send his daughter to a white school in Topeka, Kansas. The school rejected his application, remarking that a black school in his district offered the same facilities. The lower court decision, based on the "separate but equal" doctrine, held that this rejection was legal. However, in a trail-blazing unanimous judgment on 17 May 1954 the Supreme Court decided otherwise. It declared that segregated schooling was unequal in and of itself because it gave black children a feeling of inferiority with regard to their status in the community, preying on their hearts and minds in a way that could not be reversed at a later stage.

This ruling meant that the "separate but equal" doctrine that had applied since *Plessy v. Ferguson* was overruled. The segregation of schools was now unconstitutional. The judgment generated vehement opposition in the South, which persisted long after the event. On a number of occasions federal troops had to be on hand to enforce the admission of black students to white universities. Sometimes these federal troops were even opposed by state National Guards, as in Little Rock, Arkansas, in 1957. In 1964 only 2 percent of black schoolchildren in the eleven former Confederate states attended mixed-race schools, and most of these students were in Virginia and Texas. By 1970, however, the resistance had been broken. Racial segregation had ceased in 97 percent of the Southern states' 2,700 school districts. Segregated schools still existed within these districts but only 14 percent of black pupils attended purely black schools. Today there are more segregated schools in the North than in the South because segregation in the North occurs not de jure but de facto, stemming from the racial homogeneity of residential neighborhoods (Wilson 1980).

In the 1960s and 1970s desegregation led to integration, as federal courts more and more frequently made the requirement that the races should be mixed in the schools; simply allowing all to have a free choice of school was no longer enough. The Supreme Court under Warren Burger continued this pattern of legal decisions. Educational authorities were required to strive for complete racial mixing. To fulfill this aim, children had to be bused from their home neighborhoods to other parts of the town or city (John and Hoyt 1975; Sheeham 1984). Many children were no longer able to attend the school nearest to their homes. This system of busing met with vehement criticism from most of the parents affected. It remains highly controversial today, but on the instructions of the courts it is still practiced in the interests of creating a uniform school system. In the case of school busing one is able to see what the policy of creating equality of opportunity means when taken to its logical conclusion.

As late as the 1930s, the courts ruled that racial segregation did not violate the principle of equality as formulated in the Fourteenth Amendment as long as the segregated facilities offered equal opportunities—although one has to say here that comparisons between facilities were made very generously, that is, they exaggerated the quality of existing black facilities. By the end of the 1930s the judicial authorities were concerned that every black should have open to him or her the same education or training that was open to whites. At the end of the 1940s the requirement was that the education given should be of equal quality. In the first half of the 1950s the courts ruled that all racial segregation was detrimental to the equality of opportunity. And in the 1960s and 1970s the courts held that active integration was a precondition for true equality of opportunity. Although the courts long permitted state and local governments to pursue a policy of obstructing equality of opportunity, today state and local governments are required to actively establish such equality.

Yet propagating civil rights in the interests of improving equality of opportunity is not a matter that has remained confined to the courts. In the 1960s and 1970s Congress adopted an active role in civil rights policies. Although the courts initially made their decisions in opposition to a conservative majority in public opinion—as indeed they still do today on the school busing question—a swing in public opinion in favor of the liberal position was needed before Congress could take action.

The civil rights movement, which formed in the mid- to late-1950s, made its own contribution to this turnaround in public opinion (Wilson 1980; Dye 1971; Geschwender 1971; Chafe 1981). The first major move was a one-year boycott by blacks of a bus company in Montgomery, Alabama. Martin Luther King, Jr., began to make a name for himself as the movement's leader during this time. In the 1960s sit-ins, demonstrations, protest marches, and boycotts were instituted against public bodies practicing racial discrimination. In Birmingham, Alabama, in April 1963 police used force in repelling and dispersing demonstrations. On 28 August 1963, 250,000 blacks and whites participated in a civil rights march on Washington, D.C. In June 1964 three civil rights supporters in Neshoba County, Mississippi, were murdered. Under King's leadership protest marches were staged in Selma, Alabama, in the period from January to March 1965, some of which were violently broken up by the police. In the "long hot summers" of 1966 and 1967 violent demonstrations and rioting spread through many cities in the United States. On 4 April 1968 King was shot in Memphis, Tennessee.

The civil rights movement incorporated black leaders of various groups, such as Roy Wilkins of the NAACP, Whitney Young of the Urban League, and Martin Luther King, Jr., of the Southern Christian Leadership Conference. They banded together with liberal and moderate white groups. A more militant position was adopted by the Student Nonviolent Coordinating Committee (SNCC), the Congress of Racial Equality (CORE), and the Black Panther party. Black leaders did not initiate the violent riots during the 1964–68 period, but these actions probably contributed to a general swing in white public opinion in favor of integration, even if the chief concern of many whites was simply to reestablish peace and order by making concessions.

Between 1963 and 1976 support for black integration among whites increased markedly. In 1963 approximately 60 percent were in favor of integrated schools. By 1970 the figure had risen to 75 percent, and in 1972 it was 85 percent. In 1976, however, support fell to 80 percent. The falloff in support between 1972 and 1976 is presumably attributable to the controversial busing system. In 1963 approximately 50 percent of whites said they would not be opposed to having a black as a friend, 65 percent expressed this opinion in 1970, 70 percent in 1972, and 72 percent in 1976. In 1963 roughly 45 percent of whites expressed their opposition to the exclusion of blacks from white neighborhoods, 50 percent did so in 1970, 55 percent in 1972, and 60 percent in 1976. Thirty-five percent of whites objected to laws prohibiting intermarriage between blacks and whites in 1963, 50 percent in 1970, 60 percent in 1972, and 70 percent in 1976. The least support for integration was obtained in answer to the question of whether blacks should press forward into spheres in which their presence was not wanted. Approximately 25 percent opposed such moves in 1963, 18 percent in 1970, 23 percent in 1972, and 26 percent in 1976 (Taylor, Sheatsly, and Greeley 1978).

It was in the context set by the civil rights movement and the changes in white public opinion that Congress enacted civil rights legislation (Gunther and Dowling 1970; Abernathy 1980). In 1957 Congress passed a law prohibiting actions that prevented anyone from participating in a federal election. In 1960 the U.S. Attorney General was empowered to post observers to investigate cases in which blacks were prevented from exercising their right to vote. The crucial breakthrough came with the Civil Rights Act of 1964, brought before Congress on the initiative of President Lyndon B. Johnson. The Civil Rights Act prevented the use of literacy tests to keep blacks away from the polling booths, a common practice in the South. It prohibited any and all discrimination on the grounds of race, skin color, religion, or national origin in restaurants, hotels, snack bars, filling stations, movie theaters, sports stadiums, arenas, and lodging houses with more than five rooms. Furthermore, the act prohibited any discrimination on the grounds of race, skin color, religion, national origin, or sex in connection with the recruitment, dismissal, and remuneration of employees in organizations employing more than twenty-five persons. The federal Attorney General was instructed to file complaints in order to step up the pace of school desegregation, but there was no order to establish a system of school busing to bring about an improved racial balance. Federal financial aid was denied to any organization practicing discrimination.

In 1965 Congress introduced electoral examiners, who were to seek out discriminatory practices—on all levels, whether federal, state, or local—wherever fewer than 50 percent of those entitled to vote were actually listed on the electoral register. In 1968 discrimination in the purchase or renting of apartments or houses was forbidden in all cases in which real estate brokers conducted these transactions.

This civil rights legislation brought considerable results. Black participation in politics rose substantially. For example, although in the eleven Southern states only 30 percent of blacks who had the right to vote were actually entered in the electoral registers in 1960, this figure rose to 58 percent by 1971. Political representatives in the South had to take their black voters into account. In 1957 for instance, none of the Southern Democrats voted in favor of the new legislation on electoral rights. Yet when an electoral rights act of Congress came up for extension in 1970, it was approved by thirty-four out of the possible eighty-nine Southern

Democratic votes. There was a great increase in the number of black popular representatives. The total number of blacks in Congress or state legislatures rose from 182 to 316 between 1970 and 1978. In city and county positions the increase was from 715 to 2,595, in judicial and sheriff's posts from 213 to 454, and in school boards from 362 to 1,138 (Wilson 1980).

Affirmative action programs gave blacks and members of other minorities an increasing amount of governmental support in winning entry to colleges, universities, and other positions in both public and private sectors (Abernathy 1980). This program, however, generated controversy over the question of whether minorities should be given preferential treatment and compensated for the discrimination of past years by being given enhanced opportunities in general competition. The following types of programs for improving the opportunities available to disadvantaged minorities are covered under affirmative action:

1. Programs that make efforts to recruit qualified or qualifiable members of disadvantaged minorities for public service positions.
2. Training programs designed to improve the occupational qualifications of disadvantaged minorities.
3. Programs that monitor all tests to ensure their cultural neutrality.
4. Programs that monitor the qualifications required for different occupations, to avoid the disadvantages that result from discriminatory qualification rules.
5. Programs that pay special attention to members of minorities who can show in employment applications that they have the same qualifications as other applicants who are not so disadvantaged.

In practice, the affirmative action program has frequently led to quotas being established a priori for certain minorities in determining admissions to colleges and universities and in recruitment for employment. It is a practice, however, that has met with increasing criticism and is not supported by public opinion. A Gallup opinion poll showed that 77 percent of whites are in favor of training programs to improve the opportunities available to blacks but that 82 percent reject preferential treatment for blacks of equal qualification when choosing candidates for promotion. In 1974, 96 percent of whites and 83 percent of blacks were against preferential treatment at the time of recruitment. In 1977, 83 percent of the respondents were opposed to preferential treatment for women and members of minority groups when granting entry to college or filling employment vacancies. A 1976 survey asked respondents whether they approved of the fact that some large organizations were implementing affirmative action programs that sometimes gave members of disadvantaged minorities preferential treatment. The results showed that 51 percent disapproved and 35 percent approved of this policy, and among black respondents 58 percent approved and 24 percent disapproved (Lipset and Schneider 1977; Wilson 1980). These opinion survey results show quite clearly that although a large majority of Americans agree with programs to establish equality of opportunity, they strongly oppose giving preferential treatment to disadvantaged minorities if this means violating the criterion of reward according to individual performance.

Beyond basic minimum provisions for the sick, the weak, and the needy, Americans reject the notion that equality in the distribution of material goods irrespective of individual performance is desirable. However, most Americans believe that activist policy designed to bring about equality of opportunity is a fundamental task of society. The Supreme Court recognized this belief in its decision in the *Regents of the University of California v. Bakke,* handed down on 28 June 1978 (Shapiro and Hobbs 1978; Abernathy 1980; Sindler 1978). Allan Bakke, a thirty-eight-year-old engineer, applied for a place at the University of California Medical School at Davis and was rejected. Bakke then filed a complaint to the effect that the medical school's admissions procedure was unconstitutional and violated the principle of equality of opportunity as laid down in the Fourteenth Amendment. He argued that sixteen places at the school were reserved in advance for members of minorities, and that because of this policy some applicants had been accepted even though they were less qualified than Bakke. The California Supreme Court upheld Bakke's complaint and ordered that he be admitted to study medicine at the University of California. The university then lodged an appeal. However, the U.S. Supreme Court confirmed the California court's judgment by a five-to-four majority.

The majority group, which included Justices Powell, Stevens, Rehnquist, Stewart, and Burger, regarded the medical school's procedures primarily as a violation of the Civil Rights Act of 1964 and its stipulation that no one may be denied access to an institution receiving federal financial support if that denial is based on race, skin color, or national origin. Although Justice Powell reached the same verdict, he did so on the grounds that an explicit quota system was in contravention of the Fourteenth Amendment and its requirement that protection by the law of the land should be equal. Justice Powell noted, however, that a candidate's race could, per se, be one of the criteria taken into consideration.

The minority group, comprising Justices Brennan, Blackmun, Marshall, and White, argued that a quota system intended to provide redress for previous discrimination was permissible under the Constitution and under the Civil Rights Act of 1964. The Supreme Court's split decision on the *Bakke* case conveys the line of demarcation of present-day civil rights policy: although equality of opportunity should be actively brought to realization by way of training programs and special consideration should be given to previously disadvantaged groups in an effort to redress earlier discrimination, a perfect collective distribution of goods by establishing quotas is not desirable. Many regard such quota systems as reverse discrimination against persons who belong to groups that have been privileged in the past (Glazer 1975; Grass 1977). Discrimination should not be eliminated by reverse discrimination, for this too is in contravention of the Constitution.

The policy of establishing equality of opportunity has been so forcefully pursued in the United States in the 1960s and 1970s that it has continually run up against conservative opposition and, in the case of the quota system, has overshot the frame of reference of American fundamental convictions. Nevertheless, these developments have not been equaled in any other Western industrial nation and college and university admission figures for members of disadvantaged groups increased tremendously during this period. A similar trend is apparent in income levels. In 1950 blacks received wages and salaries that were only 50 percent of white salaries on average, whereas in 1973 these average earnings had increased to 73 percent of those of whites. Earnings comparisons among the female population show a still more remarkable development: black women received only 40 percent as much as their white counterparts in 1950 but 97 percent in 1975. The problem today is no longer one encompassing the black population as a whole, but primarily one of particular black groups, especially youths from broken families. The nature of the problem is illustrated by the fact that in 1977 black graduates from four-year college courses earned 94 percent of the salaries of their white counterparts but that in the same year the rate of black youth unemployment was 38 percent (Wilson 1980).

During the 1970s, the women's movement refocused national discussions of equality in the United States on the situation of women (Kraditor 1965; Flexner 1968; Stazs 1978; Theodore 1971; Treiman and Hartmann 1981; McGlen and O'Connor 1983). No other industrial country has such an active, far-reaching, and historically rooted women's movement. Although elsewhere the women's movement has remained largely confined to intellectual strata, the American movement embraces far broader strata and groups of women, including housewives.

The American woman—the housewife in particular—is much more involved in public life than her European counterpart. This is an immediate result of the private and public spheres being less sharply delineated. The fact that it was not until 1920 that women received the right to vote, through the Nineteenth Amendment, is the exception rather than the rule in the comparison between women's involvement in public life in

Europe and the United States. By the mid-1970s the women's movement had made its cause the chief focus of attention in equal opportunity policy and had also managed to achieve a number of successes in the wake of the affirmative action program. A European immediately notices how American women occupy career positions that in Europe are still a man's domain in a way that is still taken much for granted. The proportion of women in academic, industrial, and public posts is much higher than it is in European industrial countries.

6. CONCLUSION

In this chapter I began with an outline of how the idea of equal opportunity became the dominant definition of equality in American society. This definition is rooted in the relative equality of the people who built the Northern colonies. However, the idea of equal opportunity was counteracted in the Southern colonies where the idea of the natural inequality between free people and slaves dominated.

This cultural conflict eventually resulted in the victory of the Northern idea of equal opportunity, but that idea was then interpreted in both liberal and conservative ways: the liberal way called for political programs to counteract tendencies toward unequal opportunity, the conservative way opposed such programs. The development of actual equality and inequality in society has been shaped by the effects of this ongoing discourse and by economic, political, and associational processes in society itself. Many processes work unintentionally toward increasing inequality: the traditional racial, ethnic, religious, national, and class-based separation of neighborhood communities, the accumulation of unequal rewards for unequal economic achievement, the accumulation of political power in the hands of racial, ethnic, religious, national, and class-based groups, and the hierarchical differentiation of the cultures of these various groups, with the "WASP" culture in the dominant position. Additionally, there are the intentional activities of the better-off groups to maintain their position by establishing associational, political, economic, and cultural barriers against up-coming groups.

However, these tendencies toward increasing inequality are militated against by other tendencies toward greater equality of opportunity. Economic abundance, opportunities for political participation for aspiring political movements like the civil rights movement, the development of a growing middle class, mass consumption, and open communication work unintentionally toward greater equality. These tendencies are accompanied by intentional activities that aim at realizing greater equality of opportunity, namely, programs that increase the chances for disadvantaged groups to achieve in economic, political, associational, and cultural terms. Affirmative action is designed to produce such effects. The idea of equal opportunity itself exerts pressures to move society toward greater equality of opportunity. This process takes place particularly in court decision making on civil rights.

We can say that United States society, more than any other, is subject to the permanent tension of processes that work against one another. Although some processes move society toward increasing inequality, countervailing processes move society toward greater equality. In certain aspects, both inequality and equality are growing at the same time.

REFERENCES

Abernathy, C. F. 1980. *Civil rights: Cases and materials.* St. Paul, Minn.: West.

Almond, G. A., and S. Verba. 1963. *The civic culture: Political attitudes and democracy in five nations.* Princeton, N.J.: Princeton University Press.

Anderson, K. 1983. The new Ellis Island. *Time,* 13 June, 10–17.

Bannister, R. C. 1972. *American values in transition.* New York: Harcourt Brace Jovanovich.

Beard, C. A. [1913] 1968. *An economic interpretation of the Constitution of the United States.* New York: Macmillan.

Becker, G. L. 1958. *The Declaration of Independence: A study in the history of political ideas.* New York: Vintage.

Beeghley, L. 1983. *Living poorly in America.* New York: Praeger.

Berger, M. 1967. *Equality by statute: The revolution in civil rights.* Garden City, N.Y.: Doubleday.

Berthoff, R. 1971. *An unsettled people: Social order and disorder in American history.* New York: Harper and Row.

Blau, P. M., and O. D. Duncan. 1967. *The American occupational structure.* New York: Wiley.

Brown, R. E. 1956. *Charles Beard and the Constitution: A critical analysis of "An economic interpretation of the Constitution."* Princeton, N.J.: Princeton University Press.

Burkey, R. M. 1978. *Ethnic and racial groups: The dynamics of dominance.* Menlo Park, Calif.: Cummings.

Chafe, W. H. 1981. *Civilities and civil rights: Greensboro, North Carolina, and the black struggle for freedom.* New York: Oxford University Press.

Cicourel, A. 1968. *The social organization of justice.* New York: Wiley.

Cohen, L. E., and J. R. Kluegel. 1978. Determinants of juvenile court dispositions: Ascriptive and achieved factors in two metropolitan courts. *American Sociological Review* 43:162–76.

Coleman, J. S. 1966. *Equality of educational opportunity.* Washington, D.C.: Government Printing Office.

Coleman, R. P., and L. Rainwater. 1979. *Social standing in America: New dimensions of class.* London: Routledge and Kegan Paul.

Collins, R. 1979. *The credential society: An historical sociology of education and stratification.* New York: Academic Press.

Dahl, R. A. 1967. *Pluralist democracy in the United States: Conflict and consent.* Chicago: Rand McNally.

DeLeon, D. 1978. *The American as anarchist: Reflections on indigenous radicalism.* Baltimore: Johns Hopkins University Press.

Dollard, J. [1937] 1957. *Caste and class in a southern town.* Garden City, N.Y.: Doubleday.

DuBois, W. E. B., ed. [1909] 1967. *John Brown.* New York: International Publishers.

Dye, T. R. 1971. *The politics of equality.* Indianapolis: Bobbs Merrill.

Eidelberg, P. 1976. *On the silence of the Declaration of Independence.* Amherst, Mass.: University of Massachusetts Press.

Filler, L. 1960. *The crusade against slavery, 1830–1860.* New York: Harper and Row.

Flexner, E. 1968. *A century of struggle.* New York: Athenaeum.

Geschwender, J. A., ed. 1971. *The black revolt: The civil rights movement, ghetto uprisings, and separatism.* Englewood Cliffs, N.J.: Prentice-Hall.

Gilbert, J. B. 1977. *Work without salvation: America's intellectuals and industrial alienation, 1880–1910.* Baltimore: Johns Hopkins University Press.

Ginsberg, R. 1967. *A casebook on the Declaration of Independence.* New York: Crowell.

Glazer, N. 1975. *Affirmative discrimination: Ethnic inequality and public policy.* New York: Basic Books.

Glazer, N., and D. Moynihan. [1963] 1970. *Beyond the melting pot.* Cambridge, Mass.: M.I.T. Press.

Gordon, M. M. 1964. *Assimilation in American life: The role of race, religion, and national origins.* New York: Oxford University Press.

Grass, B. R., ed. 1977. *Reverse discrimination.* Buffalo, N.Y.: Prometheus.

Graven, W. F. 1949. *The southern colonies in the seventeenth century, 1607–1689.* Baton Rouge: Louisiana State University Press.

Gray, L. C. 1958. *History of agriculture in the southern United States to 1860.* Gloucester, Mass.: Peter Smith.

Grebler, L., J. W. Moore, and R. C. Guzin. 1970. *The Mexican-American people: The nation's second largest minority.* New York: Free Press.

Gunther, G., and N. T. Dowling. 1970. *Cases and materials on individual rights in Constitutional law.* Mineola, N.Y.: Foundation Press.

Jefferson, Thomas. 1905. *The writings of Thomas Jefferson.* Ed. Andrew A. Lipscomb. Washington, D.C.: Thomas Jefferson Memorial Association of the United States.

———. 1941. Notes on Virginia. In *American issues*, ed. W. Thorp, M. Curti, and C. Baker, 127–32. Chicago: Lippincott.

Jencks, C., et al. 1972. *Inequality: A reassessment of the effects of family and schooling in America.* New York: Basic Books.

John, S., and N. Hoyt. 1975. *School desegregation: Outcomes for children.* New York: Wiley.

Kahl, J. A. [1953] 1967. *The American class structure.* New York: Holt, Rinehart and Winston.

Kaufmann, R. L. 1983. A structural decomposition of black-white earnings differentials. *American Journal of Sociology* 89:585–611.

Kluger, R. 1975. *Simple justice: The history of Brown v. Board of Education and black America's struggle for equality.* New York: Vintage.

Kraditor, A. 1965. *The ideas of the woman suffrage movement, 1890–1920.* New York: Columbia University Press.

Laslett, J. H. M., and S. M. Lipset, eds. 1974. *Failure of a dream? Essays in the history of American socialism.* Berkeley: University of California Press.

Leiby, J. 1978. *A history of social welfare and social work in the United States.* New York: Columbia University Press.

Lipset, S. M. [1963] 1979. *The first new nation.* New York: Norton.

———. 1974. *Opportunity and welfare in the first new nation.* Washington, D.C.: American Enterprise Institute.

Lipset, S. M., and W. Schneider. 1977. An emerging national consensus. *The New Republic,* 15 October, 8–9.

McCord, W., J. Howard, B. Friedberg, and E. Harwood. 1969. *Life styles in the black ghetto.* New York: Norton.

McGill, R. E. 1963. *The South and the southerner.* Boston: Little, Brown.

McGlen, N. E., and K. O'Connor. 1983. *Women's rights: The struggle for equality in the nineteenth and twentieth century.* New York: Praeger.

Marx, K. 1962. *Kritik des Gothaer Programms.* In *Marx-Engels Werke,* 19:11–32. Berlin: Dietz.

Mayhew, L. 1968. *Law and equal opportunity.* Cambridge, Mass.: Harvard University Press.

Mindel, C. H., and R. W. Habenstein, eds. 1976. *Ethnic families in America.* New York: Elsevier.

Morgan, E. S. 1975. *American slavery, American freedom: The ordeal of colonial Virginia.* New York: Norton.

Murray, J. C. 1964. *We hold these truths.* Garden City, N.Y.: Doubleday.

Myrdal, G. 1944. *The American dilemma.* New York: Harper.

Navarro, E. 1971. *The Chicano community.* New York: Council on Social Work Education.

Padover, S. K., ed. 1943. *The complete Jefferson.* New York: Duell, Sloan and Pierce.

Pettigrew, T. F., ed. 1975. *Racial discrimination in the United States.* New York.

Piven, F. F., and R. A. Cloward. 1971. *Regulating the poor: The functions of public welfare.* New York: Harper and Row.

Plotnik, R., and F. Skidmore. 1975. *Progress against poverty: A review of the 1964–1974 decade.* New York: Academic Press.

Potter, D. 1954. *People of plenty: Economic abundance and the American character.* Chicago: University of Chicago Press.

Pritchett, C. H. 1979. *The American Constitution.* New York: McGraw-Hill.

Rainwater, L., ed. 1970. *Soul.* New York: Aldine.

Ratner, S., J. H. Soltow, and R. Sylla. 1979. *The evolution of the American economy: Growth, welfare, and decision making.* New York: Basic Books.

Reimers, C. W. 1984. Sources of the family income differentials among Hispanics, blacks, and white non-Hispanics. *American Journal of Sociology* 89:889–903.

Rose, P. I., ed. 1970. *Slavery and its aftermath.* New York: Atherton.

Shapiro, M., and D. S. Hobbs. 1978. *American Constitutional law: Cases and analyses.* Cambridge, Mass.: Winthrop.

Sheeham, J. B. 1984. *The Boston school integration dispute: Social change and legal maneuvers.* New York: Columbia University Press.

Sindler, A. P. 1978. *Bakke, DeFunis, and minority admissions.* New York: Longman.

Slawson, J. 1979. *Unequal Americans: Practices and politics of intergroup relations.* Westport, Conn.: Greenwood.

Stazs, C. 1978. *Female and male. Socialization, social roles, and social structure.* Dubuque, Iowa: William C. Brown.

Steiner, S. 1970. *La raza: The Mexican Americans.* New York: Harper and Row.

Sundquist, J. L., ed. 1969. *On fighting poverty: Perspectives from experience.* New York: Basic Books.

Taylor, D. G., P. B. Sheatsly, and A. M. Greeley. 1978. Attitudes toward racial integration. *Scientific American* 238:30–37.

Terry, R. M. 1967. Discrimination in the handling of juvenile offenders. *Journal of Research in Crime and Delinquency* 4:218–30.

Theodore, A., ed. 1971. *The professional woman.* Cambridge, Mass.: Schenkman.

Thornberry, T. B. 1973. Race, socio-economic status and sentencing in the juvenile justice system. *Journal of Criminal Law and Criminology* 64:90–98.

———. 1979. Sentencing disparities in the juvenile justice system. *Journal of Criminal Law and Criminology* 70:164–71.

Thurow, L. 1969. *Poverty and discrimination.* Washington, D.C.: Brookings.

Tocqueville, A. de. [1835–40] 1966. *Democracy in America.* Trans. George Lawrence. New York: Harper & Row.

Treiman, D. J., and H. I. Hartmann, eds. 1981. *Women, work, and wages: Equal pay for jobs of equal value.* Washington, D.C.: National Academy Press.

Turner, J. H. 1984. *Societal stratification.* New York: Columbia University Press.

Turner, J. H., R. Singleton, and D. Musick. 1984. *Oppression: A socio-history of black-white relations in America.* Chicago: Nelson-Hall.

U.S. Bureau of the Census. 1978. *Statistical abstract of the United States.* Washington, D.C.: G.P.O.

Verba, S., and N. H. Nie. 1972. *Participation in America: Political democracy and social equality.* New York: Harper and Row.

Wagenheim, K., and O. Jiminez de Wagenheim, eds. 1973. *The Puerto Ricans: A documentary history.* New York: Praeger.

Wilhoit, F. M. 1973. *The politics of massive resistance.* New York: George Braziller.

Wilson, J. Q. 1980. *American government: Institutions and policies.* Lexington, Mass.: Heath.

Zeitlin, M., ed. [1970] 1977. *American society, inc.: Studies on the social structure and the political economy of the United States.* Chicago: Rand McNally.

PART THREE

Modernity and General Structural and Cultural Change

Durkheim's Problem and Differentiation Theory Today

Jeffrey C. Alexander

Differentiation comes closer than any other contemporary conception to identifying the overall contours of civilizational change and the texture, immanent dangers, and real promises of modern life. As a general process, differentiation is fairly well understood, and it provides a backdrop for making sense of everyday life today. Institutions gradually become more specialized. Familial control over social organization decreases. Political processes become less directed by the obligations and rewards of patriarchy, and the division of labor is organized more according to economic criteria than by reference simply to age and sex. Community membership can reach beyond ethnicity to territorial and political criteria. Religion becomes more generalized and abstract, more institutionally separated from and in tension with other spheres. Eventually, cultural generalization breaks the bonds of religion altogether. Natural laws are recognized in the moral and physical worlds and, in the process, religion surrenders not only its hierarchical control over cultural life but also its institutional prominence.

It is in terms of these general contours of world history, and the intuitive representation of modernity they provide, that the immanent dangers and promises of modernity can be understood. Thus the need to develop flexible and independent control over social complexity leads to the emergence of large-scale bureaucratic and impersonal organizations (Eisenstadt 1963). Such centralization—political, economic, informational—provides an ever-present resource for the exercise of organized cruelty and domination. Yet precisely because it is imper-

I would like to acknowledge my colleagues in the School of Social Sciences at the Institute for Advanced Study in Princeton, New Jersey, where I was a member when this essay was composed, and particularly Michael Walzer. Parts of this paper draw on Alexander 1989.

sonal and bureaucratic rather than primordial and diffuse, that is, because it is differentiated, this centralization is experienced, even in totalitarian societies, in important new ways. Rarely is it experienced as an all-powerful and archetypical reality; more typically it is experienced as a development that challenges the existence of deeply entrenched institutions of private and public life (see, for example, Touraine et al. 1983).

The countercenters that mark private and public life are not confined to the primary groups, or life-worlds, that Habermas (1984) presents as the last bastion against colonization by rational systems. Uneven differentiation, not one-dimensional colonization, characterizes the modern world. Indeed, as Walzer (1983) has shown, it is the very existence of social and culture differentiation—not colonization—that allows social critics who are dedicated to justice in modern societies to demand ever greater autonomy and self-control for the spheres of public and private life.

But it is not enough to know the outlines of differentiation and its problems and possibilities in general terms. If the perspective of differentiation is going to produce a theory of social change, it must be brought down to earth. Obviously, not all societies and institutions differentiate. Sometimes they stagnate. Often they become brittle and reactionary, concentrated and inflexible. Why do these responses happen? Why, by contrast, is differentiation sometimes able to proceed?

Merely to describe differentiation as a general process, moreover, makes it appear to be automatic, an equilibrating mechanism that occurs whenever adjustments must be made to conflict and strain. This is not the case. The social processes that produce differentiation must be described in specific, concrete terms. When they are, the contingent nature of differentiation will be more clearly understood, as will the fact that differentiation takes different forms in different historical settings. Is a certain orienting ideology necessary for differentiation to occur? Are particular kinds of interest group formations necessary? If so, in what societies and historical conjunctures are such requirements likely to occur?

Finally, what is the relation between differentiation and the historical formations that are the traditional objects of classical theories of social change? Do feudalism, fascism, capitalism, and socialism represent a continuum of differentiation, or do they represent amalgamations of institutions that are differentiated in varying degrees? Does thinking of change as differentiation allow us to conceptualize the strains and conflicts in these formations more effectively than traditional theories do?

These questions mark the frontier of differentiation theory. They arise not just from scientific curiosity but out of theoretical competition (Wagner and Berger 1984). They are the questions that other theories put to theorists who think they see differentiation in social change. If the theory is to be maintained, it must be improved, and these questions must be answered.

In the chapter that follows I begin to formulate what some answers might be. I do this, in part, by suggesting that in the theoretical community today there is already an upsurge of investigation (for example, Alexander 1985; Alexander and Colomy 1989) directed precisely to these ends. In larger part, however, I try to provide some answers to these questions myself, or at least to produce a framework within which such answers can be more readily conceived. I begin by suggesting that the questions I have enumerated can be viewed not simply as the parochial preoccupations of recent neofunctionalist work but as issues that go back to the classical foundations of sociology itself. Indeed, I argue that, properly understood, they are generic questions that must be faced by every effort that seeks to understand social change in a serious way. I show how these questions define the achievements and limitations of Durkheim's change theory. By examining Parsons's later theorizing in these terms, I argue, we gain a new handle not only on the criticisms of the functionalist theory of change but on the efforts that have been made to improve it as well. These considerations inform my suggestions, offered in the conclusion, about what future efforts at understanding differentiation might be.

1. DURKHEIM'S PROBLEM

Although the notion that society changes through a process of institutional specialization can be traced back to ancient times, the modern theory of social change as differentiation began with Durkheim.[1] In *The Division of Labor in Society* Durkheim ([1893] 1933) put Spencer's earlier theory in a new form and started a research program that extends to the present day. Although Durkheim's first great work has, of course, become one of the classics of Western social science, the association with differentiation theory has not usually been made. In the context of the present discussion, therefore, *Division* is of particular interest. Although each of the problems I find in this classical work have been noted before, they have never been understood in reference to differentiation theory.

1. I make this observation despite the fact that Spencer articulated a wide-ranging historical classification of history as differentiation well before Durkheim's work appeared. Although Spencer had a significant influence on Durkheim, it is from Durkheim, not Spencer, that subsequent thinking about differentiation in the social sciences has drawn. Moreover, Spencer's approach to differentiation contrasts with Durkheim's in ways that are very significant for the problems and prospects of differentiation theory today. (See my discussions of Durkheim and of Parsons's neglect of war in this chapter.)

Because they have not, their theoretical interrelation has been impossible to see.

Durkheim's first great work serves as an exemplar of differentiation theory in several different ways. It can be considered the first and still one of the most powerful applications of the theory itself. It can also be seen as embodying some of this tradition's most typical and debilitating weaknesses. In other words, Durkheim's early work presents in a nutshell both the achievements of differentiation theory and the difficulties it often creates.

In Book 1 of *Division,* titled "The Function of the Division of Labor," Durkheim outlines a general portrait of social change as differentiation. Societies were once mechanically organized. They had repressive laws and were dominated by a particularistic and omnipresent collective conscience. Gradually, they have moved toward organic solidarity, where laws are restitutive and collective morality is generalized and abstract. In terms of institutional references Durkheim focuses on economic change on the one hand and the separation of religion from political and legal functions on the other hand. There is also a brief but important discussion of cultural generalization as indicating the increasingly person-centered character of the collective conscience.

This initial discussion, however, is of a particularly sweeping kind. Although this sweep confers power and scope, it makes it difficult to incorporate any real discussion of particulars, that is, the specific historical phases through which differentiation proceeds, the particular institutions and sectors on which distinct periods of differentiation depend, and the historically specific social problems that differentiation systematically might generate. Durkheim's argument in Book 1 is evolutionary rather than developmental in the sense that there are no phase-specific strains outlined. It is functional in the sense that there is no theory of how particular structures are involved. It is ideal-typical in the sense that there is no account of the processes of change by which an episode of social differentiation actually occurs.[2]

What is fascinating about this work, however, and what makes it so paradigmatic of differentiation theory as such, is that Durkheim goes on to try to supply these missing particulars in Books 2 and 3. Book 2, titled "Causes and Conditions," is his effort to supply a theory of social process. Durkheim argues that population growth leads to greater density and that greater specialization is a quasi-Malthusian response to the need for a more adaptive and efficient distribution of resources. Durkheim's Book 3, "Abnormal Forms," is an effort to discuss a particular historical

2. In developing these distinctions I am reworking and extending some of my earlier ideas about the different levels of change theory (Alexander 1983, 128–44, 259–72). In doing so I draw on the important arguments by Gould (1985) and Colomy (1985).

phase of differentiation and the problems it typically engenders. He suggests that because industrial society is not yet fully differentiated, the division of labor is coercive and disruptive. When birth is further separated from wealth, and political from economic organization, industrial relations will be mature and society less conflictual.

The fatal weakness of *Division* is that its three books cannot be related to one another in a systematic way. That demographic pressure is the principal process through which differentiation proceeds, as Durkheim asserts in Book 2, is in itself open to doubt. More significant from a theoretical point of view is that this emphasis seems to directly contradict the notion, which Durkheim argued in Book 1, that differentiation involves cultural and political phenomena. And what either demographics or systemic differentiation more generally understood have to do with the forced division of labor—Durkheim's topic in Book 3—is problematic as well. For if indeed the division of labor is anomic and coercive in 1890, there is nothing in Durkheim's general theory, or in his specific account of social process, to supply an explanation for it. What is necessary is a more phase-specific model of general differentiation and of social process alike. Only with such a theory would it be possible to stipulate the criteria for predicting the "normal" and the "pathological" outcomes of a particular social formation.

To establish links between the three parts of Durkheim's work, in other words, requires a detailed account of structures and processes and a systematic effort to link these theories to the general theory of differentiation. I argue that this is precisely the goal for which contemporary differentiation theory must strive.

2. SOCIAL CHANGE THEORY AND DURKHEIM'S PROBLEM

In order to relate this agenda for a particular research program to issues about social change more generally, one must recognize that "Durkheim's problem" was not unique to him. He used differentiation theory to grope with issues that are generic to the study of social change as such. Each of *Division*'s three parts represents one important way in which social change has been conceptualized: through the construction of general models, through developing accounts of social process, and through historically specific analyses of tensions and strains. Durkheim's problem, in other words, is an enduring one with which every perspective on change must come to grips.

In these terms I now briefly examine the principal classical theories of change with which Durkheim's must compete. Although Weber certainly defines a general theme, "rationalization," he does not emphasize the general level of his analysis in a way comparable to Durkheim. Weber's only effort to produce a general account of rationalization is the "Author's Preface" (Weber [1920] 1958, 13–31) to his collected essays in the sociology of religion, which was written only at the end of his career and which was much more an afterthought than the basis for his theoretical program. The minimalist character of the rationalization theme also can be seen from the fact that a debate is still raging about the simple definition of rationalization itself.[3] I am not suggesting that this general conception was not important for guiding Weber's thinking, for most certainly it was. But to conceptualize and elaborate it was not something with which Weber was centrally concerned.

The heart of Weber's work is his theorizing about processes of change, the role of institutions and groups in these processes, and the historically specific strains that are involved. The Protestant ethic creates capitalism in the West, patrimonialism overwhelms autonomous urban centers in the East, charismatic leadership becomes routinized and bureaucratic, priests and later legal notables have an interest in producing formally rational law. These are the middle-range propositions with which Weber is concerned. How and why these are connected to historical rationalization is implicit but never clearly spelled out. One result is that the relationship between Weber's various middle-range theories of change is never easy to see. Bendix (1961) devoted one very ambitious book to spelling out these connections, and Schluchter (1981) has recently devoted another to this same subject. But while presented as commentaries on Weber's theories, these works must actually be seen as theoretical constructions that try to fill this gap. Another result of this disarticulation of Weber's specific theories from one another and from his general perspective is that the relevance of these historical accounts for explaining other episodes of change, and for thinking about the future course of change, is far from clear.

Moreover, although Weber's historical explanations of traditional society often involve phase-specific accounts of conflict and strain—his theory of the patrimonialism-feudalism dilemma must be seen as a prototype in this regard—this genetic, or developmental, quality disappears from his treatment of the capitalist and modern periods. Again, this disarticulation between the strands of Weber's change theory leaves fundamental questions unanswered. Will bureaucratization dominate party

---

3. Here is how one of the most interesting recent contributions to this debate begins: "The idea of rationality is a great unifying theme in Max Weber's work . . . an *idée-maitresse* . . . that links his empirical and methodological investigations with his political and moral reflections. [Yet] Weber frequently uses the term 'rational' without qualification or explanation. . . . No fewer than sixteen apparent meanings of 'rational' can be culled [from his writings]. The reader may well be perplexed by what appears to be a baffling multiplicity of denotations and connotations" (Brubaker 1984, 1–2).

politics in the modern era, or will it be continuously challenged by charismatic politicians? Will formal law reign indefinitely, or will there be challenges to such formulations from different kinds of social groups, whose demands can be formulated in a substantive and historically specific way? Does the otherworldly character of Puritanism lead eventually to cultural universalism or to secularism in a purely political sense?

At the back of these problems are Weber's historicist difficulties with the concept of capitalism. Does late capitalism vitiate the processes that Weber has identified with its earlier creation? What can distinctively define late capitalism, if indeed a new postcapitalist historical phase will have to be introduced? Will this phase differ at all from the socialist form of industrial society, which at one point Weber ([1918] 1971) suggested must be seen merely as capitalism in another form, or from communist industrialism, which at another point (Beetham 1974, 46–48, 82–87) Weber believed to differ fatefully from capitalism not only in economic but in political and moral terms? Once again, my point is not that Weber has nothing to say about these issues; obviously he does. My point rather is that the failure to articulate the different levels or forms of his theorizing makes his contributions in these regards fragmentary and ad hoc. To suggest that there are paradoxes created by the rationalization of culture (Schluchter 1979) is suggestive but does not go nearly far enough. Nor is it sufficient to translate Weberian political theory into a story of the production of citizenship (Bendix 1964), even though such an effort is certainly valuable in its own right. Weber's theory remains the most perceptive theory of institutional change ever written, and it continues to inspire the most searching writing on the processes of change today (see, for example, Collins 1986b). Even for Weberian theory, however, Durkheim's problem remains.

Marxists, of course, have pointed most forcefully to these weaknesses in Weber's change theory, and when we look at Marx's approach to change, by contrast, we cannot help but admire its beauty and theoretical power. Marx united the different kinds of theorizing about social change in a coherent and compelling way. His general theme describes a dialectical movement—thesis, antithesis, synthesis—which occurs within each historical period and over the course of human history as a whole. His institutional theorizing neatly translates this dialectic by defining thesis as class domination in the service of economic production, antithesis as the struggle by classes who are exploited in production, and synthesis as the revolutionized social formation that ensues. Phase-specific strains are handled in an equally elegant and interconnected way, at least for the capitalist period: production processes rest on the forces of production; classes are established by property rights that define their relations to production; as the relations of production begin to strangle the forces of production, class conflict begins; and equilibrium can be restored only if the revolutionary transformation of property relationships is achieved.

Because Marx seems, at least in part, to provide the solution to Durkheim's problem, his theory of change has had wide appeal. In times of great conflict and anxiety, it supplies a coherent interpretation of events. It has also clearly identified some of the most specific and obvious features of contemporary social life. That there is capitalism and class conflict cannot be denied. It is also clear that the redistribution of property continues to preoccupy capitalist welfare states, and that the twentieth century has been transformed by a series of communist revolutions. Despite its intellectual power, however, Marxist change theory has, in my view, been refuted time and time again, indeed first and still most powerfully by Max Weber himself. Only when domination is experienced as intensive and relatively monolithic do Marxist theories become plausible. Insofar as social life returns to its more typically fragmented and pluralized shape, Marxism loses its attraction. We are living in such a period today. The social convulsions of the 1960s produced a renewal of Marxism but in the contemporary period Marxism is in definite decline. The centrality to change of relatively autonomous noneconomic institutions has come to be emphasized once again (see, for example, Sewell 1980; Evans, Rueschemeyer, and Skocpol 1985) and, against sweeping dialectical theories, temporal and spatial specificity has been emphasized (Giddens 1981, 1986).

As this consideration of Marxism indicates, there is more to the development of social change theories than Durkheim's problem alone. In every mode of theorizing the theorist must make specific commitments, describe empirical processes, predict conflicts, and prescribe moral possibilities. Indeed, the more explicit a theory becomes at each of the different levels of theoretical work, and the more tightly knit the interrelation it can propose, the more contestable its substantive empirical and moral commitments become. It should not be surprising that, as an advocate of more pluralistic theorizing, I find Marxism's substantive formulations implausible, even while I admire its theoretical scope. It is one thing to solve Durkheim's problem; it is quite another to solve it in an empirically and morally reasonable way. It seems to me that Weber's change theory is much closer to empirical reality than Marx's, and the moral possibilities Weber implies, although flawed in many ways, are more liberal and emancipating as well.

The challenge is to solve Durkheim's problem without giving up Weber's institutional work, which is to suggest that differentiation theory must be pushed in a Weberian direction. This was Parsons's intention. Let us see the kinds of advances he made over Durkheim's earlier theorizing before I insist, once again, that he did not really solve Durkheim's problem at all.

3. PARSONS'S CHANGE THEORY AND DURKHEIM'S PROBLEM

Parsons is generally considered, both by himself (Parsons [1960] 1967, Parsons 1971, 74, 78) and by others (Smith 1973), to have taken up differentiation theory where Durkheim left off. It is worth noting, however, that Parsons saw himself as carrying out Weber's perspective on social change as well. Although I argue that Parsons's theory is Durkheimian in its most fundamental thrust, in a certain sense Parsons's self-perception must be credited. The substantive formulations in Parsons's evolutionary writings cannibalize Weber's change theory in an extraordinary way. No one has ever taken Weber's institutional theorizing as seriously; no one has pursued the implications as strenuously or tried as hard to find a model within which they could be interrelated and explained. It is here that the paradox of Parsons's differentiation theory lies. For although Parsons finds his critical evidence and illustrations in Weber's institutional work, he never theorizes from within the institutional and processual level as such.[4] Weber's work is grist for the mill of Parsons's improved differentiation theory, but it never threatens to displace Durkheim's approach as such.

It is good grist, to be sure. Parsons's account of change is vastly superior to Durkheim's because it can be couched in the terms that Weber provides. In Durkheim there is sketchy generalization and, even in the most historical of his works (for example, Durkheim [1938] 1977), shifts from one historical phase to another are described in schematic terms. In Parsons's theory (1966, 1971), by contrast, differentiation is mapped in terms of actors, groups, institutions, social movements, civilizations, and states. As a result, Parsons is able to provide a much more intuitively compelling reconstruction of the modern world than Durkheim was able to provide himself. He can succeed in demonstrating what Durkheim merely suggested, namely, the extraordinary distance that has been traveled from band societies to the societies of the present day. In doing so, Parsons succeeds in legitimating the meaningful foundations of modern life.

4. Thus the indexes to the major works that Parsons (1966, 1971) devoted to history as differentiation include many more references to Weber than to Durkheim, and in the introduction to the second of these works he emphasizes that it "is written in the spirit of Weber's work" (1971, 2). Yet he immediately qualifies this in a telling way: "One important difference in perspective has been dictated by the link between organic evolution and that of human society and culture." Parsons refers here to the evolutionary theory of adaptation and differentiation that he drew in the most immediate sense from Durkheim's work.

It is impossible here to communicate the nuance and complexity of this Parsonian account, but I can make some indication of the scope and coherence of his generalized scheme. For Parsons historical evolution involves what might be called the defamilialization of the world. In band societies kinship ties define important social, cultural, and even psychological activity. Totemism is a good example. As an animal or vegetable symbol of ethnic identity and "religion," it fuses the band's existence with the natural world and with human kinship as well. It is no wonder, according to Parsons, that prohibitions like the incest taboo play such a socially decisive role, for the intermixing of kinship and social criteria makes behavior diffuse, particularistic, affective and, above all, prescriptive and ascribed. If societies are to become more flexible and individualized, they must make such "blood-related" qualities a much smaller part of social life. In order to do so, the significance of kinship must be drastically reduced.

This fused situation changes when one of the two lineages that usually form a band society seeks to improve its status. The equality of marriage exchange is altered; restricted intralineage marriage emerges and other resources are controlled as well. On the one hand, it is here that stratification and inequality arise. On the other hand, because power has itself become the basis for defining the extension of kinship ties, it marks the beginning of the possibility for more powerful and adaptive forms of social direction and control. Property comes into being, and kinship begins to be strategically subordinated to it. States are developed to protect the surplus wealth of the dominant lineage but, Parsons emphasizes, this is differentiation too, for from this point on the institutional structure of politics cannot be deduced from the nature of kinship itself.

These economic and political developments, moreover, cannot be sustained for any length of time without a religion that is far more elaborate and independent of kinship than totemism. This new religion must stretch over nonmarrying lineages and must explain and justify the social hierarchy and inequality. It does so not only by formulating a broader and more differentiated conception of the supernatural realm but also by developing a more generalized conception of "the people." Another result of the initial creation of stratification is the emergence, for the first time, of a nonfamilial conception of the societal community. There emerges a territorial referent for the human community that strongly emphasizes group as distinguished from lineage boundaries.

These processes continue in archaic and historical societies. Religion becomes more formalized and abstract. Cults emerge, as do other groups with specifically religious ambitions. Eventually churches, institutions with highly specialized religious personnel, develop. Politics continues to differentiate as well. It becomes more impersonal and bureaucratic, both in order to gain control for the privileged class—which involves placating lower-class groups by developing primitive welfare functions—and in order to ensure the safety of larger territories and the continuous productivity of economic life. Economic life becomes more functionally divided, and stratification increases. Within the now established range of "national" solidarity, heterogeneous groupings develop. They are arranged in horizontal as well as in vertically segmented ways. Although these developments ensure a more flexible and productive social organization, they also ensure new levels of hierarchy and inequality. Aristocracies represent the continued linkage of function to kinship, and new forms of domination emerge, like kingship and church, that fuse the control of various goods.

In the early modern and modern periods, primarily in the West, these intermediate levels of social development are pushed much further still. The Reformation moves religion toward a more abstract and less institutionally fused position. The emergence of parliaments and common law makes government more independent of social groups and economic position. With the advent of citizenship, social solidarity eventually becomes more independent of actual position in various social spheres. The advance of universal education makes culture still more generalized and accessible, regardless of one's particular group and origin. Competence rather than traditional connection or personal charisma becomes the arbiter of authority. The organization of technical knowledge through professional authority provides a systematic counterbalance to the hierarchical power derived from bureaucracies and the money power derived from markets.

Because he has one hand resting on Weber's shoulders, Parsons is able to describe the stages of differentiation with much more precision and concreteness than Durkheim himself. Even so, Durkheim's problem remains. Parsons has taken his general bearings from Durkheim, primarily from *The Division of Labor,* Book 1. Like Durkheim's before him, Parsons's general theory does not provide an account of how change occurs. To suggest that, because a differentiated institution is more effective and flexible, it will eventually develop to cope with problems posed by other spheres says little about the actual processes by which that new and more differentiated institution actually comes about. Parsons acknowledges the imbalance. He is concerned with "the structural ordering of social data," he argues (1966, 112), not in the first instance with "the analysis of process and change." He does not seem aware, however, of the intellectual difficulties that such a position presents. His insistence (1966, 111) that "structural analysis must take a certain priority over the analysis of process and change" recalls his dogged assertion in *The Social System* (Parsons 1951) that the analysis of stability must precede the analysis of change. The manifest inadequacy of this earlier claim, however, is what moved Parsons to the differentiation theory I have just described. The problem now seems to have reappeared in a new form. Even when he is committed to a theory of social change, it is the morphology of change, not its dynamics, that must come first.

But whatever Parsons's personal inclinations, this separation is impossible to make. Book 1 of *Division* was followed by Book 2, even though Durkheim could never connect them in an intelligible way. There is no second book for Parsons, but there is in fact an implicit strain of theorizing about what some of the actual processes of change might be. Unfortunately, the tone of this unwritten second book is Darwinian in a rather vulgar sense. Parsons himself has a more sophisticated parallel to Darwin in mind. He suggests that, like Darwin, he is justified in setting out a structural morphology of evolution without an explanation of just how evolution occurs. This was certainly true of Darwin's work. Because he did not have access to Mendel's theory of genetic mutation, he could only outline the macroconstraints within which species changed. But surely this situation does not apply to Parsons. Darwin could not set out a theory of evolutionary process; the knowledge simply was not there. When Parsons is writing, by contrast, a great deal of knowledge about the processes of social evolution already exists. Parsons chooses not to discuss it. The real parallel between Parsons and Darwin is less sophisticated. In Parsons's implicit theorizing about social change processes he tries to make do with Darwin's theory of macroconstraints alone. He takes over Darwin's theory of species competition and adaptation, which Spencer called the survival of the fittest. Even while eschewing an institutional understanding of process, therefore, there are suggestions in Parsons's work of how and why transitions from one form to another take place. This latent perspective, we will discover, allows Parsons to overlook knowledge about change processes that he prefers not to see.

For Parsons the world is an evolutionary field. Societies are species. They may die out, but innovations—breakthroughs to more differentiated phases—eventually occur. As a general theory of evolutionary change, there is nothing to fault this. The problem is that Parsons implies that it is a specific theory as well, that it is in order to adapt to an environment that breakthroughs in evolution actually occur. In presenting institutions and societies as problem solvers, Parsons's implicit second book takes a dangerous turn. In the long run adaptation may be the result of a given institutional innovation, but it is rarely its efficient cause (see Alexander and Colomy 1985). Because Parsons incorporated so many of Weber's specific and antiteleological explanations, this confusion could often be avoided. However, it cannot be denied that one implication of his work is that adaptation and problem solving are everywhere at work (see Smelser 1985).

The results for his change theory are often disastrous. Thinking that adaptation is both cause and result provides an ideological patina for thinking about the moral implications of rationalizing change. It also hides from Parsons's understanding the full theoretical implications of his decision to ignore real processes. These ideological and theoretical difficulties come together in Parsons's sotto voce dialogue with war.

At several critical points in his evolutionary work Parsons seems to acknowledge that the transitions between phases of differentiation can be carried out by war. In his discussion of early societies, I suggested earlier, Parsons emphasizes that upper-class lineages typically depended on religious legitimation to maintain their domination, using this fact to explain the beginnings of religious generalization. He acknowledges, however, that an exception to this dependence on legitimation exists in cases "in which a group subordinates another group by military conquest" (Parsons 1966, 44). He tries to mitigate this fact in a revealing way. Although domination through conquest may have "played an important part in *processes* of social change," he insists, military conquest cannot be considered "*differentiation* in the present sense" (emphasis mine). The conquerors in such situations are "a foreign group, not a structural segment of the original society." Moreover, it is "a rare, limiting case when such a group altogether eschews claims to religious legitimation and operates in terms of its naked self-interest alone." But Parsons's efforts to avoid the implications of his insight into the significance of war are beside the point. Of course domination through conquest is not differentiation; of course these conquerors are not part of domestic society but a foreign group; of course this conquering group will at some point need religious legitimation itself. None of this, however, denies the crucial fact that the transition toward a more complex society is often the result of war.

What if we know that the transition from band to stratified societies often involves political repression and ferocious violence? This does nothing to negate the fact that as the result of this transition more differentiation and flexibility occur. Nonetheless, this knowledge certainly changes our understanding of the meaning and implications of differentiation itself.

By underplaying process in his change theory, Parsons is able to deny the centrality of war in human history (see, for example, MacNeill 1982). Military conquest, of course, is not practiced only by conquering bands. Differentiated societies have experienced dark ages and the massive destruction of their civilizations as well. No matter what the innovations of a group, its survival is not assured. Even if a society is significantly more differentiated than those around it, one of its neighbors may be developed in a direction that is, at that historical moment, much more strategically significant in military terms.

Parsons cannot see this because he confuses differentiation with adaptive success. When he cannot avoid historical disasters, he becomes whiggish in a truly embarrassing way, discussing them from the viewpoint of the comfortable present. He writes (1966, 130), for example, that "the Nazi movement, even with its immense mobilization of power, seems to have been an acute sociopolitical disturbance, but not a source of major future structural patterns." But what does "seems to have been" mean? If a repressive system is defeated on the field of battle, this does not mean that its features were less adaptive in any short-run sense. If certain contingencies had turned out differently, historians of World War II suggest, the Nazis could well have emerged victorious. Their vicious and reactionary structures would, then, certainly have established the dominant social patterns throughout Europe for an uncertain period of time.

Because he ignores processes like war, Parsons's differentiation theory cannot understand the fundamental role of backwardness and structural fusion in creating the history of the modern world. Sandwiched between his elegiac accounts of the Renaissance and Reformation, on the one hand, and his laudatory analysis of the industrial and democratic revolutions, on the other hand, one finds scarcely four pages in Parsons's book (1971, 50–54) about the Counter-Reformation and its enormous repercussions for social and cultural life. Indeed, after his analysis of the democratic revolution in France Parsons moves directly to his analysis of how the high degree of social and cultural differentiation has stabilized American and Western European nations in our time. The clear implication is that steady progress was made, that "problems" like the Counter-Reformation came up and that they were solved by cultural and institutional adaptation.

It might well be argued, however, that quite the reverse is true. It took hundreds of years to destroy the effects of the Counter-Reformation, which was itself a response to differentiation in the early modern period. Divisions were created throughout Europe, murderous and long-lived conflicts broke out between nations, and basic patterns of cultural particularism and social authoritarianism emerged. The massive wars of the twentieth century must be seen in this context. It was not adaptation through differentiation that ended the authoritarian systems whose roots lay in the reaction to the Renaissance and Reformation, it was more or less continuous war and revolution (Maier 1975). In the twentieth century war has created not just the restabilized democratic systems Parsons extols but totalitarian and repressive states as well.

By ignoring process and war, however, Parsons does not simply commit the sin of sanguinity. He also fails to generate a powerful and coherent theory of social change. In the conclusion to his work on modern societies he acknowledges (1971, 140–41) that "there has, of course, been a great deal of conflict, 'frontier' primitivism, and lag in some of the older parts of the system relative to the more progressive parts." He even allows that "certainly the history of modern systems has been one of frequent, if not continual, warfare." The conclusion that follows has about it a stunning incongruity. "The striking point," Parsons writes, "is that the *same* system of societies within which the evolutionary process that we have traced has occurred has been subject to a high incidence of violence, most conspicuously in war but also internally, including revolutions" (emphasis in original). As I have just suggested, of course, this striking point is exactly what Parsons's history of the modern world has not explained.

I have spent a great deal of time on the unwritten second book of Parsons's change theory. One reason is that it spells out so clearly the problems with Parsons's unwritten third. In his own third book Durkheim developed a compelling, if theoretically contradictory, account of the strains that threatened the social and moral equipoise of his time. Because Parsons emphasizes adaptation through differentiation, however, he can do nothing of the kind.

It is worth noting, I think, that this was not always the case. In what I have called the "middle period" of Parsons's work, which extended from the late 1930s to the late 1940s and resulted in a series of essays on modern society (Parsons 1954b), Parsons's writing about social change had a sharply critical edge (see Alexander 1981b; Alexander 1983, 61–71). He did not write about differentiation as such, but in the light of his later work it was clearly differentiation that he had in mind. The tensions between home and office, the discontinuous and sex-linked socialization processes this separation implied, the abstraction and rationalization of modern culture, the discipline and market-orientation of labor—these were institutional developments, which Parsons would later call differentiation, that he viewed as creating enormous problems for the modern world. They led to the distortion of gender identities and relationships, to alienation and interpersonal aggression, to harsh ethnic and racial conflicts, and indeed also to war (see, for example, Parsons 1954a). In the midst of the period from the Great Depression to fascism and world war, Parsons saw differentiation as a cause of social problems and upheavals. In the period of postwar equipoise, however, he saw differentiation as a problem-solving solution.

Because the tensions of the past are underplayed in Parsons's differentiation theory, the strains of the present cannot be displayed. In

Parsons's later account the anxiety and pathos that continue to mark the twentieth century simply fail to exist. It is not that, like Durkheim, Parsons recognizes these problems but fails to integrate his account with his general theory. It is that Parsons cannot write Durkheim's third book at all. His theory lacks a developmental notion of historically specific strains and conflicts. Thus while he plausibly argues against the feudalism-capitalism-socialism trichotomy of Marx, he does not distinguish coherent phases of his own. Parsons refers to "coming phases" of modernization and to "major changes . . . in process" (1971, 141–43), but aside from vague reminders about the dangers of excessive rationality and impersonality he never tells us what these phases and changes might be.

In regard to the contemporary period it appears that Parsons is not as interested in explaining changes as in changing explanations. In the closing pages of his studies on evolution he attacks the "widespread pessimism over the survival of modern societies . . . especially among intellectuals," and suggests that the goal of his work should be understood in those terms, "To establish sufficient doubt of the validity of such views." Once again, there is a furtive backward glance at the tabooed subject of war. Parsons acknowledges "the undeniable possibility of overwhelming destruction." But the possibility of war in the future will not be pursued any more than its reality was pursued in the past.

Parsons sees the twentieth century as a period of opportunity and achievement, not a period of massive destruction and total war. In the last phase of his life he has become the "can-do" American pragmatist, the irrepressible evangelical utterly confident that the future will be shaped in a humane way. "Our view is relatively optimistic," Parsons concludes. The problem is that he cannot identify exactly the historical period he is optimistic about. His general theory certainly established the meaningful validity of "modern society." His inability to explain institutional process and to engage in more fully historical forms of explanation has made it impossible, however, to know whether this meaningful social framework will be able to survive.

In the midst of the Great Depression, classical economists predicted that Say's law remained valid. In the long run, they continued to maintain, demand would come back into equilibrium with supply and the slumping capitalist economies would revive. Keynes responded that in the long run we are all dead; the problem was in the short run. In our own lifetimes, Keynes demonstrated, there is only partial equilibrium and Say's law does not always apply. Without confronting pathologies in the short run, even the most meaningful civilizations may not survive. Durkheim's second and third books must be written, and they must be systematically integrated with the first.

4. THEORETICAL REVISION AND DURKHEIM'S PROBLEM

In the polarized political climate of the 1960s and early 1970s Parsons's version of differentiation theory became increasingly hard to sustain. It was challenged in the name of more historically specific and processual theorizing (for example, Nisbet 1969; Smith 1973). Theorists wanted to speak of specific events like the French Revolution (Tilly 1967) and of precise variations in national outcomes (Moore 1966). They wanted to explain specific phases and uneven development, for example, the emergence of the world capitalist system in early modern Europe (Wallerstein 1974) and the monopoly phase of capitalism (Baran and Sweezy 1966). They wanted to be able to talk about how modernization creates systemic conflicts and strains (Gusfield 1963; Gouldner 1979). Interactionists and resource mobilization theorists (Turner 1964, Gamson 1968) made claims for the centrality of social movements, and on this basis they developed explanations about the scope of change that went far beyond anything in Parsons's work. Conflict theorists (Collins 1975; Skocpol 1979) developed theories of state-building and revolution that were much more historically specific and comparatively precise.

There was, moreover, a pervasive shift in ideological tone. Theories became more critical and sober about the possibility that change would take a satisfactory course. These challenges insisted that Durkheim's second and third books must be written. Eventually, Marxism drew up many of these particular theories and challenged Parsons's first book as well. As I suggested above, Marxism is remarkably successful in interrelating general and specific theories of change. In the 1960s and early 1970s, a period of turbulent movements for social liberation, the elegance of Marxist theory seemed empirically compelling as well.

Empiricist philosophy of science, which continues to legitimate most social science today, holds that theories live and die through falsification. As Kuhn (1969), Lakatos (1969), and other postpositivist philosophers and historians of science have shown, however, falsification cannot—or at least in practice usually does not—disprove a general theory, even in the natural sciences. Lakatos has developed the most plausible account of how the resistance to falsification occurs (see Wagner and Berger 1985). Theoreticians differentiate between a theory's core notions, which are positions considered essential to the theory's identity, and other commitments that are more peripheral. When faced with studies that throw some of their important commitments into doubt, theorists sustain the viability of their general theories by discarding peripherals and defending the core notions. They seek to incorporate challenges by reworking and elaborating these new peripheral points. Of course this kind of defense is no more than a possibility. Whether an effective shoring-up process actually occurs depends on the empirical actors and the social and intellectual conditions at a particular time.

When differentiation theory first encountered the challenges to its predictions and its mode of explanation, it seemed as if no successful defense would be made. Parsons himself was never able to throw the weaker points of his general change theory overboard or to expand it in an ambitious way. Faced with the choice of abandoning the theory or changing it, many functionalists simply left it behind. A theory can be abandoned even if it is not refuted, and the effect on the course of scientific development is much the same.

Some of the most important early works of Parsons's students can be seen as attempts to set the theory right by writing what should have been Parsons's second book. Smelser (1959) and Eisenstadt (1963) discussed differentiation in terms of distinctive historical events and elaborated specific processes of change; Bellah (1969) and Smelser (1963) tackled the problems of specific institutional spheres. Although these studies were important examinations of change in their own right, as theoretical revisions they did not go far enough. Eventually Smelser and Eisenstadt separated the core from the periphery of differentiation theory in a much more radical way. Eisenstadt (1964) insisted that theorizing about general differentiation was impossible in isolation from concepts of specific social processes. He showed (see Alexander and Colomy 1985) that there are particular carrier groups for particular kinds of differentiation and that the interest structures and ideological visions of these groups determine the actual course differentiation will take. He insisted on the historical and comparative specificity of differentation and gave to civilizational factors such as culture a permanently arbitrating role (see Eisenstadt 1982, 1986). Smelser also initiated a fundamental critique from within. In his work on higher education in California he insisted that differentiation might be seen as a self-limiting process. He insisted on the resistances to differentiation and outlined a theory of the symbiotic relationship between differentiation and self-interested elites. Eventually, Smelser (1985) attacked the very problem-solving framework of Parsons's differentiation theory itself.

These revisions were intellectually powerful but they did not, at least at first, have a significant impact on debate in the field of social change. By the late 1970s this situation began to change. Several factors were involved:

1. The glow began to fade from the more institutional and phase-oriented theories that had initiated the response to Parsons's work. Neo-Marxist theories of the world capitalist system, for example, were challenged by rising economic growth in some Third World

nations and by the fact that the threat of imminent world economic crisis began to recede. For their part conflict perspectives appeared to have underestimated the resilience of capitalist and democratic institutions. Weber's approach to institutional process and social strain began to seem plausible once again.

2. These developments created strains between Marxism's general theory and its more specific predictions and explanations. Ideological events, moreover, lessened the political attractiveness of not only Marxism's more sweeping conclusions but also its phase-specific theory of strains.

3. A new generation of theorists emerged who had not personally been involved in the revolt against differentiation and, more generally, modernization theory; they did not, therefore, have a personal stake in continuing the controversy.[5]

By the late 1970s and early 1980s the revision of differentiation theory, which had been signaled by Smelser's and Eisenstadt's work, became both more pronounced and more widespread.[6] This work emerged in both Germany (Schluchter 1979; Luhmann 1981, 1987; Münch 1982, 1989) and the United States (Rueschemeyer 1977; Robertson 1978; Alexander 1978). These revisions proceed from the common assumption that differentiation does indeed provide an intuitively meaningful framework for understanding the nature of the modern world. But it is efforts to interrelate this general model to institutions, processes, and phase-specific strains that preoccupy most differentiation theorists in the present day.[7]

One group of efforts has been particularly directed to the issue of phase-specific conflicts and strains. Indeed, Gould (1985) first formu-

5. It is revealing of the generic qualities shared by different approaches to change that important writers in this newer generation have criticized Marxism on the same grounds that I have criticized Parsons himself. Giddens (1986) argues, for example, that Marxism is too evolutionary in its history and that it ignores the centrality of war. Indeed, the fact that Marx and even Weber (but see Alexander 1987) ignored the centrality of war to social change indicates that the problem goes beyond difficulties with Durkheim's problem to very deeply rooted blinders of an ideological kind. For other parallels between the recent criticism of Marxist change theory and the critique of Parsons, see my discussion of Marx's change theory earlier in this chapter.

6. Colomy (1989b) has provided the most extensive examination of these new developments in differentiation theory and of the criticisms to which they are a response.

7. This does not seem to apply to Luhmann's program, however. Luhmann certainly differs from Parsons in the intensity with which he has elaborated the effects of differentiation in various institutional spheres, for example, in law, religion, family, and political life. He has not, however, succeeded in linking his general theory more firmly to institutional processes or phase-specific strains. Although I cannot give a detailed consideration of Luhmann's imposing corpus here, I believe that the framework suggested in this chapter can be used to critically examine his work as well.

lated the distinctiveness of this theoretical task in his prolegomena to a theory of social crisis, and he has concretized it in a study of the capitalist and patrimonial origins of the English Revolution (Gould 1987). Lechner (1985, 1989) has used differentiation theory to find indicators for contemporary fundamentalist movements and for structural reactions against modernity more generally. Mayhew (1984, 1989) has developed a notion of the differentiated public as corresponding to the early modern origins of capitalist society.

Other developments have been directed more to Durkheim's second book, to linking differentiation to specific theories of institutional behavior and processes of change. Champagne (1989) has formulated a complex model for explaining the failure and success of differentiation in particular American Indian societies, and Rhoades (1989) has explained why the differentiation of higher education systems has been blocked by the nationally specific organization of professional and governmental spheres. Colomy (1982, 1985, 1989a) has developed the most ambitious program in this regard. Elaborating a theory of "uneven structural differentiation," he has explained the actual paths differentiation has taken in terms of the "institutional projects" developed by strategic social groups. He explains the forces that form these projects in a systematic way and distinguishes between institutional entrepreneurs, conservatives, and accommodationists.

There still remains too large a gap between this new wave of differentiation theory and the actual strains and conflicts that characterize change in the contemporary world. Obviously, social science must separate itself from the direct preoccupations of everyday life. However, a clear and identifiable linkage must be made, especially in theorizing about social change. Only this connection anchors theorizing in the effervescence of everyday life, and only this value-relevance makes such theorizing compelling as well as true. I close with some illustrations of the linkages I have in mind.

Even in relatively developed countries, the autonomy of the societal community—its differentiation from religious, primordial, political, and economic spheres—is tentative. In liberal capitalist nations, for example, the media of mass communication are often still partly fused with political, economic, and ethnic groupings (Alexander 1980). Even when a certain autonomy is achieved, moreover, social stability may not be the result. Similarly, even in societal communities that are relatively differentiated, particularistically defined core groups continue to occupy privileged positions (Alexander 1980). Because exclusion from this core on religious, ethnic, and social class grounds remains, struggles for inclusion are not bounded episodes but are permanent and inescapable features of modern life.

It is possible to argue, in other words, that in contemporary "modern" societies differentiation still has a very long way to go. Contemporary activities in virtually every social sphere can be understood in this way. Thus, although there is no doubt that kinship and blood have vastly receded in civilizational terms, the significance of gender in almost every area of modern society demonstrates that much fusion remains. Feminist movements can be seen, in these terms, as efforts to differentiate kinship and biology from evaluations of competence and hence from the distribution of economic, political, and cultural goods (see Walzer 1983, 227–42). Current struggles for workers' control and participation can be seen in much the same way. Although public governments in democratic societies have gained some independence from economic control, private governments—for example, the organization of power in factories and organizations—remain dominated by market criteria in corporate economic life (Walzer 1983, 281–312). How sharply private government can be differentiated remains to be seen, but an autonomous political and participatory sphere can certainly be extended (Siriani 1981).

To recognize that differentiation is a process that is carried by contemporary movements of social change suggests that differentiation theory needs to elaborate a conception of social polarization. Differentiation is demanded by coalitions of elites and masses, and it is opposed by other coalitions that benefit from less differentiated structural and cultural arrangements. In the course of this polarization, crises emerge (Alexander 1984). Depending on the structural setting, revolution, reform, or reaction will be the result (Alexander 1981b).

The refusal to identify differentiation with the Western status quo, and the access to a more systematic understanding of conflict that this refusal opens up, is demonstrated in the most dramatic manner when attention is shifted from the domestic to the international plane. As I have intimated above, the emergence of more powerful and adaptive social systems not only has been stimulated by war-making but has in turn laid the basis for much more continuous, widely diffused, and deadly warfare (see Collins 1986a). Not only can the intranational causes of war become an object of differentiation theory; the international social control of war can as well. The world system is not only an economic order but also a social one. Differentiation theory suggests that social systems can control conflict only through the creation of relatively autonomous regulatory mechanisms. From this perspective the contemporary world system remains in a primitive and archaic form. Primordial solidarities are dominant and the possibilities for intrasystemic regulation are only regionally conceived. The relationship between this deficient regulatory system and war constitutes a vital but virtually unexplored topic for differentiation theory. War will be eliminated only to the degree that the world system replicates the processes of differentiation—incomplete as they are—that have transformed the framework of national societies.

Contemporary struggles and strains need not be conceived only in terms of the structural and cultural fusions that remain. The achievement of differentiation does not do away with social problems, but rather shifts them to a different plane. Even when news media are independent, for example, they are subject to dramatic fluctuations in their trustworthiness (Alexander 1981a), and they can magnify and distort contemporary information as a result. The competition that ensues between autonomous media and other powerful institutions, moreover, generates manifold possibilities for corruption. Similar strains affect the relationship between autonomous universities and their host societies. Once the university has become committed to defending the autonomy of scientific or cognitive rationality, conflicts about the university's moral obligations to society can take on new and extraordinarily vexing forms (Alexander 1986).

In social science general theories are never disproved. Rather, like the proverbial soldiers of old, they simply fade away. For quite a few years it looked as if this would be the fate of differentiation theory. In this chapter I have argued that this is not the case. I have suggested that the difficulties it has faced are the same as those encountered by every ambitious theory of social change, and after examining Durkheim's classic work, *The Division of Labor in Society,* I have called these difficulties "Durkheim's problem." Parsons's revisions of Durkheim's original contribution went beyond the substance of Durkheim's theorizing in many ways, but they did not overcome Durkheim's problem in a more generic sense. Indeed, in critical respects Parsons did not face this problem nearly as well. Weberian ideas have addressed this problem in important ways but have neglected other aspects at the same time. Marxism addresses Durkheim's problem most successfully of all, but its empirical implausibility, I have suggested, undermines its considerable theoretical power. In response to these difficulties, and to internally generated revisions as well, a new round of differentiation theory has begun. That it addresses Durkheim's problem more effectively is certain. Whether it can solve his problem and retain its verisimilitude remains to be seen.

REFERENCES

Alexander, Jeffrey C. 1978. Formal and substantive voluntarism in the work of Talcott Parsons. *American Sociological Review* 43:177–98.
———. 1980. Core solidarity, ethnic outgroup and structural differentiation: Toward a multidimensional model of inclusion in modern societies. In *Na-*

tional and ethnic movements, ed. Jacques Dofny and Akinsola Akiwowo, 5–28. Beverly Hills: Sage.

————. 1981a. The mass news media in systemic, historical, and comparative perspective. In *Mass media and social change,* ed. Elihu Katz and Thomas Szecsko, 17–52. Beverly Hills: Sage.

————. 1981b. Revolution, reaction, and reform: The change theory of Parsons's middle period. *Sociological Inquiry* 5:267–80.

————. 1983. *Theoretical logic in sociology.* Vol. 4, *The modern reconstruction of classical thought: Talcott Parsons.* Berkeley: University of California Press.

————. 1984. Three models of culture/society relations: Toward an analysis of the Watergate crisis. *Sociological Theory* 2:290–314.

————, ed. 1985. *Neofunctionalism.* Beverly Hills: Sage.

————. 1986. The university and morality: A revised approach to university autonomy and its limits. *Journal of Higher Education* 57, no. 5:463–76.

————. 1987. The dialectic of individuation and domination: Max Weber's rationalization theory and beyond. In *Max Weber, rationality and modernity,* ed. Sam Whimster and Scott Lash. London: Allen and Unwin.

————. 1989. Introduction. In *Differentiation theory and social change,* ed. Jeffrey C. Alexander and Paul Colomy, 1–15. New York: Columbia University Press.

Alexander, Jeffrey C., and Paul Colomy. 1985. Towards neofunctionalism: Eisenstadt's change theory and symbolic interactionism. *Sociological Theory* 3:11–23.

————, eds. 1989. *Differentiation theory and social change.* New York: Columbia University Press.

Baran, Paul, and Paul Sweezy. 1966. *Monopoly capital.* New York: Monthly Review.

Beetham, David. 1974. *Max Weber and the theory of modern politics.* London: Allen and Unwin.

Bellah, Robert N. 1969. *Beyond belief.* New York: Random House.

Bendix, Reinhard. 1961. *Max Weber: An intellectual portrait.* New York: Doubleday Anchor.

————. 1964. *Nation-building and citizenship.* New York: Doubleday Anchor.

Brubaker, Rogers. 1984. *The limits of rationality: An essay on the social and moral thought of Max Weber.* London: Allen and Unwin.

Champagne, Dwayne. 1989. Culture, differentiation, and environment: Social change in Tlingit society. In *Differentiation theory and social change,* ed. Jeffrey C. Alexander and Paul Colomy, 52–87. New York: Columbia University Press.

Collins, Randall. 1975. *Conflict sociology.* New York: Academic Press.

————. 1986a. *Sociological theory, disaster research, and war.* Paper delivered at symposium, Social Structure and Disaster, 15–16 May, at College of William and Mary, Williamsburg, Va.

————. 1986b. *Weberian sociological theory.* Cambridge: Cambridge University Press.

Colomy, Paul. 1982. Stunted differentiation: A sociological examination of political elites in Virginia, 1720–1850. Ph.D. diss., Department of Sociology, University of California at Los Angeles.

————. 1985. Uneven differentiation. In *Neofunctionalism,* ed. Jeffrey C. Alexander, 131–56. Beverly Hills: Sage.

————. 1989a. Revision and progress in differentiation theory. In *Differentiation theory and social change*, ed. Jeffrey C. Alexander and Paul Colomy, 465–95. New York: Columbia University Press.

————. 1989b. Strategic groups and political differentiation in the antebellum United States. In *Differentiation theory and social change*, ed. Jeffrey C. Alexander and Paul Colomy, 222–64. New York: Columbia University Press.

Durkheim, Emile. [1893] 1933. *The division of labor in society.* New York: Free Press.

————. [1938] 1977. *The evolution of educational thought.* London: Routledge and Kegan Paul.

Eisenstadt, S. N. 1963. *The political system of empires.* New York: Free Press.

————. 1964. Institutionalization and social change. *American Sociological Review* 29:235–47.

————. 1982. The axial age: The emergence of transcendental visions and the rise of clerics. *European Journal of Sociology* 23:294–314.

————. 1986. *A sociological approach to comparative civilizations: The development and directions of a research program.* Jerusalem: Hebrew University.

Evans, Peter B., Dietrich Rueschemeyer, and Theda Skocpol, eds. 1985. *Bringing the state back in.* Cambridge: Cambridge University Press.

Gamson, William. 1968. *Power and discontent.* Homewood, Ill.: Dorsey Press.

Giddens, Anthony, 1981. *A contemporary critique of historical materialism.* Vol. 1, *Power, property and the state.* Berkeley: University of California Press.

————. 1986. *A contemporary critique of historical materialism.* Vol. 2, *The nation-state and violence.* London: Macmillan.

Gould, Mark. 1985. Prolegomena to future theories of societal crisis. In *Neofunctionalism*, ed. Jeffrey C. Alexander, 57–71. Beverly Hills: Sage.

————. 1987. *Revolution in the development of capitalism.* Berkeley: University of California Press.

Gouldner, Alvin W. 1979. *The new class.* New York: Seabury.

Gusfield, Joseph. 1963. *Symbolic crusade.* Champaign-Urbana: University of Illinois Press.

Habermas, Jurgen. 1984. *The theory of communicative action.* Vol. 1. Boston: Beacon Press.

Kuhn, Thomas. 1969. *The structure of scientific revolutions.* Chicago: University of Chicago Press.

Lakatos, Imre. 1969. Criticism and the methodology of scientific research programmes. *Proceedings of the Aristotelian Society* 69:149–86.

Lechner, Frank. 1985. Modernity and its discontents. In *Neofunctionalism*, ed. Jeffrey C. Alexander, 157–76. Beverly Hills: Sage.

————. 1989. Fundamentalism and sociocultural revitalization: On the logic of dedifferentiation. In *Differentiation theory and social change*, ed. Jeffrey C. Alexander and Paul Colomy, 88–118. New York: Columbia University Press.

Luhmann, Niklas. 1981. *The differentiation of society.* New York: Columbia University Press.

————. 1987. The evolutionary differentiation between society and interaction. In *The micro-macro link*, ed. J. Alexander, B. Giesen, R. Münch, and N. Smelser, 112–31. Berkeley: University of California Press.

MacNeill, William H. 1982. *The pursuit of power: Technology, armed force, and society since A.D. 1000.* Chicago: University of Chicago Press.

Maier, Charles. 1975. *Recasting bourgeois Europe.* Princeton: Princeton University Press.

Mayhew, Leon. 1984. In defense of modernity: Talcott Parsons and the utilitarian tradition. *American Journal of Sociology* 89: 1273–1305.

———. 1989. The differentiation of the solidary public. In *Differentiation theory and social change,* ed. Jeffrey C. Alexander and Paul Colomy, 294–322. New York: Columbia University Press.

Moore, Barrington. 1966. *The social origins of dictatorship and democracy.* Boston: Beacon Press.

Münch, Richard. 1982. Talcott Parsons and the theory of action. Part 2. *American Journal of Sociology* 87:771–826.

———. 1989. Differentiation, rationalization, and interpenetration: Three basic features of the emergence of modern societies. In *Differentiation theory and social change,* ed. Jeffrey C. Alexander and Paul Colomy, 441–64. New York: Columbia University Press.

Nisbet, Robert. 1969. *Social change and history.* London: Oxford University Press.

Parsons, Talcott. 1951. *The social system.* New York: Free Press.

———. 1954a. Certain primary sources and patterns of aggression in the social structure of the Western world. In *Essays in sociological theory,* by Talcott Parsons, 298–322. New York: Free Press.

———. 1954b. *Essays in sociological theory.* New York: Free Press.

———. [1960] 1967. Durkheim's contribution to the theory of integration of social systems. In *Sociological theory and modern society,* by Talcott Parsons, 3–34. New York: Free Press.

———. 1966. *Societies: Evolutionary and comparative perspectives.* Englewood Cliffs, N.J.: Prentice-Hall.

———. 1971. *The system of modern societies.* Englewood Cliffs, N.J.: Prentice-Hall.

Rhoades, Gary. 1989. Political competition and differentiation in higher education. In *Differentiation theory and social change,* ed. Jeffrey C. Alexander and Paul Colomy, 187–221. New York: Columbia University Press.

Robertson, Roland. 1978. *Meaning and change: Explorations in the cultural sociology of modern societies.* New York: Oxford University Press.

Rueschemeyer, Dietrich. 1977. Structural differentiation, efficiency, and power. *American Journal of Sociology* 83: 1–25.

Schluchter, Wolfgang. 1979. The paradoxes of rationalization. In *Max Weber's vision of history,* ed. Guenther Roth and Wolfgang Schluchter, 11–64. Berkeley: University of California Press.

———. 1981. *The rise of Western rationalism: Max Weber's developmental history.* Berkeley: University of California Press.

Sewell, William H., Jr. 1980. *Work and revolution in France: The language of labor from the Old Regime to 1848.* Cambridge: Cambridge University Press.

Siriani, Carmen. 1981. Production and power in a classless society: A critical analysis of the utopian dimensions of Marxist theory. *Socialist Review* 59:33–82.

Skocpol, Theda. 1979. *States and social revolutions.* New York: Cambridge University Press.

Smelser, Neil J. 1959. *Social change in the industrial revolution.* Chicago: University of Chicago Press.

———. 1963. *The sociology of economic life.* Englewood Cliffs, N.J.: Prentice-Hall.

———. 1973. Epilogue: Social structural dimensions of higher education. In *The American university,* ed. Talcott Parsons and Gerald Platt, 389–422. Cambridge: Harvard University Press.

———. 1974. Growth, structural change, and conflict in California higher education, 1950–1970. In *Public higher education in California,* ed. Neil J. Smelser and Gabriel Almond, 9–141. Berkeley: University of California Press.

———. 1985. Evaluating the model of structural differentiation in relation to educational change in the nineteenth century. In *Neofunctionalism,* ed. Jeffrey C. Alexander, 113–30. Beverly Hills: Sage.

Smith, Anthony. 1973. *The concept of social change: A critique of the functionalist theory of change.* London: Routledge and Kegan Paul.

Tilly, Charles. 1967. *The Vendée.* New York: Wiley.

Touraine, Alain, François Dubet, Michel Wieviorka, and Jan Strzelecki. 1983. *Solidarity: The analysis of a social movement: Poland, 1980–1981.* Cambridge: Cambridge University Press and Paris: Editions de la Maison des Sciences de l'Homme.

Turner, Ralph H. 1964. Collective behavior and conflict. *Sociological Quarterly* 5:122–32.

Wagner, David G., and Joseph Berger. 1985. Do sociological theories grow? *American Journal of Sociology* 90:697–728.

Wallerstein, Immanuel. 1974. *The modern world-system.* New York: Academic Press.

Walzer, Michael. 1983. *Spheres of justice.* New York: Basic.

Weber, Max. [1918] 1978. Socialism. In *Max Weber: Selections in translation,* ed. W. G. Runciman, 251–62. London: Cambridge University Press.

———. [1920] 1958. Author's introduction. In *The Protestant ethic and the spirit of capitalism,* 13–31. New York: Scribners.

The Infrastructure of Modernity
Indirect Social Relationships, Information Technology, and Social Integration

Craig Calhoun

SOCIAL RELATIONSHIPS AND SOCIAL INTEGRATION

During the last decade the reemergence of human geography as a vital field of social science has brought renewed attention to the spatial organization of social relationships (see, e.g., Gregory and Urry 1985). Over a slightly longer time span network studies have brought new power and sophistication to the analysis of concrete patterns of social relationships.[1] These advances draw attention to a weak spot in contemporary social theory. The study of structures of social relationships, that is, the concrete connections among social actors, has not been used to improve our understanding of social integration. Those focusing on structural analysis have failed to show how patterns of relationships constitute social life and hold social institutions and populations together; they have thrown out the problematic of social integration like a baby in dirtily functionalist bathwater. Functionalists have turned to cultural understandings of social integration, but these analyses at best

An earlier version of this chapter was presented to the Second Annual German-American Conference on Sociological Theory, "Social Change and Modernity," 26–28 August 1986. The author is grateful for comments from those who attended the conference and would also like to thank Pamela DeLargy, Bart Dredge, Anthony Giddens, and Jeffrey Weintraub.

1. The advances in network studies have been primarily methodological and only to a lesser extent empirical; it is tendentious to speak of network "theory." Contemporary network studies in sociology are often conducted in atheoretical, positivistic terms, but they draw at least implicitly on a range of structuralist and economic individualist or utilitarian theories. The modern network approach had its origins, and some of its most substantively fruitful work, in structural-functionalist anthropology. See Barnes 1954, Mitchell 1969, and Nadel 1957. Nadel, in particular, was both theoretically oriented and sophisticated. The main modern attempt to trace the theoretical foundations of network studies is that of Burt (1982).

omit and at worst obscure attention to the concrete patterns of social relationships.[2]

This failure, or even refusal, to approach social integration on the basis of patterns of concrete relationships is common to work in a wide range of otherwise divergent theoretical perspectives. Relational structures are too narrowly sociological a concern for many cultural theorists. For others the idea of social integration as a variable is too reminiscent of crude contrasts of *Gemeinschaft* and *Gesellschaft*. It seems too normative to many theorists (including some who treat utilitarianism as value free) and too vague and unmeasurable to others. In what is perhaps the foremost contemporary effort to develop a theory of social integration, Habermas (1984) focuses on a distinction between social integration/lifeworld and system integration/system in which concrete social relationships are seen as the stuff of the former, and the latter is conceived in cybernetic rather than social-relational terms.[3] In functionalist accounts integration is usually conceptualized as a system state that is partially dependent on interaction patterns but distinct from these patterns. Clearly, in Parsons's sense (e.g., 1951), the extent of integration of a social system cannot be reduced to relational structures. However, in this chapter I contend that such relational structures have been neglected compared to other aspects of integration and that they have been conceptualized in ways that focus on face-to-face interaction and obscure the fact that mediated relationships are still social relationships.

Before we can explain social change satisfactorily we need a clearer conception of the relational dimension of social integration and the beginnings of a descriptive account of variation in concrete social relationships. The contribution of social relationships to social integration may be taken loosely as the complex variable measuring the extent to which the action of each person in a population implies, depends on, or predicts that of the others.[4] Of course, the extent of social integration is not the only product

2. I refer not only to Parsonian functionalism but also to Lévi-Straussian, or linguistic, structuralism insofar as work in either vein proposes to find in culture an autonomous level of logical and/or functional integration. This point is true even of Sahlins (1978) despite his intention to break fully from the functionalist problematic.

3. "Thus there is a competition *not between the types of action* oriented to understanding and to success, *but between principles of societal integration*. . . . The rationalization of the lifeworld makes possible a kind of systemic integration that enters into competition with the integrating principle of reaching understanding and, under certain conditions, has a disintegrative effect on the lifeworld" (Habermas 1984, 342–43, emphasis in original).

4. Note that this definition in no way requires sentiments of affection or solidarity as to common purposes or values. These are perhaps likely where social integration is great (both as results and as supports) but so are dissensus, anger, and resentment. The key is stable mutual determination, not pleasure in shared company. Note also that this definition examines the contribution of social relationships to social integration. Although social

of variation in social relationships. These relationships may vary qualitatively in kind, quantitatively in density, and both qualitatively and quantitatively in pattern (including relative boundedness). The key is that we neither ignore concrete relationships nor privilege them as exclusively communal, and that we not leave large-scale organizations to representations in reified, actionless terms.[5] I argue that, by paying attention to patterns of social relationships, we can provide a strictly sociological dimension to complement accounts of the contemporary age in terms of cultural and/or economic tendencies, 'modernity' and/or capitalism.

The first part of this chapter returns to the classical conceptions of modernity, which group cultural, economic, and social structural dimensions together more or less indiscriminately. I suggest a conceptual distinction between direct and indirect relationships that can help to illuminate many of the changes evocatively suggested by *Gemeinschaft* vs. *Gesellschaft* and similar oppositions while retaining a much clearer potential for empirical specification. Taking large-scale markets and especially corporations as examples, I show the utility of this simple conceptualization by focusing on the distinctive features of key modern social institutions. At least one of these institutions, the corporation, has been given surprisingly short shrift in sociological theory. One of the constitutive features of the modern age, I argue, is the ever-increasing prevalence of indirect social relationships, that is, those relationships constituted through the media-

---

integration is a broader concept than social relationships, I am arguing that more of social integration can be understood through relational analysis than is conventionally assumed. What Parsons termed the "media of interchange" (Parsons and Platt 1973, 23–25) help to constitute an infrastructure of social integration. Even very generalized media (like money) can be understood in concretely social relational rather than cybernetic terms. Where Parsons's concept of integration thematizes the issues of internal control and self-regulation of a social system, the present argument about social relations addresses a crucial source of capacity for control and regulation without treating these cybernetically as system properties. The control and regulation may often be intentional and sometimes arbitrary exercises of power. Using the same infrastructural capacity, they may as readily be destructive of harmonious relations among actors (e.g., in Habermas's sense of the destruction of life-world integration based on mutual understanding [see n. 3]) or among subsystems of social action (in Parson's sense) as constructive of them.

5. Part of Habermas's reason for maintaining his strong distinction between life-world and system is to leave a grounding for hope that the communicative constitution of relationships in the life-world can embody the potential for social transformation or (at least) resistance against the encroachments of the system. This is problematic (a) because it tends to accept a reified view of the system rather than to theorize it in a way that aims simultaneously to reveal and explain this reification, and (b) because it tends to overestimate the extent to which actually existing concrete social relationships can be understood as manifesting the ideal of communicative action. In this connection Fraser (1985) has suggested how Habermas's conception leaves little room for recognizing the mutual constitution of life-world and system, as for example in the way in which gender relations and identities are reproduced.

tion of large-scale markets, administrative organizations, and/or information technology. More and more these relationships are coming to be the basis on which society "at large" is constituted. This does not mean, however, that direct relationships are disappearing or losing their emotional potency for individuals, only that they are becoming compartmentalized and therefore altered in sociological significance.

The second section of the chapter links this analysis of the changing patterns of social relationships to changes in infrastructural—especially transportation and communication—technologies. Sociological and economic accounts of new technologies tend to focus disproportionately on production technologies and their effects on the labor force. I suggest that infrastructural technologies are at least as important and that the infrastructural uses of such new technologies as computers hold at least as much potential for social change. Such change, however, at present (and for the plausibly foreseeable future) seems to lie primarily in the extension of the trends of the last two hundred or more years, including the increasing importance of indirect social relationships, not in a reversal of these trends. In other words, modernity continues; we are not undergoing an epochal transformation comparable to that ushered in by industrial capitalism.[6]

The third section follows directly from this point and examines why terms like "postindustrial society" are exaggerations and points out a key sociological weakness of the theories on which they rest: failure of these theories to develop an account of what constitutes society in a postindustrial (or any other) age. In other words, lacking an account of social relationships, theories such as Bell's (1973, 1979) describe features of society but not society itself. In this failure, perhaps ironically, these theories fail to make use of openings to social-relational analysis and the problematic of social integration provided by the very functionalist theories with which they are often lumped by critics and on other parts of which they (like their progenitors in theories of industrial society) depend.

The last section of the paper takes up the Marxist account of capitalism. I try to show that however strong the Marxist theory of capitalism, it must remain a theory of part but not all of social life. Marxism lacks a theory of concrete social relationships (even though it offers a powerful theory of abstract relationships such as those mediated through the commodity

6. This conclusion is true, I would suggest, in terms of both cultural and economic dimensions as well as social-relational dimensions (although there is no intrinsic reason why the three must always covary). Cultural accounts of postmodernism tend (a) to exaggerate the contemporary novelty of antimodernist movements, which in fact have a history as old as modernity, and (b) to neglect the continuing importance of such cultural tendencies as the privileging of quantity over quality or of accounts of change over those of continuity (the latter tendency being one that these accounts themselves often exhibit).

form). It offers an account of the dynamic tendencies that capitalism imposes on modern social actors, but not an account of social integration.[7]

FROM KINSHIP AND COMMUNITY TO MARKETS AND CORPORATIONS

Contrasts between country and city were a staple of nineteenth- and early-twentieth-century social commentary (Williams 1973). Nearly everyone preferred the country. The country was clean, while the chimneys of city factories belched black smoke; the country was morally pure, while cities were dens of iniquity; perhaps most important, country dwellers enjoyed true community and social order, while cities were chaotic, unregulated, and anonymous. Early social theorists believed that cities somehow embodied the core features of a new kind of society, and this new society contrasted sharply with the previous, more communally solidaristic social order. Today, however, Tönnies's (1887) *Gemeinschaft-Gesellschaft* contrast, Wirth's (1938) and Redfield's (1941) folk-urban continuum, and other contrasts of tradition and modernity are as familiar as objects of abuse as they are as mandatory bits of vocabulary in introductory sociology textbooks. Those who attack this approach generally focus on the community or tradition side of the dichotomy (e.g., Gusfield 1967, 1975). They argue that the depictions by Tönnies and others of traditional community life are nostalgic and unrealistic; they also note that the portrayal of most of the Third World as traditional rather than modern is both patronizing and predisposed to neglect the extent to which contemporary Third World patterns are produced by modern capitalism and international relations.[8]

Surprisingly, the sociological inadequacies of Tönnies's (and others') conception of *Gesellschaft* have not received comparable comment; the same goes for most of the other well-known binary oppositions.[9] The

---

7. Marxism's lack of an account of social integration is not simply the result of the fact that Marxist class theory suggests fundamental social contradictions whereas Parsons and other functionalists consider the stratification system to be primarily integrative. The problematic of social integration is not developed in Marx's work or most Marxism. Indeed, the concrete relational dimension to internal class solidarity is not much developed by Marx; when it has been studied by other Marxists, the theoretical or conceptual bases have been drawn from outside Marxism and often have been left in unclear relationship to Marx's more central categorial theory of capitalism.

8. This voluminous literature has been reviewed recently by Worsley (1985). The arguments of Wallerstein (1974, 1979) and Frank (1969, 1978) are perhaps the most prominent. Calhoun (1978, 1980, 1983) tries to salvage something of the notions of community and tradition from these critical dismissals and from the genuine nostalgia, paternalism, and error found in earlier formulations.

9. The one real exception to this contention is the Marxist critique that most of these conceptions neglect the centrality of capitalism to "modernity" or *Gesellschaft*.

impact of the transition from *Gemeinschaft* to *Gesellschaft* in Tönnies's conceptualization was largely the loss of a felt sense of belonging together in favor of an exaggerated individualism and a focus on instrumental relations. Tönnies had little social-structural foundation for his notion of changed personal experience, which accordingly remained unsatisfactorily impressionistic.[10] Simmel's analysis of "the metropolis and mental life" made a good deal more of the change in concrete social relationships that accompanied the emerging social psychology of urban life ([1903] 1971]). His attention, however, was focused on the larger issue of the development of individuality in the modern West. His characterization of cities, along with most of the other famous typologies of tradition and modernity, offered only a very general view, one that was lacking in historical specificity—or rather, one that failed to recognize the historical specificity implicit in its apparently general account (Abu-Lughod 1969). To be more precise about the experience—let alone the sociological significance—of modern urban life, we need to go beyond such broad statements about sociopsychological differences to a specific analysis of change in the structure and the kind of social relationships.

Almost all major premodern forms of social organization depended primarily on direct interpersonal relationships. Kinship, community life, and even the most stable, recurrent relationships of economic exchange all took place within the conscious awareness, and usually the face-to-face copresence, of human individuals. Such relationships might be more or less systematic and complex: for example, webs of kinship can link hundreds of thousands of members of traditional African societies. However, the actualization of each relationship, as opposed to its latent potential, was normally directly interpersonal. Although state apparatuses certainly predate the modern era (and occurred historically throughout the world), Giddens is surely right to argue that few if any were able to "govern" in the modern sense of the word; their capacity for regularized administration of a territory and its residents was very limited.[11] This limitation was largely the result of the fact that power relations could not be extended

10. It was partly to avoid this sort of impressionistic account that human ecology went to the opposite extreme in borrowing models from biology and developing a highly "objective" account that purported to treat cities as wholes without reference to their constituent interpersonal relationships. Hence the key variables in human ecology became population, organization, ecology, and technology. See Duncan 1959 and Hawley 1950, 1981. Haines (1985) has offered a cogent critique of this biological emergentism and the human ecologists' corresponding neglect of alternative "relational" approaches to their subject matter.

11. Giddens 1985, 63. Such "administrative power can only become established if the coding of information is actually applied in a direct way to the supervision of human activities, so as to detach them in some part from their involvement with tradition and with local community life" (Giddens 1985b, 47).

effectively over large distances.[12] Although their cultural variation was enormous and their variation in specific patterns of social organization was considerable, premodern peoples were only rarely able to produce the physical infrastructure and administrative practices that are necessary to build large-scale social organization of much intensity.

The direct relationships that prevailed included both "primary" and "secondary" ones, to use Cooley's language ([1909] 1962).[13] Useful though it may be for some purposes, Cooley's conceptual distinction does not differentiate the modern age adequately from its predecessors. Modernity is not constituted by the presence of secondary relationships or the absence of primary relationships; both sorts exist in a wide range of modern and nonmodern societies. Rather modernity is distinguished by the increasing frequency, scale, and importance of indirect social relationships. Large-scale markets, closely administered organizations, and information technologies have produced vastly more opportunities for such relationships than existed in any premodern society. This trend does not mean that direct relationships have been reduced in number or that they are less meaningful or attractive to individuals. Rather it means that direct relationships tend to be compartmentalized. They persist as part of the immediate life-world of individuals, both as the nexus of certain kinds of instrumental activities (e.g., the many personal relationships that smooth the way for or make possible business transactions [see Granovetter 1985]) and, especially, as the realm of private life (family, friends, and neighbors). However, direct interpersonal relationships organize less and less of public life, that is, fewer and fewer of the crucially determinant institutions controlling material resources and exercising social power. Indirect relationships do not eliminate direct ones, but they

12. This point was recognized some time ago by Innis ([1950] 1972) in his arguments about the centrality of space-transcending communications media to the building of empires.

13. Cooley's opposition was between relationships that linked people merely as the enactors of specific social roles and those that involved whole persons, linked to each other in ways that transcended the fragmentation of life into different spheres. See also the discussion in Nisbet and Perrin 1977. Cooley's version of the *Gemeinschaft-Gesellschaft* dichotomy implied a Rousseauian critique of the inauthenticity of secondary relationships. This and other criticisms that secondary relationships are less fulfilling, less meaningful, and weaker than primary relationships are central to the concepts of primary and secondary relationships as they have commonly been used. Cooley's conceptualization exists to describe an expansion in the number of relationships that is accompanied by a deterioration in their meaningful content and social strength. There may be something to this critique, but it would be better to make the issue one of the relative importance of each sort of relationship in organizing various kinds of activities, to recognize that secondary relationships are central to public life and democratic political participation, and to keep in mind the distinctive difference between both sorts of directly interpersonal relationships, on the one hand, and indirect relationships, on the other hand.

change both their meaning and their sociological significance.[14] Although they are as sociopsychologically and culturally powerful as ever, direct relationships are no longer constitutive of society at its widest reaches.[15]

The growing importance of indirect relationships was recognized by both Marx and Weber. For Marx these relationships characterized above

14. For a general discussion of some of the distinctive features of face-to-face relationships in contrast to mediated ones see Meyrowitz 1985. For example, nonmediated relationships are more easily clustered, he suggests, so that individuals can communicate in different styles and contents to different groups:

> The combination of many different audiences is a rare occurrence in face-to-face interaction, and even when it occurs (at a wedding, for example) people can usually expect the speedy resumption of private isolated interactions. Electronic media, however, have rearranged many social forums so that most people now find themselves in contact with others in new ways. . . . And the merger of different audiences and situations through radio and television has made it difficult for national politicians to say very specific things to particular constituencies or to behave differently in different social situations. (Meyrowitz 1985, 5)

This observation seems quite true, but Meyrowitz's account is biased toward broadcast media (rather than computers and other electronic media that use numbers, text, and other more abstract codes). Although broadcast media may indeed maintain a kind of surveillance over public figures that shapes their behavior and eliminates certain "privacies," two qualifications seem in order. First, earlier modes of social control may have been at least as powerful in forcing individuals to adhere to constant standards of rectitude in their behavior. Television cameras may never have invaded Victorian gentlemen's clubs or brothels to embarrass their patrons, but standards of public propriety in dress, speech, and the like allowed less flexibility in many regards even though enforcement was only through direct observation. (Giddens's [1985b] Foucault-inspired account of the growing capacity for surveillance is similarly not complemented by attention to either more informal means of social control or changing opportunities for political participation.) Second, computerized communications allow a great deal of tailoring of messages to specific audiences, as any recipient of direct-mail political advertisements knows. Where candidates speaking on television must appeal to a certain common denominator of "the general public," those targeting various population categories for funding can shape each appeal in a distinctive, perhaps quite contradictory way. An elaborate variety of statistical and other consulting services help candidates know just which issues to stress with mailing lists of churchgoers, veterans, schoolteachers, people of high incomes, parents of school-age children, or any of a hundred other segments into which the population of potential donors may be categorized. Although it is a bit dated (particularly with regard to the computerization of direct mail), Sabato 1981 is probably the best general account of this phenomenon.

15. This situation is one source of modern populist politics—the politics of local communities and traditional cultural values. It is a potent kind of politics, and it offers potentially radical and important visions of alternative modes of social organization. Many of its variants, however, are based on some combination of (1) systematic misrecognition of the opportunities for local autonomy available in a world structured largely by large-scale organizations of indirect social relationships, and (2) systematically biased analogies between the world of direct personal relationships and that of large-scale organizations of indirect relationships (e.g., "balancing the U.S. budget is just like balancing your family checkbook").

all the system of commodity production and capital accumulation. For Weber the commodity form was also key, but, characteristically, market rather than production relations were central; the "indirect exchange of money" was prototypical:

> Within the market community every act of exchange, especially monetary exchange, is not directed, in isolation, by the action of the individual partner to the particular transaction, but the more rationally it is considered, the more it is directed by the actions of all parties potentially interested in the exchange. The market community as such is the most impersonal form of practical life into which humans can enter with one another. This is not due to that potentiality of struggle among the interested parties which is inherent in the market relationship. Any human relationship, even the most intimate, and even though it be marked by the most unqualified personal devotion, is in some sense relative and may involve a struggle with the partner. . . . The reason for the impersonality of the market is its matter-of-factness, its orientation to the commodity and only to that. When the market is allowed to follow its own autonomous tendencies, its participants do not look toward the persons of each other but only toward the commodity; there are no obligations of brotherliness or reverence, and none of those spontaneous human relations that are sustained by personal unions. (Weber [1922] 1978, 636)

Weber's ideal-typical market does not correspond to any actuality, of course, any more than Marx's pure model of capitalism does. But each expresses a distinctly modern tendency.

Weber's analysis of bureaucracy suggests another such tendency: the creation of social apparatuses for rational administration. Weber tended to assume that bureaucracies would be sociogeographically concentrated; he associated them with cities and treated their development as a specification and enhancement of the role of cities as centers for the exercise of power. In fact Weber wrote at about the point in Western history when cities began to lose some of their distinctive centrality to systems of power and administration.[16] In ancient empires, dispersed city-states, and late-feudal Europe alike, cities had been at the heart not only (obviously) of civilization but also of both power relations and trade. Cities were the nodes that could anchor structures of indirect relationships in an age of minimal information technology. They could provide for mediation among participants in far-flung markets, and they were

---

16. Thus Weber was one of the many classical sociologists who together placed urban studies at the heart of sociology without recognizing the historical specificity of the centrality of cities, especially to the period of the transition to modern capitalism and nation-states. See Saunders 1985 for an argument that this error is at least partially repeated (with less excuse) by the geographers and sociologists who would make the spatial analysis of social relationships a field of its own.

the focal points for political and military control. As a result, they created networks of power and exchange stretching well beyond their boundaries. Moreover, they provided (and to a considerable extent still provide) for the direct relationships that make systems of indirect relationships work (the personal relationships that connect banking houses, for example, and the direct communications among central government officials).[17] Cities also provided for public life, which is composed of direct—although not necessarily intimate—relationships among strangers (Sennett 1977; Calhoun 1986). But the development of modern transportation and communications technologies, on the one hand, and the growing administrative organization and power of the state, on the other, meant that both economic and political activity could begin to bypass the cities.[18]

In short, state power could grow because the new forms of organization and the improved transportation and communications infrastructures (based partly on new technologies but, at first, more on heavy investments in the extension of old methods) enabled the spread of increasingly effective administration throughout the various territories of a country. This is the story Giddens (1985b) offers as the centerpiece of his critique of historical materialism, and it is a necessary complement to Marx's analysis of capitalism. It is a crucial complement, but it is not sufficient.

A full account needs to recognize, first, that the growth of the state, like the capitalist economy, developed infrastructures that could be used by ordinary people to develop connections with each other. Roads, trains, telegraphs, and telephones furthered the social integration of dispersed populations, promoted their common participation in capitalist production and exchange, and made possible their common subjection to state surveillance and administration. Class struggle itself, in the sense of the mobilization of workers organized on the same socio-

17. Ancient and early-modern cities relied much more on these direct relationships because they lacked the material and organizational infrastructures to do otherwise. Written communications were the only means of transcending the spatial and temporal limits of copresence—and literacy was not widespread, especially outside the cities. In countries of limited infrastructural technology and organization cities still appear to be largely aggregations of smaller populations linked almost exclusively by direct interpersonal relationships. Cities remain central (and often swell beyond their ready supporting capacity or their leaders' desires) because the lack of communications, transportation, and organizational infrastructures makes it all but impossible to create economic (and political) opportunities at a distance.

18. "The growing obsolescence of the city, in its traditional form, in political, economic, and military terms, is one of the most fundamental transitions initiated—although certainly not completed—as part of the emergence of the absolutist state" (Giddens 1985b, 97).

geographic scale as capital accumulation, had to wait for a communications infrastructure that was adequate to the formation of large-scale trade unions and political parties (Calhoun 1988).

Second, a full account also needs to recognize that modern states are in fact special (and critically important) instances of a more general phenomenon: corporations. As Giddens notes, the absolutist kings were distinct from other traditional rulers in the crucial sense that they not only sat at the pinnacle of state power but also incorporated the state symbolically within their own sovereign persons: "The religious symbolism of 'divine right' should actually be seen as a traditional accoutrement to something very new—the development of 'government' in the modern sense, the figure of the ruler being a personalized expression of a secularized administrative entity" (1985b, 93–94). This notion is part of what Kantorowicz (1956) meant in his brilliant portrayal of the late-medieval doctrine of the "king's two bodies," one personal and the other public. The king had begun to assume the status (still common to Roman Catholic bishops and other ecclesiastical nobles) of a "corporation sole" (see also Gierke 1934; Maitland [1900] 1958). Eventually, a doctrine of corporate personality developed that freed the corporation from any legal need for embodiment. On this and other bases corporations (starting at least as much with the state and various monastic bodies as with the urban corporations from which the lineage is usually traced) were eventually able to command routine public, jural, and even (rather unanalytical) sociological acknowledgment as unitary actors.

Oddly, the corporate form of social organization has received very little attention in sociological theory even though it is central to modern institutional arrangements.[19] A brief discussion of this remarkable form of organization is therefore in order before considering more recent information technology and the question of whether we have left, or are about to leave, modernity behind us.

The corporation is a remarkable cultural artifact. One of the most extraordinary things about business corporations—as well as the other types of corporations from religious and charitable institutions to governments and quasi-governmental organizations of various sorts—is that we so routinely reify or anthropomorphize them.[20] With minor variations and qualifications corporations throughout the Western world may own

19. Coleman 1982 is one of a handful of modern exceptions to this stricture; see also Selznick 1969. One of the best sociological treatments comes not from a sociologist but from the legal theorist Dan-Cohen (1986).

20. In *Social and Cultural Dynamics*, Sorokin (1957, chapter 18) found that the modern West exhibited a "reemergence of singularism," with continued rapid growth into the late-nineteenth and early-twentieth centuries. Sorokin's analysis links singularism—the claim of ontological or nominalist social reality for collectivities—with a "triumphant individualism."

property, litigate, and make contracts in the same way as "natural persons." They may, indeed, enter into a variety of relationships—usually highly asymmetrical—with natural persons.[21]

Such relationships are quintessentially indirect. Although real human beings are linked by them, this linkage is almost invisible. Indeed, social relationships seem to disappear in the operation of an apparently self-moving technical and social system.[22] With even a minimal communications technology the relationships constituting an organization can be rendered indirect, that is, distanced both in time and in space (e.g., by the storage, retrieval, or transmission of the written word) and socially mediated (by transmission through the official functions of other corporate agents). Thus a corporation is in one sense merely an aggregate or structure of social relationships, most (but not all) of which are indirect. In another sense, however, it is a social creature at a different level, a whole unto itself.[23] Our Western—especially American—culture grants the corporation the status of an autonomous actor, one that is capable of "responsibility," thus offering its members limited liability for their actions.[24]

Both corporations and large-scale markets depend on the flow of information through indirect social relationships, and both are accord-

21. "Asymmetrical" is Coleman's (1982) apt term for relationships between corporations and "natural persons." The relationships that spring to mind are, usually, contractual ones such as employment, the sale of goods, or credit; the ownership of shares in a corporation is perhaps a special case of contractual relationship. But corporations also enter into other sorts of relationships with natural persons, as for example when they produce or distribute toxic substances that kill them.

22. Studies have long explored the impact of mechanical analogies on our understanding of human nature. The idea of automation—self-movement—came early on to influence conceptions of social organizations. Hobbes ([1651] 1962, 81), for example, describes Leviathan as an artificial man, or automaton. The image of an artificial man suggests much of our ordinary understanding of the independence of such social automata from human action. Sociotechnical systems subject to automation not only industrial production and office work but also the control and coordination of social relations. In doing so, they create indirect relationships that are particularly conducive to reification.

23. A corporation exhibits, for example, the characteristics Durkheim ([1895] 1966) thought defining of social facts: it endures, at least potentially, longer than any of its individual members or agents; it is external to any individual (although whether it is external to all is perhaps better treated as a question of theoretical presupposition rather than one of empirical fact; see Alexander 1982); and it is capable of coercion over individuals, both conscious and intentional, and unintended and/or unrecognized on either side.

24. See the discussions in Dan-Cohen 1986, French 1984, Orhnial 1984, and Stone 1975. Attempts to apply criminal law sanctions to corporations raise particularly difficult questions about their "responsibility" and ontological status. It is not entirely clear, for example, what is meant by the notion of "punishing" a firm, as distinct from the individuals who act as its agents, own it, or otherwise create and compose it (see Coffee 1981).

ingly subject to routine reification.[25] Economists predict, and nearly everyone discusses, the economy as though it were as natural and objective a phenomenon as the weather. This tendency reflects a culture that is at once pervasively individualistic—and thus underrecognizes the social dimension in the creation of both markets and corporations—and at the same time supports a maximally "disembodied" ontology that allows people to accord some manner of unitary individual existence to bodiless social creatures. Markets differ from corporations, however, in that they lack administration. They are the aggregate of individual actions, and sometimes collective action, but they are not collective actors.

Because of this difference, corporations tend to be not only reified but also anthropomorphized. As noted earlier, we no longer find it necessary to embody states in the persons of their rulers; we attribute individuality to the disembodied state itself (see also Manning 1962; Giddens 1995b, chapter 4). Similarly, corporations are readily understood to exist, and in some sense to act, independently of their chief executives. However attractive Chrysler Corporation may find it to promote Lee Iacocca as its symbolic image or however much Ronald Reagan may appeal to Americans as a symbol of their country, no one confuses the person with the corporation. As Justice Marshall wrote nearly a hundred and seventy years ago, a corporation is "an artificial being, invisible, intangible, and existing only in contemplation of law."[26] The confusion comes in treating the corporation *as* a person.

25. Although administrative flows of information are the most obvious aspect of this dependence in corporations (including states), we should not forget that the maintenance and operation of such organizations as collective actors depends on a whole variety of "informal," that is, not specifically administered, information flows. Indeed, one of the questions that some ask about the new information technology is whether it does not subject many of these informal lines of communication to increasing surveillance or formalized administration and thus in one way weaken the organizations it more generally facilitates.

Both money and commodities can be understood as the basis of information flows in markets. Parsons (1963), Luhmann (1979, chapter 3), and Giddens (1985b, chapter 5) all offer understandings of monetary transactions as communications. Simmel ([1907] 1978, 284–85, 297–302) stresses the role of money in making possible impersonal relations between people and thus promoting individualism; he does not, however, quite develop an account of money as a medium of communications. Marx's notion of commodity fetishism has been developed in this direction (Taussig 1978; Lukács [1922] 1971). Both Lukács and Simmel draw connections between commodification and what Simmel calls "the calculating character of modern times" ([1907] 1978, 443).

26. *Dartmouth v. Woodward*, 17 U.S. (4 Wheat.) 518 (1819). See also Simmel's stress on the significance of the personal unity of the owner, including the socially created corporate owner:

Every sum of money has a different qualitative significance if it belongs to a number of people rather than to one person. The unit of the personality is thus the correlate or the pre-condition for all qualitative differences of possessions and their importance; here the assets of legal persons are, in terms of their function, on the same level because of the uniformity of their administration. Similarly, we may speak of a na-

INFORMATION TECHNOLOGY AND THE EXPANSION OF
INDIRECT RELATIONSHIPS

The past two decades have seen a near passion for labeling new ages and new kinds of society: postindustrial, technetronic, Third Wave, etc.[27] These visions of a new and different age derive substantially from the anticipated effects of new technology, most prominently computers and related information technologies. Although this technology is indeed powerful, such accounts of a qualitative break with the previous two hundred years of modernity are misleading. New technologies have extended the most basic trends in social integration more often than they have countered them, and this pattern will probably continue unless substantial social effort is invested to the contrary.

Corporations, large-scale markets, and other organizations of indirect social relationships have grown in size and importance throughout the modern era. Advances in information technology have repeatedly facilitated their extension. Computers and new telecommunications technologies continue this pattern. They not only offer a large quantitative increase in indirect relationships but also contribute to a shift in balance between two qualitative kinds of indirect relationships. By extension from Cooley's notions of primary and secondary relationships, we might conceptualize two kinds of indirect relationships: tertiary and quaternary.

Tertiary relationships need involve no physical copresence; they may be mediated entirely by machines, correspondence, or other persons, but the parties are well aware of the relationship. A tertiary relationship may be created, for example, by writing to a more or less anonymous functionary of a large bank to complain about an error in one's statement. Most ordinary citizens have only tertiary relationships with their national political representatives, relationships that are mediated by broadcast and print media, voting in elections, and, occasionally, correspondence. In a large

---

tion's wealth only if we conceive of the nation as a unified possessing subject. That is to say, we have to conceive the assets owned by the individual citizens as being unified by their interaction within the national economy, in the same way as the fortune of one individual comes together as a practical unity through such interactions—for example, distribution, the relation of individual expenditures to the total, balance between income and expenditure, etc. ([1907] 1978, 271).

For Weber ([1922] 1978, 48–52), social relationships constitute an organized or corporate group (*Verband*) only insofar as a set of specific individuals (usually together with an administrative staff) regularly enforces its boundaries. Weber refuses, however, to recognize the corporate whole as distinct from the individuals in authority. See also the discussion in Sorokin (1957, chapters 18–19).

27. Among many, see Bell 1973, 1979, Touraine 1971, Brzezinski 1977, Toffler 1980, and Naisbitt 1982; see also the review by Badham (1985) and the sampling in Forester 1986.

corporation most employees have this sort of relationship with top managers. Such relationships are more or less fully contained by their explicit purposes and systemic roles. Because they are not characterized by physical copresence, they are not as open to redefinition and expansion as are secondary relationships. The various media through which the relationship is carried out help in varying degrees to seal role performance off from the other attributes of individuals. But the relationships retain a degree of mutual recognition and intentionality; each party can (at least in principle) identify the other and the relationship itself is manifest.

Quaternary relationships, by contrast, occur outside of the attention and, generally, the awareness of at least one of the parties to them. They are the products of surveillance and exist wherever a sociotechnical system allows the monitoring of people's actions and turns these actions into communication, regardless of the actors' intentions. Quaternary relationships are created by the tapping of telephones, the theft of computerized data, or even the analysis of stored data for purposes other than those for which they were initially provided by people other than those to whom they were initially provided. Each person who uses a credit card, travels on an airplane, pays income taxes, applies for a visa, or completes employment applications—that is, nearly everyone in a modern society—provides data that can be subjected to reanalysis. Such reanalyses can be used to trace the behavior of particular individuals or groups. The purpose of such surveillance may be as benign as providing marketing information or as threatening as discovering the members of minority ethnic groups for purposes of control or persecution.[28] Modern markets and governmental apparatuses could not function in their present manners without substantial use of such data. This use nonetheless constitutes surveillance and creates very indirect, nearly invisible, but potent quaternary relationships.

As we saw in the case of markets, not all quaternary relationships depend on the administration of information. The flow of money in successive transactions is itself a form of communication; monetarization laid the basis for an extension of markets that created extremely indirect, almost invisible quaternary relationships of their own. However, the distinction between monetary communication in large markets and administered information flows is diminishing as money comes increasingly to be one version of electronically encoded information. In addition to markets a variety of noneconomic relationships are facilitated by new technologies. For example, hobbyists may use computer networks to keep in touch, a sort of semiadministered use. However, new technologies have

28. For example, the U.S. government provided supposedly confidential census data to police and legal authorities for use in finding Japanese-Americans as part of the unconstitutional program of mass detention during World War II (Burnham 1983, 20–26).

their most dramatic impacts on various kinds of more fully administered information flows.[29]

The use of writing marked the first great historical breakthrough in creating the capacity for indirect social relationships. Our present capacities still depend more on literacy than on any other invention or skill. But information technology has advanced enormously throughout the modern era, from the invention of printing presses through telegraphs, telephones, radio, television, communications satellites, cable and microwave transmission, and now computers.[30] Improvements in transportation facilities have also been vast and for centuries constituted the basis for most long-distance communications. It is worth reemphasizing how recent and how enormous transportation improvements have been. As recently as the mid-1750s, it took ten to twelve days to travel from London to Edinburgh; by 1836 less than two days were needed for the trip (Bagwell 1971); the train (which on that route is nowhere near "state of the art") now takes four hours, the plane one hour, and electronically mediated communication is virtually instantaneous. German immigrants to America after 1848 could not count on a reliable post (the International Postal Union dates from 1874) and could not expect ever again to see the family members they left behind. Yet, their great-grandchildren not only travel and phone between the two countries with ease but also own shares in corporations doing business simultaneously in both countries and depend on military coordination in which computers and satellites link commanders and staffers thousands of miles apart and monitor the entire face of the earth.

Through most of history wars of conquest and the migrations that they precipitated were among the few major vehicles of long-distance and cross-cultural communication. At considerably greater intervals wars and migrations were supplemented by waves of religious conversion. More frequently, religious pilgrimages and commercial expeditions were mounted. Trading routes provided a flow of gossip, but the everyday scale of activities was much narrower. Communications capacities grew out of the political needs of managing empires and the logistic needs of armies, drawing on the resources of clerical literacy (hence, "clerks"). In the early-modern period commerce began to compete with

29. Administration may refer to both the monitoring of information flows and the organized creation of such flows. In other words, it may refer to both phone tapping and television broadcasting as well as to the combination of both aspects in electronic credit checks.

30. Media theorists focusing on telephone, broadcast, and other electronic technologies have frequently emphasized the renewed prominence of oral communications in shaping modern culture (McLuhan 1964; Ong 1982; Meyrowitz 1985, 16–23). The role of computers in the latest wave of electronic communications technologies presages a partial reversal of this trend and a revival in the centrality of literacy.

and then surpass warfare as the occasion for international communications. It multiplied the demands for literacy and improved communications media. The growth of strong national states was tied closely to both this growth of commerce (which simultaneously provided the wealth with which to run the states and a need for the protection of trade and international boundaries) and the communications media themselves. National integration was furthered by these communications media not only through enhanced means of administration (as Giddens 1985b emphasizes) but also through the growth of cohesive national cultures and shared "consciousnesses" or ideologies. Linguistic standardization and codification was a key step in nation building (even though the histories of the German-speaking and the Romance-language countries differ somewhat in this regard) and in turn made long-distance communications still easier.[31]

Like literacy itself, new information technologies enable the transcendence of not only space but also time; fewer relationships or transactions require copresence.[32] Although it is a mundane sort of time machine and disappointingly inert, each gray metal file cabinet enables communication to take place between those who put information in it and those who take it out. Computers are able to do this, of course, on a much larger scale, with much more sophisticated procedures for matching the stored bits of information to the inquiries of future searchers. One of the most distinctive features of modern corporations is their ability to combine a high level of continuity in their patterns of operation (in the face of both environmental complexity and fluctuation and internal personnel changes) with a capacity for organized change in response to managerial decisions. Computers can be used to monitor activities in connection with very long-term plans or simply to maintain conformity with preset rhythms and routines. Communication is increasingly separated from transportation, surveillance from direct observation.

New information technologies may be used in the following ways: to organize more of social life through indirect relationships, to extend the power of various corporate actors, to coordinate social action on a larger scale, or to intensify control within specific relationships. This broad set of potentials can indeed be socially transformative; the technologies are

31. Today television is one of the central means of promoting a shared national consciousness, especially for large countries. Many Third World countries have invested heavily in it for just this reason, but few can rival China's purchase of several entire color television factories from Japanese manufacturers in order to meet its goal of one television per household by the end of the century.

32. In Innis's ([1951] 1964) sense, however, new information technologies are biased, like their forebears, toward the transcendence of space more than of time, toward reach and flexibility rather than toward permanence.

powerful and pliable. But will this transformation be a break with the trend of modernity toward an increasing reliance on indirect social relationships to organize large-scale social integration?

An excessive focus on the question of the extent to which new technologies supplant human labor in the production of material goods has obscured the deeper import of these new technologies for social integration. It is indeed true that the proportionate contribution of "artificial" (not directly human) labor to the production process has grown and is likely to grow much further.[33] This trend is important, and the potential employment impacts of computerization are not insignificant (see Jones 1982; Gill 1985). Similarly, computerization offers major advances in productivity (not only for labor, but also for capital facilities). Focusing only on these issues, however, obscures other very significant changes, including changes in the material production process itself.

The greatest changes in most production facilities are not in the numbers of people employed or even in their skill levels, but in "throughput" processes (Gunn 1982). Computerization enables not just the automation of a variety of different specific production processes (welding, say, or painting) but also the automation of the flow of goods, materials, and information through the factory.[34] At an automobile assembly plant, for example, each chassis is given a computerized identification card at the start. It corresponds to a specific car ordered by a specific dealer. The computer indicates to each worker (or robot) what parts to add to the basic chassis, what color to paint it, and what trim or finishing to give it. The computer also orders all the necessary parts and materials as needed, thus cutting down on both the clerical work force and the necessary inventory. As with assembly lines and indeed factories themselves, the change here is in the organization of the production process. Computerization's most profound industrial impact comes in increasing the scale of technically

33. This trend may shift large parts of the work forces of the advanced economies out of material production, but two qualifications need to be suggested to Bell's characterization of this shift as a move to postindustrial society (1973, 1979). First, most of the jobs created for former industrial workers (or their children or their future counterparts) are at least as mundane and often at least as manual. What could be more exemplary manual labor than typing? Yet typing is "information-sector employment." Much the same goes for such service-sector jobs as making and selling hamburgers at McDonalds. Second, proportionate declines in employment in material production industries are not mirrored by proportionate declines in investment in capital goods or value added in economic production.

34. One merit of Beniger's (1986) account of the "control revolution" is to grasp this feature of information technology, which is overlooked by many accounts. Beniger's cybernetic model for understanding this, however, tends to obscure many of the issues addressed in this chapter, as well as the matter of struggle over the course of technological change. Beniger prefers to present control as an attribute of reified "systems" rather than one of human relationships and to present increases in control as "natural" rather than chosen or created eventualities.

coordinated activity at the same time that it establishes flexibility for small-batch production. This description of the production process (based on observations in Wayne, Michigan) is part of a computerized integration of design, production, and marketing facilities in seven countries on four continents (Ford Motor Company's World Car project).

What is changed, in short, is the social integration of the production process. Just as the factory and the division of labor transformed the production of goods in the classical industrial revolution, so computerization today transforms not just individual tasks but whole organizational forms. Although automation displaces some manual workers by having machines do their jobs, it changes society more by replacing the human component in many organizational links.[35] Social organization itself is in some sense automated as computers and related information technologies help to create an artificial locus of self-movement. We call a machine automated if it can drive itself or perform autonomously. So, too, we could call the process of creating factories or even more far-flung but autonomously working organizations one of automation. We might even consider that corporations are a kind of social automaton. They are made possible by indirect relationships in which human functionaries serve as intermediaries, but they are greatly expanded on the basis of new information technologies for the mediation of relationships.

SOCIAL INTEGRATION AND
THE IDEA OF POSTINDUSTRIAL SOCIETY

In attempting to revitalize and reformulate the problematic of social integration, I am following most closely in the path of Durkheim but also in varying degrees in those of Tönnies, Weber, and Simmel. Durkheim made social solidarity and social integration more distinctively his concern than any other classical sociologist, but he did not for the most part approach these issues concretely through the study of patterns of relationships. Rather he concentrated on the sociopsychological sense of mutuality, the cognitive implications of life in society, and the functional analysis of cohesion among institutions.[36] Functional analysis of this sort

35. It is common to stress the "deskilling" of such manual workers as machinists and their partial replacement by technical specialists, who are more easily controlled (Noble 1984). Whatever the merits of this argument as to the motives behind corporate policy, it should be noted that the transformation of production organization also affects some managers. At Ford's Wayne Assembly Plant none of the managers of the facility had the ability to reprogram their robots or their throughput controls. They too had lost control to a centralized organization working through more specialized agents.

36. Durkheim's failure to develop an approach to concrete social relationships is centrally responsible for one of the most important weaknesses of his theory of social solidarity (or integration). Concentrating on differences in form between mechanical and organic

is abstract even though it is not abstract in the sense or to the extent that Marx's categorial analysis of capitalism is.[37] It is from Weber, above all, that we derive the concrete analysis of social relationships, which he understood as the probability that the actions of one person will influence the course of action of another.[38] Not all social relationships are direct, of course; many are mediated. What renders the Weberian approach concrete is its focus on relationships from the point of view of the actors (thus necessarily recognizing qualitative distinctions) rather than on the categorial nature of mediation.[39]

Ironically, although much of the structural-functionalism of the 1950s retained a focus on social integration and even on concrete social relationships (the latter perhaps more visible in the social anthropological variants), the "industrial society" theories that developed on Durkheimian and Weberian foundations as alternatives to Marxism exhibit the same neglect of social integration that characterizes Marxism. Industry is no more definitive of society than capitalism; if anything, it is less so (Kumar 1978; Giddens 1985b; Badham 1985). Industry as a way of organizing material production is clearly a feature of social life and is somewhat influential, but it is neither dynamic in itself nor the source of the basic web of relationships linking people to each other. The same problem is carried forward in Bell's theory of postindustrial society. The question of how value is produced is mistaken for the question of what society is. Regardless of the merits or demerits of Bell's notion that information

solidarity, Durkheim ([1893] 1964) reduces transformations in scale to a minor independent variable, not a major substantive feature of social change. As interesting a variable as dynamic density is, it does not substitute for an account of how dramatically different numbers of people come to be organized in a common web of social relationships or what this means for people's experiences, actions, or social structure.

37. Functional analysis is abstract in the sense that it does not study concrete interpersonal relationships or social relationships (in Weber's sense) but rather the influence of socially constructed institutional phenomena on each other. In still another sense statistical analysis is also abstract: it focuses on distributions rather than relationships. The language here is often fuzzy; statistical "relationships" are discussed where one set of distributional indicators is held to predict another. This analysis is different from the analysis (statistical or otherwise) of concrete relationships among people.

38. Simmel's work adds greatly to Weber's in this respect. Giddens's (1985a, 1985b) development of a Weberian complement to Marxist analysis almost reduces Weber to a one-dimensional theorist of power. At points Giddens focuses so predominantly on the state that social life appears as little besides economic relations with nature (analyzed in a manner primarily indebted to Marx) and power relations.

39. It is in this sense that Marxists often hold that Weber does not have a theory but only a highly systematic, formalized empirical account of history. In this view only the sort of abstract analysis I describe below for Marx's theory of capitalism counts as theory.

replaces labor as the source of value, this contention cannot be an account of the achievement of social integration.[40] Planning, one of Bell's central new institutions, seems to be charged with the maintenance of social coherence. Its failures are traced to the "cultural contradictions of capitalism" (Bell 1976), not to an analysis of social relationships or their integration as such.

It is particularly unfortunate that Bell's account should exhibit this lack of attention to social integration. This absence vitiates much of the value of what is the most serious sociological attempt to come to terms with the significance of information technology. Moreover, as I have tried to show, the notion of a fundamental discontinuity between post-industrial society (or any of its myriad synonyms) and its putative precursor is misleading. Although I have described much that is new, and a lengthier treatment of technologies and social change could describe a great deal more that is new, the set of conditions—especially social-structural conditions—we vaguely term modernity continues and appears likely to continue for some time to come (barring a material cataclysm of one form or another). There has been no basic shift in the form of social integration such that a new sort of society might reasonably be declared to exist. The changes that have occurred and are occurring are more or less of a piece with the changes that have occurred throughout the modern age. Indeed, a high rate of change and an expectation of change are among the defining features of modernity. Capitalism's relentless pushing is a major source of this continuous social (as well as technological, economic, and cultural) change. But it is not the only source, and at points it is resisted, so it should not be thought to contain the whole explanation.

40. Bell (1973, xiv; 1979, 168) shares with Habermas (1970, 104), Touraine (1971), and several others the notion of an "information theory of value" that replaces the formerly applicable labor theory of value. In each case it is remarkable that no attempt is made to revise the labor theory of value so that intellectual labor can be handled better. Habermas (1976, 1984) apparently wishes to retain a narrow sense of labor so that it can be assimilated readily into his distinction between instrumental and communicative action. The desirability of a sharp distinction for Touraine may have to do with the appeal of a "new class" analysis of workers' politics in the France of 1968 and immediately thereafter. Unlike Bell, however, Touraine (e.g., 1977) and Habermas (1984) attempt to develop an account of both social relationships as such and social integration. I conceive of the present effort to be at least partially complementary to that embodied in Habermas's recent work, which distinguishes between social integration and system integration. I wish, however, to avoid "the seducements of systems theory" (McCarthy 1985) by specifying the concrete relational basis on which the tendencies toward reification and the privileging of techne over praxis arise. Rather than ceding the "world" of formal organization and large-scale social integration to systems theory, we need to examine why it is that immediate, communicative relationships cannot account for society's integration.

MARX: ABSTRACT TOTALITY AND SOCIAL RELATIONSHIPS

The issue of concrete social relationships and the integration of social groupings is almost entirely suppressed in the works of Marx and most Marxists (Calhoun 1982; Alexander 1983). This suppression is partly because of an overemphasis on one of Marx's most fundamental insights: the totalizing drive of capitalist commodity production and capital accumulation.[41] Marx recognized in a profound way that capitalism was not established on the basis of direct interpersonal relationships. It existed only through the mediation of commodities that were produced and exchanged in the pursuit of capital accumulation. Moreover, as Giddens (1985b, chapter 5) has recently reminded us, a central feature of Marx's theory is missing from competing accounts of industrial society. The missing feature is the dynamism of capitalist production and commodification, and its ceaseless expansion into new lines of production, new areas of life, and new parts of the world.[42]

Capitalism, according to Marx, must by its nature increase its extension in the world and the intensity or completeness of its domination wherever it organizes economic activity. Capitalism drives the creation of new technology (for both production and distribution), new products, and new markets. As Giddens stresses (1985b), this analysis neglects the coeval rise of the state, which was crucial to the creation and maintenance of a distinct economic sphere. But this does not go far enough. We must both recognize the accuracy of Marx's argument for the dynamic by which capitalism

41. This is the theme of Volume 1 of *Capital* insofar as it shows how abstract forms dominate concrete relationships in modern capitalism. (For Marx, one must remember, the concrete is not the simple and the obvious but the complex and in some sense arbitrary sum of many different determinations.) The commodity form encapsulates a new kind of social mediation in which people are knit together in the most determinative ways by their production and exchange of things rather than by direct interpersonal relationships; qualitative particularity is suppressed in favor of quantitative generality. Lukács, more than any other thinker, held fast to this theme—developed in his analysis of reification—as the center of Marxism ([1922] 1971, esp. the chapter titled "Reification and the Consciousness of the Proletariat"). Although he expands the notion of totality to include many other variants of Marxist holism, Jay's (1984) analysis is very helpful on this point. For Lukács, totality is not just a tendency but an essential category that is recognizable from the abstract standpoint of the proletariat as self-moving subject-object. One of the most powerful recent attempts to read Marx's theory in this way and at the level of basic categories is that of Postone (1983). In this work totalization is seen as a historically specific tendency of capitalism.

42. "The bourgeoisie cannot exist without constantly revolutionising the instruments of production, and thereby the relations of production, and with them the whole relations of society. Conservation of the old modes of production in unaltered form was, on the contrary, the first condition of existence for all earlier industrial classes" (Marx and Engels [1848] 1976, 487).

pushes toward totality and complement it with an analysis of the concrete social relations with which capitalism (like the nation-state) coexists but which cannot be reduced to it. Capitalism, in other words, is not society. It exists in some part precisely in opposition to direct interpersonal relationships. As Marx remarked: "Their own exchange and their own production confront individuals as an *objective* relation which is *independent* of them. In the case of the *world market*, the *connection of the individual* with all, but at the same time also the *independence of this connection from the individual*, have developed to such a high level that the formation of the world market already at the same time contains the conditions for going beyond it" ([1939] 1973, 161, emphasis in original).[43] Commodities confront human beings as objectifications of human activities (in relation to nature, self, and others). Commodities mediate human relationships to create the abstract totality that is capitalism. At the same time, the commodity form reifies human activity and relationships, obscuring the fact that capitalism is the product of human labor and making it appear as an independent object. Both Marx and, especially, Engels were fond of borrowing Carlyle's phrase that capitalism left no other nexus between man and man than "callous cash payment" (e.g., Marx and Engels [1848] 1976, 487; Engels [1880] 1972, 608). Just as capitalism must disregard or even attack the irreducibly qualitative nature of commodities, so it must disregard or attack the qualitative content of human relationships (Marx [1867] 1974, chapter 1; Lukács [1922] 1971, 83–148). But capitalism can go only so far in this attack, even in Marx's theory. Commodities *tend* to the purely quantitative, but they remain physical things and thus have qualities. Similarly, capitalism cannot wholly dominate or eradicate qualitative cultural contents, interpersonal relationships, or purely personal thoughts and affects.

Indeed, it is central to at least one reading of Marx that this should be

43. "Comparison," Marx went on, takes the "place of real communality and generality: It has been said and may be said that this is precisely the beauty and the greatness of it: this spontaneous interconnection, this material and mental metabolism which is independent of the knowing and willing of individuals, and which presupposes their reciprocal independence and indifference. And, certainly, this objective connection is preferable to the lack of any connection, or to a merely local connection resting on blood ties, or on primeval, natural or master-servant relations" ([1939] 1973, 161). See the similar discussion by Engels ([1880] 1972, 627–28) and in the *Manifesto* (Marx and Engels [1848] 1976, 486–87). It is, however, above all in *Capital*, especially in the relationship between Volumes 1 and 3, that we see Marx creating a theory of a mode of totalization that makes social life appear systematically as other than it is, that is, makes capital seem the cause and not the product of human action. If we can identify capitalism with the system-world, it does not just "colonize" the life-world, as Habermas would have it, but constitutes the very severance of each from the other, the compartmentalization of the life-world and the reification of mediated action. (Whether there are other forms of mediation comparably conducive to reification remains an open question.)

so. In this reading one cannot explain the revolutionary transformation or supersession of capitalism solely on the basis of dialectical negation. That is, there must be an alternative, qualitatively separate mode or dimension of existence on the basis of which opposition to capitalism can build. Such a basis may remain outside the domination of capitalism, as in the notion, arguably suggested by Gramsci, of a counterhegemonic culture (Gramsci 1982; Boggs 1984). Or such a basis could be created by capitalism itself. Marx, for example, considered that the very concentration of workers in cities and factories (and the social organization of the factories) might provide the basis for radical mobilization (Calhoun 1983). But there is a tension between this line of reasoning in which Marx expects the coalescence of the working class as a collective actor, subjectively unified on the basis of direct relationships among workers, and Marx's more predominant analysis of how the indirect, abstract relationships of capitalism dominate and destroy direct ones.[44] In this latter line of reasoning Marx focuses on the purely categorial position of the proletariat as the negation of capitalism; the proletariat is unified by common place in the formal relations of production rather than by qualitative relationships to each other.[45]

The other side of capitalist totality in Marx's categorial analysis turns out, ironically, to be a kind of individualism. On the one hand, this is the universal individualism of utilitarianism, and Marx critiques aspects of it.

44. This tension is one that does not much trouble Engels. Where Marx (in *Capital*) has seen the anarchy of everyday capitalist economic activity as the superficial inverse of a relentless push toward totality, Engels uses similar language to contrast two levels of concrete social phenomena:

> The old bonds were loosened, the old exclusive limits broken through, the producers were more and more turned into independent, isolated producers of commodities. It became apparent that the production of society at large was ruled by absence of plan, by accident, by anarchy; and this anarchy grew to greater and greater height. But the chief means of aid by which the capitalist mode of production intensified this anarchy of socialized production was the exact opposite of anarchy. It was the increasing organization of production, upon a social basis, in every individual productive establishment. By this the old, peaceful, stable condition of things was ended. (Engels [1880] 1972, 97)

As a result, Engels can provide a more comfortable transition to an evolutionary socialist expectation that socialized production will lead naturally to proletarian solidarity and socialist society. It is this sort of Engelsian account that is revised, domesticated, and appropriated by Bell (1973) and that Galbraith (1978) and others believe they have answered by showing that modern capitalist production is not anarchic but planned, not the reckless pursuit of profit but the carefully modulated pursuit of organizational growth.

45. In different ways both Lukács and the Althusserian structuralists extend this argument from the pure categories of capitalism even further than Marx did. See Poulantzas: "Social classes are not empirical groups of individuals, social groups that are 'composed' by simple addition; the relations of these agents among themselves are thus not inter-personal relations" (1975, 17).

But, on the other hand, Marx seems to accept this "implicit" individualism as at least a partially accurate description of reality under capitalism: concrete qualitative examples of proletarian social solidarity (such as direct interpersonal relationships as opposed to political commonality or organization) are taken by Marx as nothing other than the residues of the old order. Capitalism is purely formal, impersonal, and quantitative; the working class is unified by the commonalities of a category of individuals.[46] If any relationships are held to be defining or productive of solidarity, they are the relationships of opposition to the bourgeoisie, the ruling class, not the relationships among workers. Nowhere does Marx endeavor to show that individuals in capitalist society (including capitalists as well as workers) are anything other than quantitatively interchangeable, except in potential.

It is important, however, to keep the issue of human social potential in mind. To the extent that capitalism is the object of analysis, direct interpersonal relationships are of minimal significance. In the pre-*Capital* writings where Marx envisages a communist future, however, he does not contrast quantitatively interchangeable individuals with an abstract totality. Rather he takes pains to stress that "above all we must avoid postulating 'society' again as an abstraction vis-a-vis the individual. The individual *is the social being*" (Marx [1844] 1975, 299, emphasis in original). But such a condition is a possible future to be created, not a timeless feature of human nature (other than in potential): "Universally developed individuals, whose social relations, as their own communal [*gemeinschaftlich*] relations, are hence also subordinated to their own communal control, are no product of nature, but of history" (Marx [1939] 1973, 162). Natural law and social contract theorists, Marx says at the same point in *Grundrisse*, focus their attention on "merely objective" bonds among people and mistake them for the spontaneous relationships that are not possible in the existing state of society. So long as the abstract relationships of capitalism remain determinant, the analysis of concrete relationships will be the analysis of more or less arbitrary epiphenomena. When capitalism and the human self-estrangement of private property are transcended, there will still be a difference between activities that are carried out in direct communality with others and those (e.g., science) that depend less on the immediate copresence of the group but that are nonetheless self-consciously social. But each of these activities will be self-determining in a way impossible under the domination of capitalism:

> Social activity and social enjoyment exist by no means *only* in the form of some *directly* communal activity and directly *communal* enjoyment, al-

---

46. This approach is continued in the work of many contemporary "analytic Marxists"; see, e.g., Wright 1985.

though *communal* activity and *communal* enjoyment—i.e., activity and enjoyment which are manifested and affirmed in *actual* direct *association*
with other men—will occur wherever such a *direct* expression of sociability stems from the true character of the activity's content and is appropriate to the nature of the enjoyment. ([1848] 1976, 298, emphasis in original)

In terms of Marx's own political interests, that is, his theory of revolution, there is a tension between his account of the tendency of capitalism to eradicate all interpersonal relationships not created by capitalist
commodity production and exchange and the need for a basis of social solidarity in the struggle against capitalism. Marx's few comments
on interpersonal relationships other than those constituted by capitalism itself indicate that real communality would have to be postponed
to a postcapitalist world. Thus Marx has no substantial theory of social
integration under capitalism (as opposed to system integration, in Habermas's sense, or the integration of the capitalist totality itself). Although Marx's account of capitalism is powerful, it is an account not
of the experiential or observed world of social relationships—that is,
society—but of (1) a factor pushing continuously for certain directions
of transformation in those relationships and (2) a form of mediation
producing systematic misrecognition of those relationships. Marx's
theory of capitalism is a more local or specific theory and a less universal one than is frequently claimed. It cannot be the basis for all
sociology. Indeed, in the most literal sense it is not a sociology at all.[47]
Insofar as they are composed of concrete social relationships, even
some of the most characteristic institutions of modern capitalism—
business corporations, for example—must be explained by factors
other than capitalism.

To some extent the aim of this chapter is to explore these other factors. I have offered a preliminary conceptualization of the structures of
the indirect relationships that are distinctive to the modern world. Capitalism has in part helped to produce these relationships, but, at least
equally, it depends on them. Corporations and large-scale markets are
crucial examples. Indirect relationships have been and continue to be
furthered by developments in information technology. Each relationship
is also subject to a tendency toward reification, which sets it apart from
the social institutions that are formed primarily on the basis of directly
interpersonal relationships.

The reader should not think that only Marxism suffers from the lack

47. Of course, taking Marx's theory of capitalism in this narrow sense excludes a good
deal of Marx's own work, some of which is more directly sociological. The point is that this
sociological part is not based directly on, and is still less deducible from, Marx's categorial
theory of capitalism.

of a good account of the role of concrete relationships in social integration, that a good account of social integration is to be found in the whole cloth in some other theoretical corpus, or that my argument is entirely in opposition to Marxist theory. Taking the last point first, my aim is to delimit the application of the most central part of Marxist theory, treating it strictly as a formal theory of capitalism. Marxism is a theory of capitalism as a form of mediation among human actors (again, considered abstractly as producers, consumers, and owners), not as a form of social or economic action (as it is for Weber). In this sense capitalism is dynamic and pushes toward totality.[48] Although it may need improvement, within these limits Marx's theory is powerful and still offers an almost unique insight. However, I insist that capitalism is not a form of society. Marx's theory of capitalism should not be privileged as a theory of all social life. We may grant the claim that it is the tendency of capitalism as a form of mediation to increase the extent to which a theory of capitalism will explain other aspects of social life, but many of these aspects nonetheless remain "other." Central among these other aspects for the purposes of this chapter are the various relationships through which members of populations are knit to each other and that enable the coordination of social action on a very large scale. Much the same could be said for the contents of culture.

CONCLUSION

I have argued that a dominant sociological trend of the modern era is the extension of social integration to an ever-larger scale, albeit with greater internal intensity, through reliance on indirect social relationships. I have suggested that new information technologies do not mark a break with this long-term trend. As material productivity continues to increase, so, too, do our capacities for organization through indirect social relationships. At the same time, social systems are extended further beyond the bounds of locality, and the capacity of those empowered by them to reach into the daily lives of ordinary people is extended. Issues of information technology and control are thus central for modern sociology, but this situation does not imply any qualitative break in the kind of social pro-

48. Of course capitalism never achieves complete totality. On the basis of historical experience it does not seem to come even as close as Marx imagined. We can envisage its totality by contemplating it as a purely abstract system (in the manner of Althusser), but my concern here is with concrete historical analysis. Even though the limits on the extension and intensification of capitalism have proved to be considerable, I still think it marks a qualitative break with all previous historical experience. Human organization may have seen varying scale and systematicity, but only capitalism has created the kind of abstract mediation that finds in capital accumulation not just a human desire or aim but also an apparently independent compulsion.

cesses at work at the most fundamental level. Modernity, if that is what we wish to to call our age, continues.[49]

Neither Marx's theory of capitalism nor any theory of industrial society (or postindustrial society) offers an adequate account of society itself, that is, social integration. I have offered a conceptual contribution toward this end by trying to specify the distinctive nature and modern role of indirect social relationships. Of course this discussion raises other issues that I have left untouched. New information technologies may facilitate the reversal of an ancient trend toward population concentration (at least in the rich countries of the world). Will this reversal take place? With what effects? Simultaneously, the same technologies offer an increased capacity for centralized surveillance and control. Will this be checked or balanced by new means of democratic participation? What are the meanings and potentials of direct interpersonal relationships in an age in which so much of social life is constituted through indirect relationships?

Adequate answers to these and related questions depend on our ability to analyze the varying forms and extent of social integration. This analysis in turn calls for the study of concrete social relationships. Questions of social integration cannot be addressed by purely cultural analysis or through an atomistic utilitarian individualism. Nor does the Marxist theory of capitalism suffice. Despite the centrality of its insights into the dynamic pressures for change in social integration, it remains focused on the abstract, totalizing mediation of qualitative human labor (and the qualitative activity of living itself insofar as it is "consumption" or "enjoyment" of use-values) through capitalist production and the exchange of commodities. From the more structural variants of "structural-functional" thought—especially from Weber and Simmel—we may derive an approach to the study of concrete social relationships. This approach is essential to tackling the issue of social integration, a necessary, if recently neglected, counterpart to cultural accounts of modernity and Marxist accounts of capitalism. We must not, however, limit the study of concrete relationships to the direct ones that constitute the life-world while ceding all analysis of large-scale social organization to systems theory. Rather we must extend the analysis of concrete relationships into the realm of indirect relationships, showing that large-scale organizations are still part of social integration even if they are based on relationships over which participants have little control, of which they may not even be aware, and the results of which they may tend to reify.

49. I suspect that the modern age is best characterized vaguely rather than defined precisely. In my loose-knit view certain cultural dispositions (including both compulsions to novelty and its counterpart, nostalgia) join with the capitalist push for productivity and capital accumulation and the prevalence of indirect social relationships.

REFERENCES

Abu-Lughod, J. 1969. *The city is dead—long live the city: Some thoughts on urbanity.* Center for Planning and Development Research Monograph no. 12. Berkeley: Center for Planning and Development.

Alexander, J. 1982. *Theoretical logic in sociology.* Vol. 1, *Positivism, presuppositions, and current controversies.* Berkeley: University of California Press.

———. 1983. *Theoretical logic in sociology.* Vol. 2, *The antinomies of classical social thought: Marx and Durkheim.* Berkeley: University of California Press.

Badham, R. 1985. The sociology of industrial and post-industrial societies. *Contemporary Sociology* 32, no. 1:1–136.

Bagwell, R. 1971. *The transportation revolution from 1770.* London: Batsford.

Barnes, J. A. 1954. Class and committee in a Norwegian parish. *Human Relations* 7, no. 1:39–58.

Bell, D. 1973. *The coming of post-industrial society.* New York: Basic Books.

———. 1976. *The cultural contradictions of capitalism.* New York: Basic Books.

———. 1979. The social framework of the information society. In *The computer age: A twenty-year view,* ed. M. Dertouzos and J. Moses, 163–211. Cambridge: MIT Press.

Beniger, J. 1986. *The control revolution.* Cambridge: Harvard University Press.

Boggs, C. 1984. *The two revolutions: Gramsci and the dilemmas of Western Marxism.* Boston: South End Press.

Brzezinski, Z. 1977. *Between two ages: America's role in the technetronic era.* Harmondsworth: Penguin.

Burnham, D. 1983. *The rise of the computer state.* New York: Random House.

Burt, R. 1982. *Toward a structural theory of action.* New York: Academic Press.

Calhoun, C. J. 1978. History, anthropology and the study of communities: Some problems in MacFarlane's proposal. *Social History* 3, no. 3:363–73.

———. 1980. Community: Toward a variable conceptualization for comparative research. *Social History* 5, no. 1:105–29.

———. 1982. *The question of class struggle: Social foundations of popular protest in industrializing England.* Chicago: University of Chicago Press.

———. 1983. The radicalism of tradition: Community strength or venerable disguise and borrowed language? *American Journal of Sociology* 88, no. 5:886–914.

———. 1986. Computer technology, large scale social integration and the local community. *Urban Affairs Quarterly* 22, no. 2:329–49.

———. 1988. Class, place and industrial revolution. In *Class and space: The making of urban society,* ed. P. Williams and N. Thrift, 51–72. London: Routledge and Kegan Paul.

Coffee, J. C., Jr. 1981. "No soul to damn: No body to kick": An unscandalized inquiry into the problem of corporate punishment. *Michigan Law Review* 79 (January):386–459.

Coleman, J. S. 1982. *The asymmetric society.* Syracuse, N.Y.: Syracuse University Press.

Cooley, C. H. [1909] 1962. *Social organization.* New York: Shocken.

Dan-Cohen, M. 1986. *Rights, persons, and organizations: A legal theory for bureau-cratic society.* Berkeley: University of California Press.

Duncan, O. D. 1959. Cultural, behavioral, and ecological perspectives in the study of social organization. *American Journal of Sociology* 65, no. 2:132–53.

Durkheim, E. [1893] 1964. *The division of labor in society.* New York: Free Press.

———. [1895] 1966. *The rules of sociological method.* New York: Free Press.

Engels, F. [1880] 1972. Socialism: Utopian and scientific. In *The Marx-Engels reader,* ed. R. Tucker, 605–39. New York: Norton.

Forester, T., ed. 1986. *The information technology revolution.* Cambridge: MIT Press.

Frank, A. G. 1969. *Capitalism and underdevelopment in Latin America.* Rev. ed. New York: Monthly Review Press.

———. 1978. *Dependent accumulation and underdevelopment.* New York: Monthly Review Press.

Fraser, N. 1985. What's critical about critical theory? The case of Habermas and gender. *New German Critique* 35:97–132.

French, P. A. 1984. *Collective and corporate responsibility.* New York: Columbia University Press.

Galbraith, J. K. 1978. *The new industrial state.* 3d ed. New York: Houghton-Mifflin.

Giddens, A. 1985a. *The constitution of society.* Berkeley: University of California Press.

———. 1985b. *A contemporary critique of historical materialism.* Vol. 2, *The nation-state and violence.* Berkeley: University of California Press.

Gierke, Otto von. 1934. *Natural law and the theory of society.* Cambridge: Cambridge University Press.

Gill, C. 1985. *Work, unemployment and the new technology.* Cambridge, Eng.: Polity Press.

Gramsci, A. 1982. *Selections from the prison notebooks.* Ed. and trans. Q. Hoare and G. N. Smith. London: Lawrence and Wishart.

Granovetter, M. 1985. Economic action and the problem of embeddedness. *American Journal of Sociology* 91, no. 3:481–510.

Gregory, D., and J. Urry, eds. 1985. *Spatial relations and social structures.* New York: St. Martin's Press.

Gunn, T. 1982. The mechanization of design and manufacturing. *Scientific American* 247, no. 3:115–30.

Gusfield, J. 1967. Tradition and modernity: Misplaced polarities in the study of social change. *American Journal of Sociology* 72, no. 3:351–62.

———. 1975. *Community: A critical response.* New York: Harper and Row.

Habermas, J. 1970. *Towards a rational society.* Boston: Beacon Press.

———. 1976. *Communication and the evolution of society.* Boston: Beacon Press.

———. 1984. *The theory of communicative action.* Vol. 1, *Reason and the rationalization of society.* Boston: Beacon Press.

Haines, V. 1985. Organicism, ecology, and human ecology. *Sociological Theory* 3, no. 1:65–74.

Hawley, A. 1950. *Human ecology: A theory of community structure.* New York: Ronald Press.

————. 1981. *Urban society.* 2d ed. New York: Wiley.

Hobbes, T. [1651] 1962. *Leviathan.* Harmondsworth: Penguin.

Innis, H. A. [1950] 1972. *Empire and communication.* Toronto: University of Toronto Press.

————. [1951] 1964. *The bias of communication.* Toronto: University of Toronto Press.

Jay, M. 1984. *Marxism and totality: The adventures of a concept from Lukacs to Habermas.* Berkeley: University of California Press.

Jones, B. 1982. *Sleepers wake! Technology and the future of work.* New York: Oxford University Press.

Kantorowicz, E. 1956. *The king's two bodies.* Princeton: Princeton University Press.

Kumar, K. 1978. *Prophecy and progress: The sociology of industrial and post-industrial societies.* Harmondsworth: Penguin.

Luhmann, N. 1979. *Trust and power.* Chichester: Wiley.

Lukács, G. [1922] 1971. *History and class consciousness.* Cambridge: MIT Press.

McCarthy, T. 1985. Complexity and democracy, or the seducements of systems theory. *New German Critique* 35:27–53.

McLuhan, M. 1964. *Understanding media: The extensions of man.* New York: McGraw-Hill.

Maitland, F. W. [1900] 1958. Introduction. In *Political theory of the Middle Ages,* by O. von Gierke, vii–xiv. Boston: Beacon Press.

Manning, C. A. W. 1962. *The nature of international society.* London: Bell.

Marx, K. [1844] 1975. *The economic and philosophical manuscripts of 1844.* In *Collected works,* by K. Marx and F. Engels, 3:229–348. London: Lawrence and Wishart.

————. [1867] 1974. *Capital.* Vol. 1. London: Lawrence and Wishart.

————. [1939] 1973. *Grundrisse.* Harmondsworth: Pelican.

Marx, K., and F. Engels. [1848] 1976. *Manifesto of the Communist party.* In *Collected works,* by K. Marx and F. Engels, 6:477–519. London: Lawrence and Wishart.

Meyrowitz, J. 1985. *No sense of place: The impact of electronic media on social behavior.* New York: Oxford.

Mitchell, J. C., ed. 1969. *Social networks in urban situations.* Manchester: Manchester University Press.

Nadel, S. 1957. *The theory of social structure.* London: Cohen and West.

Naisbitt, J. 1982. *Megatrends.* New York: Warner Books.

Nisbet, R. A., and R. G. Perrin. 1977. *The social bond.* Rev. ed. New York: Knopf.

Noble, D. 1984. *Forces of production: A social history of industrial automation.* New York: Knopf.

Ong, W. 1982. *Orality and literacy: The technologizing of the word.* New York: Methuen.

Orhnial, T., ed. 1984. *Limited liability and the corporation.* London: Croom Helm.

Parsons, T. 1951. *The social system.* New York: Free Press.

————. 1963. On the concept of political power. *Proceedings of the American Philosophical Society* 107:232–62.

Parsons, T., and G. Platt. 1973. *The American university.* Cambridge: Harvard University Press.

Postone, M. 1983. *The present as necessity: Towards a reinterpretation of the Marxian critique of labor and time.* Inauguraldissertation, Goethe-Universität, Frankfurt am Main.

Poulantzas, N. 1975. *Political power and social classes.* London: New Left Books.

Redfield, R. 1941. *Folk culture of the Yucatan.* Chicago: University of Chicago Press.

Sabato, L. 1981. *The rise of the new political consultants.* New York: Basic Books.

Sahlins, M. 1978. *Culture and practical reason.* Chicago: University of Chicago Press.

Saunders, P. 1985. Space, the city and urban sociology. In *Social relations and spatial structures,* ed. D. Gregory and J. Urry, 67–89. New York: St. Martin's Press.

Selznick, P. 1969. *Law, society and industrial justice.* New Brunswick, N.J.: Transaction Books.

Sennett, R. 1977. *The fall of public man.* New York: Knopf.

Simmel, G. [1903] 1971. The metropolis and mental life. In *Georg Simmel on individuality and social forms,* ed. D. N. Levine, 324–39. Chicago: University of Chicago Press.

———. [1907] 1978. *The philosophy of money.* London: Routledge and Kegan Paul.

Sorokin, P. A. 1957. *Social and cultural dynamics.* Abridged ed. Boston: Porter Sargent.

Stone, L. 1975. *Where the law ends.* New York: Harper and Row.

Taussig, M. 1978. *The devil and commodity fetishism.* Chapel Hill: University of North Carolina Press.

Tönnies, F. 1887. *Community and association (Gemeinschaft und Gesellschaft).* London: Routledge and Kegan Paul.

Toffler, A. 1980. *The third wave.* New York: Bantam.

Touraine, A. 1971. *Post-industrial society.* London: Wildwood House.

———. 1977. *The self-production of society.* Chicago: University of Chicago Press.

Wallerstein, I. 1974. *The modern world-system.* New York: Academic Press.

———. 1979. *The capitalist world economy.* New York: Academic Press.

Weber, M. [1922] 1978. *Economy and society.* 2 vols. Ed. Guenther Roth and Claus Wittich. Berkeley: University of California Press.

Williams, R. 1973. *The country and the city.* St. Albans, Eng.: Paladin.

Wirth, L. 1938. Urbanism as a way of life. *American Journal of Sociology* 44, no. 1:1–24.

Worsley, P. 1985. *The three worlds.* Chicago: University of Chicago Press.

Wright, E. O. 1985. *Classes.* London: New Left Books.

The Future of Capitalism

Johannes Berger

[Bernstein] says that capitalist development does not lead to a general economic collapse.

He does not merely reject a certain form of the collapse. He rejects the very possibility of collapse.

R. LUXEMBURG, *Reform or Revolution*

With the growing development of society, a complete and almost general collapse of the present system of production becomes not more but less probable because capitalist development increases, on the one hand, the capacity of adaptation and, on the other hand . . . the differentiation of industry.

E. BERNSTEIN, *Der kampf der Sozialdemokratie* (The Fight of Social Democracy)

Questioning the future of capitalism is nearly as old as capitalism itself. The development of this new social order was from the very beginning accompanied by concerns about both its inner stability and its overall viability. These doubts are evident not only in Marx but also in the efforts of so-called bourgeois sociology to grasp the elements of capitalism. In many quarters in the nineteenth and the early twentieth century the system was viewed in a negative light. The classical writings in European sociology reflect the view that the category of "modern" society is a transitional one; modern society has torn down the old social order but has been unable to erect a new one (Freyer 1930, 10, 165). With the coming of structural-functionalism, however, this negative diagnosis receded. But even Parsons's theory of modern society (1971) is informed by deep concerns about its future viability, and Luhmann (1984a) acknowledges that modern society both destabilizes structures and increases opportunities for criticism.

To take up once again the question of the future of capitalism is a bold enterprise. Whoever does so seems to pretend to view society and its development from an undistorted perspective. Historical materialism believed that it possessed such a viewpoint. A classic formulation of the idea that there is a special place inside society from which the social totality can be recognized in an undistorted way can be found in an early essay by Lukács: "It is only with the appearance of the Proletariat that

237

the recognition of social reality is completed. This completion is reached by having found in the class standpoint of the proletariat a point from which the totality of society becomes visible" (1923, 34, my translation). It is impossible, however, to espouse this viewpoint today because continuing social differentiation, complexity, and diversity mean that the essence of society cannot be captured by reference to its core or center.

Marx was convinced not only that a socialist society would necessarily follow a capitalist one but also that a socialist society would too represent a higher stage of civilization. In this chapter, however, I leave aside this normative dimension. Instead, I concentrate on the stability and the likely future of capitalism. I also touch briefly on the problems associated with doubts about the role of rationality in the modern world.

Because of the difficulty of investigating the future of modern societies, it is desirable to follow a famous predecessor. I choose Schumpeter as a starting point rather than Marx largely because Schumpeter created a new foundation for the study of the future prospects of capitalism. Both Schumpeter and Marx hold the view that "capitalism" is an adequate characterization of the present epoch of history. In general sociological theory there is a debate between cultural accounts of modernity, on the one hand (for example, Berger, Berger, and Kellner 1973), and Marxist accounts of capitalism, on the other hand (Bader and Berger 1976; Adorno 1969). This debate cannot be resolved here. I simply concur with Max Weber's belief that capitalism is "the most fateful power of modern life" (Weber 1920, 4). But insofar as capitalism and modernity become synonymous, it is necessary to enrich the theory of capitalism by a corresponding theory of modernity. I do not mean to fall into any kind of economic reductionism by asserting that capitalism played a central role in the "great transformation" (Polanyi 1957); I simply assert that the modernity of the economy is the model for the modernization of other institutional spheres.

I now turn to Schumpeter's central question: "Can capitalism survive?"

1. THE SURVIVABILITY OF CAPITALISM

This fateful question opens the second part of Schumpeter's classic *Capitalism, Socialism and Democracy*. He answers this question with a resounding no (Schumpeter [1942] 1962). Having answered, he has to ask, What kind of society will replace it? Schumpeter believed that socialism would follow. Although he saw socialism as a matter of evolutionary necessity, he also asked whether socialism could function as an economic system. This question he answered with a clear yes, and in doing so rejected the mainstream argument, developed by Weber and Mises, that the economic order of socialism is unstable and inefficient.

Today, after the unprecedented forty-year boom of the capitalist world economy and after the final breakdown of socialist economies, almost every student of capitalist development will find it difficult to follow Schumpeter's logic. Why is socialism supposed to be an efficient economic order? And why is capitalism supposed to be an economic system with only a limited life span? Has not the postwar period proved that capitalism is an extremely flexible and efficient economic system?

A common feature of all currents of socialist thought is that in the long run capitalism will necessarily be replaced in a revolutionary process by socialism. No doubt, Schumpeter shared with these strands of thought the idea of a shift from capitalism to socialism, but he did not believe that socialism represents a higher stage of evolution. He merely viewed socialism as a feasible economic order. For Schumpeter what distinguished socialism from capitalism was that in capitalism markets function as mechanisms for the distribution of the social product. The essence of capitalism was the combination of the functions of allocation and distribution within the framework of one economic mechanism, namely, the market. By institutionalizing markets for capital and labor, capitalist societies relieved themselves of questions of distributional equity. To abolish the markets for capital and labor, however, does not imply that in socialist societies rational economic behavior is impossible. For Schumpeter the reason for the decay of capitalism is not its economic failure. He does not substantiate his argument about the inability of capitalism to survive with the traditional argument that it is prone to crises. On the contrary, Schumpeter posits an inherent relationship between a capitalist economic order and growth. No other economic system is capable of attaining a comparable rate of economic growth. Therefore, if capitalism perishes, it is not at all because of its economic failure. In fact, it is capitalism's success that dooms it. "My thesis," Schumpeter writes ([1942] 1962, 61), is "that the actual and prospective performance of the capitalist system is such as to negate the idea of its breaking down under the weight of economic failure, but that its very success undermines the social institutions which protect it, and 'inevitably' creates conditions in which it will not be able to live and which strongly point to socialism as the heir apparent."

In this way Schumpeter puts the theory of the self-destructive tendencies of capitalism on a new basis. He wants to demonstrate that, contrary to Marx, there are no purely economic reasons for the breakdown of capitalism. He emphasizes that capitalism's self-destructive tendencies can be ascertained only if one leaves the field of economic considerations and turns to the cultural complement of the capitalist economy, namely, its sociopsychological superstructure ([1924] 1962, 198). Among the social institutions that are undermined by the success of capitalism

Schumpeter includes (1) the entrepreneurial function, (2) nonbourgeois groups, and (3) private property and the freedom of contracting. The individual entrepreneur is made superfluous by the transition from liberal to corporate capitalism: "The perfectly bureaucratized giant industrial unit . . . ousts the entrepreneur (Schumpeter [1942] 1962, 134). As to nonbourgeois groups, Schumpeter argues that the aristocracy, the craft guilds, and the peasantry are not only feudal shackles but also a precondition for the vitality of capitalism, in part because they are allies in the conflict of the bourgeoisie with the proletariat and in part because the bourgeois class, when compared with the aristocracy, is "ill equipped to face the problems, both domestic and international, that have normally to be faced by a country of any importance" (Schumpeter [1942] 1962, 138). Private property and the freedom of contracting are threatened by bureaucratization, the replacement of small firms by big enterprises, and a "tropical growth of new legal structures" (Schumpeter [1942] 1962, 191).

To analyze the future prospects of capitalism, Schumpeter uses the metaphor of a fortress under siege. Capitalism diminishes its chances to survive not only by weakening the walls that protect it but also by increasing the hostility of its enemies. Intellectuals play an important role in capitalism's creation of an "atmosphere of almost universal hostility" (Schumpeter [1942] 1962, 143). The bourgeois fortress becomes defenseless because a capitalist order is unable to control its intellectual sector, which "lives on criticism" (Schumpeter [1942] 1962, 151). This argument is far from being compelling. But even if the specific details of Schumpeter's argument are weak, the general argument is worth pursuing further. His general argument consists of two propositions: (a) capitalism will be undermined not by its failure but by the consequences of its success, and (b) these consequences are to be found not in the economic system but in the specific relationship between the economic system and its environment.

By replacing the Marxist "deterioration" perspective with a perspective that emphasized improvement and that focused on the negative consequences of success, Schumpeter revolutionized the foundations of the theory of capitalist development. However, when he speculated about the results of capitalist development, Schumpeter was quite conventional: he kept to the idea that socialism was the "heir apparent" of capitalism (even though he did not believe in socialism). Since he wrote these words, history has totally refuted Schumpeter's conviction about the inevitability of socialism; today only a small minority regards socialism as the solution to the problems that the capitalist mode of production has created. After the Second World War, the advanced capitalist countries enjoyed an extended period of prosperity for which it is impossible to find a precedent. This golden age of prosperity ended in the 1970s, but since the mid-1980s the leading industrial market economies have again experienced a period of growth. Either the social institutions that protect capitalism did not erode as Schumpeter expected or their erosion did not prevent capitalism from growing.

Although the viability of capitalist economies may be undisputed and socialist economies have failed to become a convincing alternative, it is imperative to reconsider Schumpeter's problem. Even if the industrial market economies prove to be capable of sustainable growth, it cannot be denied that this growth causes serious problems in the environment of the economic system, of which the destruction of nature is only the most obvious example. The impairment of the social and natural environment by economic growth may have repercussions on the functioning of the economy. Sociological theory must face the possibility that the economy affects its environment in a manner that makes it difficult or impossible for the economy to reproduce itself in this environment. To study the repercussions of the future prospects of industrialized market economies, a Schumpeterian framework is more apt than a Marxian one. However, two important modifications of Schumpeter's framework must be made. First, it is necessary to give up the capitalism-socialism dichotomy; socialism is in no sense the future of capitalism. Second, we must strictly separate the idea that a successful capitalist economy may endanger itself through the negative consequences that it sets off in its environment from the idea of a "general economic collapse" (Luxemburg 1937).

Insofar as the framework of the following analysis differs from Schumpeter's, it is because I assume that the viability of capitalism can be ensured by structural changes. This assumption does not serve to deny that capitalism is prone to crises. Quite the contrary. However, these crises cannot be identified with the total dissolution of the existing order or with the idea that the existing order will be replaced by an entirely different order in a way that is comparable to the transformation from feudalism to capitalism. Rather, I conceptualize crises as situations in which tensions that are inherent in the system have developed to a point where the system's central features can no longer be maintained. The structure must be transformed, but the direction of the transformation is uncertain. If we understand a crisis to be a phase of restructuring whose outcome is uncertain, this enables us to both reckon with a new prosperity and acknowledge the inherent tensions in the system. In any case sociologists should avoid forecasting with certainty the breakdown of the capitalist economy. The immense flexibility, adaptive capacity, and innovative potential that capitalist economies have displayed since World War II should prevent us from rushing to any doomsday conclusions.

I would like to approach my main question by dividing it into three parts:

1. What does capitalism mean?
2. What is capitalism's central problem?
3. Is there a solution for capitalism's central problem or will it finally collapse?

I argue that capitalism increases its viability by integrating elements that are alien to its pure form.

2. THE MEANING OF CAPITALISM

It is often asserted that the decisive feature of capitalism is that the means of production are controlled by a small group called capitalists, and that the majority of the labor force is forced to sell its labor power to the owners of the means of production in order to earn a living. Thus capitalism means the separation of the worker from the means of production. However, one may ask whether an approach that focuses on the conflict of capital and labor is not too simplistic a conception of the fundamental change that occurred during the "great transformation" (Polanyi 1957). Even if one accepts the notion that the control of the means of production is the decisive feature of the capitalist economy, it is still not clear that this description is a complete characterization of the structure of modernity. In practice the sociological theory of modernity may be read as a critique of the attempt to root the theory of society in a theory of the economy (Luhmann 1986). Taking these objections into account, I interpret the rise of the capital-labor relationship as an essential factor within the broader process of modernization. But what are the main features of this broader process?

Marx himself described modernization as a process in which the economy is set free from traditional bounds and gains autonomy. His successors did little more than work out the different aspects of this *Freisetzungsprozess* (process of setting free) that are constitutive for modernization. In traditional societies "the economic system was submerged in general social relations . . . the self-regulating market was unknown; indeed the emergence of the idea of self-regulation was a complete reversal of the trend of development" (Polanyi 1957, 67). The autonomy of the economy from the rest of society is essential for modernization. To be sure, other spheres of modern society—the state, law, science, etc.—also became relatively autonomous. For this reason I believe it is unnecessary and futile to look for a dominant structure in history. The separate spheres of politics, law, economic science, and the like cannot be deduced from the "principle of value" (cf. Sieferle 1984, 22). But these spheres differ in the degree to which they achieved autonomy from the rest of society.

Three features characterize the rise of the capitalist economy as a process of *Freisetzung:* first, the separation of society into an economic and political sphere, second, expanded reproduction (that is, ceaseless accumulation), and third, the dissolution of "communities" and "worldviews."

1. The characteristic feature of capitalism as an economic order is the liberation of economic activities from political patronage. In the course of the transition from feudalism to capitalism the economy is detached from the social order, the core of which is political authority. The separation of economic functions from the broader social context has become the model of modernization as a whole. In sociological systems theory this process has been called "functional differentiation." Western Marxism also treats this differentiation as the separation of the economic from the political sphere. The economy did not exist as an independent structure, that is, as a sphere of trade and acquisitive activities, until this separation. The emerging acquisitive society was a "free" society in the sense that economic activities were no longer fused with political concerns, as had been the case in mercantile societies. Producers in the economy were now free to focus entirely on their economic functions. This freedom meant that capitalist firms no longer based their production decisions on external (political) interests. Rather their production decisions were based on the norms of economic rationality (Weber 1972, 79).

2. Rational capitalism is not characterized by the pursuit of profit as such. We also find this in traditional societies. It is also not characterized by the appropriation of a surplus, which occurs in earlier modes of production, too. Rather, capitalism is characterized by the reinvestment of the appropriated surplus. "What is different about capitalism as a surplus-generating system is that it is the only system that invests its surplus, not in articles of personal or public luxury and adornment, but in the means to achieve more wealth" (Heilbroner 1982, 35). The business of the entrepreneur is to invest this surplus. The wealth of the societies dominated by the capitalist mode of production is entirely based on the fact that capital accumulates. If the reinvestment of surplus is to take place continuously and in a rational manner, then wage labor is needed as a precondition of accumulation. Marx described this built-in coercion of capitalist systems to accumulate as a self-determining process. In the chapters on expanded reproduction in *Capital,* Volume 2, Marx (1970) analyzed the economy of modern society as a closed, self-referential system

reproducing its elements by means of those same elements (cf. Luhmann 1984b, 315; Maturana 1979). Marx chooses the commodity as that basic element, unlike Luhmann, who designates payments to be the basic elements of the economy. If Marx is correct, the essence of a capitalist economy can indeed be characterized as the "production of commodities by means of commodities" (Sraffa 1960). Such a system is self-referential: accumulation takes place for the sake of accumulation, and it is closed in the sense that it reproduces the elements of which it consists. Thus the coercion to accumulate characterizes the mode of operation of an "autopoietic" system, that is, a system whose reproduction is based on the production of its elements with the help of a network of those elements.

3. The dissolution of existing worldviews and communities is a manifold process. At least three different aspects should be distinguished.

(a) The rationalization of worldviews (see Habermas 1981a) is a process that leads to the end of a unified metaphysics in the transition from the old to the modern world. As a result of this rationalization, the cultural value-spheres of science, morality, and art became separated. Since this time, there has been no unified belief system; at least three different belief systems have taken the place of the former metaphysics. "Since the 18th century," Habermas writes, "the problems inherited from these older worldviews can be arranged so as to fall under specific aspects of validity: truth, normative rightness, authenticity, and beauty. They could then be handled as questions of knowledge, or of justice and morality, or of taste" (1981a, 8). Whereas the philosophy of old Europe accommodated a "uniform" and "closed" society, capitalism is characterized by diverse, complex systems of belief, quite different from the unified ones in old Europe. Perhaps Lukács, in his theory of the novel ([1920] 1971) delivered the most impressive description of the "compact" world of classical antiquity and the Middle Ages. This compactness disappears when capitalism invades premodern societies. The rise of capitalism effects an opening of those closed worlds in both spatial and, above all, temporal respects. Before the rise of capitalism there is no open future.

(b) Modernization is not limited to the emergence of separate subsystems, such as the economy, with specific functions. Of equal importance is the tendency for the "system" and the "life-world" to diverge (Habermas 1981b). In the course of modernization the sphere of (bourgeois) society is set free from "communal" ties. But in the very same process the meaning of "community" changes. Habermas's life-world concept stands for the same phenomenon that Parsons referred to as "societal community" and that Tönnies was trying to get at in his distinction between "society" and "community." Tönnies remarked that not social life per se but communal social life vanishes and a new social life develops (1982, 38). In sociological systems theory this process has been described as the uncoupling of society from its interactions (Luhmann 1984a). Undoubtedly there is already some difference between society and its interactions in primitive society, but the gap increases in the course of development; with the French revolution the existence of the gap became obvious. Since that time the belief that society is controlled by personal interactions has turned out to be illusory (Luhmann 1984a, 577, 579). The communications that are part of daily life are subject to principles and normative orientations that differ from communications in the functionally differentiated subsystems of society. In modern society normative orientations, which may be predominant in interactions, diverge as a rule from the dominant values and orientations of actions in the field of science, the economy, and politics (Luhmann 1975). In the modern economy the separation between society and its interactions amounts to the detachment of capitalism from normative contexts. Because of this detachment from normative contexts the market becomes an "impersonal order"; it is not an accident that such different thinkers as Marx and von Hayek use this term to describe the essence of the market order. Markets are distinguished from other realms of society by the fact that they only need a minimal morality to function. In Streissler's words, the market is an economic mechanism that could function even among devils (1980).

(c) Capitalism leads to the disintegration of all forms of communal life. The classical description of this process can be found in Marx's *Grundrisse* (1973). In the famous chapter on "forms which precede capitalist production" (1973, 471–79, 483–514) Marx outlines a discontinuous view of historical evolution that differs radically from the evolutionary scheme he posits in the *Foreword to a Critique of Political Economy* (1969), which places capitalism on a continuum of forms of society that stretches from slavery to socialism. Capitalism involves a fundamental structural break in history. This break may be characterized as a switch from a "natural" (*naturwüchsig*) to a "pure" mode of social integration (Breuer 1983). Through this decisive shift in the mode of social integration, all social structures become contingent. Because each social phenomenon in modernity is "made" or "produced" (*gesetzt*), it can in principle be arranged differently (see Touraine 1977).

Having distinguished between the three essential features of modernity, the question arises whether these features have a common root. I believe that this common root is the "liberation from the past," which results in the autonomy of the components of a modern society. A modern society differs from a premodern one in that there is no longer a social bond that keeps the parts of society from drifting apart. In premodern societies community acted as that social bond. Certainly community has not vanished in modern society but it has become another subsystem. To belong to a community today is not an all-embracing process that leaves little room for individuality. On the level of individual behavior this change in the "status" of community is reflected in an increase in the number of "options" and a decrease in "ligatures" (Dahrendorf 1979). During the transition to modernity the cultural net that held together different activities in traditional societies starts to disintegrate. In modern societies a comparable core of normative values that restricts the range of options does not exist.

In the economic realm Marx's concept of the "self-valorization of value" as a "ceaseless movement" had already formulated the fundamental process by which the economy was being freed from traditional life-orders. "All that is solid melts into air." This short sentence from the *Communist Manifesto* captures the essence of modernization (Berman 1982). But it would be misleading to regard this process exclusively as a negative one; on the level of society as a whole modernization means not only disintegration but also the development of productive forces, the increase of adaptive capacity, and the like. Moreover, on the level of the individual it means emancipation and self-development.

3. THE CENTRAL PROBLEM OF CAPITALISM

Political economy examines the problems of capitalism that result from its inner weaknesses and instability. Unlike the crisis-theoretical approach of political economy, a theory of self-destructive tendencies (à la Schumpeter) emphasizes that the decisive problems of capitalism result from its continuing stability and strength, which is, for example, demonstrated by its ability to penetrate preexisting forms of social life. Although one may question whether the history of capitalism is the history of progress, obviously this mode of production is evolutionarily superior in the sense that it substitutes for premodern forms of economic organization and that socialism is not a stable or promising alternative to it. If one follows this line of thought, the "contradictions" that are capable of endangering the advanced capitalist economies—if they exist at all—do not stem from the weakness but from the strength of the economy. From this point of view a capitalist economy generates systemic problems primarily by its functional efficiency and success, not by its functional deficiencies.

I have been arguing that the evolutionary core of the "great transformation" consists of a process of "freeing," "becoming autonomous," and "achieving independence" from different components of social life. Polanyi summarized this development with his concept of "disembeddedness." Only a disembedded social system is able to mobilize the energies needed to penetrate and disintegrate all given forms of social life, be they communities, life-worlds, worldviews, etc. The question is, How can one show that a mode of production based on *Freisetzung* contains self-destructive tendencies?

The only way to identify such self-destructive tendencies is to show that when capitalist economies are set free from normative bonds and instead pursue their own expansion, they destroy the preconditions for their functioning. These preconditions are located in the natural and cultural environment of the capitalist system. Insofar as a capitalist system does not keep within "reasonable" limits, it endangers itself by endangering its environment.

This argument is pitched at a very general level. The general idea that expanding markets destroy the resources on which a market economy relies is one of the most fundamental contributions of social theory to the analysis of the functioning of a market economy. But to point to this feedback loop is not sufficient to demonstrate that the destruction of the environment of a capitalist economy threatens its reproduction. To make the argument compelling, one has to demonstrate the mechanism by which such a self-threatening situation can evolve. A lot must happen before a robust economy is endangered. Given that the fundamental problem of a capitalist economy is not its inner weakness but its strength, in principle such a situation can only evolve if (a) a capitalist economy is crucially dependent on external resources and (b) these resources are being exhausted by capitalist growth.

Apropos the first issue, the radical ecologists contend that capitalist systems expanded in the past only because they found a variety of previously undiscovered natural resources (Immler 1989). But this interpretation may be disputed. It conflicts with the view that capitalist expansion is caused mainly by endogenous factors. This view is held by mainstream economics and even the neo-Ricardian interpretation of Marx does not deviate very much from it, stating that surplus labor "can play no essential role in the theory of why profits are positive" (Steedman 1977, 50). According to this view the viability of the capitalist economy relies on its productivity. An economy is productive if it produces more commodities than it consumes. Mainstream economics maintains that the productive quality of the capitalist system is owing to its technology. Neo-Ricardians add, And to the level of its real wages.

Apropos the second issue, the main problem consists in specifying the limits beyond which the destruction of external resources endangers the reproduction of the economy. Self-destructive tendencies can remain unnoticed for a long time because they vary with the ability of the environment to cope with impairments, not with the adaptive capacity of the system. Provided that one can quantitatively specify the amount of pollutants nature can cope with, these quantities need not indicate a limit for the functioning of the economic system producing this pollution. Before the natural limits to growth are attained, presumably normative limits make themselves felt. Whether and to what degree the destruction of the natural environment has repercussions on the functioning of the economy largely depends on a collective decision about the normative issue of how much pollution a society is willing to accept.

But attempts to substantiate the idea that the ongoing destruction of nature "in the long run" will impair the functioning of the economy have to take into account not only the indefiniteness of objective limits to the destruction of nature but also the problem that the economic system—as far as the consequences of the destruction of the environment are concerned—is less sensitive than other parts of society. Public opinion, new social movements, and the societal community react with more sensitivity to ecological issues because a central value of those systems, the quality of life, is endangered by the deterioration of the environment. That ecological issues lack resonance (Luhmann 1986) in the economic system is mainly the result of the fact that the economic system succeeded in realizing a high degree of autonomy vis-à-vis its environment. It disposes of a system-specific meaning of action—the provision for future needs—a system-specific criterion of selection—efficiency—a system-specific medium of communication—money—and a system-specific code—the price system. These system-specific features, which underlie the stable expansion of the economic system, may also explain why the economy tends to perceive environmental problems in a distorted way. For instance, the "language of prices" (Luhmann 1983) can comprehend problems that arise from the exhaustion of natural resources only if these resources have a price and even then it can only map the price aspect of the problem in question.

So far I have discussed the question of whether the destruction of external resources may impair economic expansion only with reference to natural resources. I left aside the destruction of normative and cultural resources and the possible repercussions of their destruction on the economy. Hirsch (1976) has studied the "depleting moral legacy" of capitalism. He regards the market system as an attempt "to erect an increasingly explicit social organization without a supporting social morality" (1976, 12). According to Hirsch the

> social morality that has served as an understructure for economic individualism has been a legacy of the precapitalist and preindustrialist past. This legacy has diminished with time and with the corrosive contact of the active capitalist values. . . . The system has thereby lost outside support that was previously taken for granted by the individual. As individual behaviour has been increasingly directed to individual advantage, habits and instincts based on communal activities and objectives have lost out. (1976, 117–18)

As Hirsch emphasizes, welfare losses and increasing difficulties in managing capitalist economies are the direct consequences of the weakening of traditional social values.

Although Hirsch's argument is appealing, I do not propose to discuss it at length. The only point I want to make is that in order to study the repercussions of the exhaustion of external resources on the economy, it is reasonable to give ecological arguments preference over moral ones. The main reason for this preference is that a capitalist order not only destroys the moral order it has inherited from the past but also creates a new one resting on capitalist foundations. As Axelrod (1984), for instance, has shown, self-interest may act as a source of cooperation. Whereas a capitalist order can create a social morality that is capable of supporting the functioning of the system, the same is not true for natural resources. The economy may lower its consumption of natural resources and there may be substitutes for them, but no economic system is able to create them. Thus there is a strong case for focusing on ecological problems if the fundamental problems of a capitalist market economy, which are connected with its strengths and not its weaknesses, are at stake.

To summarize, in order to make the search for possible solutions to the ecological problem an imperative, it is only necessary to make two assumptions:

1. An expanding economy is capable of destabilizing nature. It is not necessary to assume that its expansion relies on the exploitation of natural resources.

2. There is a need for action even though the economy may be less concerned by the consequences of the destruction of the environment than other social systems, for example, the societal community.

4. POSSIBLE SOLUTIONS

If we assume that the ecological problems arising from the "ceaseless movement of accumulation" supersede the problems occurring on the labor-capital front, then the key question is whether this accumulative movement can be restrained and made sensitive to its side effects. A satisfying answer to the question of which strategies are successful in steering an economy toward a path of no or less harm to the ecology would require an examination of the different steering mechanisms a modern society disposes of (markets, the state, community, corporations, etc., see Streeck and Schmitter 1985). This task, however, is far beyond the objective of this chapter. I confine myself to some sketchy remarks on the question of whether democratization could help. I also want to point out that self-control (self-regulation) and an increase in self-responsibility seem to be a promising way to cope with the ecological problem.

In a stimulating article on the reasons why "big rare whales still die," Gonigle (1980) describes the conflict between ecology and economy as the consequence of the "economizing" of the ecology. For him ecology means more than merely the protection of the natural environment. "Economy" and "ecology" stand for different sets of "decision rules." The difference between the two sets of decision rules is defined by the different time horizons each implies. Because they provide for future needs, economic decisions are directed to the future (Weber 1972, 31, 35). But their time horizon is restricted to the short term. Long-term problems are not considered in rational investment decisions. The investor, neglecting the future, pursues a strategy of maximizing returns, even if this leads to the exhaustion of the natural resources on which he depends. In contrast to economic decision making, ecological decision making acknowledges that the earth has to be preserved for future generations. Therefore, present needs have to be weighed against future ones. From the ecological point of view economic behavior can be regarded as an attack of the present on the future. In terms of economics market allocation is suboptimal in intertemporal and intergenerational respects.

In its evolutionary aspect the main problem of the economic mode of decision making is that it threatens the balance between economy and ecology. For this reason it is short-sighted to regard the transition to socialism as a solution to this problem. The distinction between capitalism and socialism does not capture the essence of the problem. Gonigle sees the extermination of big whales as connected with the general problem of the lack of integration between the economic system and its natural environment. For him the solution to the problem lies in the politics of ecological transition. The result of such a transition would be the institutionalization of a radically changed mode of decision making. Gonigle describes this in conventional terms as "democratic" decision making that should take into consideration the interests of the natural environment. But Gonigle does not explain what he means by "demo-

cratic." Usually, democratic decision making is identified with the participation of the workers in the investment decisions of the firm. Following
this conventional definition, one would have to explain how the participation of the workers is necessarily a means to integrate the interests of the
natural environment. Quite the opposite can happen. The postwar
growth of the European welfare states was based on a capital-labor accord that included the reckless disregard of the consequences of growth
to the natural environment.

The problem of how to control ecological risks in decision making
leads to a more emphatic and more radical idea of democratization. This
idea is present in Marx's projection of a postcapitalist type of association
that enables people to control their *Lebenszusammenhang* (social life) instead of being controlled by it. Heilbroner, with reference to Branko
Horvat's book *The Political Economy of Socialism*, describes this radical
democratization of decision making as the "complete lodging of decision
making and responsibility for the labor process in labor, and the complete lodging of political responsibility in citizens" (1982, 39). Considering the degree of differentiation in modern societies, it is unclear what
type of institutional change would be required to effect such control. It is
not enough to refer simply to the principle "only the persons concerned
ought to decide" as a general rule for decision making. This rule is
impracticable because one cannot separate the persons concerned from
the persons not concerned. Who, for instance, is affected by an economic
decision? Moreover, this rule could be repudiated for normative reasons,
not to mention the decline of efficiency it would probably cause.

If we want to minimize ecological risks, more than a vague appeal to
democratic decision making is required (cf. Perrow 1984). We must explore the available strategies to sensitize the economic system to the
destructive consequences that "ceaseless accumulation" has on the environment of the system. The recent literature on control strategies and
social planning attempts to explore the potential of institutional change
by "self-control" (*Selbststeuerung*). Self-control replaces state intervention,
but it is not the same as deregulation. Under self-control the political
system helps to increase the capacity of the economy to organize itself.
The principle of self-control may be summarized as follows: the economy is restructured in a way that enables it to become aware of the side
effects of economic decisions in the environment of the economy. As the
capacity of self-control increases, the economic system stops maximizing
efficiency without regard to the environment: the standards of a healthy
environment are taken into account in economic decision making. By
this measure, the purposive rationality of economic decision making is
increased insofar as the purposive rationality of decisions depends on
the capacity of a system to be aware of the consequences of its actions.

These consequences may be indirect, remote, or noneconomic in nature. To internalize standards of rationality that include the environment does not imply giving up in toto the pursuit of self-interest or of system-specific goals. Rather it means that these goals must be pursued in such a way that the side effects of pursuing these goals are taken into account from the beginning (Teubner and Willke 1984).

Each reorganization of the economy that is based on self-control amounts to an increase in the perceptive faculty of the economy. One possible way of attaining the required institutional change is to monetarize the ecology, that is, ecologize the economy by economizing the ecology. As long as nature is a free good, rational decision making has to treat it as such.

One must not confound this opening of the economic system for environmental problems with "dedifferentiation." Dedifferentiation occurs if the economy pursues noneconomic goals (for example, education). In contrast, to include environmental effects in economic decision making does not concern the functional specialization of the economic system. Rather it concerns the autonomy of the economic system. A model for the opening of the economy to its environment is social policy. Heimann ([1929] 1980) describes the principle of social policy as the realization of social welfare ideas in capitalism *against* capitalism. Social welfare ideas are inherently anticapitalist insofar as their realization amounts to the revolutionary restructuring of the capitalist economy. However, the implementation of social welfare ideas stabilizes demand and attenuates opposition to the capitalist order. Thus social welfare ideas contribute to the survival of capitalism, and social policy is at the same time both revolutionary and conservative (Heimann [1929] 1980).

One can now argue that the politics of realizing ecological ideas in capitalism against capitalism is analogous to Heimann's definition of the contradictory nature of social policy. Provided that ecological politics finds normative consent, the most important question is whether ecological ideas should be realized by means of external control or an increase in the spontaneous self-control of the economy. In the latter case "control" means to increase the empathy of the system and to bind its autonomy by "heteronomizing" it. As a result, an ecologized economy would prevent both the further deterioration of the natural environment and the disintegration of life-spheres. Such a transformation to an ecological economy would imply a rearrangement of the relationship between the economy and the other social orders. It would also allow a greater variety of modes of production and life-styles. In this manner "reflexive" types of control are compatible with the autonomy of the economy. By reflexive types of control, I refer to the types of control that reflect the negative consequences of system operations on its environment. Because of reflexive types of control, a system becomes aware of the disturbing effects of its operations; this awareness is a necessary precondition for the readiness to decrease the level of such effects.

I argue that autonomy (a lack of common bonds) is, on the one hand, a necessary condition for the efficiency of the economy and, on the other hand, leads to a neglect of the environment. Therefore, skepticism vis-à-vis the possibility of an ecologically sensitive capitalist economy is advised. One can certainly argue that given the self-referential mode of operation of the economy, reflexive forms of control are rather improbable. In my opinion, at least two preconditions must be fulfilled to render self-control effective:

1. Governments must give priority to environmental policy, and
2. Social movements that are trying to win influence over economic decision making by means of public discourse must exist.

However, in order to ensure that the environment appears on the "screens" of the subsystem, it is worthwhile to make use of the medium specific to the particular subsystem. In the case of the economy this medium is money.

As recent ecological catastrophes have repeatedly demonstrated, there is still a crucial lack of self-control and reflection. But does the autonomy of the economy necessarily imply its inability to learn? If the answer is yes, then the question of capitalism's survival turns into one of whether capitalism can ride out a political discussion about the costs and benefits of a type of production that purchases growth by destroying the environment; not much imagination is needed to depict a situation in which the refusal of the economy to take ecological concerns into account renders state intervention which restricts the autonomy of the economy inevitable.

REFERENCES

Adorno, T. W., ed. 1969. *Spätkapitalismus oder Industriegesellschaft? Verhandlungen des 16. Deutschen Soziologentages in Frankfurt, 1968.* Stuttgart: Enke.

Axelrod, R. 1984. *The evolution of cooperation.* New York: Basic Books.

Bader, V. M., J. Berger et al. 1976. *Einführung in die Gesellschaftstheorie: Karl Marx und Max Weber im Vergleich.* Frankfurt: Campus.

Berger, P., B. Berger, and H. Kellner. 1973. *The homeless mind.* New York: Random House.

Berman, M. 1982. *All that is solid melts into air.* New York: Penguin.

Bernstein, E. 1897–98. Der Kampf der Sozialdemokratie und die Revolution der Gesellschaft. In *Die Neue Zeit,* no. 18, 548–57.

Breuer, S. 1983. *Sozialgeschichte des Naturrechts.* Opladen: Westdeutscher Verlag.

Dahrendorf, R. 1979. *Lebenschancen.* Frankfurt: Suhrkamp.

Freyer, A. 1930. *Soziologie als Wirklichkeitswissenschaft.* Leipzig: Teubner.

Gonigle, R. M. 1980. The "economizing" of ecology: Why big, rare whales still die. *Ecology Law Quarterly* 9:120–237.

Habermas, J. 1981a. Modernity versus postmodernity. *New German Critique* 22:5–18.

———. 1981b. *Theorie des kommunikativen Handelns.* Frankfurt: Suhrkamp.

Heilbroner, R. L. 1982. The future of capitalism. *Challenge* 25:32–39.

Heimann, E. [1929] 1980. *Soziale Theorie des Kapitalismus: Theorie der Sozialpolitik: Mit einem Vorwort von Bernhard Badura.* Frankfurt: Suhrkamp.

Hirsch, F. 1976. *Social limits to growth.* Cambridge, Mass.: Routledge and Kegan Paul.

Horvat, B. 1983. *The political economy of socialism.* New York: M. E. Sharpe.

Immler, H. 1989. *Vom Wert der Natur.* Opladen: Westdeutscher Verlag.

Lukács, G. [1920] 1971. *Die Theorie des Romans: Ein geschichtsphilosophischer Versuch über die Formen der grossen Epik.* Neuwied: Luchterhand.

———. 1923. *Geschichte und Klassenbewusstsein: Studien über marxistische Dialektik.* Berlin: Malik-Verlag.

Luhmann, N. 1975. Interaktion, Organisation, Gesellschaft. In *Soziologische Aufklärung,* ed. N. Luhmann, 2:9–20. Opladen: Westdeutscher Verlag.

———. 1983. Das sind Preise: Ein soziologisch-systemtheoretischer Klärungsversuch. In *Soziale Welt* 34:153–70.

———. 1984a. *Soziale Systeme. Grundriß einer allgemeinen Theorie.* Frankfurt/Main: Suhrkamp.

———. 1984b. Die Wirtschaft der Gesellschaft als autopoietisches System. *Zeitschrift für Soziologie* 13:308–27.

———. 1986. *Ökologische Kommunikation: Kann die moderne Gesellschaft sich auf ökologische Gefährdungen einstellen?* Opladen: Westdeutscher Verlag.

Luxemburg. R. 1937. *Reform or Revolution.* Trans. Integer. New York: Three Arrows Press, 1937.

Marx, K. 1953. *Grundrisse der Kritik der politischen Ökonomie.* Berlin: Dietz-Verlag.

———. 1969. *Zur Kritik der politischen Ökonomie.* In *Werke,* by Karl Marx and Friedrich Engels, 13:3–160. Berlin: Dietz Verlag.

———. 1970. *Das Kapital: Kritik der politischen Ökonomie.* Vol. 2, *Der Zirkulationsprozess des Kapitals.* In *Werke,* by K. Marx and F. Engels, vol. 24. Berlin: Dietz-Verlag.

———. 1973. *Grundrisse.* Foundations of the critique of political economy. Ed. M. Nicolaus. New York: Vintage.

Maturana, H. 1979. *Autopoietic systems: A characterization of the living organization.* Urbana: University of Illinois Press.

Mises, L. V. 1932. *Die Gemeinwirtschaft: Untersuchungen über den Socialismus.* Jena: G. Fischer.

Okishio, N. 1977. Notes on technical progress and capitalist society. *Cambridge Journal of Economics* 1:93–100.

Parsons, T. 1971. *The system of modern societies.* Englewood Cliffs, N.J.: Prentice-Hall.

Perrow, C. 1984. *Normal accidents: Living with high-risk technologies.* New York: Basic Books.

Polanyi, K. 1957. *The great transformation: The political and economic origins of our time.* Boston: Beacon Press.

Schumpeter, J. [1942] 1962. *Capitalism, socialism and democracy.* New York: Harper and Row.

Sieferle, R. P. 1984. *Fortschrittsfeinde?: Opposition gegen Technik und Industrie von der Romantik bis zur Gegenwart.* Munchen: C. H. Beck.

Sraffa, P. 1960. *Production of commodities by means of commodities.* London: Cambridge University Press.

Steedman, Ian. 1977. *Marx after Sraffa.* London, New Left Books.

Streeck, W., and P. C. Schmitter. 1985. Community, market, state, and associations? The prospective contribution of interest governance to social order. *European Sociological Review* 1:119–38.

Streissler, E. 1980. Kritik des neoklassischen Gleichgewichtsansatzes als Rechtfertigung marktwirtschaftlicher Ordnungen. In *Theorie markwirtschaftlicher Ordnungen,* ed. E. Streissler and C. Watrin, 38–60. Tübingen: Mohr.

Teubner, G., and H. Willke. 1984. Kontext und Autonomie: Gesellschaftliche Selbststeuerung durch reflexives Recht. *Zeitschrift für Rechtssoziologie* 6:4–35.

Tönnies, F. 1982. *Gemeinschaft und Gesellschaft.* In *Handwörterbuch der Soziologie,* abridged ed., ed. A. Vierkandt, 27–38. Stuttgart: Enke.

Touraine, A. 1977. *The self-production of society.* Chicago: University of Chicago Press.

Weber, M. 1920. *Gesammelte Aufsätze zur Religionssoziologie.* Vol. 1. Tübingen: Mohr.

——. 1972. *Wirtschaft und Gesellschaft: Grundrisse der verstehenden Soziologie.* Textbook ed. Tübingen: Siebeck und Mohr.

Cultural Change and Sociological Theory

Robert Wuthnow

The study of cultural change enjoys a long and venerable history in sociological theory. Going back in time, one thinks immediately of Comte's characterization of the evolution from theological culture to metaphysical culture to scientific culture. Or one thinks of the more dynamic aspects of Malinowski's treatment of culture or the work of Herbert Spencer on cultural evolution. Marx, Weber, and Durkheim all come to mind as having painted broad canvases depicting the contours of modern cultural change. Turning to more recent theorists, we confront Sorokin's model of the cyclical dynamics of ideational and sensate cultures and Parsons's specification of pattern variables as a way of modeling the cultural developments associated with social differentiation. Parsons's stage theory of societal evolution finds expression as a model of cultural evolution in the writings of Bellah, Eisenstadt, Dobert, and Habermas. Peter Berger, Thomas Luckmann, and Hans Blumenberg have made significant statements on the subject of cultural modernization. In the Marxist tradition such figures as Lukács, Althusser, and Therborn have contributed rich offerings. And we have a host of more focused empirical studies and specific theoretical inquiries by scholars such as Michel Foucault, Anthony Giddens, Niklas Luhmann, Neil Smelser, and Wolf Lepenies.

In contrast with most historians' approaches to cultural change, sociologists have been interested in generating broad theoretical models. Rather than focusing on the descriptive details of specific episodes of cultural change, they have tried to identify recurrent patterns that depict long-range directions of change or that stylize the main sources of change. Whereas the historian tends to be skeptical of broad generalizations of this kind, sociologists have been audacious enough to try to formulate vast theoretical panoramas on the basis of deductive logic and comparative inquiry. Presumably, these panoramas have been based on the historical "facts," but their purposes have been as much normative as descriptive. Their role has been not only to summarize some of what we know about the past but also to tell a story about where we have been and where we are going. As such, sociological theory functions as a guide that influences the very selection of issues on which to focus. Especially in theories of cultural change, the very framework that is adopted dictates the kinds of questions that can be asked. In sociology this aspect of the functioning of theoretical perspectives is usually made explicit. The same role, however, is often evident in the work of historians, even though they may be less inclined to acknowledge it.

Much has been written, of course, about the respective roles of historical inquiry and sociological theorizing and about the more specific interface between social history and historical sociology. The distinctions that have been drawn in that literature are quite relevant to the issue of cultural change as well. In addition, however, the problem of culture is plagued by a number of difficulties of its own. As soon as we enter its domain, our feet seem to sink into a quagmire of conceptual and empirical perplexities. We not only face the usual problems of selecting appropriate evidence and developing plausible theoretical generalizations but also seem to embark into a never-never land of subjective notions about beliefs and motivations that have only vague referents in the world of observable empirical evidence. We run into endless debates about epistemology, ontology, and interpretation that pit scholars against one another before the research task ever gets under way. The very meaning of "culture" itself, not to mention questions about the ways it changes, seems to evoke little consensus.

My intention here is not to address the more general issues of definition and theoretical method that surround the study of culture. Rather I reconstruct—and then examine critically—the main assumptions on which the two leading theories of cultural change have developed in sociology. First, I show that these two perspectives are clearly identifiable in the sociological literature, that they both grow out of classical sociological theory, and that they continue to influence much of our present thinking about cultural change. Second, I propose several criteria that can be used to judge the adequacy of these theories and demonstrate that both theories fall short of the mark on these counts. Finally, I briefly discuss an alternative approach to cultural change toward which some of the recent work on this topic appears to be moving.

One point of clarification is in order at the outset. Cultural change can refer to many different things, so many that the subject has to be defined more precisely if fruitful discussion is to ensue. For convenience three varieties of cultural change can be distinguished. First, there are many instances of cultural change that are part of a specific social movement and seem to do little more than reinforce or challenge a particular idea. An example would be the new emphasis that has been placed on nature in recent years by the environmentalist movement. Second, in some discussions cultural change is depicted primarily as a gradual, incremental process, apparently occurring largely as a result of imperceptible shifts in socialization patterns. An example of this kind of cultural change would be the presumed long-term decline in superstition over the past five hundred years or so. Finally, cultural change sometimes appears to happen fairly abruptly, on a large scale, and as part of a relatively distinct social movement or set of social movements. The Protestant Reformation might serve as an example. These distinctions are scarcely meant to stand as tight deductive categories but will nevertheless serve for present purposes. The theoretical perspectives I examine in this chapter focus primarily on the third kind of cultural change. At points I address aspects of the first two as well but my emphasis is on historically identifiable cultural changes of major proportions that are associated with a specific group of people, a movement, or a set of movements.

1. CULTURAL ADAPTATION THEORY

Cultural change has often been characterized in sociological theory as a developmental or evolutionary process that occurs in a sequence of analytically distinct stages in response to changing societal conditions. Variously described as institutional differentiation, growing societal complexity, or in terms of more specific tendencies such as urbanization and industrialization, social conditions are said to create problems that lead to new patterns of culture. These processes, moreover, are generally not entirely neutral with respect to subsequent developments but are thought to enhance the society's adaptive capacity to accomplish tasks necessary to its survival. Consequently, the cultural changes that become theoretically interesting are those that contain evidence of "adaptive upgrading," to use Talcott Parsons's (1971, 27) term, or "adaptive modification," as Marshall Sahlins (1960, 12) has suggested.

An early formulation of the theory of cultural adaptation can be found in Durkheim's *The Division of Labor in Society* ([1893] 1933). This formulation links cultural change specifically with the increasing institutional differentiation that comes about as societies grow larger and become more complex. In a relatively undifferentiated society, Durkheim ([1893] 1933, 287) argues, everyone is related to things "in the same way," so cultural expressions remain tied to the concrete ("this animal, this tree, this plant"). In a larger, more diverse society experiences are more varied, so people must shift to a higher level of abstraction in order to generate shared understandings (not "such an animal, but such a species"). Durkheim summarizes his general thesis in the following formula: "[The common conscience] changes its nature as societies become more voluminous. Because these societies are spread over a vaster surface, the common conscience is itself obliged to rise above all local diversities, to dominate more space, and consequently become more abstract" ([1893] 1933, 287). As an example, he suggests that religious conceptions become increasingly abstract and internally differentiated as societies grow more complex. In the simplest settings sacredness is an attribute of concrete objects rather than of separate gods. "But little by little religious forces are detached from the things of which they were first only the attributes. . . . Thus is formed the notion of spirits or gods who . . . exist outside of the particular objects to which they are more specifically attached . . . [and] are less concrete" ([1893] 1933, 288). Christianity, for instance, articulated a sharper distinction between God and nature than did earlier Greek polytheism. The Christian God was also more abstract and universal: the God of humanity rather than the God of the city or clan. As general correlates of the division of labor in modern societies, Durkheim also suggests a tendency toward greater cultural rationality and individuality. Rationality is associated with having general principles that permit communication across different situations, individuality with the fact that generalized cultural abstractions can be applied in different ways by different individuals. For example, science is a rational mode of communication that transcends local and national cultures; when we say, "In my view" or "I believe," we individuate science so it can mean different things to different people.

Directly or indirectly, the perspective formulated by Durkheim has found its way into the work of a variety of more recent theorists. Parsons, for example, describes cultural change as a process of "value generalization" that is specifically induced by the growing complexity of social patterns: "When the network of socially structured situations becomes more complex, the value pattern itself must be couched at a higher level of generality in order to ensure social stability" (1971, 27). As examples, he cites changes in religious conceptions, the development of empirical and theoretical knowledge, and changes in legal codes. Together these developments constitute, in Parsons's view, the critical form of cultural change: "The generalization of value systems, so that they can effectively regulate social action without relying upon particularistic prohibitions has been a central factor in the modernization process" (1971, 15). Much the same argument has been outlined by Niklas Luhmann, who until recently has borrowed heavily from Parsons's general theoretical perspective. In a succinct statement about cultural change Luhmann explains: "The reason for . . . the rise of ideologies lies in . . . an increase in the range of possible actions among which choices can be made, and thus in a heightening of the complexity of society—a heightening that, in turn, is attainable only when more effective mechanisms for the reduction of complexity can be institutionalized" (1982, 101). Others who have adopted this general view of cultural change include Robert Bellah, whose stage theory of religious evolution represents a major effort to depict broad patterns of cultural change, and Jürgen Habermas (1979), particularly in his scattered formulations on cultural evolution (which in many respects resemble Bellah's [1970] theory). Both formulations depict cultural evolution primarily as a response to increasing societal complexity.

Although the notion of societal complexity usually remains abstract in these formulations, two specific kinds of social change are frequently mentioned as prime sources of cultural adaptation. One is urbanization. Durkheim, for example, singles out rapid urbanization as a particularly likely source of increased cultural abstraction, rationality, and individuality. In rapidly growing cites, he observes, the population consists of large numbers of immigrants. Their experience is characterized by two overriding conditions: they must adjust to social circumstances that are much different than those in which they were reared, and the composition of the city is more varied because of the migrants' different backgrounds. Both, he suggests, encourage new outlooks and habits of thought.

The other specific kind of social change identified in the literature as a leading source of cultural adaptation is economic expansion. Economic growth causes dramatic effects on culture, especially when such growth occurs rapidly. Although the exact sequence of causation varies from one formulation to the next, the breakdown of established social relations that presumably accompanies rapid economic growth is frequently identified as an important factor. Durkheim, for example, articulates this notion, particularly in emphasizing the uprooting of community and the potential for disorientation that comes with the transition to industrial society. During this transition, he suggests, people are especially susceptible to new ideas.

Although the emphasis in cultural adaptation models has been on gradual, continuous evolutionary change, specific historical episodes have often been identified as major exemplars of such change. Durkheim alludes briefly to three such periods. The first, beginning in the fifteenth century, consisted chiefly of the breakdown of the communal bonds between masters and workers that accompanied the growing specialization of artisan labor. "Beginning with the fifteenth century," Durkheim observes, "things began to change." Prior to this time, "the worker everywhere lived at the side of his master." They shared a common experience and a common culture. But after the fifteenth century, "a sharp line is drawn between masters and workers." The two became "an order apart" and are forced to develop a more differentiated set of cultural abstractions. The second period Durkheim identifies is the industrial revolution of the late seventeenth and eighteenth centuries. And the third period of rapid social change was, in Durkheim's view, his own—the end of the nineteenth century.

In other formulations these periods of rapid social change have also been identified as particularly salient moments in the evolution of modern culture. Parsons, for example, identifies the breakup of the feudal mode of social integration during the late medieval period as the social change that culminated in the Renaissance and Reformation. The Reformation in particular serves in Parsons's evolutionary framework as a key example of cultural adaptation. It was, he suggests, "a movement to upgrade secular society to the highest religious level" (1971, 48). In a brief passage Parsons also focuses on the eighteenth century, particularly prerevolutionary France, as a time of rapid growth in societal complexity owing to the state's efforts to extend the political system to the entire nation. This growth in complexity, he suggests, set up the conditions that necessitated the rising emphasis on empirical knowledge and mass education that came about as a result of the Enlightenment. Similarly, the rapid industrial expansion of the late nineteenth century seems, in Parsons's view, to exemplify the relations between increased societal complexity and cultural upgrading. He suggests that the emergence of socialist ideology in this period, for example, was a response to the fact that capitalism had not fully extended the conception of rights and equality to all social strata; socialism was facilitated by the erosion of ascriptive social ties and in turn assisted in the process of mobilizing "government power to institute fundamental equality" (1971, 97).

2. CLASS LEGITIMATION THEORY

The alternative to evolutionary theories of cultural adaptation has tended to focus on class legitimation. In this approach cultural change comes about as a result of the shifting position of social classes relative to one another. As a new social class becomes more powerful, it allegedly needs to legitimate itself both in relation to segments of the older ruling class and in relation to subordinate segments of the population. New ideologies come into being at these moments in history in order to provide this legitimation. Cultural change is adaptive as far as the rising ruling class is concerned, but in contrast with the other approach, this change is thought to come about more abruptly and in the service of a specific set of social interests. The leading source of this theory of cultural change has, of course, been Marx. However, similar arguments are also evident in Weber's discussion of the role of status groups in bringing about cultural change.

In Marxist theory the need for ideological legitimation arises primarily from the fact that any rising social class is faced with opposition from existing elites. If this rising class is to succeed, it must develop a broader coalition of support. As Marx and Engels write in *The German Ideology*, "Each new class which puts itself in the place of one ruling before it, is compelled, merely in order to carry through its aim, to represent its interest as the common interest of all the members of society" ([1846] 1947, 40–41). This is the impetus that leads to the articulation of a new ideology, that is, a set of ideas that are framed in universalistic terms and disseminated broadly throughout a society.

The specific content of a new ideology is shaped, in the Marxist view, by two conditions: first, by the fact that new ideas reflect the particular historical experience of the rising ruling class, and second, by the fact that the new ruling class controls the means of ideological production. In explaining the rise of new political doctrines during the Enlightenment, for example, Marx and Engels state that the idea of a separation of powers reflects the bourgeoisie's actual experience of contending with the aristocracy and monarchy for power. They also liken the production of ideas to the production of goods, thereby making control over the means of cultural production a decisive factor. As they write, the class that has "the means of material production at its disposal, has control at the same time over the means of mental production, so that, thereby, generally speaking, the ideas of those who lack the means of mental production are subject to it" ([1846] 1947, 39).

Elements of the class legitimation argument can also be found in Weber, for example, in his remarks on the social sources of the Reformation. Weber's main interest in the Reformation lay, of course, in the effects of Protestantism on capitalism, rather than in the origins of the Reformation itself. But he commented extensively on the role of social conditions in bringing about the Reformation. In *Economy and Society* he argued that the Reformation was "codetermined," at least indirectly, by economic factors, namely, the rise of the bourgeoisie as a class characterized by a more rationalized ethic, a preoccupation with self-justification, and less exposure to "organic natural events" than rural classes had. It was, he wrote, "the peculiar piety of the intensely religious bourgeois strata that made them side with the reformist preachers against the traditional ecclesiastic apparatus" (1978, 1197). Moreover, it was the relative power of the bourgeoisie that determined which of the different branches of the Reformation were to prevail in different areas. Wherever the bourgeoisie gained the upper hand, the "ascetic varieties of Protestantism" prevailed, but wherever princes and the nobility retained power, the situation was more conducive to the rise of Anglicanism or Lutheranism.

Much the same line of reasoning is evident in Weber's scattered remarks about the Enlightenment. Here his concern is, again, more with the consequences of Enlightenment teachings for subsequent economic development than with giving a full account of their origins. Accordingly, he suggests in passing that charisma played a role in initiating the Enlightenment. Nevertheless, he also suggests that the growing importance of ethical rationality among the bourgeoisie contributed to the principal doctrine of the Enlightenment—the basic rights of the individual—and that the Enlightenment was reinforced over time by its affinities with the advance of capitalism. Specifically, he suggests that the eighteenth century was characterized by a heightened sense of individual rights in the economic sphere, including "the right to pursue one's own economic interests," "the inviolability of individual property," "freedom of contract," and "vocational choice." These ethical norms, he suggests, "find their ultimate justification in the belief of the Enlightenment in the workings of individual reason which, if unimpeded, would result in the at least relatively best of all worlds." Weber, in fact, likens the Enlightenment doctrine of the rights of man to that of ascetic Protestantism, suggesting that it had a corrosive effect on traditional patrimonial norms, that it "facilitated the expansion of capitalism," and "made it possible for the capitalist to use things and men freely" (1978, 1209).

In explaining the rise of socialist ideology Weber again stresses the role of status groups and economic interests. Here, however, it is no longer the laissez-faire bourgeoisie but the "bureaucratic literati" whose interests are advanced by the new ideology. He writes: "It is this sober fact of universal bureaucratization that is behind the so-called 'German ideas of 1914,' behind what the literati euphemistically call the 'socialism of the future,' behind the slogans of 'organized society,' 'cooperative economy,' and all similar contemporary phrases. Even if they aim at the opposite, they always promote the rise of bureaucracy" (1978, 1400). The unintended consequence of socialist ideology, in his view, was to legitimate an extended rationalization of society, an enlarged conception of rights and responsibilities (for public welfare, full employment, old-age insurance, and so on) that would require a growing cadre of bureaucrats to administer. It was in the interest of this cadre, therefore, to advance some version of socialist ideology.

In a more general sense the theoretical themes evident in these arguments are also apparent in Weber's lengthy treatment of the relations between status groups and religious ideology. Throughout this discussion Weber is primarily concerned with tracing the origins of a rational ethic in religion. Consequently, many of his specific assertions about the propensities of different status groups toward cultural innovation must be interpreted with this specific reference in mind. Nevertheless, he also offers numerous remarks of a more general sort that reveal his broader perspective. Like Marx, Weber assumes that class position has a strong influence on the character of beliefs. Although Weber's term "status group" is considerably broader than Marx's concept of class (which allows Weber to refer to social strata in precapitalist as well as capitalist societies), he frequently refers to Marxist categories, such as proletariat, bourgeoisie, and petty bourgeoisie. These and other status groups have, he asserts, distinctive ideological characteristics: the peasantry has an ideology rooted in nature and magic with a relative lack of rational ethical orientations; the nobility (especially "warrior nobles"), a belief in fate, divine protection against evil, and righteous causes; bureaucrats, a highly rational ideology that scorns magic and superstition, focuses on sober and disciplined order, and lacks interest in personal salvation; the bourgeoisie, a skeptical, this-worldly orientation; the petty bourgeoisie, a penchant for personal piety and congregational religion; and the proletariat, a secular ideology that stresses dependence on social influences. On the surface Weber's examples often appear haphazard and inductive. His point, however, is to demonstrate that an even closer affinity exists between social positions and ideologies than that suggested by class relations alone. However, as modern class relations emerge, they increasingly become a predominant influence on beliefs.

Like the cultural adaptation perspective, class legitimation theories have been greatly elaborated beyond their initial formulations in classical theory. Rather than simply tracing the development of these literatures, however, it will prove more efficient to discuss the various contributions in the context of raising critical issues related to both perspectives. As criteria for assessing the theoretical adequacy of the two approaches, I use the following considerations: (1) the concept of culture implicit in each approach; (2) the clarity of the explanatory variables in each; (3) the variations in the rate and timing of cultural change; (4) the mechanisms of cultural change; and (5) the relation between theory and history.

3. CRITICAL CONSIDERATIONS

3.1 The Concept of Culture

The concept of culture that implicitly informs both the cultural adaptation and class legitimation models of cultural change casts primary emphasis on the subjective features of culture. This emphasis is evident in the very terms used to identify culture: "collective conscience" (Durkheim), "orientations that guide action" (Parsons), "class consciousness" (Marx), "beliefs and conceptions" (Weber), "mental structures" (Mannheim). Although there are other more objective aspects of ideology in these conceptions as well, the basic orientation tends to derive from a variant of subject-object dualism in which ideas are associated with the subjective realm while behavior and social structure are conceived of as objective realities. One of the difficulties of this conception, of course, is that culture ceases to have readily available empirical referents. Instead of consisting primarily of observable artifacts, it remains a matter of beliefs and outlooks, of moods and motivations that are in the best of cases difficult to pin down in instances of historical change. In addition, much of the emphasis in these theoretical traditions has been on the psychological functions of ideology for the individual.

Weber, for example, clearly grounds his discussion of cultural change in psychological arguments. In discussing the relation between social stratification and religious belief he states that the hunger of the disprivileged classes for worthiness, for instance, is a "psychological condition." He also suggests that the legitimating beliefs of privileged classes are "rooted in certain basic psychological patterns." And he goes on to say that "everyday experience proves that there exists just such a need for psychic comfort" (1978, 491). Or to take a different example, Lukács ([1922] 1971, 50) makes it quite clear that subjectivity is a crucial aspect of his formulation of class consciousness when he writes: "[Class existence] is *subjectively* justified in the social and historical situation, as something which can and should be understood, i.e., as 'right.' " And later he notes that class consciousness consists of what people "thought, felt and wanted at any moment in history" and that it manifests itself essentially as the "psychological thoughts of men about their lives" ([1922] 1971, 51, emphasis in original).

In seeking the sources of cultural change, then, one is forced to rely heavily on assumptions about psychological processes. Ideas are bent, as it were, to fulfill psychological needs. The actual sequence by which this bending occurs remains vague, but theorists implicitly assume that the internal processing of individuals plays a key role. Weber, for example, in discussing salvationist religions, suggests that although they may originate in the privileged strata or be articulated by a charismatic prophet, their nature undergoes serious modification when these ideas reach the disadvantaged. In the process, he suggests, religion "changes its character." Elsewhere, he describes the change as a "form of adaptation." How does this change occur? Apparently in the decisions that autonomous individuals make about their beliefs. Consequently, the changes come about gradually ("by the most numerous transitional stages"). Individual interpretations reflect individual needs, and these needs change the character of individual convictions, which in turn affect the appeals that leaders may articulate.

A process of this nature is difficult to observe. But even on formal theoretical grounds, it clearly contains deficiencies. It treats individuals as autonomous entities, rather than recognizing the importance of social interaction among them. It ignores other constraints that are likely to influence the ideas that leaders articulate, that is, it focuses too much on audience "demand" rather than emphasizing the conditions of ideological "supply." And it necessitates the assumption that there is a close fit between individual needs and ideological content, whereas in fact this fit may be only partial or may be determined by a wide range of other needs and interests.

3.2. The Clarity of Explanatory Variables

Implicit in the fact that theories of social change have often utilized psychological explanations is the tendency in the literature to rely on highly general, if not vague, conceptions of social change in order to account for specific manifestations of cultural change. In the cultural adaptation literature the most general source of cultural change is identified as increasing societal complexity. But complexity has a host of diverse empirical indicators: population size, population density, occupational diversity, urbanization, cultural heterogeneity, institutional differentiation, technological specialization, and so on. In class legitimation theories the concept of class is equally vague. It ranges from distinct conceptions of social position in capitalist societies to vague notions of economic process to highly general ideas about power, authority, prestige, and status. In attempting to account for specific episodes of cultural change, therefore, concepts often appear to be evoked more on the basis of convenience than in any rigorous fashion. Virtually any event since the sixteenth century can become subject to explanation as a product of either increasing social complexity or the dynamics of "bourgeois class formation."

In some formulations of the cultural adaptation model the logic of explanation also exemplifies the fallacy of teleological reasoning. Cultural adaptation, it is argued, is necessary for further societal development; the logic of some formulations implies that cultural change occurs *because* it facilitates development. A variant of this problematic form of argumentation is evident in Durkheim's discussion of cultural change. Although Durkheim circumvents a purely teleological form of functionalist reasoning, he nevertheless runs into some difficulty in actually formulating a causal argument about the sources of cultural change. Durkheim specifically argues against a teleological explanation. He notes that the development of culture is generally found to be societally functional but argues that "it is not the services that it renders that make it progress." He also observes that it is false "to make civilization the function of the division of labor"; instead, he insists that the correct wording is that civilization is strictly a "consequence" of the division of labor. But he is somewhat at a loss, if a functionalist argument is disallowed, to say how this connection comes about. Having argued that cultural innovations should not be attributed to hereditary factors such as genius or innate creativity, he nevertheless falls back on an essentially physiological explanation of a different kind. Increases in social complexity lead to new ideas, he suggests, "because this superactivity of general life fatigues and weakens our nervous system [so] that it needs reparations proportionate to its expenditures, that is to say, more varied and complex satisfactions" ([1893] 1933, 337). Although it avoids teleological reasoning, this formulation serves as a clear example, of course, of the tendency toward individualistic, psychological interpretations of cultural change, which I have already mentioned.

Turning to Weber, we find a somewhat more sophisticated set of social explanations for cultural change, but unfortunately these remain inadequately developed. Weber emphasizes both the specific role of status groups and the more general effects of economic and political development on culture. He also identifies—but never treats systematically— two other facilitators of cultural change (see Habermas 1984, 217–42): social movements, which, as Habermas suggests, "were inspired by traditionalistic and rather defensive attitudes, as well as by modern conceptions of justice, that is, by ideas of bourgeois and, later, of socialist provenance" (Habermas 1984, 217); and differentiated institutions oriented to the production of culture. Habermas (1984, 217) somewhat misleadingly calls these "cultural systems of action" but is clear in identifying scientific academies, universities, artistic groups, and religious bodies as obvious examples.

The picture that emerges, albeit dimly, from Weber is one of greater theoretical complexity than is typically recognized in the literature on cultural change. General economic and political developments certainly must be taken into consideration, but if Weber is correct, specific social movements and culture-producing institutions must also be incorporated into any adequate theoretical explanation. Otherwise, explanatory variables are likely to remain improperly specified.

An illustration of this problem is evident in Marx's discussion of the English and French Enlightenments. Marx singles out several particular aspects of the eighteenth-century social experience of the two countries and relates them to the content of a few writers of the Enlightenment. But Marx's discussion clearly fails to develop a more systematic or comprehensive view of the relationship between the bourgeoisie and the Enlightenment. He seems more intent on illustrating certain biases in utilitarian theory than in articulating a theory of the effects of bourgeois class position on enlightened culture. What he provides, therefore, is only a general sense of these effects. At most, it becomes possible to infer that the rise of the bourgeoisie in England and France was associated with certain economic problems being given special intellectual attention in the work of scholars such as Locke and Holbach. What is lacking in Marx's argument is any sense of whether the bourgeoisie as such is essential to this argument or whether it is sufficient to suggest only that commercialization had a general influence on eighteenth-century thought.

In the class legitimation literature more generally, there is, as Martin Seliger (1977, 151–56) points out, considerable ambiguity over the concept of class itself as an explanatory variable. This ambiguity revolves around the question of whether class is a conceptual category or an action unit. In viewing it as a conceptual category theorists have tended to consider it an aggregation of individuals, whereas as an action unit it has been regarded as an organized entity in which the majority of its members are joined together in a single organization. Both conceptions can be found in Marx and in Weber and in more recent writers such as Lukács and Mannheim. Curiously, however, both conceptions represent only the most extreme possibilities. Consequently, many of the intermediate levels of organization (within or across class boundaries) that may also affect ideological change have been neglected. This point, again, bears an affinity with Weber's underdeveloped arguments about the necessity of paying more attention to social movements and culture-producing institutions.

3.3. Variations in the Rate and Timing of Cultural Change

A careful reading of the specific statements on cultural change of Marx, Durkheim, Weber, or more recent theorists such as Parsons or Mannheim, reveals another persistent ambiguity: although some attention is devoted to specific episodes of notable change in cultural systems, such as the Enlightenment or the rise of socialism, theoretical statements also tend to give the impression that cultural change must be conceived of as gradual, linear, and for the most part continuous. The latter emphasis in particular works against offering satisfactory theoretical explanations for specific variations in the rate and timing of cultural change. If cultural change is simply incremental, then only the broadest sources of its general direction can be of interest.

In some measure this issue arises from ambiguities concerning the appropriate level of generality at which to examine cultural change. If culture is conceived of as the most general patterns or orientations underlying social behavior rather than as specific symbolic expressions, then attention is inevitably drawn to prevailing forms rather than to particular episodes of cultural change. Weber, for example, can be interpreted as having identified rationalization as the most general tendency underlying the development of modern culture. In examining the process of rationalization, Weber is led to discover it everywhere in the Occident: in law, music, economic relations, science, bureaucracies, museums, the state, religion, and military organization. Given this prevalence, it becomes bootless in a sense to inquire into the sources of any of its particular manifestations. One instance of rationalization simply reinforces another.

At this high level of generality, each manifestation of cultural change ceases to be important in its own right. Rather, it becomes significant only as an indication that some deeper process is at work. Understanding the origins of a particular cultural episode becomes less interesting than interpreting its meaning in relation to some larger pattern. Habermas, in discussing Weber's contribution to the sociology of music, for example, suggests that it is less important to know how rational musical structures originated or became institutionalized than to recognize that this development was a symptom of the increasing differentiation of autonomous cultural spheres, the increasing differentiation of aesthetic and technical realms, and the increasing differentiation of theoretical and practical reason (1984, 161–62). This sort of argument is conducive, of course, to an interpretive style of social science that is concerned with discovering the meanings of events rather than explaining their sources. Such an approach, however, depends mainly on having an a priori conception of the master tendencies in modern culture (for example, differentiation). With such a conception in mind, the investigator merely has to find instances of cultural change that seem to fit into the overall pattern. But the processes by which cultural changes actually become institutionalized remain unilluminated. This tendency is related, I will show below, to an increasing bifurcation in the study of cultural change between purely theoretical and more historical or empirical approaches. For the moment it will suffice to say that efforts to relate these general perspectives to specific historical cases, while numerous, have proven less than satisfactory. Two examples illustrate this point.

Although (as already discussed) the Enlightenment is often regarded as a key instance of cultural change coming about in response to changing needs for class legitimation, one of the most recent and most extensive studies of the Enlightenment straightforwardly rejects the notion that cultural change in this period was in any way connected with a rising bourgeoisie or its need for class legitimation. "A new vision of the future certainly emerged," the author states, "but its apostles were to be found among both nobles and bourgeois—of the famous *Philosophes* of the Enlightenment most were either born or bought themselves into the nobility—and the first people who tried to translate the enlightened ideas into practice were members of the government, all of whom, apart from Necker, were nobles" (Behrens 1985, 9). Behrens goes on to assert that commercial and industrial wealth did not constitute more than a small share of the eighteenth-century economy, that the nobility and the bourgeoisie were largely indistinguishable in terms of the sources of their wealth, and that the nobility did not suffer any relative or absolute decline. The author's veracity, evidence, or indeed, understanding of the theoretical perspective at issue may, of course, be questioned. She is, however, scarcely alone among historians in drawing this conclusion.

The rise of socialism also provides an example. Of all modern cultural changes, this development, perhaps ironically, seems to have created the most difficult explanatory problems, especially for the class legitimation model. These problems may be partially attributable to the fact that some of the theoretical formulations in this tradition are themselves associated with the rise of socialism. But other problems also seem to be evident. At the simplest level class legitimation models attribute the rise of socialism to the emergence of the proletariat as a new class in need of legitimation. More sophisticated versions, however, have not been content with this explanation. Wanting to maintain the significance of socialist ideology as a precursor of the proletarian struggle, these arguments have taken a different view. Lukács, for example, writes that "nothing has changed in the objective situation" and that only the "vantage point from which it is judged" has changed ([1922] 1971, 150). This kind of argument, of course, undermines the basic thrust of the class legitimation model. For if nothing changes in objective social relations, then how is the change in "vantage point" to be explained?

3.4. The Mechanisms of Cultural Change

I have already implied at several points that both the cultural adaptation model and the class legitimation model are less than satisfactory in specifying the actual processes by which broad societal changes result in specific episodes of cultural change. Because many of the more general formulations are concerned primarily with broad evolutionary tendencies, they specify a general relationship between increasing societal complexity or increasing economic capacity and ideas but do not provide an explanation of the intervening processes by which these changes influence culture. In this respect these approaches serve best as models of macro-level comparisons rather than as models of actual processes of change. With these macro-level approaches it is possible to make hypotheses based on static, cross-sectional comparisons of societies at different levels of complexity or development or on comparisons of a single society at two or more widely separated periods. But the manner in which change in complexity or development actually leads to cultural change is likely to remain unspecified.

Symptomatic of the lack of specificity about intervening social mechanisms is the tendency in these approaches, already mentioned, to resort to explanations rooted in assumptions about individual psychology. Even if psychological processes are involved, however, these processes cannot substitute for a more explicit consideration of the conditions under which they operate. Marxist theory, in particular, emphasizes the fact that individuation, and therefore, individual psychology, is itself contingent on the nature of the productive process. If ideology is conceded to change primarily because of changes in individual experience, this experience is nevertheless a product of particular social conditions. Individual experience occurs under conditions in which market relations and "the principle of rational mechanization and calculability" have permeated society to such an extent that the "atomized individual" has come into existence. Also it tends to be limited to those aspects of ideology that concern an individual's self-perception as an externally governed commodity (Lukács [1922] 1971, 83–92). Within this formulation of the class legitimation model, individual experience can provide only a partial explanation of cultural change. To the extent that market relations remain incomplete (that is, subject to noncontractual constraints) and to the extent that individuals function in collective settings rather than being totally atomized, ideology will be shaped by other factors. The subjective, experiential determination of ideology, in short, operates only under extremely limited conditions—in much the same sense that classical economics assumes that economistic behavior applies when "all other things are equal." According to this version of the class legitimation theory, therefore, social mechanisms other than direct individual experience need to be considered in any effort to account for real historical episodes of cultural change.

The alternative to identifying psychological states as the intervening mechanisms connecting societal changes and cultural changes is to assert a simple mechanistic connection. This sort of connection is especially evident in the more macroscopic levels of analysis that focus on broad patterns of social evolution. These analyses simply assert that one kind of change leads to another; they do not even raise the question of how these changes are effected. Some of the functionalist imagery I cited earlier has failed in this way. Deterministic imagery is also evident in some formulations. Durkheim, for example, is particularly adamant about the deterministic connection between social change and cultural development. "Civilization," he asserts, "is itself the necessary consequence of the changes which are produced in the volume and density of societies." He goes on to suggest that the development of science and art comes about because of "a necessity which is imposed." The advance of modern culture, therefore, should not be attributed to the values or desires of individuals. Nor should it be understood in terms of its attractiveness or as something toward which people strive. Rather, culture is moved along by the increasing size, density, and diversity of society: "It develops because it cannot fail to develop" ([1893] 1933, 336).

More recent discussions have naturally taken issue with this extreme form of sociological determinism, arguing for the value of seeing a dialectical relationship between social and cultural change. Therborn (1980), for example, has argued not only for a more dialectical view but also for one that gives greater attention to process and competition. In emphasizing process Therborn places importance on the fact that ideologies develop in interaction with social conditions over a period of time. In emphasizing competition (among different ideologies) he also wishes to stress the fact that the outcomes of these interactions are to a degree indeterminate. Rather than envisioning a straightforward ideological outcome associated either with rising social complexity or with changing class relations, he prefers to consider the specific situations that provide room for new ideologies to develop, how these ideologies influence one another, and what the eventual outcome of a particular sequence of action may be. Therborn's approach, therefore, inevitably leads to a greater consideration of the actual processes and the more immediate conditions that link broad societal changes with specific episodes of cultural innovation.

3.5. The Disjuncture between Theory and History

As a final critical observation, I note that both the cultural adaptation and the class legitimation literatures have shown an increasing tendency toward bifurcation between theoretical specification, on the one hand, and historical analysis, on the other hand. Indeed, much of the interest in cultural change among sociological theorists appears to have moved in the direction of abstract, normative, or reconstructive models, which in some discussions are specifically regarded as having no connection with historical analysis. A variety of reconstructive formulations of cultural evolution have emerged from the cultural adaptation tradition, and the class legitimation literature has produced an increasing number of philosophical and epistemological specifications, especially in the Marxist and neo-Marxist traditions. Studies of concrete historical episodes of cultural change have not abandoned the assumptions of these more general traditions entirely, but they have increasingly expressed dissatisfaction with them and have worked from what might be called a more ad hoc, inductive, or deconstructionist perspective.

Both tendencies—toward raising theoretical questions and toward more inductive historical approaches—probably reflect the growing awareness in epistemological thought of the hermeneutic circle in which the social analyst is caught. Nevertheless, there has also been a tendency for the two variants of scholarship to grow farther apart. Indeed, a virtual impasse has been reached in some of the more philosophical discussions. Even as long as a half century ago, we find Lukács categorically asserting that it is "not possible to reach an understanding of particular [historical] forms by studying their successive appearances in an empirical and historical manner" ([1922] 1971, 186). Thus, for Lukács it is only by constructing a purely universalistic, philosophical model of evolutionary materialism that scholarship can be advanced; in short, historical studies had nothing to contribute. Among more recent theorists, Habermas, Therborn, and Seliger have all in various ways espoused a version of this argument.

The relevance of this kind of argument for empirically oriented studies of cultural change is both positive and negative. On the positive side it underscores the fact that any such inquiry will inevitably be guided by broad assumptions and questions implicit in the investigator's view of history. Much of the attractiveness of the cultural adaptation and class legitimation models has undoubtedly rested more on the nature of their assumptions than on their explanatory value alone. Philosophical criticism only underscores the importance of giving greater explicit recognition to these assumptions. On the negative side the high ground that philosophical discussions have staked out for themselves inevitably casts a long shadow over the valley to which empirical studies have been consigned.

4. TOWARD AN INSTITUTIONAL APPROACH

Several of my remarks, apart from being critical of the prevailing traditions, point in what might be regarded as a common direction for reinvigorating the empirical study of cultural change. Specifically, some of my arguments point toward multifactoral rather than unicausal explanations of cultural change and highlight the importance of considering the specific contexts, processes, and mechanisms that translate broad societal changes into concrete episodes of innovative cultural production. In the remaining space it is not possible to fully follow up on these suggestions. I can, however, indicate some of the directions in which such a discussion might go.

As a starting point, we should recognize that a considerable amount of rethinking of the basic concept of "culture" has taken place since the cultural adaptation and class legitimation models came into prominence. Rather than viewing culture primarily as a subjective set of beliefs, values, or orientations current treatments of this concept increasingly focus on the observable features of culture, namely, discourse and other kinds of symbolic acts. Once culture is understood in this fashion, it becomes more apparent that the study of culture must pay attention to speakers and audiences, discursive texts, the rituals in which discourse is embedded, and the social contexts in which it is produced. As something that is not simply affirmed subjectively but produced collectively, culture clearly depends on social resources, and the availability and distribution of these resources is likely to play a major role in influencing the direction of cultural change. Cultural change necessitates, even more so than before, an approach that focuses on the institutional contexts in which it is produced, enacted, disseminated, and altered.

That cultural change comes about not simply as a result of the disparate pressures of social experience on individuals but as the product of culture-producing organizations has generally been de-emphasized in the cultural adaptation and class legitimation literatures. But it has not been entirely overlooked. One can, for instance, find suggestive passages in Marx that point toward this conception of culture. Writing in the *Communist Manifesto* about the creation of a world market for economic goods, Marx and Engels ([1848] 1967, 84) add: "As in material, so also in intellectual production. The intellectual creations of individual nations become common property. National one-sidedness and narrow-mindedness become more and more impossible, and from the numerous national and local literatures, there arises a world literature." They also liken cultural production to material production in their discussion of the problem of oversupply in advanced capitalism, stating that there is "too much civilization, too much means of subsistence, too much industry." They also speak of cultural change in these terms, asking rhetorically: "What else does the history of ideas prove, than that intellectual production changes in character in proportion as material production is changed?" ([1848] 1967, 102).

But if culture is produced and cultural production requires social resources, then we must ask about the range of variables that may be relevant for understanding changes in the form and content of this product. For heuristic purposes it may be useful to divide these variables into three categories: the institutional contexts in which culture is produced, the broader environmental conditions that influence the kinds of social resources available to these institutions, and the specific action sequences within institutional contexts by which culture is produced.

Institutional contexts serve as the immediate settings in which culture is produced. Of particular relevance are the roles occupied by the direct producers of culture, their relationships with other producers (both colleagues and competitors), and the nature of their contact with relevant audience groups. Beyond the immediate interests and experiences of these actors, their relationships with broader sets of organizations, coalitions, and interest groups are also likely to be important. Because resources are crucial to the production of any cultural activity, the relationship of cultural producers to the state, to economic elites, and to other cultural authorities is likely to be especially important.

The broader social environment subsumes many of the variables that have been identified in the traditional literature—social complexity, rates of economic growth, distributions of power among social classes, etc.—but it is particularly concerned with the character of the resources that may influence the institutional configurations in which cultural activities are produced. Rather than positing that these variables have a direct, unmediated influence on culture, the institutional perspective conceives of a mediated form of influence, channeled through the institutional contexts in which cultural production takes place.

Finally, the idea of "action sequences" highlights the fact that even within institutional contexts the production of culture is a process. Among the questions encountered in examining this process are questions about agency, the activities of cultural producers, their responses to crises and other contingencies, and the manner in which their responses are limited by the institutional structures in which these responses take place. By bringing questions of cultural change to this level of specificity, investigations can also focus on the ways in which different ideological formulations compete with one another, how social relations are imbedded in the "texts" produced, and how these texts are mirrored in the social interaction that ensues.

An institutional approach of this kind implies a great deal of indeterminacy in identifying the broad factors generating cultural change. This indeterminacy, however, appears to be truer to the historical record than the tight theoretical formulations with which sociologists have labored in the past. If anything, the cultural adaptation and class legitimation models have suffered from ambiguity because their simpler formulations strain the bounds of credibility. In contrast, combinations of institutional variables, environmental variables, and action variables leave room for considerable diversity in the factors that operate to produce cultural change in different times and places.

To suggest that theories of cultural change move in the direction of looser, more multifaceted models does, of course, not imply any radical deviation from the empirical work that has already been under way for some time. It merely affirms what the more insightful of these studies have already begun to show.

REFERENCES

Behrens, C.B.A. 1985. *Society, government, and the Enlightenment: The experiences of eighteenth-century France and Prussia.* New York: Harper and Row.

Bellah, Robert N. 1970. *Beyond belief.* New York: Harper and Row.

Durkheim, Emile. [1893] 1933. *The division of labor in society.* New York: Free Press.

Habermas, Jürgen. 1979. *Communication and the evolution of society.* Boston: Beacon Press.

———. 1984. *The theory of communicative action.* Vol. 1, *Reason and the rationalization of society.* Trans. Thomas McCarthy. Boston: Beacon Press.

Luhmann, Niklas. 1982. *The differentiation of society.* New York: Columbia University Press.

Lukács, Georg. [1922] 1971. *History and class consciousness: Studies in Marxist dialectics.* Cambridge: MIT Press.

Marx, Karl, and Friedrich Engels. [1846] 1947. *The German ideology.* New York: International Publishers.

———. [1848] 1967. *The communist manifesto.* Baltimore: Penguin.

Parsons, Talcott. 1971. *Societies: Evolutionary and comparative perspectives.* Englewood Cliffs, N.J.: Prentice-Hall.

Sahlins, Marshall D. 1960. *Evolution and culture.* Ann Arbor: University of Michigan Press.

Seliger, Martin. 1977. *The Marxist conception of ideology: A critical essay.* Cambridge: Cambridge University Press.

Therborn, Goran. 1980. *The ideology of power and the power of ideology.* London: Verso.

Weber, Max. 1978. *Economy and Society.* 2 vols. Ed. Guenther Roth and Claus Wittich. Berkeley: University of California Press.

PART FOUR

Evolutionary Themes

The Direction of Evolution

Niklas Luhmann

Since its beginning in the eighteenth century, reasoning about social and cultural evolution has taken two forms. On the one hand, it has become a more-or-less elaborated scientific theory, reflecting the scientific and theoretical requirements of the day. On the other hand, it has served as a self-description of the entire society. The latter form has to be elaborated by social communication within the society of which the observers are a part. In other words, social science tries to look at society from an outside position, but inevitably its descriptions are part of society, always changing the objects that are described. It is not a matter of objective versus subjective knowledge; rather it is a matter of whether or not social science is able to reflect its own position[1] by describing the ways in which it contributes to the self-description of society.

During the eighteenth and early nineteenth centuries such self-descriptions drew on the imagery of Newtonian science. Scientific research on social issues was stimulated by its supposed relevance for comprehending civilization, commercial societies, and modern states. Although cognitive theory was troubled by the issue of its own "conditions of possibility," this did not prevent the development of increasing trust in science. Even history moved from the traditional narrative style toward a scientific model, at least in Germany after the second half of the eighteenth century.

This new scientific history broke radically with former traditions, giving new meanings to terms like development, evolution, and history itself (see Koselleck 1975). In the context of the aristocratic societies of the past histories reflected the needs and the interests of the leading groups. They were stories told to instruct the hereditary prince or the king himself.

1. A "third position" in the sense of Bråten 1986.

They were histories of heroes and villains, kings and military leaders, their ladies and daughters, and their advisers. They were histories of interaction within a framework of destiny. And they referred to the religious meaning of the world. The guiding distinction was between virtue and self-control, on the one hand, and fate, on the other, that is, between the internal and the external causes of events. Only events and actions were thought of as changing within a world of stable essences, species, and forms.[2] The notions of mutation, vicissitude, and change referred to this level of events, not to the levels of structures, time, or eternity. In regard to the form of the narrative, one had to distinguish between history and poetry, that is, between real versus fictional narrative, both of which served rhetorical and educational functions.

All this disappeared by the second half of the eighteenth century. The histories of interaction were replaced by the history of society, *histoire de la société*, as Bonald would have it.[3] Destiny was now no longer outside of history but inside of it. History became fatalistic, or at least observers disputed the extent to which intentional action was important *in* history (but certainly not *as* history) (see Hoeges 1984).

My hypothesis in this chapter is that the change from the histories of interaction to the history of society reflects a radical transformation of the structure of society. The societal system itself changed its primary mode of differentiation from a hierarchical to a horizontal or functional order (see Luhmann 1982, 229–54).

Society's primary subsystems are no longer based on strata but on functions. Social order is now maintained by the adequate functioning of politics, scientific research, economic care for the future, family-building, public education, etc., and no longer by living life according to one's inherited position in society. This does not mean that stratification has vanished, but it does mean that it loses its legitimacy. Stratification is no longer the social order per se but a consequence of the way social order is reproduced, particularly by the rational workings of the economic and educational systems. Inequality is no longer simply ascribed to the different qualities of people living in God's creation. For writers of the eighteenth century inequality became a problem of "civilization" (as distinguished from "nature"). Inequality was not created by God. Rather, it was a deplorable necessity of civilized social life—*vel ratione imperii, vel ratione dominii*, as Gundling says—anticipating the need to distinguish between force and property or *Staat und Gesellschaft*

2. Crucé states the following as a common opinion of his time: "Les actions et evenemens sont nouveaux en leur individu, mais les especes ont tousiours esté comme à present" ([1623] 1909, 285).

3. "Ce n'est que dans l'ensemble ou la généralité des faits qu'on peut étudier l'histoire de la société" (Bonald [1858] 1982, 91).

(Gundling 1736, 40).[4] Nineteenth-century writers adapted the self-description of society to this new situation through the notion of "class society"[5] and its ultimate projection of a society without class (albeit within the constraints of the division of labor).

The substitution of functional differentiation for stratification implies a radical break, completely changing the basis on which social order is built. The people in a system undergoing such a transition cannot observe or describe this transition. They may perceive it as a catastrophe or as leading eventually to a utopian future. For Bayle and Voltaire, as for all who participated in the Enlightenment, their perspective on history had already changed. History became the prehistory of reason, a prehistory of opinions (including religious opinions) that would not stand the test of reason. A few decades later history is perceived as crisis. Herder, for instance, explicitly said that his interest in a new concept of history was a reaction to what he called a crisis of the human mind.[6] One occasionally has to live for a while in a society that cannot be easily described. Because the descriptions of society vary so much it soon becomes clear that all descriptions are either prejudiced or serve latent interests or functions. The sense of reality is shaken at the level of "second order observations," that is, observations of observations. Essence and reality—the old *kosmos*—are replaced by ideology, that is, by descriptions of what others cannot observe.

1. TEMPORAL DESCRIPTIONS OF SOCIETY

These sketchy considerations are a prelude to my main topic. I want to suggest that in a situation characterized by declining belief in stratification, vanishing essence of beings (in the sense of essential, i.e., the being that explains what the being is), and disputed descriptions of reality, time becomes important as a dimension of describing the society in terms of the past and of the future, in terms of a "no longer" and "not yet." The present is no longer seen as mediating "this time" (*tempus*) of human life with eternity. It is now the terra incognita between the past and the future, fostering the paradox of the simultaneous presence of the no-longer and the not-yet.[7]

In Christian cosmology there was a long-standing debate about whether time tends toward decay followed by final salvation. But this

4. For the retreat from the idea that the unequal distribution of power and property is a reflection of the will of God, see also Koehler [1735] n.d.; Burlamaqui 1747.

5. For a view on the semantics of "social classes" see Luhmann 1985.

6. "Niemand in der Welt fühlt *die Schwäche des allgemeinen Charakterisierens* mehr als ich" (Herder [1774] 1967, 36, emphasis in original).

7. For the continuing semantical problems of "the present," see Oesterle 1985.

debate was related to the level of *tempus,* of vanishing times, of human life, not to eternity. At the end of the eighteenth century the similar topic of the direction of time assumed a very different meaning. Observers used it to compensate for the ontological emptiness of a present that was between an obsolete past and an unknown future. What gave meaning to the present was no longer eternity, with its implication of life after death, but the direction of time. In modern times there is no other level of temporal order outside of the fluid concept of time that connects the past, the present, and the future. This new one-dimensionality of time eliminates easy explanations that refer to the variety of times (in distinction from eternity).[8] Time no longer exists outside of history. The direction of time is the direction of history, and the nineteenth century came to the conclusion that no ethical principles, cognitive forms, or natural laws exist outside of history.

Moreover, we can temporalize this temporal description of modern society. It is itself a result of historical changes that emerged not before the second half of the eighteenth century.[9] Time becomes historical because every present constitutes its own past and its own future, and history itself is the movement of the present on the difference of past and future states, so that new pasts and futures emerge. The *Zeitgeist* (Herder [1774] 1967) is historically situated, looking at the past and the future. As historians since the eighteenth century have known, history must now be rewritten for every generation. But how? Arbitrarily or according to national interest and political fortune?

Historians have given a great deal of methodological reflection to these issues and have tried to avoid being completely relativistic. But this is not the point. Considerable time has passed since the beginning of the historization of history and by now we can detect the structuralism of conceptions of time. Looking back three hundred years, we can distinguish at least three different periods. In each period observers conceived of modern society in temporal terms. The meaning of the direction of evolution, however, changes from period to period. Each period is marked by a different semantics of societal self-description, and the change of these semantics follows a certain pattern: As soon as the new consequences of functional differentiation become visible, the self-description of modern society has to change. Although the new self-description does not allow for a view into the future, except in the most general optimistic or pessimistic terms, it does require a continuous adaptation of descriptions to the realities that have to be accepted as features

8. The variety of times was supposed to explain why previously helpful medicines do not help any more (Malvezzi 1635, 148).

9. See Koselleck 1979. See also my essays "The future cannot begin" and "World time and system history" in Luhmann 1982.

of modern society. I hesitate to use the Hegelian terminology about the self-revealing character of society because of its theoretical premises and "end of history" results. But at least the awareness of structural consequences of the modern system of society has increased during the last two centuries, and new insights have to be continually incorporated into any attempts to describe society.

Different modes of describing modern society in temporal terms produce, of course, different views of the past and the future. They stimulate different ways of reflecting history within history and temporal horizons over time. History becomes the main mechanism for collecting information about the new society. This is why the "history of society" has replaced the traditional "histories of interaction." Even the term "new" and its derivatives (for example, *Neuzeit*) take on a new meaning.[10] Now, different ways of conceiving the direction of history become possible.

The question of what constitutes the unifying tendency of history for a given period, linking the past and the future by an intrinsic direction, leads us to observe the ways in which the self-descriptions of modern society adapt to new experiences. We can distinguish three different ways of connecting different phases, stages, or epochs in social history. The first uses the idea of progress. The second describes history in structural terms as increasing differentiation and complexity. The third describes history and, in particular, evolution as increasing improbability, for instance, considering the concept of thermodynamic "negentropy," that is, negative entropy, or the idea of the increasing artificiality of social institutions that are the solutions of problems that are the consequences of previous solutions to previous problems. To some extent these three ways of understanding represent different expressions of the same idea. My hypothesis, however, is that since the late nineteenth century the emphasis has changed from progress to differentiation and complexity and from there to improbability. This semantic change reflects an increasing awareness of the problematic nature of the structures of modern society. The sequence of semantic "discourses" from progress to differentiation and complexity to improbability does not simply reflect a change in the history of ideas. Rather, it is rooted in processes of industrialization and technological development, political democratization, and the provision of mass education in schools. Moreover, this semantic sequence corresponds to the slow process of discovering the contours of modern life.

The idea of progress became *idée directrice* in the second half of the seventeenth century. At first, however, the term "progresses" was used

---

10. In medieval Latin *novus* simply meant "deviant," and even in seventeenth-century French *nouveautéz* was a term for something unworthy of approbation in matters of religion and politics in the sense that it deviated from the accepted order. See Spörl 1930; Freund 1957; Koselleck 1979.

and referred to the arts and sciences only, not to society as a whole. Only during the eighteenth century did progress become a concept used mainly in the singular, referring to a generalized range of objects such as the economy, science, civilization (mankind) and commercial society. The main reason for this change seems to have been a new kind of discourse that attributed progress to the economic system, or more accurately, to the political economy. In other words, the semantic change was caused by the differentiation of the economy as a functional subsystem. This semantic change, however, could not describe the functional differentiation of society as an all-encompassing system. No concept (except "mankind") was available to describe the change in the total social system. Instead, the very concept of society changed, shifting from a political and legal meaning to an economic one. During the second half of the eighteenth century the term "society" took on connotations of exchange and commerce (including the *doux commerce* of social relations) and eventually became a term for the system of needs and need-satisfaction, of property, money, and labor. Society was now identified with the economic system in distinction to the state, which was identified as the political system.

Because progress was observed in the framework of society in the new, economic sense, the meaning of the term became ambivalent, particularly in French writings. The Marquis de Mirabeau, to give an example, speaks of "*dégradations nécessairement résultant des progrès même de notre perfectibilité possible.*"[11] Progress became a mixed blessing and civilization (in distinction to nature) an ambivalent term. These developments paved the way for the ideological disputes of the nineteenth century. Progress remained a promising idea for about a hundred years but the ways to achieve it (and therefore the ways society described itself) were judged differently, according to different political and ideological preferences.

Since the notion of progress was now contested, the fledgling discipline of sociology had to look for other foundations. For a while "differentiation" became the substitute term (Simmel 1890; Durkheim [1893] 1930). This notion had many advantages. It could explain the phenomenon of individualism, that is, the increasing emphasis on the individuality of the human being in the wake of the increasing division of labor and differentiation of roles. It could also explain cultural developments by assuming a correlation between structural differentiation and symbolic generalizations. And after Darwin differentiation could be conceived as a necessary outcome of social evolution. Darwin had explained the immense differentiation of species by one or eventually a few simple mecha-

11. See L. D. H. [L'ami des hommes] [Victor de Riqueti, Marquis de Mirabeau] 1774, xxi. See also Robinet: human perfectibility is "aussi fertile en mal que en bien" and society, in comparison with nature, produces "plus de biens et plus de maux" (1766, 1:75ff.).

nisms. In the long run the complexity of the phenomenal world could be reduced to one genetic principle: natural selection. Historical "conjectures" and "doubtful periodizations" were no longer needed and were in fact artificial assumptions. From a "scientific" base the new theory of evolution combined genetic simplicity with phenomenal complexity. It was no longer necessary to identify decisive events (such as the invention of artillery or the printing press, the discovery of the Americas, or revolutions) to articulate the direction of time. The identification of decisive events was replaced by the concept of evolution,[12] a mechanism that produces increasing differentiation and complexity.

If this replacement was the starting signal for sociology and the point of departure of the up-to-now unmatched theoretical performances of its classics, the general public was not prepared for this type of theory. Unable to steer the mass media, sociology could influence but not control the self-description of society (Heintz 1982). A strange new mixture of hopes for progress called Social Darwinism was prepared for the general public by sociologists during the last decades of the nineteenth century, but it was soon replaced by a new emphasis on social values (Hofstadter 1945; Francis 1981). Looking back at this time, we find sociology more on the social side of the battle (Ross 1907).[13] We also find disputes about accepting or rejecting the idea of social evolution and disputes about whether structure or process should serve as the guideline of theory-building. However, the level of the theoretical development of sociology was still too low to resolve these issues, let alone impress the general public with new ideas. Within the social sciences evolution, then as now, was conceptualized as a theory of phases or periods of development.[14]

During this period, which ended only after World War II, the presuppositions of society's self-description were defined relatively strictly. The consequences of the industrial revolution fascinated contemporaries to such an extent that theories were considered useful only if they had a direct relation to the so-called social question. The concern about the social question reflected the general uneasiness about class structures, working conditions, technological developments, problems of welfare and social security, and, above all, the passing away of a whole set of traditional structures and views. Weber and Durkheim directed their intellectual energies toward the metatheoretical virtues of objectivity,

12. This was true at least for sociologists of the time, who then overemphasized "structure" in response to an overemphasis on "process," and vice versa. Historians, however, continued for a while to be preoccupied with questions of periodization. See Faber and Meier 1978; Gumbrecht and Link-Heer 1985.

13. This book is a strange mixture of the condemnation of public opinion and the hope to influence it.

14. Complaints about such a conceptualization are very recent indeed. See Blute 1979.

methodological control, causal explanation, and value-free research. And they were quite successful at founding a particular academic discipline, namely, sociology. But there were also strong demands for a self-description of society that takes sides on political issues, defines situations, copes with difficult and unfamiliar aspects of modern life, and offers remedies. In this regard it became more and more difficult to maintain the idea of a direction in history. The consequences of social evolution, differentiation, and complexity were still widely discussed, but this discussion occurred not under the heading of progress, but under the heading of obstacles to planning and social control.

The social scene finally changed in the 1960s. At this time it became clear to a larger audience that the theory of system differentiation did not have enough conceptual space to include all the negative statements about modern society one wanted to make. Nobody took the trouble to refute Parsons. He simply became obsolete as a theorist focusing on the functional differentiation of the system of action. For a while "complexity" became a conservative topos (and particularly a topos for right-wing people in left-wing parties).[15] In search of a better theory, many intellectuals turned to the "cheeky teenage years" (roughly 1850–80) of the social sciences and, in particular, to Karl Marx.

However, this interest in outdated theories did not last long. It faded away as a result of a remarkable shift of interest in societal self-description. New ecological topics, anxiety about the future, daily news about technological advances, and disasters tend to catch people's attention. The inequalities of economic distribution continue to exist, but the risks inhering in the day-to-day functioning of the economic system seem to be more relevant from the short-term vantage point of daily news-making. Examples of these risks include the international credit system, free-floating money flows (sometimes several hundred billions of dollars a day), unemployment, the destructive consequences of free trade for local economies, and the destructive consequences of national trade barriers for the international economy. New fields of scientific reasearch, such as nuclear physics and biogenetic engineering, offer both great prospects and terrible fears. "Orientation"[16] is the futile demand of the day. Symptomatic of the embarrassment of the public, commissions on ethics are invoked to act as if they are in control of the situation. Sociology has responded with more or less untheoretical discussions about the fashionable terms of postindustrialism or postmodernity, trying either to catch up to the train of social movements or to run business as usual, that is,

15. For more recent discussions in this regard see LaPorte 1975; Lanzara and Pardi 1980; United Nations University 1985; Bocchi and Ceruti 1985.

16. For the semantic history of this word see Lübbe et al. 1982.

conduct empirical research. Does this mean that we are losing all sense of direction in social history? It seems as if the temporal self-descriptions of modern society and increasing complexity only leave us with the certainty of the uncertainty of the future.

2. EVOLUTION AND IMPROBABILITY

A short look at the larger context of scientific developments and interdisciplinary discussions does not confirm such a desperate conclusion. On the contrary, we can easily find many theoretical attempts to give new meaning to evolution. They provide the conceptual space for describing modern society as a highly selective arrangement of unusual accomplishments. We can characterize this state of modern society by its evolutionary improbability.

As an introduction to this idea, consider the following example, or "paradigm." We can say that an organism that needs a constant internal temperature even when the temperature in its environment changes is in a more improbable state than an organism that adapts its own temperature to the variations of its environment. Organisms that are in a state of higher improbability can afford other differences between the system and its environment. Such a difference is not a sharp one; it can evolve gradually. But once there is a sufficient guarantee of bodily temperature and blood circulation, other improbable states of being can develop and stabilize. This means that more and more variables can be controlled by the system in relation to its environment. The "range of correspondences," to use a term of Herbert Spencer, grows. As the complexity of the relevant environment increases, new forms of complexity emerge within the system.

Biologists commonly describe the incredible stability of life on earth in terms of statistical improbability. The only controversial question is whether this stability is explained by the capacity for adaptation or by the capacity for detachment (Roth 1986). The evolution of society can also be conceptualized in these terms. Evolution accumulates improbabilities and leads to results that could not have been produced by planning and design. The point, however, is that the improbabilities once attained are preserved in the form of highly structured complexity. Complexity implies a highly selective arrangement of elements (see Luhmann 1984, 45ff.). It retains the possibilities of other combinations passed over in its morphogenesis. Complexity is based on repression or inhibition[17] and

---

17. Barel characterizes inhibition very aptly as "potentialisation," the mode of pure possibility, to be used, however, if circumstances change (1979, 185ff.).

readmits the unused combinatorial possibilities as limited potentials for structural change.

From the perspective of information theory structured complexity contains information in the sense of a choice between possible states and redundancy in the sense of connections between different choices. Thus it is not completely arbitrary to expect certain elements if you have information about others. Information is a measure of improbability, and redundancy is a measure of probability (Atlan 1979). Concrete systems are always mixtures of probabilities and improbabilities. If we add, however, the genetic perspective and describe the system, starting with entropy, in terms of its probability here and now, it becomes extremely improbable.[18]

Of course this improbability is a matter of observation and description. Whatever we observe and describe has the following characteristics: it is as it is; it is neither probable nor improbable; it is neither necessary nor possible; it is not different from what it could have been; and it has neither past nor future. These modalizations are instruments of observation and description. Therefore they depend on the ability of systems to observe and to describe, to use negations and distinctions, and to project unity onto what they perceive as highly complex. For our purpose, however, these epistemological caveats do not matter because we are discussing the self-description of modern society, something that is a description anyway. A society cannot know what it is. It can only know what it describes and why it prefers certain descriptions to others. But do we, in fact, describe our society in terms of evolutionary improbability, and if so why?

To begin with, I list a few indicators of such a change in description.

1. Immanuel Kant proposed to elaborate a new kind of metaphysics, one that was based on a new type of question, namely, "How is *x* possible" (Kant 1783, preface). The new metaphysics did not develop, but the way of putting the question remained influential. Nobody doubts that *x is* possible. The question *how*, then, refers to the improbability of quite normal and accepted facts. For example, when referring to the Hobbesian problem of order, the question becomes "How social order is possible" (Parsons 1949, 87ff.; see also O'Neill 1976; Luhmann 1981). This formulation of the question tends to move the problem from rational to empirical

18. It is easy to demonstrate this following a calculation of Eigen 1985. A gene with the length of 1.000 symbols (a quite normal length) contains about 10^{600} possible recombinations. The age of the universe is supposed to be 10^{18} seconds. The conclusion seems obvious: The evolution of the universe increases its own improbability. In this sense it is an unrepeatable historical entity.

grounds. Habermas in particular objects to such a shift. For our purposes, however, the interesting fact is the disjunction between *that* and *how,* representing the distinction between the normal world as we take it for granted and the improbability of its present state. As a very recent consequence of this disjunction, modern cognitive sciences tend to transform "what" questions into "how" questions.

2. The famous distinction between entropy and negentropy has fostered the interest in improbability and probability. However, the former distinction is not identical with the latter one because the first distinction presupposes an observer "in between." In the direction of entropy the observer sees the probability of the improbability of an equal distribution of indistinguishable entities. In the direction of negentropy the observer sees the diminished possibility of randomness in the social order. In both directions the observer has to use a paradoxical technique of observation.[19] Otherwise the observer cannot make use of what physicists present as an "objective" distinction that is based on the laws of thermodynamics.

3. Recently, there has been a shift in the meaning of "noise." It is no longer a technical problem that involves the disturbance of the transmission of information and that is solved by redundancy. Now, noise is a necessary condition for the development of order (von Foerster 1960; Atlan 1972).

4. A similar upgrading has occurred with "randomness." Only since the twentieth century have we been trying hard to produce randomness, be it in mathematics or in art (Brok 1967). This seems to indicate that we need, for whatever reasons, access to randomness as a position from which we want to see order. And because the world is in an ordered state, we utilize highly sophisticated techniques to produce the counterfactual state of randomness. Mere accidents do not suffice. They are not random enough.

5. At the beginning of this century observers generally assumed that an evolutionary development violating the second law of thermodynamics would require a nonphysical, that is, teleological, explanation. Today, this problem seems to have been solved by theories about nonequilibrated thermal processes. With respect to teleological explanations, one has to accept the dictum of Warren McCulloch: "The circuit must be closed to be purposive" (1965, 41).

19. Using a more rigorous interpretation, we could also say that the cosmology of entropy and negentropy *excludes* the observer who estimates probabilities and *includes* the observer at the same time as a physical, chemical, biological, psychological, and social being.

6. Although throughout history the elements of nature were considered stable, changeable only by divine intervention, our century has reversed this view. Ilya Prigogine takes the discovery that elementary particles are generally unstable to be "one of the most extraordinary discoveries of this century" (1981, 42). To support this point, he refers to a lecture of Steven Weinberg titled "The End of Everything."

By observing observers who use the six devices just discussed, we can extrapolate a common tendency to look at natural and social facts as if they were highly improbable. This approach does not dramatically shake our confidence in everyday expectations, but it adds the new dimension of observing what others do not observe: the improbability of the bases of their observations.

To be sure, such a formula remains paradoxical: we observe observers who do not know that they do not know that they observe improbable probabilities. Although a paradox, it might be a creative paradox, suggesting strategies of "unfolding" that might lead to theoretical advances.[20] The advantage of this instruction for "observing systems"[21] is that it directs attention to time and history by using the asymmetry of time to dissolve this paradox.

In this sense terms like "higher improbability" connote a temporal description of states of nature or society. The concept of evolutionary improbabilities refers to the dimension of time. It indicates that time is needed to build up systems that presuppose themselves in the course of further developments. The arrow of time, then, points from more probable (easy to generate) to more improbable states that feed on previous developments. This description of temporal direction includes progress in the sense that we may or may not want to live in, maintain, and develop the improbable states we find ourselves in. This description also includes the ideas of differentiation and complexity in the sense that the modern type of differentiation, namely, functional differentiation, is a highly improbable state with more positive and more negative aspects than either segmentation or stratification. The new framework of temporal description encompasses the old ones. Moreover, it also reevaluates them and provides conceptual space for including actual feelings of insecurity and risk, distrust in optimizing strategies and good intentions, and unavoidable alienation.

---

20. A review of the research on this question of "creative paradoxes" is presented in Krippendorf 1984.

21. I cite the intentionally ambiguous title of Heinz von Foerster (1981).

REFERENCES

Atlan, Henri. 1972. Du bruit comme principe d'auto-organisation. *Communications* 18: 21–36.

———. 1979. *Entre le cristal et la fumée.* Paris: Seuil.

Barel, Yves. 1979. *Le paradoxe et le système: Essai sur le fantastique sociale.* Grenoble: Presses Universitaires.

Blute, Marion. 1979. Sociocultural evolutionism: An untried theory. *Behavioral Science* 24: 46–59.

Bocchi, Gianluca, and Mauro Ceruti, eds. 1985. *La sfida della complessità.* Milan: Feltrinelli.

Bonald, Louis de. [1858] 1982. De la manière d'écrire l'histoire. In *Oeuvres Complètes*, 78–112. Reprint. Geneva: Slatkin.

Bråten, Stein. 1986. The third position: Beyond artificial and autopoietic reduction. In *Sociocybernetic paradoxes: Observation, control and evolution of self-steering systems*, ed. Felix Geyer and Johannes van der Zouwen, 193–205. London: Sage.

Brok, Alfred M. 1967. Randomness and the twentieth century. *Antioch Review* 27: 30–61.

Burlamaqui, J. J. 1747. *Principes du droit naturel.* Geneva: Barrillot.

Crucé, Emeric. [1623] 1909. *Le nouveau Cynée.* Reprint, with English translation by Thomas W. Balch. Philadelphia: Allen, Lane and Scott.

Durkheim, Emile. [1893] 1930. *De la division du travail social.* Paris: Presses Universitaires.

Eigen, Manfred. 1985. Homunculus im Zeitalter der Biotechnologie—Physikochemische Grundlagen der Lebensvorgänge. In *Geistige Grundlagen der Medizin,* ed. Rudolf Gross, 9–41. Berlin: Springer.

Faber, Karl Georg, and Christian Meier, eds. 1978. *Historische Prozesse.* Munich: Deutscher Taschenbuch Verlag.

Foerster, Heinz von. 1960. On self-organizing systems and their environments. In *Self-organizing systems,* ed. Marshall C. Yovits and Scott Cameron, 31–50. London: Pergamon Press.

———. 1981. *Observing systems.* Seaside, Calif.: Intersystems Publications.

Francis, Emerich K. 1981. Darwins Evolutionstheorie und der Sozialdarwinismus. *Kölner Zeitschrift für Soziologie und Sozialpsychologie* 33: 209–28.

Freund, Walter. 1957. *Modernus und andere Zeitbegriffe des Mittelalters.* Cologne: Böhlau.

Gumbrecht, Hans-Ulrich, and Ursula Link-Heer, eds. 1985. *Epochenschwellen und Epochenstrukturen im Diskurs der Literatur und Sprachhistorie.* Frankfurt: Suhrkamp.

Gundling, Nicolaus Hieronymous. 1736. *Jus naturae ac gentium.* 3d ed. Halle-Magdeburg: Renger.

Heintz, Peter. 1982. *Die Weltgesellschaft im Spiegel von Ereignissen.* Diessenhofen, Switzerland: Ruegger.

Herder, Johann Gottlieb. [1774] 1967. *Auch eine Philosophie der Geschichte zur Bildung der Menschheit.* Frankfurt: Suhrkamp.

Hoeges, Dirk. 1984. Der vergessene Rest: Tocqueville, Chateaubriand und der Subjektwechsel in der französischen Geschichtsschreibung. *Historische Zeitschrift* 238: 287–310.

Hofstadter, Richard. 1945. *Social Darwinism in American thought, 1860–1915*. Philadelphia: University of Pennsylvania Press.

Kant, Immanuel. [1783] 1893. *Prolegomena zu einer jeden künftigen Metaphysik*, ed. I. H. von Kirchmann. 3d ed. Leipzig: Dürr.

Koehler, Heinrich. [1735] n.d. *Juris naturalis . . . exercitationes*. 2d ed. Jena: Ritter.

Koselleck, Reinhart. 1975. Geschichte, Historie. In *Geschichtliche Grundbegriffe: Historisches Lexikon zur politisch-sozialen Sprache in Deutschland*, 2: 593–717. Stuttgart: Klett.

———. 1979. *Vergamgene Zukunft. Zur Semantik geschichtlicher Zeiten*. Frankfurt: Suhrkamp.

Krippendorf, Klaus. 1984. Paradox and information. In *Progress in communication sciences*, ed. Brenda Dervin and Melvin J. Voigt, 45–71. Norwood, N. J.: Ablex Publications.

Lanzara, Giovan Francesco, and Francesco Pardi. 1980. *L'interpretazione della complessità: Metodo sistemico e scienze sociali*. Naples: Guida.

LaPorte, Todd R., ed. 1975. *Organized social complexity: Challenge to politics and policy*. Princeton: Princeton University Press.

L. D. H. [L'ami des hommes] [Victor de Riqueti, Marquis de Mirabeau]. 1774. *La science ou les droits et les devoirs de l'homme*. Lausanne: Grasset.

Lübbe, Hermann, Oskar Köhler, Wolf Lepenies, Thomas Nipperdey, Gerhard Schmidtchen, Gerd Roellecke. 1982. *Der Mensch als Orientierungswaise? Ein interdisziplinärer Erkundungsgang*. Freiburg: Alber.

Luhmann, Niklas. 1981. Wie ist die soziale Ordnung möglich? In *Gesellschaftsstruktur und Semantik*, by Niklas Luhmann, 2: 195–285. Frankfurt: Suhrkamp.

———. 1982. *The differentiation of society*. New York: Columbia University Press.

———. 1984. *Soziale Systeme: Grundriß einer allgemeinen Theorie*. Frankfurt: Suhrkamp.

———. 1985. Zum Begriff der sozialen Klasse. In *Soziale Differenzierung: Zur Geschichte einer Idee*, ed. Niklas Luhmann, 119–62. Opladen: Westdeutscher Verlag.

McCulloch, Warren. 1965. *Embodiments of mind*. Cambridge: MIT Press.

Malvezzi, Virgilio. 1635. Ritratto del privato politico christiano. In *Opere del Marchese Malvezzi*, by Virgilio Malvezzi. Milan: Mediolanum.

Oesterle, Ingrid. 1985. Der "Führungswechsel der Zeithorizonte" in der deutschen Literatur. In *Studien zur Ästhetik und Literaturgeschichte der Kunstperiode*, ed. Dirk Grathoff, 11–75. Frankfurt: Lang.

O'Neill, John. 1976. The Hobbesian problem in Marx and Parsons. In *Explorations in general theory in social science*, ed. Jan J. Loubser, Rainer C. Baum, Andrew Effrat, and Victor Meyer Lidz, 1: 295–308. New York: Free Press.

Parsons, Talcott. 1949. *The structure of social action*. 2d ed. Glencoe, Ill.: Free Press.

Prigogine, Ilya. 1981. Order out of chaos. In *Disorder and order: Proceedings of the Stanford International Symposium (September 14–16, 1981)*, ed. Paisley Livingston, 41–60. Sarotoga, Calif.: Anma Libri.

Robinet, Jean Baptiste. 1766. *De la nature.* 3d ed. Amsterdam: van Harrevelt.

Ross, Edward A. 1907. *Sin and society: An analysis of latter-day iniquity.* Boston: Houghton and Mifflin.

Roth, Gerhard. 1986. Selbstorganisation—Selbsterhaltung—Selbstreferentialität: Prinzipien der Organisation von Lebewesen. In *Selbstorganisation: Die Entstehung von Ordnung in Nature und Gesellschaft,* ed. Andreas Dress, Hubert Hendrichs, and Günter Küppers, 149–80. Munich: Piper.

Simmel, Georg. 1890. *Über sociale Differenzierung.* Leipzig: Duncker and Humblot.

Spörl, Johannes. 1930. Das Alte und das Neue im Mittelalter Studien zum Problem des mittelalterlichen Fortschrittsbewusstseins. *Historisches Jahrbuch* 50: 297–341, 498–524.

United Nations University. 1985. *The science and praxis of complexity.* Tokyo: United Nations University.

The Temporalization of Social Order

Some Theoretical Remarks on the Change in "Change"

Bernard Giesen

Anyone who does not wish to confine the analysis of social change to merely sketching temporal variations in social phenomena but insists on aiming to propound an autonomous theory of social change is soon confronted with the suspicion that to indulge in such a hope is to indulge in speculation. Social change, it might be argued, is no more and no less a specific object for theory-construction than is history itself. Moreover, it might be argued that explanations for the sequence of and relationships among the events that make up history and social change have already been provided by the theories of action and structure; consequently, there is no need for any separate theoretical concepts.

However, any such attempt to decouple the analysis of social change from autonomous theoretical concepts overlooks the tacit categorial assumptions made in all analysis of social change. Although "temporality" has to be regarded as a universal presupposition for experience, conceptions of temporality and change are themselves subject to alteration over time. The observations that follow are concerned with social change and the evolutionary development of these categorial preliminary assumptions regarding change and development.

These reflections start with the assumption that it was necessary for certain differentiations and structural transformations to have occurred during the course of the history of ideas before alterations over time could be conceived of as "social change." If one pursues the story of how the concept of social change came about, there is some evidence for the supposition that "social change" as a sociological term already represents a further transformation of the temporal structures that underlay the his-

I am indebted to Wolfgang Schneider and Uwe Sibeth for stimulating criticism and assistance in investigating the conceptual history of "change."

torical theory of the modern era or, before that, the history-of-salvation models in Christian philosophy (see Löwith 1953). Consequently, these differentiations set out a repertoire of possible approaches to the subject of social change that delimits and structures any theoretical treatment. The following evolutionary-theoretical outline is guided by the notion that the switch from historical to social change transforms temporal structures in a manner analogous to the process of secularization in which the problem of social change is differentiated from that of social order.[1]

1. THE ANALYSIS OF TEMPORAL STRUCTURES

The basis for the remarks in this chapter is the following model for the analysis of interpretational patterns.[2] According to this model, analyses of worldviews, interpretational patterns, and categorial structures can be developed along three dimensions. The first dimension involves the depiction of various systems for classifying the world. These systems are characterized by the spatial-topological distinction between different spheres, occurring in its most basic form in the dichotomous differentiation of internal and external, near and far, above and below.[3] The second dimension is concerned with various models for the production, genesis, and temporal linking of events. These process models, which are incorporated in interpretational patterns, can be traced back to the elementary experience and shaping of temporality as actions are performed. The third dimension is concerned with the forms and methods by which a subject reflexively verifies and adopts a posture toward the world (the matter of whether that subject is an individual or a collective is irrelevant). In analyzing interpretational patterns or categorial structures I assume that all interpretational patterns of whatever kind incorporate a structural, a processual, and a reflexive dimension.

1.1. Topological Structure

As is true of other models, models of temporality and change can only be conceived of with great difficulty in the absence of points of reference. In this instance, the structural and topological reference is represented by a fundamental difference on which our awareness and conception of

1. For a discussion of the process of secularization see Blumenberg 1974 (75ff.); Lübbe 1965. M. Weber refers to religious secularization as a part of the process of rationalization. See Weber 1963 (1:11) and Schluchter 1980 (9–40).

2. For the concept of interpretational structure see Oevermann 1973; Giesen 1987; Arnold 1983.

3. Structuralists usually refer only to the topological dimension of symbolic systems and ignore the equally important dimensions of process and reflective interpretation.

change depends: the difference between a sphere of stability, continuity, and identity, on the one hand, and one of variability, transformation, and dynamism, on the other hand. Change can only be perceived against a constant background just as continuity can only be recognized against the sphere of change. In an elementary form this difference between stability and continuity occurs as the boundary between the continuity of the subject having the experience and the chaotic change in that which he is experiencing in the "world." Naturally, positions providing a guarantee of identity and continuity may also develop outside the experiencing subject in the world. Thus the development of differences in temporality between different spheres and the topology of those spheres constitutes the first axis in an evolutionary-theoretical reconstruction of models of change.[4]

1.2. Process Models

Process models have been given particularly close attention to date by those who propound historical theories and metatheories of social change.[5] Observers draw distinctions between cyclical and recurrent conceptions of the course of time, on the one hand, and cumulative models of progress and purposive development, on the other hand. A third concept of temporal sequence has gained less attention: the idea that events succeed one another chaotically and at random, the idea of chance and indeterminacy.[6]

Such elementary experiences as purposive action, aging, the sequence of day and night, and uncertainty about events in the world provide the ontogenetic basis for process models. The nature of such processes provides a second important means of distinguishing between the models: change can be kept in motion by action-type processes or it can be determined by natural events. The increasing differentiation between natural, objective processes and those in which action is involved represents an important line of development in the evolution of temporal structures.

No society has confined its concept of change exclusively to one particular process model; several such models have always been used simultaneously, even though they were of course differentiated on the basis of spheres. Together with differentiation according to tempi, that is, according to the speed of change, then, the differentiation of spheres according to the cyclical, cumulative, or chaotic sequences involved is a further area of attention in an evolutionary analysis of models of change.

4. For the evolution of levels of time see Fraser 1982. M. Schmid (1986) also argues in favor of an evolutionary-theoretical conception of time.

5. Chemistry, however, was the first scientific discipline that applied the notion of "process." See Roedgers 1983.

6. However, the concept of randomness has recently gained more attention in the philosophy of history. See Koselleck 1968; Meier 1978; Troeltsch 1913; Lübbe 1977, 54–68.

1.3. Reflexive Forms

The subject of processes of change can adopt three possible responsive postures. One alternative is that change is actively and purposefully driven on by the subject, accelerated or decelerated by him. Another alternative is that the subject experiences change as inevitable and uncontrollable, even though his own action is affected by it. The third posture is that the subject experiencing change is insufficiently affected by it and perceives it with an attitude of indifference. Of course no society confines itself exclusively to just one attitude to processes of change, but attitudes are invariably differentiated to suit particular spheres. For example, even if they accept change in the majority of spheres fatalistically, actors may nevertheless adopt an activist attitude to carrying out their everyday actions and remain indifferent toward the changes in natural phenomena that they perceive but by which they are not clearly affected. Thus the attention of evolutionary-theoretical analysis is directed toward change as it is distributed between spheres in which it evokes activist, fatalistic, and indifferent attitudes.

2. THE CHANGE IN "CHANGE"

2.1. Time as the Action Period

An analysis of this kind starts out from an interpretational pattern that makes no distinction between processes of social action, on the one hand, and processes of social order and social change, on the other hand. There is no recognizable social order standing out above processes of interaction within the framework of this interpretational pattern. The perception of change and temporal alteration is limited to the time-period one has lived through and remembered, to the *durée* of social action.[7] Hence the "narrative" logic by which action is recounted both frames and structures the logic underlying the passage of time.[8] The "stories" recalled are kept in motion by interaction among a number of actors, and the stories' beginnings and ends are determined by how the theme of interaction is dealt with.[9]

Both the change experienced in the world during the course of action and the change experienced in the subjects themselves that they remember as they consider their own personal experience of getting old are of

7. The phenomenological conception of time focuses solely on the mental representation of time as action period. See Bergmann 1981.

8. For the narrative conception of historical method see Louch 1966; Danto 1965; Olafson 1970.

9. In a magical understanding of the world nature is also composed of entities with whom it is possible to interact—although it occasionally may be difficult to do so. Such interactions do not involve a separate level of change or experience of time.

course limited as long as there is no social structure differentiating among time periods. Aging processes take place synchronously and therefore hardly give cause for the social differentiation of periods of time or of temporal levels. Beyond the period of action and the lifetime as directly experienced the world is experienced as something timeless and ultimately chaotic.

Primitive classifications, which by definition are not systematized by any superordinate principle, clearly show the unordered complexity of the world. They barely offer a topological "toehold" for identifying time that reaches beyond one's own lifetime or beyond the actions of the present (Lévi-Strauss 1962). The only way in which primitive classification allows a number of lifetimes to be linked together is via the kinship link of conception and birth; this pushes the temporal horizon back into the past and creates an awareness of continuity and change independent of the experience of the present. Evidently, the extension of such a genealogical model of time marks out a line of development running from the action-period notion of time to the socially differentiated notion of time.

2.2 Historical Time

2.2.1. The differentiation of temporal levels.
It is only possible for such a socially differentiated notion of temporality to exist and to be capable of grasping change even when change occurs beyond the course of action or individual experience if the structure of social order breaks free from processes of interaction to take on a duration and scope that is cast more broadly than individual interaction processes. In early high cultures the topological structure of such an order emerges as a vertical hierarchical ranking of a number of levels distinguished according to the tempo of change and according to the forms of process (see Kanitscheider 1974, 27; Lämmli 1962). The highest level in the hierarchy is generally timeless and infinite: the sphere of the gods, the sacred and the cosmic order. This realm preserves continuity and stability, instills time with unity and cohesion, determines change in the world, and determines the fates of human beings. This celestial sphere was initially—and for a considerable time afterward—conceived of in terms of acting personages: almighty and immortal gods who created the world, who guide the history of humankind by their active involvement, and who command the laws of the world as its supreme rulers. The fact that the reference of continuity had been detached from the individual human subject did not yet mean that the action scheme had been abandoned as a process model.[10]

10. Greek philosophy was the first to depersonalize this level, understanding it, on the one hand, in terms of elementary building blocks and principles of nature and, on the other hand, in terms of everlasting ideas. Both the pre-Socratic and the Platonic alternatives mark a decisive and momentous structural transformation.

Below the eternal, infinite order of the sacred, but still determined by it, change takes place in the political passage of time, that is, in the rise and fall of empires. When set against the eternal order of the cosmos, the rhythm on this level takes the form of a short-term cyclical sequence, remaining a series of mere "histories" in which cohesiveness can be found only on the uppermost level (Hager 1974; Meier 1975; Koselleck 1973). However, when set against the action period experienced by the individual, the processes by which states and unions are formed, i.e., the passage of time on the political level, represents long-term growth and development. It serves as a reference point to lend "superordinate meaning" to the parallel courses and the chaotic multifariousness of individual lives.

This middle level of historical and political change was separated from the eternal order of the cosmos, on one side, and the juxtapositions and sequences of the actions of the present, on the other side. But these separations still do not rule out the possibility that superordinate historical processes were understood in terms of the familiar model of the action period. Action-theoretical metaphors continued to set the scene: struggle and conflict, victory and defeat, ambition and avarice. The development of historical time initially takes place as a topological differentiation of tempo, but not of forms of process.

Beneath politically constituted "historical time," that is, on the level of social action and interaction, change continues to occur according to the principles of the action period. However, having recourse to the historical time-axis makes it easier to recall past action situations.[11] The hierarchical construction of temporal levels means time can be perceived in a special way and more keenly: rapidity, fleetingness, and transitoriness are no longer perceived only via contrast with the continuity maintained by the subject. Individuals become able to be aware that their own lifetimes and actions are transitory, fleeting, and solitary. It is via this solitude and isolation of human action that conceptions of human individuality then come into view, in Roman thought, for example (see Seneca 1969; Boethius 1974). At the same time, the desire to transcend one's own short-lived existence and attain the level of immortality becomes a powerful motivating force for human action and the central theme of the high religions.

As divine order, historical change, and human action diverge from one another, a final essential aspect is that the acting subject must adopt some posture: activism and fatalism then diverge from each other. Activism is

11. Koselleck has recently suggested a threefold differentiation of levels of time that separates the before-after of historical action events from the supraindividual historical processes and the metahistorical "conditions of historical possibility." See Koselleck 1984; Braudel 1958.

limited to the subject's relationship to processes occurring on the same
temporal level or on the next level down, whereas fatalism applies to the
attitude toward higher levels. The assumption here is that, although interaction between "neighboring" levels is always possible, differences in temporality generally prevent control being exercised upward from below.
Human action is too short-lived to be able to determine historical processes, and the course of history has no influence on the gods. An indifferent attitude to change, the final alternative, cannot develop until certain
levels have been depersonalized and objectivized, when, for example, the
responsibility for ensuring the unity of the world and maintaining the
progress of history no longer lies with the will of an eternal God but with
an impersonal cosmic order. As long as action-type processes keep the
world in motion, the predominant forms of response remain fatalism and
activism.

2.2.2. The history-of-salvation model.   It is now common to view Judaeo-
Christian eschatology as having transcended the cyclical concepts of history that prevailed during the classical period. The Christian promise of
deliverance meant that the tension between life on earth and the hereafter, between the eternal kingdom of God and the finite and changeable
terrestrial realm, was to become the driving force for an irreversible and
linear history of salvation. At its conclusion, by the grace of God and the
striving of the chosen, life on earth and the hereafter would be reconciled. In this view it is the task of humankind to drive on this history-of-
salvation by sacralizing the here and now and to make progress with a
view to the return of the holy spirit. It was the agreement to fulfil this
task that separated the chosen people from the damned.

The original Judaeo-Christian eschatology still conceives history
within the bounds of a model based on the action period. By virtue of
its covenant with a mighty God and the intervention of his Son, a
people remembers and experiences its history as the path toward a
salvation that, to begin with, was understood in quite earthly terms.
This ultimately magical pattern of interpretation was not so much
based on the separation of different temporal levels as on the topological difference between the chosen people and the heathens. It was not
until after it became obvious that the return of the Redeemer could not
be expected within a single lifetime that—under the influence of classical philosophy—the time horizon and the topological difference between life on earth and the hereafter, between God and the world,
between the immortal soul and mortal flesh, and between the terrestrial
and heavenly realms were expanded and thus diverted attention away
from the division between the chosen people and the heathens. There
was an added topological difference between the individual and the

world historical levels of explanation. The individual was able to make progress along the path to salvation; the world, via the sequence of the three realms (paradise, life after the fall, and salvation), carried out God's promise of deliverance.[12]

Another development of momentous significance was the new form taken on by the process model for change in the secular sphere. The cyclical view of the rise and fall of empires was supplemented by the perspective of the unilinear and irreversible development of the world and progress toward salvation.

Moreover, for history to be seen as the history of salvation, it was also necessary for humankind to be active in its approach and to strive for salvation. Redemption and the reconciliation of earthly life with the hereafter were not solely the work of God but involved humanity as well. This eschatological dualism introduced a comprehensive, positive moment of tension into historical change. No longer was change merely short-term unrest without underlying hope. It now had as its goal and ultimate end the perfection and redemption of the world. The beginning and end of history were in turn determined by the timelessness of paradise, past and future. Naturally, the eschatological process at first remained completely within the bounds of action-theoretical notions: the world had been created by a personal God who issued commandments, and if humanity followed these it would ensure its own progress to salvation.

2.2.3. Secularization as the structural transformation of the history of salvation.   When the rediscovery of classical philosophy occurred in the twelfth century, a topological differentiation began that laid the foundations for the secularization process of the modern era within the hierarchical model of temporal levels (Hoffmann [1926] 1960; Baeumker 1927; Beierwaltes 1969; Bredow 1972). The secular sphere now became more markedly and more clearly differentiated along two lines. First, the course of history and the prevailing social order was separated from the individual striving for salvation and morality. Second, the sphere of action and history was separated from the natural order. Nature, however, was no longer seen as unredeemed, unholy, barbaric, and the source of the base desires of the flesh. Rather, it was seen as the creation of God, a creation that reveals the eternal principles of the divine. The individual, by actually withdrawing from the spheres of worldly interests and the changing times into his or her inner being,

12. See Augustin 1955, 1:35, 10:32, 15:1, 5, 21, 10:14. See also Aquileia 1864, chapter 43, 246A: "Perfectio non in annis, sed in animis"; and Aquin 1934, 1, 2 qu. 106, art. 4c: "Unde non potest esse aliquis perfectior status praesentis vitae quam status novae legis: quia tanto es unumquodque perfectius, quanto ultimo fini propinquius."

becomes an equally timeless stage for encounters with God and gaining knowledge of the truth.

The "dehistorification" of nature as a reflection of the divine and the dehistorification of the individual as the locus of the search for salvation and knowledge have the corollary effect of making the level of historical processes appear particularly secular, profane, and time-bound. As the level of individual action comes under increasing pressure from the history of salvation and as the eternal laws of the creator are sought in nature, history and the sphere of politics are gradually freed from their eschatological ties and are treated as a specific field of unrest in human action with a dynamism of their own. Even the final attempts to provide history with a theological intent in the sixteenth and seventeenth centuries (by Bossuet and the Protestant universal historians) could not avoid making the assumption of inner-worldly regular patterns in their presentation of the course of history (see, for example, Carion [1532] 1966; Bossuet 1964; Klempt 1960, 8). Following Guicardini's and Machiavelli's historiographies of the Renaissance, active intervention by the eternal God recedes into the background. God no longer reveals himself to the faithful. Rather the faithful experience him through their own reason. Nature follows the unalterable, eternal laws of its maker, and history becomes the stage for interests and politics functioning according to their own secular principles (Machiavelli [1532] 1962; Bodin [1583] 1961; and Pufendorf [1744] 1967).

In modern thought, too, the level of historical time, which lies above that of action-period time, is primarily constituted by politics and law. Political interests are what move history, and the principles of legality and the state are what constitute the order of society. The legitimation of the law and authority by God through his grace, by reason via enlightened monarchy, by nature via the notion of natural law, or by individual freedom via the concept of contractual agreement thus become the central problems in conveying continuity or discontinuity. The "detheologization" of history and dehistorification of nature bring about a fundamental transformation of the temporal levels. The level of timelessness is no longer conceived of as a level involving acting personages. The place of the eternal God is now taken by the objectivity of reason, natural law, and the laws of nature.

In contrast to this, the social level, which includes customs and common usage, initially appears incoherent and random, to be made up of illusions and mere fashions, to be "irrational" (see Fontenelle [1686] 1908). The differences between the sphere of the social, on the one hand, and the principles of nature and morality, on the other hand, nevertheless provide an avenue for analysis and explanation. "The external circumstances which cause the differences in human customs and may be supposed to favour them further should be divided into natural and moral circumstances," according to Walch's *Philosophical Lexicon*, published in 1726 (Walch [1726] 1968). The main natural causes are taken to be physical constitution and climate, and differences in upbringing and education are thought to be the main moral causes (Montesquieu [1758] 1950). The education of humankind by enlightenment thus offers itself as a paradigm of historical change and progress.[13] The idea of progress was to develop in the wake of the famous *querelle des anciens et des modernes*," that is, the argument about the respective merits of ancient and modern learning, into the central concept of historical theory in the eighteenth century (Bury [1932] 1955). By applying reason and gaining knowledge of nature, observers believed that it was possible to repeal superstitions and misconceptions to an ever greater degree and to make history itself rational.

The new model and paradigm of history, then, is academic and scientific progress, which many believe will allow the fortunes of humanity to be planned in a society of the enlightened. "The perfectibility of man knows no factual bounds, and can never reverse into decline," writes Condorcet in 1793 ([1793] 1963, 27, my translation). The conception of infinite progress had as its opposite number the universal expansion of history's area of concern as proposed by Voltaire in his famous *Essai sur les moeurs*. Europe and Christendom were no longer the self-evident reference points for historical change. Shortly before this, Vico, in his *Szienza nuova*, had made the *mondo civile* the object of a special branch of science investigating social action and societal order. This investigation was not conducted, as before, with reference to moral precepts or the history of salvation but with respect to actual conditions. Once the future had been opened up as offering the prospect of never-ending progress, the space under consideration was extended and the "social" was discovered as an object of empirical science. The confines of the hierarchical model were overcome once and for all.

Apart from the extension of historical space in Voltaire's philosophy of history, the natural sciences' concept of time in the eighteenth century also broke through the barriers of the hierarchical model of temporal levels. The concept of an objective measurable passage of time determined and moved by the laws of nature gradually asserted itself as a point of reference. Against it, historical time appears limited, imprecise, and inconstant. The temporality of the world, on the one hand, and that of the passage of history and experience, on the other hand, are hence ever more sharply delineated by different process models. "Objective"

---

13. Löwith (1953, 74) names Pascal as the first who—albeit still with a Christian intent—saw history in terms of a learning process.

time moves according to the eternal laws of nature, whereas historical time is kept in motion by the progress of the human race (Elias 1984).

2.3. The Emergence of "Social Change"

2.3.1. The temporalization of the topological structure. The years of the late eighteenth century and the early nineteenth century are regarded by historians today as a threshold period. This applies equally, indeed especially, to the understanding of temporality, history, and change. The hierarchical topology of different temporal levels, where change and adjustment form part of a comprehensive and stable order, is replaced by a model that understands change as an abstract, universal process that reverses the relationship between order and change. No longer is change contained within the framework of an order guaranteeing continuity, but order is the continually new product of a comprehensive, persistent process of change.

The "temporalization of order" as part of the consciousness of progress in the nineteenth century is initially recognizable in a changeover from fundamentally synchronously arranged topologies to a series of consecutive developmental stages.[14] The stage that comes later in time is regarded as superior and accorded a higher rank. Historical change no longer finds unity and a reference point guaranteeing continuity in an upper level of timelessness but rather in the infinite future that should be made a reality "as quickly as possible." From the point of view of the modern consciousness, change becomes the normal state. Moves to consolidate processes of change in stable orders are pushed to the verge of the pathological, and the modern order's legitimacy consists primarily in its capacity to be systematically revised and refashioned. Progress, history, development, and finally evolution are the comprehensive "collective singulars" (Koselleck 1972, 1973). Their processes and their courses provide the material for the differentiation of different forms of order as "developmental stages" (Koselleck 1972, xvii). Although one could talk of progress in the sciences at the beginning of the eighteenth century, neither the terms development nor progress, nor even history, would normally be found in philosophical dictionaries. But by the first half of the nineteenth century these terms were part of the recognized inventory of philosophy (see Krug [1832–38] 1969, 1:776, 2:591, 216).

The temporalization of order is also apparent in the change in meaning over time of the term "revolution" (Koselleck 1984). Kepler still used the term *"revolutio"* to describe the orbits of the planets. In the seventeenth and eighteenth centuries the term referred to the renewed estab-

---

14. See Luhmann 1978 for the analytically inverse concept of "temporalization of complexity." Luhmann discusses the process of temporalization at the level of general systems theory in his *Soziale Systeme* (1984). See also Luhmann 1975b and 1980.

lishment of the old, just order as history, having lost its innate order, completed another cycle. Yet in the nineteenth century revolution was understood in terms of the acceleration of history. The old order stands in the way of change and progress and so must be smashed to clear a path for history. Finally, in the following century, "permanent revolution" marks the attempt to prevent any tendency of history, having once been accelerated, to become settled enough to produce a new order. In this latter case change in itself is thought to be enough to ensure that reason prevails.

In the view we hold of social structure today the temporalization of order is brought out by the metaphor of the avant garde, which is now beginning to replace the concept of societal rank and honor: It is no longer one's traditional rank but one's ability to preempt whatever is new and of the future that creates social respect. The concept of avant garde is temporalized to the core. An attribute that is avant garde today will be generally known tomorrow, and shortly after that will even be seen as "backward" (Eco 1984, 77).

Neither the principles of a societal order as a whole nor its laws and politics can be made comprehensible except when placed in terms of time: The contradistinction between progressive and conservative is an allusion to historical orientations. The working class does not build its interests on old claims that have been disregarded in the past but on the societal order of the future. And the law as it exists is under the notorious suspicion that it is "outmoded" and that it impedes the march of history. The classical theory of society, from Comte and Hegel to Marx and from Spencer and Mill to Durkheim, is determined by this model of the temporalization of social order. Observers can only analyze and understand a social order by contrasting it with its past and future stages of development and by conceiving of it as the product of historical development. No longer do monarchs, as symbols of either state unity or God, guarantee a society's unity. Their place is taken by the future and the orientation of action toward the project of creating a society of the future.

This temporal relativizing of the social order obviously caused problems for a purely moral approach to the social, which was still emphasized in the eighteenth century, for example, in the Scottish School of Moral Philosophy. The focus of attention was not now on a historical institution's relationship to the universal order of reason or morality but on its temporal relationship to preceding and succeeding developments.

The temporalization of the topological structure is backed up by the cumulative process model, which the late-eighteenth-century philosophers of history retained from the phase of secularization. Within this model every event and every state of rest is accorded its own position in the flux of time. History, therefore, is unique; it is a sequence of historical individuals who can only be understood and placed in order according to a single, timeless principle: the principle of temporal consecutiveness itself (Meinecke 1959a; Meinecke 1959b, 118–20; Faber 1982, 45–65).

The temporalization of order thus also cleared the stage for a theory of society that was intended to be "positive science," that is, for an autonomous theory of social change that could no longer be reduced to terms of action theory or to the theory of social order but could claim to be a fundamental theory of the social in its own right. Since that time the theory of society has no longer been the theory of contract but the theory of evolution.

With the turn toward the theory of society in the nineteenth century there is also a change in the topological relationship between the individual, on the one hand, and the sphere of the social on the other hand. Until the Enlightenment the old European tradition contrasted the individual, in whom universal reason and natural morality were located, with the sphere of customs, fashions, errors, and variations that went to make up things social. In Hegel, at the latest, although probably earlier (in Proudhon and Turgot), this relationship begins to be turned on itself. The individual now appears to be myopic, governed by particularized interests and blind passions, and incapable of comprehending what reason underlies societal development and the march of history. It is only through the cunning of reason that the historical forces that stand behind the backs of acting individuals (Marx) and that also assert themselves against the will and without the understanding of acting individuals shape historical progress. Reason in history might be discerned by scrutiny, and the important point is to unveil the essential and general aspects beneath the surface of particular individual actions.

2.3.2. Functional differentiation as a process model. The temporalization of topology is complemented by the rebuilding of the process model so that the dynamism for change no longer derives from the relationship of tension between unequal levels in a hierarchy but from the relationship between equally ranked units of society. The individual striving for salvation gives way to the dynamics of functionally differentiated subsystems.[15]

In the context of the old European temporal-level model the political functional aspect had already emerged in differentiated form for the level of historical change. This point of reference was formulated in terms of action theory and the theory of order as, respectively, the logic of the rational pursuit of political interests and as the question of just rule and authority. The "self-thematization" of society as it entered the

---

15. Luhmann (1980) notes that the temporalization of complexity is closely connected to the functional differentiation of society.

modern era is a clear reflection of this differentiation of politics. The theory of society was indeed political theory, an identity that can also be inferred from the increasing "legalization" of social action and societal processes. The demand that authority claims be legally regulated long represented the focus of modern conceptions of progress and the central theme of political movements.

The theory of society during the Enlightenment, with its orientation to knowledge gained by science, reason, and natural morality, presented an obstacle to the dominance of politics. Scientific advances caused political authority and legal stipulations to seem backward and wanting in justification. Progress had now changed horses: the differentiated sphere of science and culture, not politics, was in the vanguard of history. (Even in Comte, the highest level of historical development is still characterized by the rule of positive science.)

At the turn of the nineteenth century another functional sphere provided the theme for the theory of society: the economy. A considerable part of the nineteenth-century theory of society consisted of the analysis of society using the terminology and guiding concepts of economics. The terms "division of labor" and "functional differentiation" became the fundamental structural concepts of the theory of society, and the notion of progress was interpreted more and more as increasing economic productivity. In this movement the orientation to economic goals seemed to envelop and regulate all other conceptions of progress. The raising of production levels signified prosperity and happiness for the individual and progress in the sciences and became a guiding conception of politics and the law. This fascination with economic dynamism as the fundamental driving force for societal motion can be felt in an exemplary way in Marx, who wrote that history is held in a state of unrest by the contradiction between the dynamics of the forces of production and their enchainment by the law, politics, and ideology, that is, by the backward spheres. Not until ideology, the law, and politics have made up for this developmental lag is history able to come into its own. Thus, as Löwith (1953) has shown, the old motif of the history of salvation is taken up anew, and, in addition—especially when communist society ceases to be a realistic historical expectation—a new process model is documented, one that will take on an increasing significance as time moves on.

Once politics, science, and the economy had been identified and differentiated, both symbolically and institutionally, different societal spheres came into existence and interrelated in such a way that unrest in even one of these spheres caused relations among spheres to become fundamentally imbalanced and loaded with tension. Establishing relations among spheres that have differing dynamics presents us with a new way to experience time. If temporality and change are the fundamental givens of history, specific fixed points can no longer be used as the guarantors of continuity: everything is always in motion, and the only constant is change itself. The relativistic perception of time only remains in the relationship that different processes of change have with one another, in the differences in dynamism between spheres, and in the gap between advanced and retarded spheres.[16]

If these differences in dynamics do not occur, and the various spheres develop "in time," that is, synchronously, then the possibility of historical time also disappears. When developments accelerate and a particular "pace-making" sphere triggers a societywide take-off because of its own dynamism, then history and change have their chance. Consequently, order in any particular society can never be a concrete and ultimate phenomenon. Order is always a process-generated, provisional, and transitory structure that has its continuity solely in the infinite nature of the process itself and in the lack of simultaneity among different spheres. As society undergoes conversion from a stratified to a functionally differentiated structure, the models of temporality are likewise fundamentally reconstructed. Within the framework of the order that guarantees continuity change is replaced by the temporalization of order, and the social hierarchy is replaced by the market as the model of history and change.

An analogous paradigmatic switch occurred in biology when the Linnean classification of natural processes was succeeded by the Darwinian theory of evolution. Darwin's theory of the origin of the species by natural selection, which was to prove extraordinarily momentous for the theory of society that followed, brings out, in its very name, the temporalization of order. A number of observers have noted that Darwinian theory itself took as its model certain economic theories of the day.[17]

2.3.3.The objectification and moral neutralization of the social realm. The changed makeup of the topological structure and the switch in the process model that occur in the modern theory of change have as a counterpart alterations in the prevailing reflexive forms in change. These alterations primarily involve moral aspects giving way to cognitive aspects in society.

16. This is a point that Schlegel has already noted: "The proper problem of history is the unevenness of progress in the different components of the total human education, particularly, in the large divergence with repeat to the degree of intellectual and moral education" (cited in Koselleck 1975, 391, my translation). More recent theorizing on the system-relative experience of time has adopted this point of departure (Bergmann 1981, 171).

17. It was not until Darwin read Malthus's essay on population in October 1838 that he found a theoretical model that integrated his observations. See De Beer 1964. Marx originally intended to dedicate the first volume of *Das Kapital* to Darwin. For a general discussion of the several links between social theories and Darwin's theory of evolution see Burrow 1966.

This movement, which forms part of the comprehensive process of rationalization in modernity, is brought out in the value-neutral attitude adopted by scientific observation. This changeover is as apparent in the alteration of the concept of society during the nineteenth century as it is in the objectification of social structures, which become ever more markedly separated from the level of individual social action.

In the seventeenth century "society" still largely refers to particularized societies in the sense of organized groupings serving a specific purpose. It later takes on the additional sense of a community of educated and civilized persons.[18] Only during the course of the nineteenth century does "bourgeois society" lead to the concept of society as a comprehensive social system that cannot be reduced to the terms of its constituent parts (see Riedel 1975). The objective structures of history and society, on the one hand, and the processes of individual and collective action, on the other hand, take on their own separate identities. The progress of history and the development of the individual or the development of a collective subject, e.g., mankind, the nation, followed one and the same pedagogical principle in the philosophy of the Enlightenment, and in the model of the theory of contract the structure of the state always remained bound to the interests of contracting parties. But in later times the collective singulars (see Koselleck 1972, 1973), i.e., history, society, and progress, became a set of impersonal, abstract, and objective interrelations actually developing in contrast to both subjectivity and particularized organizations. The levels of interaction, organization, and society part company (Luhmann 1975a, 1984, 551ff.).

This objectification of the societal is especially evident in the nature of the relationship linking the various levels of society. In premodern hierarchical historical models the relationship was one of command and obedience, of moral prescription and adherence to precepts. The notion of an action-type relationship between various actors that was capable of being moralized was still a binding one for the Enlightenment's idea of history. However, it should be noted that these relationships were viewed in reverse: in the conflict between rulers and the ruled, the apologists of the ancien régime and those of the revolution, and later between society and the individual, the higher level in the hierarchy bore the taint of immorality.

In the nineteenth century the concept of society begins to separate from the notion of intentional action that one has to relate to in moral terms, whether in the form of rebellion or obedience. Society is comprehended as an objective structure that is only linked to the action level via

18. See "Gesellschaft" in Zedler 1735, col. 1260; "Societät" in Zedler 1743, col. 171; "Societät (öffentliche)" in Zedler 1743, col. 180; "Gesellschaft" in Walch [1726] 1968, 1:col. 1659–63; "Societät" in Walch [1726] 1968, 2:col. 916; "Gesellschaft" in Adelung 1775, 617; "Gesellschaft (societas)" in Krug [1832–38] 1969, 2:238–42; and Kaupp 1974, col. 459–66.

the unintentional consequences of action or, more frequently, via the preconditions for action that are not necessarily conscious. As structure and action or, stated in a different terminology, system and life-world or, to use yet another famous phrase, society and community part company, this tendency is initially treated morally—as an opportunity to register critical complaints against modernity. But it is later treated theoretically—as a theme and point of departure for sociological reflection. Although Marx criticizes the commodity form and the abstractness shown by social relations, he still systematically uses the parting of societal conditions, individual consciousness, and societal consequences of action in his own conception of crisis. In comparison with the impersonal and objective mechanisms of the process of capital exploitation, the individual consciousness, and indeed the collective consciousness of particular classes, appears to be of secondary significance. Yet even the economic relations involved in the process of capital exploitation are themselves those of a tacit and more deep-seated relationship that of course must be understood in the Enlightenment tradition as authoritarian and as an impediment to the realm of freedom.

In Durkheim, however, the noncontractual elements of contract are made the constitutive structures for society and the moral foundation of society is drawn away from the sphere of individual or collective action. No longer does action provide the explanation for societal structures; rather action is now explained as a product of those same structures. At the same time the objectivity of societal structures is delimited by its forms of manifestation in culture, religion, and the economy. Thus the relationship between knowledge and society has changed fundamentally since the Enlightenment. No longer does the dynamism—or the backwardness—of knowledge govern changes in customs; instead, the structure of society explains the variation in knowledge and religion.

Since Durkheim, society has irrevocably become an objective and empirical reality that can no longer be adequately grasped in moral reflection or controlled by political action. Rather, as an empirical system in reality, society needs to be approached scientifically and cognitively in an effort to ascertain the principles peculiar to all that is social. Sociology comes on the scene as an empirical and positive science. The posture adopted toward change by science rests primarily on the impartiality of the observer, who is at pains to be objective. Although activism remains the predominant attitude of the citizen within society, this orientation necessarily recedes into the background when the scientific examination of the actual situation begins. Weber's theory of sociological science, in particular, documents this attitude of impartiality toward social reality. His work, in which social action becomes the comprehensive concept commanding the subservience of economic action, marks the end of a line that reaches from the idea of the irrationality and randomness of customs to that of a distinctive logic of the social providing the foundation for the multifariousness of historical change. Finally, the modern sociological theory of social change comes forward with the claim to assume the position of the theory of history and to take over the legacy of secularization.

3. ON THE CURRENT SITUATION OF THE THEORY OF SOCIAL CHANGE

Contemporary theories of social change are confronted with a scenario that has not only developed beyond the temporal structures of the secularized history-of-salvation model but also beyond the evolutionism of the nineteenth century. The topological differentiation of various temporal levels is supplemented and overlaid by the unregulated juxtaposition of several equal-ranking subsystems. Societal structures are no longer simply seen as a reflection or consequence of individual or collective action, but as a comprehensive determinant basis for action.

Nor is the interpretation of the process of change itself any longer reliant on a secularized version of the history-of-salvation model. History has lost sight of its goal, and the concept of a cyclical passage of events is also no longer able to offer a plausible overall interpretation of the historical process. Unrest and change in societal structures are no longer solely the product of the contingencies and interweaving of individual action; they are also the product of the unregulated relationships social systems have with one another as they attempt to maintain and reproduce their structures in the face of insecure environments. Although stratified structures and cyclical sequences do occur in processes that are temporally and structurally limited, they do not occur in the overall process of societal change itself.

The overall process of change is no more than the most general, empty frame of reference for the development and decline of structures. In this extreme formulation change is synonymous with temporality. This generalization, together with the dilution of the concept of change, is reflected by the switch from the experienced and recalled action-period time, via the time reflected in the course of history, to the objective time used in physics, which also provides the self-evident frame of reference for the sociological analysis of change. This time is infinite, vacuous, reversible, equally divisible, and measurable.

There are a number of ways in which sociological theory may react to this situation. I outline the two most important options.

1. The first option is to abandon the aim of achieving an autonomous theory of social change because temporality and change form a

general determinant of the social realm. The category of change is too empty and unspecific to serve as a worthwhile object of specific theory-building. The sociological analysis of change should therefore be confined to investigating certain empirical aspects of specific processes of change. Thus this option completes—after a certain amount of delay—the turn away from the ambitious theory construction already carried out by the historical sciences. The obvious gain from such a strategy is that the methodological approach would be between quantitative historical science and the empirical analysis of social change. The price would be the underdevelopment of the theoretical concepts implicit in this option and the surrender of the subject of time to the natural sciences.

2. In contrast to this, a number of theoreticians insist on a second option that continues to treat the question of change sociologically but does so within the framework of simple—sometimes too simple—temporal structures.

One can initially conceive of four options in terms of a theoretical strategy for analyzing and explaining social change in the context of premodern temporal structures. Two of these fall within the model of action-period time and do not make any strict distinction between the themes of social action, social order, and social change. Two other options, although they establish differentiated levels with regard to social action and social order, nevertheless still treat the question of social change in a frame of reference defined by a theory of order. In these two cases the background is provided by a model of temporal levels.

1. Individualistic explanations and analyses of social change give primacy to theories of instrumental, or strategic, action, even when it comes to answering questions of social order and social change (see Schmid 1982, 58–92). Although it is true that individualistic theories, in their topologies, set the action level apart from the structural level or level of order, the only factor admitted as a process model is the dynamism of individual, utility-oriented action. The interconnection and interweaving of these actions on a larger scale, resulting in unintentional effects, are, however, not generally treated using specific theories of social order. Rather they are explained by a theory of instruments of action. Similarly, social change is seen as change in structures that is generated by action. Hence it is explained in action-theoretical terms. Consequently, social change is taken to have been adequately explained only if it can be traced back to the actions of empirical subjects.[19] Just as a

19. The idea of a structural mechanism of change is contrary to the individualistic social ontology. See Alexander and Giesen 1987.

social order or a social structure is inconceivable without the individuals who compose it, so too social change is incomprehensible without the actors who are its moving force. Because this involves temporally breaking down the process of change into actions and their consequences, the analysis of long-term structural change is impaired. The pursuit of far-reaching results of action is tortuous from a theoretical point of view and painstaking from an empirical one.

2. Interactionistic analyses of social change also have difficulty in using theory to trace the differentiation between social action, social order, and social change. Indeed, the very ambition of interactionistic theory is to present social order and structure as the fragile and fleeting result of a continual process of social interaction and construction.[20] Change is directly located on the action level and does not require any special theoretical question to be posed. If lasting structural relations have any part to play at all in the context of interactionistic analysis, it is as symbolic structures of knowledge that form the prerequisite for communication. Of course change and adjustment in these structures are entirely bound up with an action-type process model.

3. In contrast to individualistic or interactionistic analyses, classical system-theoretical and conflict-theoretical explanations do not start out from the theme of action but from that of social order. They comprehend social change as either instability on the part of structures or adjustments to solutions to the problem of order. Associated with the shift in primacy from the theme of action to that of order is a similar shift in temporal structures: action-period time gives way to the model of temporal levels. The common objection to the classical functionalist theory of society that it is incapable of delivering an appropriate explanation for social change may be reformulated at this point. Traditional functionalist analyses are in fact in a position to analyze social change but in doing so they always start out from a general assumption of social order.[21] Change is produced when actors attempt to eliminate disturbances in equilibrium, maladjustments, or tensions arising from within the system

---

20. Schmid (1982, 104) states that, after investigation, he was not able to detect an interactionistic theory of social change. See also Turner 1974, 182.

21. See Parsons 1951 and 1967. Münch is completely right in defending Parsons against the usual criticism that the assumption of consensus and order is *empirically* false, but the very idea of considering social order as an analytical point of reference supports the thesis that the theories of the "middle" Parsons have to be considered as giving primacy to the problem of order. See Münch 1982, 108. The most comprehensive elaboration of the problem of social action and social order is presented by Alexander 1982–83.

and to restore a state of relative order or relative equilibrium. In this case change always occurs within the context of order and with regard to the creation of order. The concept of different systemic levels where change may take place points to the model of temporal levels as a topological structure. This concept means that action-theoretical assumptions concerning the process of change are no longer necessary. Change occurs as a process of seeking equilibrium or adapting to a changing environment.

4. Conflict-theoretical analyses of social change maintain the use of action-type process models but apply these models to the relations between collective actors. Again, the problem of order is placed in the foreground. Conflicts between societal groups and contrary interests emerge out of the existing social order, and change can only be conceived of as a result of the conflicts surrounding social order (see, for example, Dahrendorf 1958). It is difficult to imagine any original conception of social change independent of the theme of order in this situation. The conflict-theoretical analysis of change also moves within the framework of the model of temporal levels. An indicator of this model is provided by the topological difference between the ruling class, which is presumed to have conservative interests, and the groups over which it rules, which are regarded as the sources of change and the conveyers of interest in seeing some alteration to the status quo.

5. In contrast to classical systems and conflict theories evolutionist theories in sociology take the temporalization of order in the modern worldview into account but shift theoretical primacy from the theme of order to that of change. A fundamental distinction needs to be drawn here between two evolutionist conceptions. One encompasses the materialistic theories of evolution, which see the dynamics of societal evolution in terms of a progression in the relationship of society to nature (see, for example, Lenski and Lenski 1970; White 1959; Sahlins and Service 1960; Harris 1977). The other includes idealistic evolutionary theories, which analyze societal evolution as a pedagogic relationship between the members of society, or even between the intellectual vanguard and the people, a learning process, or the rationalization of worldviews.[22] Both materialistic and idealistic variants of evolutionism, however, assume that there is a topological difference between a universally valid motor of evolution, on the one hand, and the spheres it moves, with their tendency toward backwardness, on the other

22. Habermas 1976; Schluchter 1979. According to the (oversimplified) scheme of classification offered in this chapter, Parsonian neoevolutionism and the neo-Parsonian theories of J. Alexander and R. Münch have to be classified here as idealistic evolutionary theories.

hand. Of course there are various and frequently contradictory interpretations of which is the motor and which are the backward spheres. Societal evolution, then, is perceived as a progressive relationship, as growth and unilinear development. One such view focuses on thermodynamic efficiency and growth in productivity; another focuses on the development of the moral consciousness, progress, and the differentiation and rationalization of knowledge. Both variants of evolutionism have recourse to models of progress from the Enlightenment and the nineteenth century, and both have been the targets of fierce criticism from the empirical, historical, methodological, and theoretical standpoints (see Smith 1973; Schmid 1982; Giesen and Lau 1981).

6. If one wishes to take note of these criticisms yet not to abandon the temporalization of order, another concept of evolution understands functional differentiation as a process model and regards the concept of directed development as inappropriate to societal change as an all-embracing phenomenon.

Theories that are based on the analytical primacy of the question of change and assume a polycentric and relativistic conception of history have to reject the idea of progress and development in global history. They must replace the concept of global and unilinear modernization and progress with a relativistic conception of rationality, that is, with the idea of the structural "epigenesis" of the temporally limited emergence and decay of structures. History and progress dissolve in a diversity of contingent histories and progresses that are, however, interconnected and intermingled in a global process of change.

The radicalization of the modern pattern of temporality and change finally engenders a "postmodern" view of society. The topology of postmodern models of change abandons the moral opposition of individual subject and society and renounces the evaluative differentiation of backward and progressive spheres of society. Instead it conceives the realm of the social as being composed of objective structures existing above and beyond the acting subjects and focuses attention on the internal and external relationships of structures. Postmodern topology centers on the differences between system and environment, between structure and situation, and between text and context, and it temporalizes these differences: the emergence and disintegration of structures are at the core of the postmodern paradigm of change.

Even if the elaboration of this postmodern paradigm is still in its infancy, two alternative theoretical options can be discerned. The first option is represented by attempts to apply advanced theoretical concepts from the sciences—in particular from either the biological theory of autopoietic systems or the theory of dissipative structures—to social processes (Luhmann 1984). The second option for a postmodern paradigm of change is the "poststructuralist" analysis of texts and related concepts that aim at the transformation of symbolic systems (see Lyotard 1984; Baudrillard 1983). Both options dramatically increase the objectification of social reality and the temporalization of social order resulting from modernity. One may doubt, however, whether a discipline that is deeply rooted in modernity and that considers Max Weber as one of its founding fathers will be able to survive in the thin and cool air of postmodern conceptions of change.

REFERENCES

Adelung, J. C. 1775. *Versuch eines vollständigen grammatisch-kritischen Wörterbuches.* . . . Vol. 2. Leipzig: Breitkopf.

Alexander, J. 1982–83. *Theoretical logic in sociology.* Vol. 4, *The modern reconstruction of classical thought: Talcott Parsons.* London: Routledge and Kegan Paul.

Alexander, J., and B. Giesen. 1987. Introduction. In *The micro-macro link,* ed. J. Alexander, B. Giesen, R. Münch, and N. Smelser, 1–42. Berkeley: University of California Press.

Aquileia, Paulinus von. 1864. *Liber exhortationibus, vulgo de salutaribus documentis.* In *Patrologiae cursus completus, seu bibliotheca universalis,* chapter 43. *Series Latina.* Ed. J.–P. Migne. Vol 99. Paris.

Aquin, Thomas von. 1934. *Summa theologica.* Katholischer Akademikerverband. Salzburg: Anton Pustet Verlag.

Arnold, R. 1983. Deutungsmuster: Zu den Bedeutungselementen sowie den theoretischen und methodologischen Bezügen eines Begriffs. *Zeitschrift für Pädagogik* 6: 893–912.

Augustin. 1955. *Vom Gottesstaat [De civitate dei].* 2 vols. Zurich: Artemis-Verlag.

Baeumker, C. 1927. Der Platonismus im Mittelalter. *Beiträge zur Geschichte der Philosophie des Mittelalters* 25, nos. 1–2.

Baudrillard, J. 1988. *Selected writings.* Ed. M. Poster. Cambridge: Polity Press.

Beierwaltes, W., ed. 1969. *Platonismus in der Philosophie des Mittelolters.* Darmstadt: Wissenschaftliche Buchgesellschaft.

Bergmann, W. 1981. *Die Zeitstrukturen sozialer Systeme.* Berlin: Dunker and Humblodt.

Blumenberg, H. 1974. *Säkularisierung und Selbstbehauptung.* Frankfurt am Main: Suhrkamp.

Bodin, J. [1583] 1961. *Les six livres de la republique avec l'apologie de R. Herpin.* Reprint. Aalen: Scientia.

Boethius. 1974. *Consolatio philosophiae.* Ed. F. von Hermann. Reprint. Aschendorff.

Bossuet, J. B. 1964. *Discours sur l'histoire universelle.* Paris: Garnier-Flammarion.

Braudel, F. 1958. Histoire et sciences sociales: La longue durée. *Annales* 13: 725–53.

Bredow, G. v. 1972. *Platonismus im Mittelalter.* Freiburg: Rombach.

Burrow, J. W. 1966. *Evolution and society: A study in Victorian social theory.* Cambridge: Cambridge University Press.

Bury, J. B. [1932] 1960. *The idea of progress: An inquiry into its origin and growth.* New York: Peter Smith.

Carion, J. [1532] 1966. Chronica durch Magistrum Johan Carion. In *Die Anfänge der reformatorischen Geschichtsschreibung,* ed. H. Scheible. Gütersloh: Güterslohes Verlagshaus G. Mohn.

Condorcet, M. J. A. [1793] 1963. *Entwurf einer historischen Darstellung der Fortschritte des menschlichen Geistes,* ed. W. Alff. Frankfurt am Main: Europäische Verlagsanstalt.

Dahrendorf, R. 1958. Toward a theory of social conflict. *Journal of Conflict Resolution* 2: 170–83.

Danto, A. C. 1965. *Analytical philosophy of history.* Cambridge: Cambridge University Press.

De Beer, G. R. 1964. *Charles Darwin: Evolution by natural selection.* New York: Doubleday.

Eco, U. 1984. *Nachschrift zum Namen der Rose.* Munich: Hauser.

Elias, N. 1984. *Über die Zeit.* Arbeiten zur Wissenssoziologie, ed. M. Schröter. Frankfurt am Main: Suhrkamp.

Faber, K.–G. 1982. *Theorie der Geschichtswissenschaft.* Munich: Deutscher Taschenbuchverlag.

Fontenelle, Bernard La Bouyer de. [1686] 1908. *Histoire des oracles.* Paris: L. Maigron.

Fraser, J. T. 1982. *The genesis and evolution of time.* Brighton: Harvester.

Giesen, B. 1987. Natürliche Ungleichheit, Soziale Ungleichheit, Ideale Gleichheit. In *Theorien sozialer Ungleichheit,* ed. B. Giesen and H. Haferkamp, 314–45. Opladen: Westdeutscher Verlag.

Giesen, B., and C. Lau. 1981. Zur Anwendung darwinistischer Erklärungsstrategien in der Soziologie. *Kölner Zeitschrift für Soziologie und Sozialpsychologie* 33: 229–56.

Habermas, J. 1976. *Zur Rekonstruktion des historischen Materialismus.* Frankfurt: Suhrkamp.

Hager, F. P. 1974. Geschichte, Historie. Part 1. In *Historisches Wörterbuch der Philosophie,* ed. J. Ritter and K. Gründer, 3:344–45. Darmstadt: Wissenschaftliche Buchgesellschaft.

Harris, M. 1977. *Cannibals and Kings.* New York: Random.

Hoffmann, E. [1926] 1960. *Platonismus und christliche Philosophie.* Rev. ed. (original title: *Platonismus und Mittelalter*). Zurich: Artemis-Verlag.

Kanitscheider, B. 1974. *Philosophisch-historische Grundlagen der physikalischen Kosmologie.* Stuttgart: Reclam.

Kaupp, P. 1974. Gesellschaft. In *Historisches Wörterbuch der Philosophie,* ed. J. Ritter and K. Gründer, 3:459–66. Darmstadt: Wissenschaftliche Buchgesellschaft.

Klempt, A. 1960. *Die Säkularisierung der universalhistorischen Auffassung.* Göttinger Bausteine zur Geschichtswissenschaft. Vol. 31. Göttingen: Musterschmidt.

Kosselleck, R. 1968. Der Zufall als Motivationsrest in der Geschichtsschreibung.

In *Die nicht mehr schönen Künste: Grenzphänomene des Ästhetischen,* ed. H. R. Jauss, 129–41. Poetik und Hermeneutik, no. 3. Munich: Fink.

———. 1972. Introduction. In *Geschichtliche Grundbegriffe,* ed. O. Brunner, W. Conze, and R. Koselleck, 1:xiii–xxvii. Stuttgart: Klett-Cotta.

———. 1973. Geschichte, Geschichten und formale Zeitstrukturen. In *Geschichte, Ereignis und Erzählung,* ed. R. Koselleck and W. D. Stempel, 211–22. Munich: Fink.

———. 1975. Fortschritt. In *Geschichtliche Grundbegriffe,* ed. O. Brunner, W. Conze, and R. Koselleck, 2:351–423. Stuttgart: Klett-Cotta.

———. 1984. Die unbekannte Zukunft und die Kunst der Prognose. In *Soziologie und gesellschaftliche Entwicklung,* ed. B. Lutz, 45–59. Frankfurt: Campus.

Koselleck, R., C. Meier, J. Fisch, and N. Bulst. 1984. Revolution. In *Geschichtliche Grundbegriffe,* ed. O. Brunner, W. Conze, and R. Koselleck, 5: 653–788. Stuttgart: Klett-Cotta.

Krug, W. T. [1832–38] 1969. *Allgemeines Handwörterbuch der philosophischen Wissenschaften.* Vols. 1 and 2. 2nd ed. Reprint. Stuttgart: Frommann-Holzboog.

Lämmli, F. 1962. *Vom Chaos zum Kosmos.* Schweizerische Beiträge zur Altertums wissenschaft, vol. 10. Basel: F. Reinhardt.

Lenski, G., and J. Lenski. 1970. *Human societies.* New York: McGraw.

Lévi-Strauss, C. 1962. *La pensée sauvage.* Paris: Plon.

Louch, A. R. 1966. *Explanation and human action.* Oxford: Blackwell.

Löwith, K. 1953. *Weltgeschichte und Heilsgeschehen.* Stuttgart: Kohlhammer.

Lübbe, H. 1965. *Säkularisierung: Geschichte eines ideenpolitischen Begriffs.* Freiburg: Alber.

———. 1977. *Geschichtsbegriff und Geschichtsinteresse.* Basel: Schwabe.

Luhmann, N. 1975a. Interaktion, Organisation, Gesellschaft. In *Soziologische Aufklärung,* by N. Luhmann, 2: 9–20. Opladen: Westdeutscher Verlag.

———. 1975b. Weltzeit und Systemgeschichte. In *Soziologische Aufklärung,* by N. Luhmann, 2:103–33. Opladen: Westdeutscher Verlag.

———. 1978. Temporalization of complexity. In *Sociocybernetics,* ed. R. Felix Geyer and Johannes van der Zouwen, 2: 95–111. Leiden: Kluwer Academic.

———. 1980. *Gesellschaftsstruktur und Semantik.* vols. 1 and 2. Frankfurt am Main: Suhrkamp.

———. 1984. *Soziale Systeme.* Frankfurt: Suhrkamp.

Lyotard, J. F. 1984. *La condition postmoderne.* Paris: Minuit.

Machiavelli, Niccolò. [1532] 1962. *The prince.* New York: Airmont.

Meier, C. 1975. Geschichte II. In *Geschichtliche Grundbegriffe,* ed. O. Brunner, W Conze, and R. Koselleck, 2: 595–610. Stuttgart: Ulett-Cotta.

———. 1978. Fragen und Thesen zu einer Theorie historischer Prozesse. In *Historische Prozesse,* ed. K.–G. Faber and C. Meier, 11–66. Munich: Deutscher Taschenbuchverlag.

Meinecke, F. 1959a. *Werke.* Vol. 3, *Die Entstehung des Historismus.* Ed. C. Hinrichs. Stuttgart: Oldenbourg.

———. 1959b. *Werke.* Vol. 4, *Zur Theorie und Philosophie der Geschichte.* Ed. E. Kessel. Stuttgart: Oldenbourg.

Montesquieu, Charles de. [1758] 1950. *De l'esprit des lois oeuvres complètes.* Ed. André Masson. Vol. 1. Reprint. Paris: Les Belles Lettres.

Münch, R. 1982. *Theorie des Handelns.* Frankfurt: Suhrkamp.

Oevermann, U. 1973. Zur Analyse der struktur von sozialen Deutungsmustern. Johann-Wolfgang Goethe Universität, Frankfurt am Main.

Olafson, F. A. 1970. Narrative history and the concept of action. *History and Theory* 9: 265–89.

Parsons, T. 1951. *The social system.* Glencoe, Ill.: Free Press.

———. 1967. A paradigm for the analysis of social systems and change. In *System, change and conflict,* ed. N. J. Demerath III and R. A. Petersen, 189–212. New York: Free Press.

Pufendorf, S. F. v. [1744] 1967. *De jure naturae et gentium.* Ed. Q. Mascovius. 2 vols. Reprint. Frankfurt am Main: Minerva.

Riedel, M. 1975. Gesellschaft, bürgerliche. In *Geschichtliche Grundbegriffe,* ed. O. Brunner, W. Conze, and R. Koselleck, 2: 719–800. Stuttgart: Klett-Cotta.

Roedgers, K. 1983. Der Ursprung der Prozessidee ous dem Geiste der Chemie. *Archiv für Begriffsgeschichte* 27: 93–157.

Sahlins, M. D., and E. R. Service. 1960. *Evolution and culture.* Ann Arbor: University of Michigan Press.

Schluchter, W. 1979. *Die Entwicklung des okzidentalen Rationalismus.* Tübingen: J. C. B. Mohr.

———. 1980. *Rationalismus der Weltbeherrschung: Studien zu Max Weber.* Frankfurt am Main: Suhrkamp.

Schmid, M. 1982. *Theorie sozialen Wandels.* Opladen: Westdeutscher Verlag.

———. 1986. Zeit und sozialer Wandel. In *Zeit als Strukturelement von Lebenswelt und Gesellschaft,* ed. F. Fürstenberg and I. Mörth, 259–306. Opladen: Westdeutscher Verlag.

Seneca, J. A. 1969. *De providentia.* In *Philosophische Schriften,* ed. Manfred Rosenbach, 1:1–42. Darmstadt: Wissenschaftliche Buchgesellschaft.

Smith, A. 1973. *The concept of social change.* London: Routledge and Kegan Paul.

Troeltsch, E. 1913. Die Bedeutung des Begriffs der Kontingenz. In *Gesammelte Schriften,* 2: 769–78. Tübingen: J. C. B. Mohr.

Turner, J. 1974. *The structure of sociological theory.* Homewood, Ill.: Dorsey Press.

Walch, J. G. [1726] 1968. Naturell der Völker. In *Philosophisches Lexicon.* 4th ed. 2: col. 233. Reprint. Hildesheim: Olms.

Weber, M. [1920] 1963. *Gesammelte Aufsätze zur Religionssoziologie.* Vol 1. Tübingen: J. C. B. Mohr.

White, L. A. 1959. *The evolution of culture.* New York: McGraw.

Zedler, J. H. 1735. *Grosses vollständiges Universallexicon.* Vol. 10. Halle/Leipzig: Zedler.

———. 1743. *Grosses vollständiges Universallexicon.* Vol. 38. Halle/Leipzig: Zedler.

Contradictions and Social Evolution
A Theory of the Social Evolution of Modernity

Klaus Eder

1. A CRITIQUE OF MODERNIZATION THEORY

1.1. The Key Concepts: Differentiation and Rationalization

The classical theory of modernization is based on the general evolutionary assumption that modernization is the result of differentiation and rationalization. However, the extent to which these processes are necessary aspects of modernization is an open question. Discussions of modernization must at least ask about the extent to which dedifferentiation and derationalization are also developmental processes that characterize modern societies.[1] If these counterprocesses can be shown to be part of modernization, then differentiation and rationalization are only two among the many possible results of the evolution of modern society. They then lose the explanatory power that is attributed to them in classical modernization theory.

The real problem is that differentiation and rationalization are not variables explaining modernization, but processes needing explanation. In other words, I propose that differentiation and rationalization are not causes, but effects of modernization. My strategy is to look for the processes producing and reproducing these effects. The theoretical starting point is to look first for the modus operandi, a generative structure of

---

1. For recent contributions to the theory of modernization in terms of differentiation see Smelser 1985 and Luhmann 1982; for modernization theory in terms of rationalization see, among others, Habermas 1981 and Schluchter 1981. For the theoretical problems posed by the processes of dedifferentiation and reenchantment see Tiryakian (this volume); pleas for reenchantment are found (among many others) in Berman 1984 and Moscovici 1976.

modernity, and then for the opus operatum, that is, differentiation and rationalization as possible outcomes.[2]

I start by restating two classical problems of sociological theorizing. The first is the Durkheimian problem of relating the process of social differentiation to the conditions producing it.[3] How does differentiation come about? What forces underlie the process? Durkheim's answer is unsatisfactory: he takes demographic growth and increasing social density as the central causal variables for the progressive dissolution of collective consciousness (and the individualization resulting from it). Thus the key to explaining modernization is ultimately demography, something nonsocial (but as we know, socially produced!).

The second problem is the Weberian problem of relating the process of rationalization to the social conditions producing it.[4] How does rationalization come about? Weber gives a historical answer. He identifies specific social groups as the carriers of the process and then relates these groups to the general social structure, that is, the system of status, class, and power. Thus modernization is explained through the more or less contingent historical emergence of specific social groups. For Weber it is history that ultimately explains modernization.

The alternative theoretical approach to Durkheim and Weber is that of Marx. Marx's theory states that the evolutionary change of society (a change that has been conceptualized by later theorists as differentiation and rationalization) is the product, first, of the contradictions between the forces of production and the social relations of production and, second, of the contradictions between social classes. Ultimately, contradictions are the causes of modernization.[5]

Within the Marxian theoretical framework social development is a process based on two types of contradictions. The first type is a contradiction between social actors, that is, the conflict between social classes. As long as contradictions are understood as contradictions between social groups, the theory explains the development of society through genuinely social factors. The second type refers to a more abstract concept of

2. Such a macrosociological focus on the conditions generating society is prominent in French sociology. For two (very different) versions see Touraine 1977 and Bourdieu 1984. I take the distinction between modus operandi and opus operatum from the latter.

3. Alexander (this volume) describes this Durkheimian problem as being one of relating general models, social processes, and historical analyses of specific strains and tensions. My chapter can be read as an attempt to relate these levels.

4. For a treatment of the Weberian problem see Schluchter 1979, 1981. Going beyond Weber, Schluchter tries to develop the general model of rationalization, leaving the question of social processes and historical analyses more or less aside.

5. See Godelier 1973 for a systematic discussion of Marx's distinctions between levels of contradiction.

contradiction. In it social structures rather than social actors are seen to contradict each other.[6] The configuration of social structures is supposed to set into motion the evolution of society. This abstract use of the notion of contradiction has become relatively important in more recent theoretical thinking: contradictions between systems are seen as leading to self-blockading situations and contradictions within systems as generating incompatible functions that the systems fulfill.[7]

But these functionalist reinterpretations run the danger of an analytical nominalism that is empty of any social theory. I consider communication theory to be a more promising theoretical approach to a reinterpretation of the Marxist approach of explaining social change because it is more adequate to the study of modernization than functionalist and neofunctionalist reinterpretations of Marx. In communication theory the analyst can give a systematic place to the concept of contradiction.[8] Reformulated in this way, the concept of contradiction becomes the starting point for a more adequate theory of modernization.

1.2. Evolutionary Theory and Modernization

I propose the following preliminary theoretical assumption: contradictions are mechanisms that initiate or continue communication. Insofar as societies are the most complex system of communication, contradictions can be treated as the mechanisms for the evolution of such systems.[9] This hypothesis entails an evolutionary theory that draws from beyond the old alternatives of an epigenetic mysticism and a Darwinistic functionalism.[10] It takes contradictions as the mechanism producing modernizing processes like (functional) differentiation and rationalization.

6. This structural notion of contradiction has often been criticized as being "objectivistic." Such a critique can be found in Habermas 1979, who relates this type of contradiction to the problem of system integration as opposed to social integration. See also Sahlins 1976, who distinguishes two "historical materialisms," one of which is guilty of the objectivistic sin.

7. See Sjoeberg 1960; Offe 1972.

8. A systematic treatment of the notion of contradiction is found in Elster 1978, (esp. chapters 4 and 5); Luhmann 1984, (488ff.); Miller 1986, (esp. 296ff.).

9. Evolution is not to be conceived as the change of society or some of its subsystems—to do so would be a case of misplaced concreteness—but as the evolution of structures that regulate the construction of the system (and its subsystems). Such structures are assumed to be on the level of social evolution structures regulating communication.

10. The differences between Darwinistic and epigenetic theories can be reduced to differences in the concept of contradiction. Either evolution is conceived of as the resolution of contradictions between systems and their environments (the old Darwinistic explanatory strategy) or it is conceived of as the resolution of a general contradiction underlying the history of humankind (an idea that is related to the old progressivist thinking in social theory).

This hypothesis changes the evolutionary assumptions underlying modernization theory in a fundamental way. I discuss two modifications here. First, modernization theory should not be tied to the idea of a fixed and unidirectional path of development to modern society. Differentiation is not an explanatory variable but only a descriptive category that says that there are increasingly more fields of social conflict and struggle. Differentiation must therefore be described as the structural by-product of collective practices that produce a modern social order. Second, modernization theory is not to be tied to the idea of a self-propelling force (reason or unreason for example) that pushes social development. Rather, rationalization is the cultural by-product of collective practices that construct a cultural order through learning processes and symbolic struggles, both of which together establish legitimate authority and generate the symbols society needs to reproduce itself as a legitimate social order.

As a substitute for the two evolutionary assumptions that modernization is self-propelling and unidirectional,[11] I propose the idea that contradictions open up diverging and even incompatible paths of development. There is no prescribed way to and through modernity. There are as many ways into modernity as there are historical developments. Therefore, modernization theory cannot be constructed by conceptualizing its outcome but only by conceptualizing the way this modern order is produced.

The problem then is to conceptualize and explain the social production of modern society. The conception I propose is threefold. First, it suggests looking at the learning processes of those social groups that create a new collective consciousness, that is, political and social ideas, to orient individual and collective social action.[12] But because these learning processes are part of a larger historical environment, we must also look further.

Second, we must consider the idea of class conflict. Class conflict should be conceptualized on the level of the system of status and power. In order to reproduce a given system of status and power, social classes engage wherever possible in struggles to classify and reclassify each other. They struggle to have "right" on their side. The symbolic universe of right, the idea of morality, sometimes even universal morality, has to be mobilized to secure the reproduction of the class structure.[13]

---

11. For an analysis of the pitfalls of old evolutionary theories see Habermas 1979. For a critique of Habermas's alternative see Schmid 1982. But the alternative Schmid (1982) proposes also remains unsatisfactory.

12. The following discussion is an attempt to locate the formal structures of learning processes, as described by Miller 1986, within a historical context. For an extensive discussion see Eder 1985a.

13. The role of the symbolic dimension in Marxist thinking has already been elaborated by Godelier. For a short and instructive account see Godelier 1978. For an interesting theoretical reformulation of this problem see Bourdieu 1984.

Third, my conception examines how differentiation and rationalization are related to the evolution of modernity. I explain them as the structural by-products, that is, the combined effects, of learning processes and class conflict that in turn reproduce these generating conditions. Learning processes and class conflict change the social and cultural dimensions of the structure of society. They lead to what Weber has called the differentiation and rationalization of *Wertsphären*.[14] This modern differentiation between moral, aesthetic, and theoretical symbols restricts the possible images of a legitimate social order to the moral sphere. In modern times this differentiation of the moral sphere (which structurally is probably the most important one) can no longer be grounded on a holy order, that is, a hierarchy, but only on the abstract and formalistic idea of a social order based on the equal agreement of those belonging to it.

With this theoretical program the reformulation of the notion of contradiction in communication theory should allow for the revision of the theoretical assumptions underlying the conceptualization of differentiation and rationalization as the paths to modernization and offer new grounds for describing the processes of modernization. And on a more general level it should allow for the revision of the implicit evolutionary assumptions of modernization theory.

In the following sections I discuss how the concept of the social production of modernity can be made fruitful in a systematic (not historical) reconstruction of developmental processes in modern society. First, I discuss the role of learning processes in the social production of modern society. These processes take place first in "enlightenment societies" (*Aufklärungsgesellschaften*) that call themselves "associations" in order to differentiate themselves from "corporations" and from the corporate groups of traditional society such as guilds, estates, etc. These associations contain the elementary structures of specifically modern collective learning processes. Next, I attempt to locate this evolutionary new type of association within the social structure of early-modern society. Here the specificity of modern social classes and the corresponding class conflict become the analytical focus.

This analysis then allows me to describe the evolution of modern society as one that is generated by learning processes and class conflicts and reproduced by processes of differentiation and rationalization. Differentiation is the key part of the mechanism that reproduces these generating conditions. But differentiation is in itself insufficient; it must also mobilize symbolic resources in order to continue reproducing differ-

14. See Habermas 1981, who uses Weber's distinction of *Wertsphären* for his own attempt to differentiate between various irreducible claims of validity constituting communicative action.

entiation. Rationalization is the process producing the symbolic resources needed for this reproduction. The analysis of the reproduction of modernization by differentiation and rationalization gives some preliminary answers to two central problems in modernization theory: the problem of alternative paths to modernization and the problem of the rationality of these different paths to modernization.

2. THE SOCIAL PRODUCTION OF MODERNITY

2.1. Association and Communication

Since the beginning of modernity certain social groups that are characterized by an evolutionary new form of communication have had a profound effect in triggering modernization processes. Such groups try to organize their mode of organization according to the principles of the equal and discursive handling of disputes.[15] This type of discourse is based—ideally—on the free and equal exchange of arguments, that is, on *Aufklärung* (enlightenment). Associations are the social contexts within which this evolutionary new type of discourse can take place.

I would like to distinguish among three historical manifestations of associations in modern society. The first is tied to the rise of groups that since the eighteenth century have identified themselves as the bearers of enlightenment.[16] Within these groups social and political life is discussed in a way that differs fundamentally from the past. This form of collective discussion, which is learned in small political and private associations, forces these associations to describe themselves in a way that is independent of their place in a hierarchy. They begin, instead, to describe themselves as part of a social movement, as *Aufklärungsbewegung.*

A second historical manifestation of the modern type of associations is that found in the working class movement.[17] The culture of discussion found in the working class movement continues the tradition of the Enlightenment. The difference between the associations of the working class movement and the earlier associations of the Enlightenment is in the content of the discussion. The discourse organized in the associations of the working class allows for learning the competence needed for

15. This observation should not be mistaken for the claim that these associations have actually functioned in this manner. I only claim that these principles define the structural model of these associations.

16. Important descriptions of this phenomenon are Nipperdey 1972 and Koselleck [1959] 1973. For a systematic sociological treatment see Eder 1985a, (67ff.).

17. The idea of treating the working class movement as a collective learning process is an old idea in the socialist tradition. See, e.g., Na'aman 1978 and Vester 1970, who utilize this concept for a reconstruction of the labor movement; see also Thompson 1978. Also relevant in this context is Tilly 1978.

organizing the workers as a collective social force. Thus the specific social experiences of the workers modify the contents, but not the form, of the discourse of the eighteenth-century associations.

A third historical manifestation of the modern type of associations is the associations that have emerged since the end of the last century in the petit bourgeois classes. But the social experiences necessary for these "middle" classes to produce an autonomous discourse arise only in the second half of the twentieth century when the old petit bourgeoisie is complemented and strengthened by a new petit bourgeoisie[18] that is the result of the increasing professionalization of work. The associations of these new social groups describe themselves today as "new" social movements. These new associations defend a private "life-world" that differs from both the just society defended by the working class and the public sphere defended by the bourgeois/*citoyens*. This new life-world is their own private world, their own psychic and physical integrity. Thus the specific experiences of these groups modify the content of discourse, but they do not modify its logic.

In all these groups a reflexive use of communication is practiced. As people learn to communicate about communication, they revolutionize the traditional order. The evolution of modern society becomes dependent on the communication that is the subject of communicative relationships. Reflexivity in communication is the starting point for the social production of modern society. Those who participate in modern associations know that they are taking part in a collective learning process. In the *Aufklärungsgesellschaften* of the eighteenth century (the Jacobin clubs were their radical variants), the *Arbeiterbildungsvereine* of the nineteenth century (the associations for the self-education of the workers), and the therapy groups of the late-twentieth century, the function of learning has become part of the process of communication. The mechanism constituting the modern associations since the eighteenth century can therefore be defined as discursive communication.[19]

The form of communication practiced in these associations throughout modernity changes the form and the content of the learning processes taking place in these associations. Thus the idea of an evolutionary new type of learning is the theoretical key to the cultural consequences of the emergence of associations since the beginning of modern society. Cultural change in modern society is produced by a collective learning process whose logic is defined by the logic of discursive com-

18. For a controversial discussion of the social-structural basis of the new social movements see Offe 1985; Eder 1985b; Bourdieu 1984.

19. The concept of discursive communication has been elaborated by Habermas (1981). The following text can also be read as an application of this type of sociological theorizing to the theory of modernization.

munication. Cultural change, then, is bound to the logic of modern discourse.

2.2. Collective Learning Processes

The constitutive element of discursive communication is a "generative," or "deep," structure. This structure is defined by two principles: equality and the discursive handling of conflicts. The logic of discursive communication is structured according to the principles that we ascribe as being central to modernity.[20] The logic underlying the modern discourse thus allows for learning processes that are fundamentally different from traditional ones. These modern learning processes are based on the principle of ceaselessly testing the universalizability of the normative order of civil society. Their mechanism is the resolution of contradictions by argumentation or "critique." They are modeled according to the logic of a universalization procedure.

A universalization procedure is defined as the impartial consideration by everybody concerned. The basic structure of an impartial judgment is "equality more geometrico." Equality more geometrico means to consider only the behavioral manifestation of an act, not its motivations or circumstances. This basic structure must then be applied to a specific case. First, impartiality can be described as giving everyone an equal chance to act in his or her own interest. This condition is the equality of opportunity. A second way to construct a situation of impartiality is to distribute chances to act in such a way that all possible positions within the distribution are acceptable to all. This condition is the equality of differential chances to act. The logical structure of the operation of the principle of the equal consideration of everybody becomes logically more complex in both cases. In the first case it is applied to an abstract other; in the second case the relevant other becomes somebody with needs that clash with yours, a situation that has to be taken into account within the procedure of universalization. Going from the first to the second level, the hypothetical operation takes additional empirical parameters into account. The problems inherent in these approaches result in a third way of describing impartiality: the unequal distribution of chances to claim the universality of wants and interests within a process of collective discussion. This condition is the equality of communicative relationships.

Thus we can distinguish three steps in the development of the logic of

20. For an interesting theoretical treatment of the model of civil society see Dumont 1967, 1970. For an early treatment of its discursive aspects see Habermas 1962. For a systematic use of both notions for a reconstruction of modernization processes see Eder 1985a (87ff.).

universalization[21] that underlies collective learning processes since the eighteenth century. The form of communication invented and practiced by the early associations (the societies of enlightenment) has become the foundation for the model of modern society. This model is civil society. This model sets forth the characteristics of association—the equal rights to free thinking, speech, and association—as basic to civil society. The more this complex learning can be organized, the more the idea of a democratic organization of civil society can be radicalized into the postulate of the democratic organization of the well-being of society. This idea culminates in the idea of the democratic realization of the good life by civil society.[22] The theoretical proposition is that these increasingly complex forms of a civil society are incorporations of the logic of the learning processes that have been going on since the eighteenth century. This development, then, can be conceptualized as the manifestation of collective learning processes using the logic of universalization as its basic mechanism.

2.3. Social Class and Class Conflict

The concept of discursive communication is insufficient for explaining the production of a social order in modern society because discursive communication cannot control its institutional environment. On the contrary, it sometimes even serves ends contradictory to its intentions. Associations do not exist merely in the thin air of discussion. Being part of a wider social context, they are not independent of the power system inherent in the social order. They are bound to an institutional framework. And the symbolic universe produced by discursive communication is used for legitimating purposes within this institutional framework. To grasp this aspect of the social reality of modern society, we have to look for the social struggles accompanying and controlling the processes of discursive communication.

Associations are part of the class structure of society. This being so, contradiction comes into play as a mechanism of class struggle. Class conflict thus constitutes a social reality beyond the collective learning processes initiated in associations. This social reality has been described

21. Habermas's theory of communicative action (1981) can be read as the theoretical program of the reconstruction of this type of universalization procedure. A theoretical solution to the problem of developmental logic is the idea of a permanent social contract (Eder 1986a). This solution offers an alternative to Kohlberg's (1981) psychological conception of developmental logic. See also Eder 1985a (67ff.); Tugendhat 1980.

22. For a discussion of the development of democratic rights see the classic work of Marshall (1950). But it should not be forgotten that these ideals are taken from the theoretical work of intellectuals, who are tied more or less to the different social and political groups and movements producing modern society.

since the beginning of the nineteenth century as a reality structured according to class-specific opportunities and rights. Whether such classes correspond to concrete groups has been the object of controversy.[23] But in modern societies class has become a specific way of describing social differences in society. How far the implicit self-description is adequate varies historically.

Since the eighteenth century the classification of the objective positions that separate social classes has followed a different logic from that underlying the previous classification of estates. The transition in early-modern society to a new logic of classification was a result of freeing the social order from traditional bonds and was part of the process of commercializing agriculture and handicrafts. The new social order became different from traditional bonds because the unifying hegemony of the church was broken.[24] Without the church a society without religious bonds arose. In order to substitute for hierarchical classification, a new classification system had to be built into the social structure.

During the transformation of traditional society into early-modern society social relations remained organized around the bonds of patron-client relationships. Class relations were established, as Thompson puts it,[25] between the patrician culture and the plebeian. The patrician culture was organized around the idea of autonomy and self-determination in private life. The plebeian culture, however, was organized as a "moral economy." The moral economy was opposed to the market economy; it defended "just" prices against market prices and the principle of concrete reciprocity against the principle of subjective rights. Taking the example of eighteenth-century England, the structure of these class relations can be described as gentry-crowd reciprocity.[26] The gentry, which is defined as a polite culture dissociating itself from the plebeian culture of the crowd, employed the classical means of control: the majesty and terror of law and the symbolism of their cultural hegemony. Both contributed to the theatrical representation of patrician culture. The plebs, however, had at their disposal the elements of a traditional culture: the

23. For a new sociological look at the concept of class see Luhmann 1985. Luhmann treats classes as emerging from processes that make interactive relations increasingly secondary for social structure. But his discussion suffers because he confuses class structure and differentiation-as-stratification.

24. For the English example see Thompson 1978 (133ff.).

25. Thompson 1974 (382ff.).

26. For this "cultural" definition of class relations see Thompson 1974 (397–98). This definition is formulated in opposition to those definitions of class society that are too narrow and too economic in nature. The same may be said of Calhoun 1982. It is important to see not only "class" but also "class relations." This point has been emphasized by Kumar (1983), who points out that class action cannot be explained when classes are seen as isolated entities with no relationship to other classes.

moral economy. The struggles between social classes were still struggles for the reconstruction of the traditional good society and were struggles between traditional status groups. Thus the conflict between these class cultures functioned like a bridge between the old and the new.

As soon as class conflict is identified as being concerned with the social organization of industrial work the classification underlying class conflict becomes more clearly defined. Social classification starts to be thought of as the result of individual effort. But the classification of social reality can still be reduced to a dichotomy: to the contradiction between capital and labor. Classes are constructed around the contradiction between those who sell wage labor and those who buy it.[27] But contrary to the preindustrial phase of modern society, both factors, capital and labor, are defined in ways that are independent of cultural or political traits. Culture and politics become the superstructure, something actually secondary in describing the class structure of industrial society. The further development of modern society, however, has called this dichotomy into question.

Later, with the withering away of the industrial model of development and the coming of "postindustrial" society, a new contradiction appears between social groups defending technocratic progressivism and those defending a communicative life-world. Today class conflict is being transformed into a fluid antagonism that reaches into every aspect of social life. Class conflict has expanded in time as well; it has become permanent class conflict. The social reality created by this permanency is a system of classification that radicalizes the individualist premises of the modern system of classification. This system of classification that compares individuals and that counts the (economic and cultural) capital they own results in the highly individualized class structure of modern society.[28]

These ways of classifying people create a power discrepancy between social groups that has to be shown to be normal; the discrepancy must be seen as being legitimate.[29] Class conflict necessarily is accompanied by practices that generate the legitimating symbolic order. The purpose of

27. This interpretation of classes differs from the conceptions that see classes as concrete social groups. Rather than trying to identify the groups that constitute a class, my theoretical approach constructs classes theoretically and tries to find out whether historically these classes actually emerged. I expect that any identity between theoretical constructs and historical classes will be an exceptional case.

28. This development can only be grasped by a theoretical approach that constructs classes as clusters of indicators that are shared by individuals. When such indicators become diversified, empirical classes are increasingly less bound to a single or several concrete social groups. Today, classes can be described as highly "individualized." For this point see Beck 1983.

29. Bourdieu (1980, 1984) has developed at length the idea of collective illusions as systematically distorted visions of the world. Theoretically, this notion is, so far, the most interesting sociological reformulation of the old concept of ideology.

legitimating practices is therefore to make the existing relations between individuals appear to be normal relations. Resolved in this way, legitimating practices allow for the symbolic reproduction of the class structure of a society. The symbols favored by those who are on top are the symbols claiming universal validity because such symbols produce the most perfect image of legitimacy for the class structure of modern society. Thus on the level of class conflict, another logic of cultural change intervenes. Cultural change is not only the result of learning processes but also the result of class-specific symbolic practices.

2.4. Legitimating Practices

The production and reproduction of class structure is dependent on the symbolic practices by which classes try to maintain their differences. For this purpose symbolic resources are used to legitimate the class structure.[30] Class conflict produces not only a social relation but also a symbolic relation. This symbolic relation serves as a specific mechanism for organizing and reorganizing the symbolic universe that legitimates modern society. A look at modern history might clarify this point.

In the sixteenth and seventeenth centuries princes and the newly established parliaments tried to break the sovereignty of religious authority by postulating a new basis for legitimizing political domination: the welfare of the people.[31] This secular ground for domination legitimated either the absolute sovereignty of the king or the representative sovereignty of the estates. The plebs still lived in the old world of the moral economy, which was culturally opposed to both the world of the absolute prince and the world of the new estates. The ensuing struggles on the symbolic level were struggles between the modern and the traditional world. Thus the symbolic practice of the absolutist state (constructed as the practice of the rule of law) was opposed to the symbolic order of traditional life (defined as the practice of customary law) that was defended by the lower classes.

At the beginning of the industrial revolution a new field of symbolic struggle was added. The dominance of the old class cultures was broken by the rising bourgeoisie, which transcended these cultural worlds with its idea of an individualistic and competitive society, a society based on

30. For a systematic treatment of processes of classification in modern societies see Bourdieu 1984. My analysis implies a critique of Touraine's central assumption that the concept of society is no longer adequate as a description of modern social life. Touraine's idea of centering social theory on a modified version of class conflict is insufficient to tackle the developmental processes going on in the cultural representations of society. For this perspective see Touraine 1981.

31. The collected papers of Hintze (1970) is still the best systematic analysis of this period. For a more recent treatment see Mousnier 1974, 1980.

"industria." It was legitimated by a radically individualistic ethic, the Protestant work ethic, and its telos of never-ending maximization and perfection. This class made the individualistic society of a market economy the symbolic world shared by both the upper and the lower classes. The legitimating practices based on this symbolic world led to the model of class relations that was created in nineteenth-century Europe between the labor movement, on the one hand, and the organizations of the industrial elites, on the other hand. This model conceived of this relationship as a game between pressure groups bent on maximizing power and interests.[32] It conceived of the capital-labor relationship as a bargaining one. This symbolic world created the illusion that was necessary for the reproduction of this individualistic and competitive society. This illusion helped to reproduce—at least for a time—the class structure of modern society in its industrial phase of development.

The developmental dynamic of advanced industrial societies again changes its field of symbolic struggle. The world of the unlimited development of the industrial forces of production is replaced by a new legitimating practice: the programming of the economic, cultural, and social reproduction of society. The cultural world opposing such an encompassing program developed in both the working class and the bourgeois classes. This development took the form of a romantic culture emphasizing naturalistic sentiments that are opposed to the "coldness" of modern economic and political life. In late-modern society a new "green" philosophy, which is trying to develop another moral image of the good world, carries on this tradition of a culture that is opposed to a world controlled by the bureaucratic welfare state. The "new" social movements are explicitly opposed to the welfare state; instead they speak of health, green nature, and aesthetics, and they generalize the idea of the "good life" into all fields.[33] The ensuing symbolic struggles between different "modernities," that is, between modernity and romanticism, legitimate a society with a highly individualized class structure.

The winners in these symbolic struggles try to produce the image of defending claims that are universally valid. The claim of universalism is, at least in modern societies, the most promising strategy to reproduce a given class structure of society. If symbolic struggles arrive at defining the symbolic world of the upper classes as the legitimate one, the lower classes have to see their own existence as an illegitimate one. The degree

32. A history of the labor movement seen from a trade-unionist perspective is contained in Kendall 1975.

33. The new social movements manifest a conflict about the type of professional knowledge that should be used for the reproduction of society. See Eder 1982. For the green movement see Galtung 1986. Theories of postindustrial societies—with the exception of Touraine 1981—generally miss this point.

of legitimacy becomes the reference point for distinguishing social groups. The history of legitimating practices[34] is therefore the key to an understanding of the processes that constitute the symbolic universe of modern class society.

The symbolic universe of law offers the exemplary case of the processes of legitimating the class structure of modern society. On the one hand, legal norms fix the objective classification of legal rights. On the other hand, law has symbolic power because it claims to have morality on its side.[35] Law is a mechanism that is used in different contexts for the symbolic reproduction of an institutional order. In order to analyze this function of the symbolic universe of the law, I use examples from the history of legal and political thought.[36]

At the beginning of the sixteenth century both traditions adopted the new premises that there no longer existed a metaphysical order on which political and social life could be built and that the anthropological nature of man is the basic fact. These new premises emerged from the reflexive structure of modern social thinking: social thought had become dependent on the thinker (and his nature) as such. Hobbes's Leviathan and the radical Puritan theories of the covenant are examples of this radically new kind of social thinking; they mark the beginning of the evolution of modern representations of society.

The symbolic authority of the modern legal order is based on these new normative grounds. There are three key ideas: the idea of the maintenance of order by the rule of law; the idea that the state's function is to maximize the welfare of its constituents; and the idea that a good way of life must be defended against the consequences of uncontrolled progressivism. Order, welfare, and a good life are the normative grounds for the symbolic authority of modern law.

The images of a legal order constructed on such principles are the most effective mechanisms for producing the illusion that is necessary for the reproduction of society. The more complex the social structure of modern society becomes, the more complex these images become. The first idea, the idea of a formal legal order founded on the universalistic principle of the reason of state, structures and legitimates the absolutist

34. For a sociological approach to the history of social movements and cultural struggles in modern society see Eder 1986b. See also Eisenstadt 1981 and his contribution to this volume, which focuses on the complementary aspect of the elites.

35. The old and polemicized problem of the relationship between the moral and the legal is restated here in a new way. For the classical sociological treatment see Durkheim 1950.

36. For a history of political thought that takes this perspective see Skinner 1978. For legal history see the abundant nineteenth-century German literature. For the sociological use of this literature see Eder 1985a (329ff., 396ff.).

state that ended the religious wars by guaranteeing indifference to religious and social differences, thus creating order through law. The second idea of a legal order takes into account the fact that the modern state has taken on the regulation of the economic sphere, which up to that time had been integrated into traditional forms of living. The telos of a legal order is maximizing the welfare of a society through law. The third idea emerges from the dysfunctional consequences of maximizing social welfare. Because perfect order is no longer produced by regulative law, "progress" has to be corrected or, better, planned "by the people." The law then distributes the chances to participate in the planning of society. Law, conceived primarily as procedural law, becomes the incorporation of the democratic creed.[37]

Against the majesty of such a law the lower groups either mobilize a cultural world beyond the law or—and this is the normal case—they subject themselves to the law, accepting its authority and thereby contributing to its authority. Thus law is one of the foremost mechanisms of legitimating class structure. Legal practices are the most important among the symbolic practices reproducing the power structure of society.

3. THE EVOLUTION OF MODERNITY

3.1. The Social Reproduction of Modernity

In the preceding section I laid the foundations for a theory of the social production of modernity. I identified the mechanism that launches processes of social and cultural change, but I have not yet described the specific nature of the processes launched. The processes of social and cultural change that are seen as crucial by traditional modernization theory are (functional) differentiation and (formal) rationalization. Whether they are the master trends of change in the course of modernization is a question that must be answered now. My answer has two aspects. First, differentiation and rationalization can take different courses than those ascribed to them in classical modernization theory. Second, there are differences in the "functionality" and "rationality" of these processes that have to be explicated.

The first of these processes, differentiation, is a structural arrangement to meet the functional consequences of two types of modernizing forces: modern associations and modern class structure. This structural arrangement has to reproduce these generating forces. Otherwise, modernization cannot go on. Thus differentiation can be defined within my theoretical framework as the mechanism for the social reproduction of

37. A short description of the stages of legalization can be found in Habermas 1981 (2:527ff.).

these modernizing forces. A theory of differentiation describes how the opus operatum reproduces the modus operandi.

Classical modernization theory says that in modern societies differentiation takes on the course of functional differentiation, a course that is different from the traditional course of stratificational differentiation. The decisive innovation is the functional autonomy by which structural arrangements are equally and without external constraints able to accommodate[38] the functional consequences of the modernizing mechanisms. By separating and multiplying the fields in which the construction of modern society can take place, functional differentiation makes this accommodation possible.

Thus differentiation allows modern societies to accommodate learning processes and class struggles by structurally separating the specific spheres of action that are the objects of these collective actions. For example, the economic system and the religious system are based on functionally specific ways of accommodating the consequences of modernizing activities. Economic class struggle is no longer logically adapted to enactment in the religious sphere of action (as in traditional society). But there are still social struggles within the religious sphere, for example, in conflicts between religious professionals and the lay public. Specific class conflict occurs in the economic sphere and is manifest in the distance between capital and labor. And there are analogous struggles in the political and the cultural spheres. The most conclusive example is the effect of differentiating the educational system from other systems. The modern educational system reproduces the class structure of modern society much more efficiently than before, at the same time guaranteeing the cognitive skills a complex, modern society needs for its reproduction.[39] Functional differentiation is the mechanism by which the dominant elites reproduce their positions in an increasingly complex modern society.

But such differentiation is not a master trend; it is the trend of the masters. This observation implies that there is more than one path of differentiation in modern society. Functional differentiation, I propose, reproduces class structure by producing a distinctive structure for the

38. The concept of "accommodation" has been proposed by Smelser (1985, 124). This concept allows for the development of a more adequate idea of the functionality, or "success," of differentiation.

39. The functional differentiation of class conflict is normally thought of as the end of class conflict. This notion, however, presupposes a realistic definition of class, that is, it implies that we already know what a class consists of. I argue that differentiation allows for the reproduction of class structure. The best example of this phenomenon is the role of the educational system. For the reproductive role of the differentiated educational system see Bourdieu 1984.

formation of relatively autonomous elites and for the deformation of the people as the clients of these elites. Whether dedifferentiation takes place depends on whether social forces are strong enough to get rid of their confinements to the specific social spaces that, from the perspective of the elites, are rational and to redefine the social space in which they act. Such dedifferentiation mobilizes class conflicts that generate collective action beyond the established networks of communication to involve those who do not yet communicate with each other.[40]

Thus those who argue that the formation of elites is the most important function of structural arrangements have to plead for functional differentiation. Those who argue that the organization of the collective interests of the lesser classes is the most important function must plead against functional differentiation. Ultimately, functional differentiation is an option, not a fate. It is a possible but not a necessary trend of modernization. Using it as a master trend implies a value judgment. To give theoretical distinctiveness to it contributes to its image of being "rational."

3.2. The Cultural Reproduction of Modernity

The ability of functional differentiation to dominate the process of modernization depends on its ability to reproduce the image of an egalitarian social order. Thus a second form of the reproduction of modern society has to be taken into account: Rationalization allows for the cultural reproduction of modernity.

As I have already indicated, in modern society rationalization is the result of a double production of culture: learning processes and practices that legitimate class differences. Collective learning processes constitute the discourse within which modernity is made possible. Symbolic practices try to mobilize the universe of discourse produced in these learning processes to legitimate existing distributions of power and positions in modern society. The mechanism generating rationalization is, first, discourse in associational life and, second, the interest on the part of social classes in legitimating their own position and illegitimizing the positions of others.

Rationalization is the result of two types of generating conditions and can assume different forms. What holds for differentiation also holds for rationalization: there is more than one path of rationalization in modern society. Rationalization is made possible by both the disenchantment and

---

40. An interesting concept trying to mediate between differentiation and dedifferentiation is the concept of "uneven" differentiation. See Colomy 1985. But, ultimately, he remains tied to the elitist perspective complemented by the idea that there must be structures providing a refuge or haven for critical (i.e., powerless) elites.

the reenchantment of the world.[41] The social preconditions for this difference are the differences between the high and the low cultures of modern society; both cultures are rationalized in different ways. Their differences consist in the differential use of the symbolic resources that are at a society's disposal. There are two ideal types of rationalization: disenchantment, which is related to the dominant groups in society, and reenchantment, which is related to the dominated groups. Both processes produce different images of the modern world, images that I refer to as "official" and "unofficial." What looks, when seen from the Weberian perspective, like historical vacillation between rationality and irrationality can be seen as the rivalry between an official and an unofficial type of rationalization. This difference has become central in deciding the course of modernization.

Among the best examples of the official version of rationality is legal rationality. There are, however, other symbolic universes based on this type of rationality. For example, the symbolic universe of political discourse and that of scientific discourse contribute in their specific manners to the official rationality of modern society. Rationalization triggered by these forms of rationality ends up, as Weber has argued, in disenchantment.[42]

Rationalization takes a different course when strong cultural movements put a society's accepted practices and ways of thinking, that is, its hegemonical symbolic order, into question.[43] Such movements can be brought about by psychic or ecological crises that cannot be resolved by purely political or economic means. Rationalization that takes a direction other than the official one ends up in reenchantment. Whether rationalization really takes this direction depends on the developmental paths set by such cultural movements.

Reenchantment does not necessarily mean "irrationalization." Reenchantment can be based on the old symbolic resources of religious orientations.[44] For example, we know the extent to which Catholic and Protestant ideas still influence individual and group choices in the continuing path to modernization. We know the effect of non-Western religious

41. The discussion about disenchantment and reenchantment refers above all to the religious aspects of rationalization. See Tiryakian (this volume). Lechner (1985) also takes reenchantment into account but reduces the conditions leading to reenchantment to discontent, that is, to a negative orientation toward social action. Thus the elitist theoretical stand can be kept.

42. These examples of rationalization are ones identified by Weber. For a systematic discussion of the different aspects of rationalization see Habermas 1981 (1:114ff.).

43. Cultural movements and countercultures are a difficult subject for theoretical treatment. For one attempt see Yinger 1982.

44. Reenchantment, conceived as the development of posttraditional religion, is a counterprocess to the process of secularization. For such a restatement of the notion of secularization see Werblowsky 1976.

traditions on the process of the social production of the modern social order. Weber has proposed the difference between this-worldy and other-worldy orientations to distinguish between different symbolic logics.

Beyond such religiously based forms of reenchantment another form of reenchantment is the attitude toward nature. This form of re-enchantment challenges the productivist image of modernity, which is defined by its instrumental relation to nature, with a romantic image of another modernity that is defined by the integration of society into na-ture. This reenchantment leads to a rationalization of a more moral kind. Weber called this moralization "material" rationalization.[45] It ques-tions the dominance of formal rationality and serves as the vehicle, as Weber saw it, of an irrational rationalization.

But Weber's interpretation is misleading. Both processes are contradic-tory forms of rationalizing the modern world. In traditional societies cultural differences center around the poles of orthodoxy and hetero-doxy. In modern societies they center around the poles of formal and material rationality. But how do we decide on their respective degrees of rationality?

3.3. Falling Short of Modernization

The question of rationality comes up on both levels of the reproduction of modernity: on the level of differentiation and on the level of rationaliza-tion. When functional differentiation is substituted by segmentary forms of differentiation, a social structure emerges that is unable to reproduce the class structure of modern society. Moreover, when rationalization is replaced by a new magical image of the world, a cultural system emerges that is unable to reproduce the collective practices underlying the produc-tion of modernity. In this case a manifest regression occurs. But can we describe such a development as "irrational"? In addition, on the levels of differentiation and rationalization we are also confronted with antagonis-tic paths to modernization. Whether one of these paths is more rational than the other becomes a problem for a theory of modernization.

The key to these problems is not the theory of differentiation but the theory of rationalization because this theory contains the double prob-lem: to look at the way the social order is rationalized and to identify the criteria for distinguishing what is to be considered as rational. Thus the theory of rationalization cannot escape the process of rationalization of which it is part.[46]

---

45. The concept of material rationalization was originally developed by Weber using the example of the legal postulates for justice.

46. The reflexivity built into the idea of rationalization has been treated by Habermas 1981 (1:106–13).

There are only two ways out of this problem: either to postulate a substantive normative criterion of rationality or to identify the social conditions that are necessary for rationalization to occur. The first solution is tautological because such a postulate itself becomes part of the symbolic struggles pushing rationalization in whatever direction. The second solution is to see the social conditions of rationalization as the "procedural" norms[47] that are necessary for rationalization and to examine whether they are in evidence and, if so, to what extent.

Reduced to its procedural form, the ultimate ground of the rationality of modernity, then, is that we can choose our symbolic orders, that we are not stuck with any one type of rationality, and that we can at any time abandon what we have ceased to accept rationally. Whether or not such a rational outcome is to be expected has to be treated as an open question. Classical modernization theory seems to have already decided this question by describing modernization as rationalization. In the following section, however, I show that this modernization is not necessarily a rational one. Therefore, modernization theory has to incorporate a more explicit notion of rationality into its conceptual framework. I suggest that we look for procedural rationality on the level of the conditions generating what has been called rationalization.

As I have shown, rationalizing the modern social order is dependent on two mechanisms. First, rationalization is the net result of social struggles between social classes. Second, these social struggles are dependent on collective learning processes to reproduce the cultural conditions of their existence. Thus two mechanisms are necessary to arrive at a modern social order. Although difficult to achieve, such a social order is even more difficult to reproduce. It has to be assured that learning processes and class conflict can go on. When reproduction fails, then social development regresses or is rigidified. The historical process becomes "pathological." The result of blocked class conflicts and blocked learning processes is the pathogenesis of modernity.[48]

Historically, pathological processes seem to predominate. Collective learning processes are more often blocked than released. Associations more often turn into forms of interaction producing enemies rather than forms favoring learning processes. The history of modern associations is much more a history of private feuds than a history of learning.

47. The concept of procedural norms has close links with communication theory. This point is examined later in this chapter.

48. The pathogenesis of modernity has been the topic of the classical discussion concerning the "German road to modernity." The central problem of this discussion has been whether there is such a thing as a "normal" road to modernity that can be attributed to a country.

The same applies to class conflict. Often class conflict is neutralized by populist appeals or reduced to an elitist struggle.[49]

Either way, the result is cultural conflicts that try to mobilize either the moral majority or the moral minority. Fascism radicalizes the moral majority: it offers integrative formulas with racist, nationalist, or imperialist orientations. Terrorism is the radicalization of a moral minority and is exemplified by the Jacobin terror after the French Revolution, the terror of Stalin, and that of the Khmer Rouge. Whether class conflict ends up as fascism or moral terror depends on the cultural logic of a modern society.

This conceptualization allows us to tackle the problem of pathological developments in a more promising way. Although associations "learn" and social classes "struggle" with each other, modernization nevertheless fails. Nationalism mobilizes expressive resources that are not rationalized by the former factors. Fascism mobilizes sentiments that cannot be controlled by the modern political and social movements. But why do such pathological developments occur? Why are learning processes blocked? Why is class conflict negated? What are the cultural foundations that make possible such outcomes?

A provisional answer to these questions can be given here. Ultimately, it is the symbolic universe in which a society lives that seems to be the decisive factor in determining whether modernization, once triggered and set into motion, will actually succeed or not. Variations concerning the degree of associational life and class conflicts in modern societies raise secondary questions: Why is there no socialism in the United States? Why is there such a strong tradition of class conflict in England? Such factors determine the tempo of modernization and the injustice tied to it. But they do not block modernization.

The crucial question, then, is why modernization in some societies within this reach of variations fails—at least for some time. It does so because there are cultural traditions that become dominant in specific phases of modernization. An example is the German modernization experience in the second half of the nineteenth and the first half of the twentieth centuries.[50] Although starting modernization like the other European nations, collective learning processes and social struggles over the cultural orientation of modernization were blocked in favor of a civil society that was controlled by the state. The state took tight control over associations, thereby controlling collective learning processes. The state also neutralized class conflict, thereby imposing a symbolic order on

49. This critique of an elitist or populist transformation of class conflict is found, for example, in Touraine 1981.

50. For a discussion of the concept of social pathology see Eder 1985a; for the idea of blocked learning processes as indicators of social pathology see Miller 1986.

modern society. The modern culture was created in an authoritarian manner. And as long as this type of creation remains dominant the possibility of pathological cultural evolution exists.

Therefore, the key to explaining the path of development leading into modernity lies in the learning processes and the symbolic practices in the sphere of culture. These processes and practices determine not only the type of rationalization (disenchantment or reenchantment) that will take place, thereby restricting the possibilities of structural differentiation, but they also determine the degree of rationality. Thus we will be able to regard the counterprocesses to functional differentiation and formal rationalization not as simple aberrations[51] from the path of modernization but as possible outcomes of modernization. The normality of differentiation and rationalization is precisely not the point. The question of normality and pathology is rather a question of the social conditions generating differentiation and rationalization. Only by taking into account the conditions that block collective learning processes and symbolic struggles will we be able to explain pathogenetic forms of differentiation or dedifferentiation, of disenchantment or reenchantment.

The description of modernizing processes as pathogenetic developments, which is much in vogue today, is a communication about the conditions that trigger collective learning processes and change the universe of discourse used in class conflict as a means of legitimating practices. Such communication, defined as the condition of rationality, about the pathogenesis of modernity cannot exclude, but can minimize, the possibility for the pathogenesis of modernity.

4. CONTRADICTIONS AND EVOLUTION

4.1. A Theoretical Treatment of Contradictions

The foregoing analysis of the social production of modernity has led to an analysis on three levels: collective learning processes, class conflict, and reproductive structures. This analytical distinction of levels allows for localizing both the structure and the functioning of contradiction as the mechanism for originating and reproducing communication. This implicit notion of contradiction must be clarified in the following sections.

Contradiction can be defined as a social event where somebody opposes what somebody else says. This definition leads to a first thesis: the notion of contradiction presupposes the notion of communication. Without communication contradiction is a meaningless category. Only within

51. Although it has often been mentioned that different paths to modernization cannot be reduced to aberrations from a master trend leading to modernity, seldom have the necessary theoretical consequences of this observation been considered.

a communicative relationship can contradiction occur at all.[52] This thesis leads to the following corollary: contradictions work on different levels of social reality.

On the level of associations contradiction is the mechanism by which participants in a collective discourse can construct a shared world of meanings. Such a shared world relies on concrete interaction, which forces those engaged in it into a logic that transcends their personal involvement and egoistic interests. A communication on the level of concrete interaction that uses the mechanism of contradiction is bound to the logic of argumentation. Argumentation is in turn a mechanism that binds all engaged in it to a collective reality, one defined by the learning process triggered by communication. Thus contradictions are fundamental for a first type of social reality: the reality of social groups. On this level we have to deal with concrete actors trying to communicate with each other.

But contradiction can be pushed to the point where argumentation is itself put into question: one side can argue against further argumentation and start to resort to power. The reproduction of communication in the group is interrupted. A substitute for the social basis of communication must therefore be found. The new basis is constituted not by social relations between persons but between classes of persons. On this level communication is a mechanism for locating and relocating classes in relation to each other. The mechanisms that force social classes to communicate, that is, to struggle, with each other are those of the marketplace because those who do not participate are necessarily the losers of the game. But at the same time this situation forces institutional agreements in order to reproduce the marketplace. Generating distinctions, that is, a world of social classification, is the result of communication on this level. Thus contradictions are fundamental for a second type of social reality: the reality of social classes.[53] On this level we have to deal with social classes communicating by struggling with each other.

But there is still another type of contradiction that escapes the description of contradictions given so far. These are the contradictions built into the structural effects of group and class action, into differentiation and rationalization. This level of contradiction is not the same as a contradiction between society and its environment because society cannot contradict its environment:[54] the environment is defined by the fact that it does

52. For the centrality of the concept of communication for a sociological theory see—each following different intentions—Habermas 1981 and Luhmann 1984. For the cultural anthropological point of view see Leach 1976. In the following I draw heavily on Miller 1986.

53. To insist on the difference between group and class implies the critique of classical conflict theory as developed by, for example, Dahrendorf (1959).

54. This point is one that Luhmann especially emphasizes. See Luhmann 1984 (191ff., 498ff.).

not communicate. The contradiction I mean is still within society. Thus we arrive at the broadest and most fundamental level of social contradictions: the level of structural contradictions that constitute the social reality of society. Structural contradictions do not constitute communication. But because they are communicated they allow for the reproduction of communication both on the level of group and on the level of class.

The levels of the communicative constitution of social reality can be summarized as follows:

—The first level concerns contradictions between actors communicating with each other. This level constitutes the social reality of the group and the learning processes triggered by communication between actors.
—The second level concerns contradictions between groups engaged in classifying and reclassifying each other. This level constitutes the social reality of class and the social struggles going on between classes.
—The third level concerns contradictions built into the developmental processes that are the structural effects of learning and class conflict. This level constitutes the social reality of society.

Contradictions on all three levels work together to produce social evolution. The implications of this conceptualization for the theory of social evolution can now be clarified.

4.2. Contradictions and Social Change

This discussion of the communicative function of contradictions on different levels of social reality shows that contradictions are the medium and the telos of communication. The telos of communication is not the resolution of the contradiction—for that would imply the end of communication. Rather it is to reproduce communication, to assure an ongoing stream of communication. This ongoing stream of communication means that social reality is something that is always in flux.

This relationship between contradiction and communication opens up a new theoretical perspective on social change. The second thesis concerning a theory of social change follows: contradictions generate social change and these changes are the mechanisms of evolution.[55] This proposition differs from usual conceptions of social change in one fundamental respect: it tries to explain change not by changes in factors outside the system but by internal generating mechanisms. Social change is

55. The difference between my approach and the Marxist strategy consists in differentiating between the changes produced and the evolutionary process that handles these changes. My approach avoids the problem of "misplaced concreteness," which is tied to theories that try to deduce social developments directly from observed actions.

itself a social product. A corollary of this general assumption is as follows: contradictions are constitutive of social change; they produce social change in the process of constituting social reality.[56]

Social change is constituted on the level of association by the very fact of contradicting. Communication exerts a specific constraint: it forces those participating in communication to learn or not to learn. Contradictions can be used to reinterpret the world; if this use is declined, those engaged in the communication must explicitly negate the possibility of learning that is offered to them. In either case social reality changes. In this problem, the theory of practical discourse has its generic field of application: it is an ideal model of the constitution of social reality. It leaves the other levels of social reality to other theories, such as systems theory.[57] Contradictions on this first level produce social change by triggering collective learning processes.[58]

But these learning processes do not suffice to explain social change because not every learning process survives on the level of the institutional order. Social change can therefore be seen on the level of the institutional order as the result of struggles between groups interested in classifying or reclassifying others or themselves. Contradictions on this second level produce social change by forcing social classes into class conflicts.[59]

These conflicts, whether they are described as class struggles or as forms of status politics, have structural effects beyond their intended effects. The structure of communication producing these effects gives rise to a type of contradiction beyond the actors and classes of actors. Contradictions on the level of the reproduction of the conditions generating society produce social and cultural change by mobilizing antagonistic models of reproduction (i.e., differentiation and rationaliza-

56. Here, some possible misunderstandings should be mentioned. The centrality of contradiction does not imply that contradiction is the guarantor of rationality; those who contradict do not necessarily understand those whom they contradict. This also applies to contradictions in class conflict; the result of class conflict is not rational per se. And the same applies for the idea of rationalization; the empirically given process of rationalization (what is real) is not necessarily rational. None of these empiricist presuppositions has to be made. The only thing that counts is the fact of contradiction. Reality is nothing but the environment, which is a continual resource for changing the conceptions of reality.

57. This is the theoretical strategy of Habermas (1981), who is working with two different theories at the same time; the difference between these theories is established by their normative difference.

58. A systematic account of this term is given by Miller 1986. See also Eder 1985a, 1986b.

59. The theoretical treatment of classification leaves open the question of the mode of differentiation used in classification. Whether there is functional, segmentary, or other differentiation remains to be seen. For a special treatment see Schwartz 1981.

tion) that take for their theme the structural basis of communication.[60] Thus Marx's idea of the contradiction between the social relations of production and the forces of production is abstracted to become a contradiction between the antagonistic forms of differentiation and rationalization that are to be specified on each level of the evolution of society.

4.3. Evolutionary Mechanisms

This discussion still leaves open the problem of how contradictions on the different levels of reality are related to one another. How are contradictions that generate learning processes related to contradictions on the level of class conflict? And how are the contradictions on this level related to contradictions on the level of the reproduction of society? This problem leads to a third thesis: the social changes on these different levels are the mechanisms of social evolution.[61] Evolutionary changes are the result of the combined effects of contradictions producing changes on different levels of social reality.

This thesis implies that it is neither collective learning processes nor class conflict nor structural strains alone that explain the evolution of society but their evolutionary interaction. Collective learning processes function like the mechanism of mutation, offering varying patterns of social reality produced in various social groups. Class conflict functions like the mechanism of selection, favoring the patterns of social distinctions that will be integrated into the institutional system of society. Differentiation and rationalization function like the mechanism of reproductive isolation, stabilizing the system of society.

But there is a problem in grafting such an evolutionary-style theory, well designed though it may be for biological evolution, onto the process of social change. The processes described are not tied to a specific evolutionary mechanism. The evolutionary mechanisms these processes serve are interchangeable. This implies that learning processes, class conflicts, and structural antagonisms can all be selection environments. And mutations can result from any of the social processes mentioned. The same reasoning is valid for the mechanism of reproductive isola-

60. This observation points to the central place that a theory of reproduction has for sociological theorizing. A sociology of culture is a necessary and important part of such a theory of reproduction, but it has to be complemented by a sociology of social structure. A new approach to such a sociology can be found in Bourdieu 1980, who works with the concept of a social topology. He speaks, in a manner similar to the language of differentiation theory, about the logic of different fields of action, and of the homologies concerning the social positions in these fields and the homologies of these fields within the general society—both of which reproduce a classified reality.

61. For these discussions on the relevance of the biological model see Plotkin 1982; for a sociological application see Eder 1987.

tion (stabilization). The possible recombinations of mechanisms and processes thus strongly suggest a theory of evolution with a highly complex structure.

An important corollary goes along with this theory of evolution: given these mechanisms, a strict Darwinian theory, which may be defined as a theory that assumes no relation between mutation conditions and selection conditions,[62] is not feasible. A Lamarckian theory would work better. The Lamarckian approach, which assumes a strong relation between mutation conditions and selection conditions, is better suited for explaining the interchangeability of mechanisms and processes in the theory of social evolution. It would allow us to anticipate that the mechanism of stabilization could be transformed into the mechanism of mutation as soon as structural antagonisms became the topic of communication in groups. Or it would allow us to anticipate that the mechanism of stabilization could be transformed into the mechanism of selection as soon as the description of structural antagonisms became a weapon in the hands of one class of actors against another class of actors.

The analysis of modernization, then, demands a much more sophisticated theory of evolution. Evolutionary theory, itself a product of modernization, is a way of describing modern society. As such, it must take into account the force of collective action. It must also take into account the dimension of social and cultural conflict. And it must be able to account for the success or failure of historical developments. It would seem that only an evolutionary theory that leaves open the question of what a modern order is about and that concentrates on the question of the social production of modernity will be able to grasp the changes occurring in society. These are changes that, after all, often contradict the theory of modernization that sociologists have formulated concerning this type of society. But perhaps this contradiction is still another mechanism of change in modern society.

REFERENCES

Beck, U. 1983. Jenseits von Stand und Klasse? In *Soziale Ungleichheiten. Sonderband 2 der Sozialen Welt,* ed. R. Kreckel, 25–73. Göttingen: Schwartz.

Berman, M. 1984. *The reenchantment of the world.* New York: Free Press.

Bourdieu, P. 1980. *Le sens pratique.* Paris: Les Editions de Minuit.

———. 1984. *The distinction: A social critique of the judgment of taste.* Cambridge: Harvard University Press.

Calhoun, C. 1982. *The question of class struggle: Social foundations of popular radicalism during the industrial revolution.* Chicago: University of Chicago Press.

62. See Harré 1980 (293ff.).

Colomy, P. 1985. Uneven structural differentiation: Toward a comparative approach. In *Neofunctionalism,* ed. J. Alexander, 130–56. Beverly Hills: Sage.

Dahrendorf, R. 1959. *Class and class conflict in industrial society.* 6th ed. Stanford: Stanford University Press.

Dumont, L. 1965. The modern conception of the individual: Notes on its genesis and that of concomitant institutions. *Contributions to Indian Sociology* 8:13–61.

———. 1967. *Homo hierarchicus.* Paris: Presses Universitaires de France.

———. 1970. Religion, politics, and society in the individualistic universe. *Proceedings of the Royal Anthropological Institutions of Great Britain and Ireland, 1970,* 31–41.

Durkheim, E. 1950. *Leçons de Sociologie. Physique des moeurs et du droit.* Paris: Presses Universitaires de France.

Eder, K. 1982. A new social movement? *Telos* 52:5–20.

———. 1985a. *Geschichte als Lernprozeß? Zur Pathogenese politischer Modernität in Deutschland.* Frankfurt: Suhrkamp.

———. 1985b. The "new social movements": Moral crusades, political pressure groups, or social movements? *Social Research* 52:869–90.

———. 1986a. Der permanente Gesellschaftsvertrag. Zur Kritik der ökonomischen Theorie des Sozialen. In *Gerechtigkeit, Diskurs oder Markt? Die neuen Ansätze in der Vertragstheorie,* ed. L. Kern and H.-P. Müller, 67–81. Opladen: Westdeutscher Verlag.

———. 1986b. Soziale Bewegung und kulturelle Evolution. Überlegungen zur Rolle der neuen sozialen Bewegungen in der kulturellen Evolution der Moderne. In *Die Moderne—Kontinuitäten und Zäsuren. Sonderband 4 der Sozialen Welt,* ed. J. Berger, 335–57. Göttingen: Schwartz.

———. 1987. Learning and the evolution of social systems. An epigenetic perspective. In *Evolutionary theory in social science,* ed. M. Schmid and F. M. Wuketis, 101–25. Dordrecht: Reidel.

Eisenstadt, S. N. 1981. Cultural traditions and political dynamics: The origins and modes of ideological politics. *British Journal of Sociology* 32:155–81.

Elster, J. 1978. *Logic and society.* New York: Wiley.

Galtung, J. 1986. The green movement: A socio-historical explanation. *International Sociology* 1:75–90.

Godelier, M. 1973. System, Struktur und Widerspruch im Kapital. In *Ökonomische Anthropologie. Untersuchungen zum Begriff der sozialen Struktur primitiver Gesellschaften,* by M. Godelier, 138–72. Reinbek, W. Ger.: Rowohlt.

———. 1978. Infrastructures, societies, and history. *Current Anthropology* 19: 763–68.

Habermas, J. 1962. *Strukturwandel der Öffentlichkeit.* Neuwied: Luchterhand.

———. 1979. *Communication and the evolution of society.* Boston: Beacon Press.

———. 1981. *Theorie des kommunikativen Handelns.* 2 vols. Frankfurt: Suhrkamp.

Harré, R. 1980. Social being and social change. In *The structure of action,* ed. M. Brenner, 287–312. Oxford: Blackwell.

Hintze, O. 1970. *Staat und Verfassung.* Göttingen: Vandenhoeck and Ruprecht.

Kendall, W. 1975. *The labour movement in Europe.* London: Allen Lane.

Kohlberg, L. 1981. *The philosophy of moral development: Moral stages and the idea of justice*. San Francisco: Harper and Row.

Koselleck, R. [1959] 1973. *Kritik und Krise. Eine Studie zur Pathogenese der bürgerlichen Welt*. Frankfurt: Suhrkamp.

Kumar, K. 1983. Class and political action in nineteenth-century England: Theoretical and comparative perspectives. *Archives Europeennes de Sociologie* 24:3–43.

Leach, E. 1976. *Culture and communication: The logic by which symbols are connected*. Cambridge: Cambridge University Press.

Lechner, F. J. 1985. Modernity and its discontents. In *Neofunctionalism*, ed. J. Alexander, 157–76. Beverly Hills: Sage.

Luhmann, N. 1982. *The differentiation of society*. New York: Columbia University Press.

———. 1984. *Soziale Systeme. Grundriß einer allgemeinen Theorie*. Frankfurt: Suhrkamp.

———. 1985. Zum Begriff der sozialen Klasse. In *Soziale Differenzierung*, ed. N. Luhmann, 119–62. Opladen, W. Ger.: Westdeutscher Verlag.

Marshall, T. H. 1950. *Citizenship and social class*. Cambridge: Cambridge University Press.

Miller, M. 1986. *Kollektive Lernprozesse—Studien zur Grundlegung einer soziologischen Lerntheorie*. Frankfurt: Suhrkamp.

Moscovici, S. 1976. Die Wiederverzauberung der Welt. In *Jenseits der Krise. Wider das politische Defizit der Ökologie*, ed. A. Touraine et al., 94–131. Frankfurt: Syndikat.

Mousnier, R. 1974. *Les institutions de la France sous la monarchie absolue*. Vol. 1, *Société et Etat*. Paris: Presses Universitaires de France.

———. 1980. *Les institutions de la France sous la monarchie absolue*. Vol. 2, *Les classes sociales*. Paris: Presses Universitaires de France.

Na'aman, S. 1978. *Zur Entstehung der deutschen Arbeiterbewegung. Lernprozesse und Vergesellschaftung, 1830–1868*. Hannover: SOAK.

Nipperdey, T. 1972. Verein als soziale Struktur in Deutschland im späten 18. und frühen 19. Jahrhundert. In *Geschichtswissenschaft und Vereinswesen im 19. Jahrhundert*, ed. H. Boockmann et al., 1–44. Göttingen: Vandenhoeck and Ruprecht.

Offe, C. 1972. *Strukturprobleme des kapitalistischen Staates*. Frankfurt: Suhrkamp.

———. 1985. New social movements: Challenging the boundaries of institutional politics. *Social Research* 52:817–68.

Plotkin, H. C., ed. 1982. *Learning, development, and culture*. Chichester: Wiley.

Sahlins, M. 1976. *Culture and practical reason*. Chicago: University of Chicago Press.

Schluchter, W. 1979. The paradoxes of rationalization. In *Max Weber's vision of history*, ed. G. Roth and W. Schluchter, 11–64. Berkeley: University of California Press.

———. 1981. *The rise of Western rationalism: Max Weber's developmental history*. Berkeley: University of California Press.

Schmid, M. 1982. Habermas' theory of social evolution. In *Habermas: Critical debates*, ed. J. B. Thompson and D. Held, 162–80. London: Macmillan.

Schwartz, B. 1981. *Vertical classification: A study in structuralism and in the sociology of knowledge.* Chicago: University of Chicago Press.

Sjoeberg, G. 1960. Contradictory functional requirements and social systems. *Journal of Conflict Resolution* 4:198–208.

Skinner, Q. 1978. *The foundations of modern political thought.* 2 Vols. Cambridge: Cambridge University Press.

Smelser, N. J. 1985. Evaluating the model of structural differentiation in relation to educational change in the nineteenth century. In *Neofunctionalism*, ed. J. Alexander, 113–30. Beverly Hills: Sage.

Thompson, E. P. 1968. *The making of the English working class.* Harmondsworth: Penguin.

———. 1974. Patrician society, plebeian culture. *Journal of Social History* 7:382–405.

———. 1978. Eighteenth-century English society: Class struggle without class. *Social History* 3:133–64.

Tilly, C. 1978. *From mobilization to revolution.* Reading, Mass: Addison-Wesley.

Touraine, A. 1977. *The self-production of society.* Chicago: University of Chicago Press.

———. 1981. *The voice and the eye.* New York: Cambridge University Press.

Tugendhat, E. 1980. Zur Entwicklung von moralischen Begründungsstrukturen im modernen Recht. *Archiv für Rechts- und Sozialphilosophie* (beiheft neue Folge) 14:1–20.

Vester, M. 1970. *Die Entstehung des Proletariats als Lernprozeß. Die Entstehung antikapitalistischer Theorie und Praxis in England, 1792–1848.* Frankfurt: Europäische Verlagsanstalt.

Wallace, A. F. 1972. Paradigmatic processes in culture change. *American Anthropologist* 74:467–78.

Werblowsky, R. J. 1976. *Beyond tradition and modernity: Changing religions in a changing world.* London: Athlone Press.

Yinger, J. M. 1982. *Countercultures: The promise and the peril of a world turned upside down.* New York: Free Press.

World Society Versus Niche Societies

Paradoxes of Unidirectional Evolution

Karl Otto Hondrich

Catastrophes cause people to learn; the same is true of innovations. It follows that catastrophes that are innovative in the sense that they are without precedent have a strong didactic effect. Indeed, in the wake of the meltdown of the Chernobyl nuclear reactor in the Soviet Union, some European countries learned very quickly that nuclear energy could and should be replaced by a new combination of other forms of energy, particularly solar energy, as well as energy-saving innovations. In contrast, some have cited a different lesson that should be learned from this catastrophe, namely, that it is supposedly both futile and impossible to extricate oneself from a trend that has become established on a global scale.

I do not want to discuss the question of energy resources but rather that of worldwide inevitability. Some sociocultural and technocultural patterns have become so pervasive worldwide that no country is in a strong enough position to ward them off. Markets, mass media, modern weaponry, sports competitions, blue jeans, pop music, government legitimation by majority consent, equal rights for men and women, nuclear power plants, and the nuclear family all belong to this set of technical and normative patterns. Global patterns such as these create the impression that societies all over the world are becoming ever more alike and that this trend is ineluctable.

This pattern may seem regrettable to us in some respects, but in other respects it is a source of hope. "Good" norms, such as mutual understanding and nonaggression in the framework of world government, may be disseminated and generally accepted as desirable future solutions to the world's most dangerous and potentially destructive conflicts, including thermonuclear war.

Rather than seeing such patterns solely as a source of hope, I argue that the risks inherent in the prevailing trends toward world unity, socio-cultural homogeneity, and efficiency in all areas outweigh the advantages. The more established such trends become, the more paradoxical their effects.

From this point of departure the question as to the ineluctability of prominent patterns becomes all the more crucial. Are there no other possible courses of development? I pose this question with the sociological classics in mind but get no answer. As I see it, there is no alternative to Spencer's and Durkheim's vision of social evolution as a unidirectional process of functional differentiation. I interpret the theories put forward by Marx, Weber, and Adam Smith as different versions of this same answer. I must turn to evolutionary biology in order to find two models of evolution within one paradigm.

Thus, in my short analysis of functional differentiation as *the* motor of modernity I point in particular to the paradoxes and pitfalls the concept entails. Reality protects itself against risks by resorting to segmentation, the counterpole to functional differentiation. The reality of modernization is to an increasing extent characterized not by functional differentiation replacing segmentation but by both principles cooperating in very subtle combinations. Biology and ecology, which both emphasize the evolutionary function of niches, take us one step further toward the rehabilitation of the principle of segmentation. Taking societies as the units of analysis, I juxtapose functional differentiation and segmentation in terms of their expression in the notions of "supersociety" and "niche societies" respectively. I understand the prevailing concept of modernization to mean the transformation of niche societies into supersociety by means of functional differentiation. In other words, the concept of modernization is theoretically one-sided, to say the least, and does not take into account its own risks and political implications. Although strong empirical, political, and moral support exists for the concept of modernization, a countervailing concept is in order that would, politically speaking, represent the interests of niche societies against those of the large and dominant societies. This concept, however, would present a far from satisfactory theory of evolution if it could not claim to be in the interest of evolution itself.

1. PARADOXES OF FUNCTIONAL DIFFERENTIATION

The sociological tradition makes use of a simple and convincing paradigm of *Vergesellschaftung* or social evolution: two or more small and relatively self-sufficient hordes merge—whether as a consequence of one dominating the other, outside pressure, or "free choice"— and form a new and larger social unit. Internally, this new unit tends to subdivide into functions and functional subgroups. This model of social evolution has a threefold advantage with regard to survival: it increases the power of the whole unit vis-à-vis its environment, it increases its internal power by providing a new and stronger form of integration, and it increases its efficiency by introducing the social division of labor.

The model of evolution has become the core of the theory, first elaborated by Spencer and Durkheim, that sees social evolution as an ongoing transformation from segmentary to functional differentiation. When we look at world society today, we see that the power of functionally specialized economic, scientific, and cultural subsystems is eroding the boundaries of the segments of national societies. Thus we may conclude that the process of functional differentiation is still under way.

It is useful to reconceptualize this "transformational model" into the terminology of systems theory, making it an ideal type, free of historical connotations:

1. Two or more social systems merge into one system. However, one can also consider the status quo ante as "one" system, consisting of several loosely connected segmentary subsystems. In any case, this transformation amounts to an increase in power and size.

2. A variety of either dissimilar segments or loosely connected systems is replaced by a variety of dissimilar functions and functional subsystems within one strong system. This view is certainly not in accordance with the popular conception of functional differentiation. Nor is it in accordance with the view put forth in the classics. Durkheim and Spencer proceeded from the assumption that social segments are similar or homogeneous from the very beginning. Indeed, the clans and tribes of primitive societies may look similar when seen through our eyes, but in terms of their own self-description they are meaningfully distinct from each other and constitute a variety of social systems that are both heterogeneous and independent of one another. For them, functional differentiation means the transformation of their own particular sociocultural structures into more general ones. The same is true for these new systems. They have transformed heterogeneity into homogeneity. Spencer's dictum that evolution is the progression from homogeneity to heterogeneity is only true with respect to functions. As for sociostructural arrangements, there is an increase in homogeneity.

3. The reduplication of any function or set of functions in two or more systems or subsystems is reduced. The principle involved is that functional differentiation must progress as far as possible, which

means that it continues up to the point where there is only one structural representation (or one subsystem) remaining for each function in the system. The redundancy of functions and structural subsystems is transformed into uniqueness. This amounts to an increase in efficiency. Adam Smith's famous use of the example of pin production to illustrate the division of labor is a case in point. Thus, an increase in efficiency and a tendency toward the increasing uniqueness of functions and corresponding structural subsystems is implied in functional differentiation.

The list of the implications of functional differentiation as an ideal type can be extended to include the transformation of internal power relations, personalities, and micro-macro relationships. Our insights into functional differentiation are as yet very poor. Nevertheless, I end the list here for the time being and turn to the question of risks. What risks do social systems encounter as they approach the ideal type of modernization represented by functional differentiation? Following the order of the three points outlined above, I discuss the risks of largeness and power, the risks of homogeneity, and the risks of uniqueness and efficiency. In order to change the emphasis somewhat, I at times speak not of risks but rather of paradoxes or paradoxical developments. What is paradoxical is that social systems grow weak owing to their own largeness and strength.

The fact that systems are weakened by their very strength is the "paradox of largeness and power." Similarly, the "paradox of evolution" is that functional differentiation not only creates variety but also creates homogeneity and that homogeneity threatens to decelerate evolution. And it is also a paradox that the increasing efficiency that results from decreasing redundancy makes systems more vulnerable because the slightest disturbance in one of the subsystems dramatically decreases the efficiency and viability of the whole system. I call this tendency the "paradox of efficiency."

1.1. The Paradox of Largeness and Power
The weakness of strong systems may be explained in several ways.

1. As systems grow in size and elements, their contacts with other systems decrease because they have sufficient opportunities for a wide range of contacts within themselves. In large societies, as Peter M. Blau (1977) has argued, the ratio of internal to external interaction is higher than it is in small societies. This holds true for economic, cultural and social interaction. In other words, the amount large societies have to learn from small countries is not as much as small countries can learn from them. This analysis also

suggests that large countries are more "closed" toward the flow of information from other countries and that small countries are more "open." This is true despite the fact that some large countries understand themselves to be "open societies" in the Popperian sense. This may also explain the greater incestuous conformity of sociocultural patterns within large societies as compared with smaller societies. Large numbers of elements thus have a negative effect on the receptiveness and diversity of large systems.

2. Even if large systems do exchange information with smaller ones, they do not learn as much from small systems as small systems learn from them. For example, in the case of five million Americans having five million contacts with five million Swiss people, only about 2 percent of the population of the United States learns something about Switzerland but about 90 percent of the total population of Switzerland learns something about the United States.

3. Inasmuch as large systems are powerful and power amounts to "the ability to afford not to learn" (Deutsch 1966, 111), large systems do not have to learn as much as small systems must in order to survive. Furthermore, the consciousness of being powerful enough not to have to learn may have an additional effect: lowering the tendency to learn. I call this tendency the "stubbornness" of large power systems.

4. As Gödel has shown for mathematics, Turing for computers, and Hofstadter (1979, 101) has reminded us, all systems are incomplete and contradictory insofar as they cannot know or prove the consistency and completeness of themselves without resorting to assumptions from outside. From the point of view of cybernetics, one can add that systems cannot be self-steering if they do not receive information about their goals from outside. Large systems, which process less information from outside than do small systems, learn less about themselves and about their own contradictions than small systems and are therefore less in a position to determine an appropriate set of goals. In the extreme case of a supersystem that has absorbed all other systems to the point that it alone remains, the system completely loses any ability to set appropriate goals. As a consequence, it is also stripped of its self-steering capacity. This would hold true for a world state that had swallowed all other nation states.

1.2. The Paradox of Evolution

To understand the paradox of evolution, it is necessary to resort to a generalized version of the model of evolutionary biology. Evolution may be understood either (1) from the perspective of an ecological system, as increasing or maintaining the variety of all species, or (2) from the perspective of each species, as increasing its population and the variety of different individuals within this population. Each of these two perspectives puts the other in a dilemma. Additionally, a contradiction also exists between increasing numbers and variety. It is therefore wrong to confuse the evolutionary success of one species with that of a system of species. It is also misleading to measure the success of a species by its increasing numbers alone. Evolutionary "success" is an ambivalent and diffuse quality, and it is so for good reasons.

Living systems—among them, societies, as one form of social system—can be considered a species if they (1) possess a common set of features, and (2) reproduce themselves by the recombination and mutation of a certain number of basic elements (genes) drawn from a common genetic pool. There is a variety within this common pool, and the recombination and/or mutation of its elements makes for continuing and ever-new variety. However, selection reduces variety by increasing the number of individuals in a given population that are similar in the sense that they are best equipped for survival in a given environment. Such a tendency toward homogenization within a population takes a long time to assert itself and thus cannot be detected easily in very large and segmented populations, for example, the human species.

Species with small populations, however, are different. With a population of only 160—if we take membership in the United Nations as a rough indicator—the species of nation-states is exceptionally small. Thus, applying the paradox of evolution, the tendency of a species to destroy its own internal variety by homogenization of its population may be particularly strong within the species of nation-states. Homogenization by functional differentiation and homogenization by selection both work in the same direction. Should they be considered as two sides of the same phenomenon? As yet I am not sure. I am inclined to see a parallel, or even a synonymity, between the sociological notion of functional differentiation and the biological concept of a recombination and mutation of elements (genes). If this approach is correct, it makes the case for homogenization even stronger. Biologically speaking, homogenization does not commence with the process of selection. Rather it is triggered by the process of recombination and/or mutation.

1.3. The Paradox of Efficiency

The paradox of efficiency can be understood as the result of competition among several systems or subsystems that all fulfill the same function. The most efficient one will endure and incorporate the work done by the others. The realization of the principle "one function, one system" brings about maximum efficiency, not only because the most efficient system is the one that survives the competition but also because the energies of the embracing, higher-level system are applied most effectively. Monopolization processes in markets are a case in point. The paradox arises not so much from an abuse of power but from the increased safety risks inherent in the unification process. If there is only one system left to handle each function or set of functions, a defect in that system causes an inversion from highest efficiency to highest inefficiency.

An even stronger version of the paradox of uniqueness and efficiency may be derived from the theory of the hypercycle (Eigen and Schuster 1979), an explanation of the origin of life. Molecules that start reproducing themselves do so not on their own but in cooperation with others. This process, a hypercycle of reaction cycles, has many variants, but the "fittest" soon forces its competitors out of existence. This analysis explains the uniqueness of the genetic code for all living beings on earth. If we apply this to societies, their propensity to gradually merge—via functional differentiation and homogenization—into the uniqueness of one supersociety would eventually bring the process of societal reproduction to an end. In a species with a population of one there can be no self-reproduction in a cooperative hypercycle. In terms of cybernetics, a system that has no other systems of the same species left is highly endangered because it lacks not only cooperation but also competition. It is only through "cooperation by competition" that a system comes to know the possibilities open to it and the restrictions on it with regard to setting realistic goals. A "lonely system" loses its capacity for self-organization and condemns itself to death.

2. SEGMENTATION AND NICHE SYSTEMS

Fortunately, the evolution of systems, and social systems in particular, does not follow the risky path suggested by the ideal-typical theory of functional differentiation. On the contrary, it makes great use of segmentary differentiation as a supplement to and a safeguard against the dangers of functional differentiation. Segmentation does the following:

1. It breaks large systems down into small ones and reduces the power of the subsystems.
2. It maintains and increases a variety of functionally equivalent structures with dissimilar sociocultural patterns despite the tendency toward homogenization.
3. It creates redundancy in the form of similarity as a counter to the pressure toward uniqueness.

We are mistaken to look at segmentation as an alternative that replaces functional differentiation and leads to dedifferentiation. At least in the case of social systems, it would seem improbable that such systems simply "forget" the level of functional differentiation that they have already attained. Thus, even if there were a planned dedifferentiation of structures, second-level, underground structures that retain and preserve a higher degree of functional differentiation would remain.

But this is not my main point. What is crucial is that any step toward more functional differentiation invariably produces more segmentation as well. This is true at all levels of the system. At the level of society, functional differentiation has been pushed forward particularly by the formation of political and economic subsystems. Because of its increase in size, homogeneity, and uniqueness, the political subsystem can be regarded as a paradigmatic example of functional differentiation. And yet at the same time the very same process has led to the contrasting program of a socioemotional subsystem composed of families, friendships, private acquaintances, and intimate relationships, a subsystem segmented into many small systems, each with a high variety of structural patterns and a high degree of functional redundancy.

Within the second-level functional subsystems, segmentation is an ongoing process. In the political system we usually find a variety of parties and interest groups and regional and local governments. In the economic system segmentation occurs mainly among enterprises and households. In the single family segmentation comes to an end because of the smallness of the unit; instead we find different patterns of functional differentiation, both emotional and economic. In summary, *Vergesellschaftung* as societal evolution leads to an "architecture of complexity" (Simon [1969] 1981, 193), which is characterized not only by a hierarchy of systems, subsystems, subsubsystems, etc., but also by a typical mixture of functional differentiation and segmentation, a mixture different for each subsystem and each level of subsystem. There is strong evidence that the range of freedom to change this mixture is very limited. It would not make sense to organize emotional-affective functions at the level of society by applying principles of functional differentiation. And yet conversely, to start organizing the economic and political spheres by segmentation would result in a tremendous loss of efficiency. Thus for all functional subsystems, there seems to be an appropriate (if not optimum) combination of the two principles of differentiation and segmentation. Social planning may change the weighting within this mix. In its attempt to "modernize" social structures, it often overemphasizes the functional principle, as in kibbutz education or in the central planning of an economy. As a result, segmentation is pushed into the underbelly of society, into unofficial structures such as black markets, informal groups, and secret networks of communication.

Generally speaking, any step toward changing social differentiation creates its opposite: diffuseness, a repository that embraces all those functions and relations that are no longer or still not accounted for or thematized by differentiation. The forms in which these functions and relations exist is unclear, uncertain and undetermined as well as covert, unconscious, and only latent. But exist they do. They are "the other side of the coin." Sociology does not look at this obverse side too often.

As differentiation does not destroy, but rather generates diffuseness, so the relationship between functional differentiation and segmentation is one of two opposing yet collaborative principles of evolution. Functional differentiation represents the dynamic, innovative, expanding, and risky aspects of evolution. Segmentation stands for preservation, stability, and the reduction of risks. We must abandon the classical model of social evolution that envisions progress from segmentation to functional differentiation. And we should also question the analogous model of modernization.

Such a revision of the transformational model opens up a wider range of interpretations of problems of evolution. Some of these problems arise not because there is "still too much" segmentation but because there is "not yet enough" segmentation in evolving social systems. Segmentation cannot be regarded as completely rehabilitated if it is only thought of as the companion of functional differentiation. It is more than that because it is an originating source of evolution itself. To understand this more fully, let us again consult the biological and ecological model of evolution. As explained above, the evolutionary process that leads to the homogenization and/or the extension of the population of a species is only one alternative within the transformational model. Another would be evolution through the formation and isolation of niches.

Niches are the set of conditions by which a part of the population of a species lives in relative specialization, isolated from the rest. To find a niche means to find or establish boundaries preventing the unlimited exchange of contacts with the rest (or majority) of the population. Thus the recombination of genes is restricted to the niche population, which is another way of saying that this group is protected from having to compete with the rest of the population on their terms.

> In a number of isolated ecosystems each will unquestionably follow evolutionary dynamic processes of its own as a result either of random shocks or of environmental differences. This will lead to a very much larger number of different species in totality [that is, different ways of life in the total population] than would a single, large ecosystem, in which many of the mutations that have survival value in the small system would not have survival value in the large. (Boulding 1978, 113)

This model of niche development amounts to "evolution by segmentation." The niche forms the segment in which one or a few individual systems develop their own peculiarities independently of the other systems.

The isolation of niches, therefore, leads to a variety of systems that are functionally equivalent but structurally distinct from one another. As societies, the United States, the Soviet Union, Sweden, and South Africa all have the same function but each fulfills this function via totally different sociostructural patterns. As elements of the "higher" system of international society, however, these societies fulfill different functions or play different roles, such as competing superpowers, neutrals, even outcasts (see Luard 1976, 259ff.). Redundancy exists within this higher system in the sense that the functional subsystems—the economic and political spheres, the socialization system, etc.—are each replicated many times, in both similar and different forms. The similarity of patterns has its survival value. If one system disappears, others make sure that the pattern endures. And yet the variety of patterns has its survival value too. Systems can choose between different patterns, they can recombine different patterns, or they can learn from the differences in one another's patterns.

Certain conditions must be fulfilled in order for niche-produced variety to become important in terms of evolution:

1. Niches should not be too small. Large systems have a better chance of producing improbable mutations and of protecting these against outside interference.

2. Adaptation to niches should not go too far. Niches are in a continual state of change. If the niche shrinks too much, the population that is too well adapted to this niche will cease to exist as a distinct entity. Adaptability, however, increases the capacity of a given population to expand niches or to find new niches. Catastrophe favors adaptability and eliminates the previously well-adapted but unadaptable (Boulding 1978, 111, 114).

3. Mutations or innovations that generate increased complexity, especially those that increase adaptability, have a better chance of discovering new niches than do those that reduce complexity.

4. Niches that are too open to their environment will be invaded by populations that are either more complex or greater in size and power and will thus lose their distinctness.

5. Niches that close themselves off too much forfeit the chance to become more complex by absorbing innovations from outside; they will not be able to expand.

Opening and closing are important strategies for increasing and preserving variety (Klapp 1978). Evidence for this point is provided by socialist countries in Eastern Europe; they have become open societies today by admitting many new elements of political and economic culture, thus increasing their internal variety.

3. THE PROSPECTS FOR THE EVOLUTION OF WORLD SOCIETIES

How strong are the trends in the international system of societies toward functional differentiation? And what are the chances for niche societies to oppose this tendency?

Society may be seen as an interesting species of living systems. It appears late in the history of evolution, which moves from the physical to the biological to the societal level (Boulding 1978, 29–30). Among social systems, society is also a latecomer. It is characterized by its degree of coordinative or synthesizing power: "More inclusive of controls over action than all others . . . , a type of social system, in any universe of social systems, which attains the highest level of self-sufficiency as a system in relation to its environment" (Parsons 1966, 2, 5). Today we would be critical of such a definition, knowing that all living systems are self-sufficient in the sense that they are self-organizing and that they are not self-sufficient because in order to reproduce themselves they require the cooperation of many other systems at numerous different levels.

Thus, the most important difference between society and other social systems is the symbolic social meaning attributed to society. It represented a "higher" social system that symbolized the unity of social organization at a time (in the eighteenth century) when such a unity was already fragmented and continually endangered by ongoing functional differentiation. In this situation the search for society as the symbol of unity had completely contradictory results. On the one hand, the unity and identity of the whole seemed to be best represented by the political subsystem as the locus of control over a territory with visible geographical boundaries. On the other hand, Hegel viewed society as something that included both the family and the economy, two subsystems with different boundaries that were otherwise overlooked in the political understanding of the term. The paradox of society is that it came into being as a symbol for unity at the very time that unity was disappearing.

The species "society," although comprising less than 200 "individuals," shows a remarkably high degree of dissimilarity. These dissimilarities include (1) both very big and very small individuals in terms of territorial boundaries; (2) both growing and shrinking individuals that result from the reproductive strength or weakness of their respective elementary parts; (3) both strong and chaotic individuals with respect to internal normative control, self-organization, and outlook; and (4) both independent and dependent individuals.

It is peculiar to the species "society" that it may reproduce itself either by segmentation, that is, by increasing its population and decreasing the size of its individuals, or by means of (frequently coercive) functional differentiation, that is, by decreasing the population in favor of ever larger individuals.

Both segmentation and functional differentiation can be perceived in world society today. Segmentation took place particularly after World War I (the division of the Austro-Hungarian Empire) and World War II (the division of Germany and Korea) as well as in the course of decolonization. Within the same period Soviet and Chinese societies grew larger in size. Contemporary societies in Western Europe have retained their territorial identity but seem gradually to be merging their norms and control mechanisms. Some African cases, however, illustrate reproduction by territorial integration without a corcomitant successful integration of control norms. What has been most remarkable, however, has been the development of three superpowers, each characterized by its large size, its large population, and its high degree of complexity—although each superpower is complex in different ways. All three illustrate the paradox of largeness. Chinese society has made recent attempts to overcome this paradox by means of birth control, by opening its borders to knowledge from abroad, and by introducing market segmentation. The result has been an increase in the degree of segmentary independence and learning within China. In the Soviet Union, however, the paradox continued to flourish unabated until the system practically broke down. The traditional insularity of the system and its overemphasis on functional differentiation have led to the centralization of political and economic activity without the concomitant exploitation of the learning potential inherent in independent and competitive segments (parties, enterprises, and interest groups). These characteristics lead to the kind of inflexibility and deficient adaptability expressed by the paradox of largeness. The United States may be proud of its openness and the philosophy and structures of conflicting and competitive segments that it upholds, but this trust that these structures are the best suited to solve problems can prevent Americans from seeing that such structures cannot solve the paradox of largeness and power. As a consequence of its largeness, the United States has developed many self-steering mechanisms at the local and regional level. The attention of the public—and of the politicians who rely on public consent—is focused on these events, and not on what is going on outside. Compare, in this respect, the ratio of international and local information contained in American and in Swiss or Dutch newspapers.

The "inner-directedness" of the social self-sufficiency of large societies would not in itself pose a problem if these societies were not in the position of being superpowers in relation to small societies. Virtually all societies in Western and Eastern Europe are protectorates of the superpowers, inasmuch as they are not able to defend themselves against the superpower that represents the other side. Nobody likes to have to depend on somebody else, especially if the other person is powerful and as a consequence of his size-induced self-centeredness does not really understand and care about the other. This is not a moral dilemma that can be solved by an effort on the part of the powerful "to understand others." It is, as the paradox of largeness teaches us, a sociostructural "dilemma of asymmetrical understanding," which resists even the best intentions of the powerful systems. As a consequence, they run into a threefold complex of misunderstandings. First, they do not understand the small and dependent systems to the same degree that these systems understand them. Second, they do not understand that they cannot understand the small societies sufficiently, even if they were to make an effort to do so. Third, they do not understand why the small societies think that they are misunderstood, and small societies do not understand why they are not sufficiently understood. As a result, everybody gets angry.

Turning to the paradox of evolution, at first glance there seems to be no empirical evidence that supports its existence in world society. The number of independent state-societies is increasing and the variety of their cultural patterns is very great. However, there is some diffusion of common norms—for instance, where child labor or discrimination against women is concerned—all over the world. The work of international organizations such as ILO and UNCTAD gives us an idea of what the increasing body of commonly accepted norms is like.

The trend toward a homogenization of technocultural and sociocultural patterns is even more striking, a trend that persists in both official and unofficial forms. Some might argue that in the course of the gradual expansion of homogeneity throughout world society, there has been an expanding of cultural heterogeneity as well, that is, the mixture of the diffusing modern elements with the remaining traditional elements in each society creates new and specific sociocultural patterns and lifestyles. This heterogeneity, however, is only meaningful to a certain degree because at another level of abstraction the new patterns and lifestyles that result from the mixture of the modern and the traditional merely lead once more to the homogenization of societies. They all become multifaceted societies, permitting the existence and practice of many different life-styles at a time. This coexistence of the traditional and the modern, of individualized and standardized life-styles can be described, albeit incompletely, using the concept of the "dual society." In most countries this has increasingly given way to a "multifold society."

In many countries of the Third World the modern "international" sector is declared to be the official one, whereas in others (such as Iran) and in countries of the socialist camp it forms an unofficial structure, a "second society" (Hankiss, 1985). Be this as it may, those goods, norms, and social patterns that bring about homogenization among and within societies are and must be considered to be the most modern, dynamic, and important ones—or, from the point of view of the traditionalists, the most dangerous ones.

The most remarkable aspect of societal homogenization is its asymmetric character. Unlike human reproduction, in which both sides have an equal chance to be represented in the recombination of genes, one side is almost always disadvantaged in the recombination of technocultural and sociocultural patterns. The side that offers the highest degree of complexity or the strongest combination of complexity and power dominates. In world society today this is the side of the United States. American society is the leading society in the sense that it diffuses its sociocultural patterns and products in what amounts to a one-way process. Other big countries, such as the Soviet Union, China, Japan, and Europe, do not send as many or such important things back to the United States as they receive from it. And countries in the Third World do not copy as many patterns and things from other leading societies as they do from the United States.

One explanation for this one-way dynamism is the fact that the United States, as an immigrant society, is traditionally open to the most dynamic elements of other countries. It does not import them as products or institutions but integrates them in the form of the personal "know-how" of the pizzamaker, the rocket engineer, or the scientist. World society receives the dynamic elements imported into the United States back from the United States in a transformed and enriched form.

The last step in the homogenization of world society would, of course, be the disappearance of state borders. In reality, the borders are only being eroded, not abolished. Diversity is covertly being eroded while officially the diversity and independence of state societies is respected.

If the significant variety of different societies is decreasing, then evolution must also be losing its capacity to recombine and select variety at the level of society. But why should recombination and selection not be going on "below" and "above" the level of state society? Below—or, rather, in addition to—the level of state society exist functionally specific segments of enterprises and households, universities and schools, etc., that could still exist in the absence of the nation-state. They could maintain their selectivity by competing with one other: one scientific community pitted against another, and both against religious communities. The public, be it by means of market or quasi-market procedures, could be the arbiter in such processes of selection. But could not a world state play the role of arbiter in exactly the way that the existing nation-state does? After all, the nation-state at present already takes care of the functioning of markets, protects the family, allocates research funds to different scientific enterprises, and so on. An evolutionary superstate could quite plausibly guarantee the maintenance of the evolutionary potential for diversity.

However, a world state could not substitute for the regulatory functions of the state itself. Where politics and the judiciary are concerned, a loss of diversity seems inevitable. Legitimately, there can only be one political and legal order prevalent in one place at one time (although there may be federal and communal substructures). Thus, a supranational world state would mean the end of existing alternatives and competition with regard to political and judicial cultures. In other words, only a variety of nation-states or camps of nation-states can guarantee the evolution of political and legal structures by recombination and selection of alternatives.

A superstate efficiently enforcing common norms in the face of the conflicting interests of nation-states is one of the most hopeful visions for world peace. Unfortunately, this vision is inextricably bound up with the paradox of uniqueness and efficiency. The more efficient a world state is, the more it destroys its own functional alternatives, that is, the environment of systems of the same kind that have to cooperate as one learning system in order to find out what the appropriate functions and limitations of the state are. In addition, as far as nonstate functions and institutions are concerned, even a superstate aiming at diversity runs the risk of favoring either the wrong alternatives or too few alternatives. Finally, in view of the accumulation of regulatory power necessary for the management of world society, a superstate simply magnifies the risks implied in social largeness and power.

In opposition to the prevailing trends in world society toward both large supersociety and a decreasing variety of technocultural and sociocultural patterns among societies, is there a chance for niche societies to escape the paradoxes of largeness, evolution, and uniqueness, even if only to a certain degree?

Niches, at the level of societal evolution, do not exist by virtue of nature or fate alone; they can be made by social effort. An effort certainly is necessary if niche societies are to become a successful alternative to the supersociety. This effort has to take into consideration the conditions, mentioned earlier, under which niche systems arise, if these systems are to be relevant from the point of view of evolution. Niche societies should not be so small, powerless, and niche-adapted that they are reduced to an existence of museumlike preservation. They should be complex and open enough to enter into a limited but fruitful exchange with the supersociety.

Primitive societies may be so far removed from modern societies in this respect that they do not even belong to the same species, as Giesen (1980) has argued. Consequently, the chances of finding niches that are meaningful to evolution increase with the levels of complexity and power of societies. And niches cannot be found within the boundaries of the nation-state or a federation of states alone; the concept of variable niches presupposes a flexibility of changing coalitions. For example, there may be a European-Arab niche with regard to the development of solar energy but not in terms of a common religious pattern.

The concept of niche evolution at the societal level has its own paradox: It is successful to the extent that niche systems are powerful enough to protect themselves against world trends and that they have complex alternatives to offer to complex mainstream problems. Unfortunately, the success of niche systems serves also to reproduce the paradoxes of largeness and power and of evolution within the niches.

But these are the problems of the day after tomorrow. The problem facing niche societies today is the extreme difficulty of developing alternative technocultural and sociocultural patterns in opposition to the dominating and homogenizing trend that emanates from and favors the leading societies. There seems to be a law of increasing power differences. Innovations that are disseminated by the leading countries to the rest of the world strengthen the superiority of the leading societies for three reasons.

1. The leading societies are superior in terms of resources and so their own innovations and follow-up innovations have a competitive edge.
2. The leading societies also have a competitive advantage inasmuch as the innovation is a product of their own societal culture, which is likely to encounter difficulties or "implantation costs" in other societies.
3. The leading societies have, in most cases, an advantage of power: power is the chance to promote a solution to the disadvantage of better solutions.

In this situation the development of niche societies not only amounts to creating a countervailing power. It also means a change in competition in the sense that niche societies reject the worldwide competition for those patterns and solutions that are offered by the leading societies. For the reasons just outlined, to accept this competition would be to continually strengthen and increase the differences in power and welfare between the leading societies and the rest of the world. The chance open to the niche society is not to avoid all competition but to offer indirect competition in the form of different sociocultural patterns problem-solving devices. Niche societies want to be free in their choice of realms of competition.

Although most of us cherish values of pluralism and multiculturalism, in the final instance we are hardly prepared to accept the images of niche societies that are really their own. Fundamentalism in Iran is usually interpreted as a backlash against modernization processes that were enforced in that country too quickly and too strictly. The common view is that it constitutes a temporary obstacle to further modernization. But perhaps we should accept it as a valid and valuable sociocultural pattern of its own.

As I see it, the concept of niche evolution is a necessary theoretical and political complement to the prevailing concept of a functional differentiation that culminates in the vision of a supersociety. Admittedly, the obstacles and resistances to the realization of niche societies are stronger than the forces in its favor. Any planned effort will probably not be enough if it is not supported by the tacit work of the paradoxes I discussed in this chapter, paradoxes that can be seen as the self-regulating mechanisms of social systems and that function to ensure that the "trees do not grow up into skies," as a German saying would have it.

REFERENCES

Blau, Peter M. 1977. *Inequality and heterogeneity: A primitive theory of social structure.* New York: Free Press.

Boulding, Kenneth E. 1978. *Ecodynamics: A new theory of societal evolution.* Beverly Hills: Sage.

Deutsch, Karl. 1966. *The nerves of government.* New York: Free Press.

Eigen, Manfred, and Peter Schuster. 1979. *The hypercycle: A principle of natural self-organization.* Berlin: Springer.

Giesen, Bernard. 1980. *Makrosoziologie: Eine evolutionstheoretische Einführung.* Hamburg: Hoffmann und Campe.

Hankiss, Elemer. 1985. The "second society": The reduplication of the social paradigm in contemporary societies: The case of Hungary. Budapest. Working Papers, Institute of Sociology, Hungarian Academy of Sciences.

Hofstadter, Douglas R. 1979. *Gödel, Escher, Bach: An eternal golden braid.* New York: Basic Books.

Klapp, Orin E. 1978. *Opening and closing: Strategies of information adaptation in society.* Cambridge: Cambridge University Press.

Luard, Evan. 1976. *Types of international society.* New York: Free Press.

Parsons, Talcott, 1966. *Societies: Evolutionary and comparative perspectives.* Englewood Cliffs, N.J.: Prentice-Hall.

Simon, Herbert A. [1969] 1981. *The sciences of the artificial.* Cambridge: MIT Press.

PART FIVE

International and Global Themes

External and Internal Factors in Theories of Social Change

Neil J. Smelser

One of the hallmarks of human history in the late twentieth century is the increasing internationalization of the world: in production, trade, finance, technology, threats to security, communications, research, education, and culture. One major consequence of this trend is that the mutual penetration of economic, political, and social forces among the nations of the world is increasingly salient. And it may also be the case that the governments of nation-states are progressively losing degrees of direct control over the global forces that affect them. For social scientists the phenomenon of internationalization poses a conceptual challenge: to rethink the fundamental assumption, long established in our disciplines, that the primary unit of analysis is the nation, the society, or the culture.

In light of these circumstances it might be helpful to take a look at a number of theoretical strands in the study of social change over the past century to see how theorists have addressed the issue of the relative importance of external and internal factors in the genesis, course of development, and consequences of social change. This is what I propose to do in this chapter. I examine these strands in the broadest sense and will not consider theoretical details or empirical studies that have flowed from them. One of my conclusions is that the history of the theory of social change in the past century has been something of an oscillation—perhaps even a dialectic—between theories stressing the endogenous and theories stressing the exogenous. Toward the end of the chapter I turn to the theme of increasing internationalization and give an indication of the major dimensions involved in the study of external and internal forces of change.

Initially, I would like to clarify the use of the terms "external" and "internal"—or "endogenous" and "exogenous." Some theorists use "external" to refer to nonsocial determinants of social change, determinants such as climate, availability of resources, and biological forces. My usage differs from this. I use the term "external" to refer to influences emanating from the presence of other societies in a given society's environment, and I concentrate on international, intersocietal, and intercultural forces. By "internal" I refer to the mutual interrelations of values, social structure, and classes as they are institutionalized in a given society. In making this external-internal distinction, however, I would like to be clear that it cannot be regarded as a fixed, dichotomous one; some of the most interesting questions to be raised about the two kinds of forces are how they interact with each other and how the distinction sometimes breaks down as the two kinds of forces fuse to generate or block social change.

1. THE STARTING POINT: CLASSICAL EVOLUTIONARY THEORY

The fundamental presumption of evolutionary theory, which has dominated social thought in the last half of the nineteenth century, is the notion that civilization has progressed by a series of stages from a backward to an advanced state. The characteristics of the stages differ from theorist to theorist—Comte, Maine, Bachofen, etc.—but the central idea of progress informs them all. To distill out the essential themes of this approach, I sketch the line of argument taken up in Lewis Henry Morgan's *Ancient Society* ([1877] 1963).

The subtitle of *Ancient Society* reveals its essence: *Researches in Lines of Human Progress from Savagery through Barbarism to Civilization.* Morgan, like other evolutionists, regarded human history as advancing through several stages. These stages constitute "a natural as well as a necessary sequence of progress" ([1877] 1963, 3). The main defining characteristic of each stage is the type of inventions that society used to gain its subsistence. Thus, the lower stage of savagery extends from the beginnings of the human race to the time that people began to rely on fish for subsistence; the middle stage of savagery began with fish subsistence and the use of fire and moved into the upper status of savagery with the invention of the bow and arrow. The analysis continues in a similar fashion through three stages of barbarism to the state of civilization, which began with the use of a written alphabet. In addition to technology, other institutions also developed by stages. In the period of savagery government was organized into gentes, or clans, and "followed down, through the advancing forms of this institution, to the establishment of political society" ([1877] 1963, 5). And a parallel story of progress is to be found in religion, architecture, property, kinship, and other institutions. In fact, most of Morgan's efforts were devoted to presenting evidence of "human progress . . . through successive periods, as it is revealed by inventions and discoveries, and by the growth of ideas of government, of the family, and of property" ([1877] 1963, 6).

For the purposes of this chapter the characteristics of this kind of theory are the following:

1. The linearity and regularity of change through distinct stages.
2. The presence of a mechanism (for example, technology) that is internal to society as the impetus to change.
3. The assumption of a functional fit in society such that different institutions cluster consistently at each stage and substage.
4. The absence of assumptions regarding any kind of influence of one society on others. In fact, Morgan was not interested in societies but rather society considered as a whole.
5. The implicit compression of comparative study and the study of social change. Other contemporary societies (for example, aboriginal Australia or tribal North America) are regarded as resting at some earlier stage of evolution when compared with the more advanced societies.

One interpretation of the works of Marx is that his theory shares many of the fundamentals of classical evolutionary thought. His thinking is characterized by a distinctive number of stages (Asiatic, feudal, capitalist, etc.), and there is a distinct internal mechanism for transition from one stage to another. This mechanism, the development of economic and societal contradictions, is of course very different than that stressed by others. In his work on the evolution of the family and the state, Engels ([1884] 1969) relied heavily on Morgan's evolutionary scheme. Elsewhere in Marx, as I note later, we see evidence of his appreciation of the international dimension of economic forces.

2. REACTIONS TO CLASSICAL EVOLUTIONARY THOUGHT AND NEW FORMULATIONS

One does not choose classical evolutionary thought as a starting point because of its theoretical sophistication or its empirical adequacy (indeed, it is one of the few identifiable traditions of thought that can be said to have been definitely discredited); one chooses it because of its intellectual dominance at the time, and because its distinctive features set the agenda—the issues to be addressed—for a great deal of theoretical work in social change that has been created since that time. This latter point is more clearly observed by the range of theories of social change that appeared in the early part of the twentieth century. Consider the following illustrations:

2.1. Diffusionism

The implication of an evolutionary theory like Morgan's is that a cultural item or institutional complex appears when a given society is "ready" for it in terms of its evolutionary stage. The diffusionists' challenge to this point of view was to demonstrate that many cultural items did not develop independently in different cultures but were borrowed from abroad, sometimes at a great geographical distance. Very painstaking studies were made, showing how myths, calendars, costume styles, maize cultivation, and other items have traveled in intricate paths around the world. Kroeber (1923, 197–98) summarized the force of the principle of diffusion as follows:

> The vast majority of culture elements have been learned by each nation from other peoples, past and present . . . even savages shift their habitations and acquire new neighbors. At times they capture women and children from one another. Again they intermarry; and they almost invariably maintain some sort of trade relations with at least some of the adjacent peoples. . . . There is thus every *a priori* reason why diffusion could be expected to have had a very large part in the formation of primitive and barbarous as well as advanced culture.

Viewed in relation to classical evolutionary thought, diffusionist theory constituted simultaneously a polemic and a revision along three lines: first, consistent with the positive upswelling in the early decades of the twentieth century, it eschewed the speculative heights of evolutionism and insisted on careful, limited, empirical descriptions; second, it constituted a fundamental critique of the linearity of evolutionists' conceptions of change by arguing that stages could be modified or even skipped through the borrowing and adopting process; and third, it explicitly introduced an intercultural dimension, showing that change was a product of importation. That emphasis has survived to the present; it is evident in studies that are preoccupied with the transfer of technology.

Yet the emphasis on the borrowing of things led the diffusionists toward a very limited conception of social change. They seldom asked why certain items diffused and others did not, how items were modified after being incorporated into a new cultural setting, or what new internal changes were stimulated by borrowed items, even though a theorist such as Lowie (1937) was aware of these issues. In short, diffusionists inquired very little into the social-system contexts of either the originating or the borrowing cultures. In particular, other types of intercultural or intersocietal influences on change, such as economic or political domination, were almost completely absent from diffusionist theory.

2.2. Classical Functionalism

The classical functional anthropologists and sociologists shared with the diffusionists the conviction that evolutionary theory was speculative and ignored actual history, but their chief polemic was of a different sort. They believed that the evolutionists were asking the wrong kinds of questions in their efforts to explain the presence, absence, or clustering of cultural and institutional elements in societies. It is not important, functionalists argued, to know about the historical origin of a particular element; this tells us nothing about how the structure fits into and contributes to the ongoing life of the society. It tells us little about the structure's current functions. Radcliffe-Brown stated the functionalist argument in general terms as follows:

> Individual human beings . . . are connected by a definite set of social relations into an integrated whole. The continuity of the *social structure,* like that of an organic structure, is not destroyed by changes in the units. Individuals may leave the society, by death or otherwise; others may enter it. The continuity of structure is maintained by the process of social life, which consists of the activities and interactions of the individual human beings and of the organized groups into which they are united. The social life of the community is here defined as the *functioning* of the social structure. The *function* of any recurrent activity, such as the punishment of a crime or a funeral ceremony, is the part it plays in the social life as a whole and therefore the contribution it makes to the maintenance of structural continuity (1952, 180, emphases mine).

The criticisms of the position of the functionalists from the standpoint of the study of social change are well known. Because of their stress on stability, integration, and social equilibrium, functionalists were not interested in theories of social change and lacked the conceptual tools to analyze or generate such theories. (Radcliffe-Brown [1935, 395–97] contended that this criticism was not justified because there is no more reason why the functionalist approach precludes the study of the growth of civilizations than there is reason why physiology—the study of functioning organisms—precludes the study of embryology, paleontology, and evolution.) Also because of these preoccupations, functionalists were less likely to study various kinds of conflict in society, especially conflict as a particularly powerful engine for change. The same preoccupations also intensified the functionalists' focus on the internal relations of culture and institutions in the life of a society. External impingements played little or no role in their theory or empirical studies. Be that as it may, it might be instructive to refer to two theorists with functionalist presuppositions: Ogburn and Malinowski. Both of these theorists were interested in processes of social change and one, Malinowski, incorporated both a dimension of conflict and a dimension of international domination (colonialism) into the picture.

Ogburn was hostile to classical evolutionary theory, asserting that "the inevitable series of stages in the development of social institutions has not only not been proven but has been disproven" (1922, 57). He further argued that the basis for the disproof is found in the hard facts of history and ethnography, which show that the evolutionists' generalizations are faulty (1922, 66). Furthermore, any conclusions about evolution must rest not on impressionistic history and anthropology but on a review of the "actual facts of early evolution" (1922, 66).

In place of grand theories of evolution Ogburn proposed a theory that was simultaneously positivistic and functionalist. It was positivistic because it stressed measurable facts and trends, eschewed speculative theory not based on these, and insisted on theories of limited range. It was functionalist because it stressed the systematic interrelatedness of social institutions. In addition, Ogburn's theory discarded the functionalist theory of short-term equilibration and substituted for it the notion of "cultural lag," summarized as follows:

> Not all parts of our organization are changing at the same speed or at the same time. Some are rapidly moving forward while others are lagging. These unequal rates of change in economic life, in government, in education, in science, and religion, make zones of danger and points of tension. (President's Research Committee on Social Trends 1933, xiii)

More particularly, Ogburn argued that changes in "material culture" (technology and economic organization) forever outrun changes in "adaptive culture" (religion, family, art, law, and custom), and the consequences of this chronic lag are a parade of social problems and the danger of social disorganization.

The Ogburn formulation is instructive for the student of social change because it demonstrates how the elimination of one fundamental functionalist premise and the substitution of another permits Ogburn to generate a theory of social tensions or contradictions that is not totally removed from Marx's theory of contradictions, which, although derived from a different set of first premises, also involves the notion of increasing discrepancy and the relationship between material and institutional forces. At the same time Ogburn retained the functionalist view that society is bounded. Although he acknowledged the international diffusion of technology, the dominant thrust of his theory is on the internal consequences of change and social stability in societies.

Malinowski, one of the founders of classical functionalism and not especially noted for his contributions to the theory of social change, turned his attention to cultural change in his last work (1945), published posthumously. The setting of this work was intersocietal, dealing with the subject of culture contact and change in the African colonial societies. In his analysis Malinowski retained one assumption of the functionalist perspective, namely, that cultural traits cannot be studied as if scattered and unrelated to one another because they cluster in institutions that have interrelated material, legal, and cultural elements. This assumption implies that change occurs in patterns of elements, not single elements alone. At the same time, however, he admonished against treating a colonial society as a "well-integrated whole"; it is a multiplicity of contrasting and conflicting cultural elements. Any conception of a well-integrated community in the contact situation would "ignore such facts as the color bar, the permanent rift which divides the two partners in change and keeps them apart in church and factory, in matters of mine labor and political influence" (1945, 15).

The first basis for instability in colonial societies is that they are dominated politically, which refers to the "impact of a higher, active culture upon a simpler, more passive one" (1945, 15). But this impact is not a matter of the simple transfer of Western prototypes or the retention of African prototypes. Rather it is a dynamic fusion of the two types into qualitatively new forms:

> The concept of the mechanical incorporation of elements from one culture into another does not lead us beyond the initial preparatory stages, and even then on subtler analysis breaks down. What really takes place is an interplay of specific contact forces: race prejudice, political and economic imperialism, the demand for segregation, the safeguarding of a European standard of living, and the African reaction to this. (1945, 23)

Accordingly, Malinowski viewed colonial societies in terms of what he called his "three-column approach," which delineated three kinds of social forces: (1) "the impinging culture with its institutions, intentions, and interests"; (2) "the reservoir of indigenous custom, belief, and living traditions"; and (3) "the processes of contact and change, where members of the two cultures cooperate, conflict, or compromise" (1945, vii).

Malinowski viewed the relations among these several forces as unstable for two reasons. First, the intruding European culture and the surviving African cultures are not evenly matched. He described the European culture as "higher" and "active" and the African cultures as "simpler" and "passive." Second, the existence of conflicting institutional patterns makes for cultural contradictions and pressures for change:

> The African in transition finds himself in a no-man's land, where his old tribal stability, his security as to economic resources, which was safe-

guarded under the old regime by the solidarity of kinship, have disappeared. The new culture, which has prompted him to give up tribalism,
has promised to raise him by education to a standard of life worthy of an
educated man. But it has not given him suitable and satisfactory equiva-
lents. It has been unable to give him rights of citizenship regarded as due
an educated Westerner; and it has discriminated against him socially on
practically every point of the ordinary routine of life. (1945, 60)

Malinowski predicted that the incessant pressures of European culture
and the various forces of culture contact and change would "sooner or
later . . . gradually . . . engulf and supersede the whole of [the surviving
African tradition]" (1945, 81).

Malinowski's theory of culture contact and change constitutes an
especially interesting recombination of ingredients of the following
sort: (1) the theories of classical evolution were largely irrelevant by
now to his enterprise; (2) like the classical functionalists, he adopted the
postulate of societal interrelatedness, but, unlike them, he built in a
postulate of constant conflict and contradiction, with equilibrium never
reached; and (3) like the diffusionists, he acknowledged the salience of
intercultural or international contact as a determinant of change, but
unlike them, he concentrated on patterns of culture rather than dis-
crete cultural items, stressed the systemic context into which they are
incorporated, and emphasized the dimension of political, economic,
and cultural domination that colonialism implies.

2.3 Marx-Lenin

Earlier I noted some resemblances between classical evolutionary theory
and Marxian thought, particularly on the internal genesis of change.
That picture is clearly incomplete. Marx forever stressed the international character of capitalism and its bourgeois and proletarian classes.
And he provided more specific insights than this. Competition provides
the impulse for capitalist expansion, and the most potent strategy in the
competitive struggle is to increase productivity through technological
advance. Before this strategy reaches its ultimate limit, one final strategy
is available. Marx found the limits for any given innovation—or set of
innovations—in the size of the market. No market can sustain feverish
overproduction and this inhibits a market's capacity to absorb increased
production. Industrial expansion creates both the need for more raw
materials for itself and the need for larger markets for its own products.
The natural consequence is to internationalize capitalism. Capitalists destroy the handicraft industries of backward countries with their cheap
products and force them into the production of raw materials. In this
way a "new international division of labor, a division suited to the requirements of the chief centers of modern industry springs up, and converts

one part of the globe into a chiefly agricultural field of production, for supplying the other part which remains a chiefly industrial field" (Marx [1867] 1949, 451).

In applying this principle to India Marx interpreted the British efforts to unify that country politically and to build a network of railroads as a strategy to convert India into a supplier of cotton and other raw materials for British industries (1853a). Marx also predicted that the introduction of railways should set the stage for a more general growth in India that would, in turn, dissolve the caste system that had posed such obstacles to economic development. With respect to China, Marx (1853b) attributed the political upheaval in mid-nineteenth-century China to the economic penetration of the mainland by capitalism. In addition, Marx commented on the vulnerability of the international dependency that arises from the establishment of trade between the capitalist nations and their economic suppliers of raw materials (1853b).

Lenin ([1917] 1939) carried the theme of internationalization further. The starting point of his analysis was that competition as the driving engine of capitalism was disappearing. The main reason for this was the development of monopolies that controlled raw materials, prices, and production by virtue of the gigantic size of firms. (Marx also foresaw this kind of concentration in his later works.) Banks had also become monopolized and formed links with industry to create a system of finance capital. Through the export of capital—as contrasted with the earlier pattern of the export of goods—this system had "divided up the world" economically. This development was accompanied by a political division of the world through colonial domination, which "*completed* the seizure of unoccupied territories on our planet" ([1917] 1939, 76, emphasis in original). In keeping with the fundamentals of earlier Marxian formulations, however, Lenin described the imperialist developments of the late nineteenth and early twentieth centuries as "the highest stage of capitalism" (invoking the evolutionary logic of Marx), found these developments to be "parasitic" and replete with contradictions peculiar to capitalism (such as the high cost of living and the oppression of the cartels arising from monopolization), and argued that imperialism was a transition "from the capitalist system to a higher social-economic order" (again reminiscent of the evolutionary imagery and ultimate optimism of Marx).

The Marx-Lenin perspective moves furthest in the international direction, envisioning the world as a single sytem at least temporarily dominated by a single economic system (capitalism). The viewpoint tends to regard internal economic and class developments—for example, the destruction of the Indian caste system and the "embourgeoisment" of the British working classes in the late nineteenth century—as a more-or-less

direct result of external developments occasioned by the internationalization of capitalism. The internationalism of the Marx-Lenin perspective
differs from the internationalism of both the diffusionists and Malinowski
with respect to the causal mechanisms involved: it identifies specific economic mechanisms (the export of goods, the export of capital) supplemented by specific political mechanisms (colonialism), whereas the diffusionist perspective rests on the imagery of borrowing or transfer and
Malinowski's perspective envisions the operative mechanisms as mainly
political domination (colonialism) and the accompanying cultural contact.

2.4 Weber

Weber, too, was engaged in a certain dialogue with classical evolutionary
thought (including its Marxist variant). His particular complaint was that
such formulations are too general and abstract (and therefore unrealistic) because they do not take the variations found in historical and
comparative study into account:

> [Weber's image of "economy and society"] drew the lines against Social
> Darwinism, Marxism and other isms of the time. Weber rejected the preva-
> lent evolutionary and mono-causal theories, whether idealist or materialist,
> mechanistic or organicist; he fought both the reductionism of social scien-
> tists and the surface approach of historians, both the persistent search for
> hidden "deeper" causes and the ingrained aversion against historically
> transcendent concepts. He took it for granted that the economic structure
> of a group was one of its major if variable determinants and that society
> was an arena for group conflicts. (Roth 1968, xxix)

This polemical position, of course, posed a challenge for Weber, namely,
to formulate some kind of general statements about society and social
processes while at the same time respecting historical and comparative
variations. Weber took a middle position in relation to this challenge,
identifying relatively coherent historical constellations of economic, political, and social arrangements. With respect to processes of social
change, Weber identified a number of ideal-typical processes, which are
best characterized as semiautonomous developments arising from particular group, institutional, or cultural constellations. Among these ideal-
typical processes are (1) the tendency for charismatic leadership to become routinized; (2) the aggrandizing and leveling tendencies associated
with bureaucracy; (3) the transformational tendencies associated with
belief systems such as ascetic Protestantism; and (4) the general tendencies of coherent cultural systems (religious tenets, musical styles) to move
in the direction of rationalization. Considerable controversy remains,
however, as to how far these processes identified as typical should be
interpreted as implying a more general or evolutionary emphasis.

All four of the developmental directions noted in the foregoing paragraph are internal in the sense that they involve the unfolding of certain cultural or organizational principles, sometimes in relation to exigencies that are encountered. A broader reading of Weber's comparative-historical studies and economic sociology reveals, however, that he was fully sensitive to intersocietal and international influences and that he gave them a central place in his analyses. His historical analyses make reference to war, population movements, international economic developments, and the diffusion of religion as the directional forces of change. His "general economic history" (Weber [1920] 1950) lectures systematically included international factors such as trade in antiquity and medieval times, changes in the prices of the "international" metals, gold, and silver, colonial exploitation in the eighteenth century and the rise of the great colonial companies. And, to give Weber equal time with Marx, his diagnosis of India in 1916 stressed the British penetration:

> Today the Hinduist caste order is profoundly shaken. Especially in the district of Calcutta, old Europe's major gateway, many norms have practically lost their force. The railroads, the taverns, the changing occupational stratification, the concentration of labor through imported industry, colleges, et cetera, have all contributed their part. The 'commuters to London,' that is, those who studied in Europe and who freely maintained social intercourse with Europeans, used to become outcasts up to the last generation; but more and more this pattern is disappearing. And it has been impossible to introduce caste coaches on the railroads in the fashion of the American railroad cars or waiting rooms which segregate 'White' from 'Black' in the Southern States. All caste relations have been shaken, and the stratum of intellectuals bred by the English are here, as elsewhere, bearers of a specific nationalism. They will greatly strengthen this slow and irresistible process. (Weber [1916] 1970, 397)

Even down to the peculiar importance of railroads, Weber's diagnosis bears a striking resemblance to Marx's, even though there were divergencies in identifying causal mechanisms and the general dynamics of change.

This brief review of the major theories of social change and development, most of which had crystallized by the early decades of the twentieth century, reveals that they contained virtually all the elements of the theories of social change that were to develop in the post–World War II period. Among these elements are the neoevolutionary perspectives embodied in some versions of modernization theory, the consequences of irregular development, international political and economic domination, the crucial role of international finance and capital, and international dependency. The originality of the later period lies not so much in the discovery or invention of new elements of change but rather in novel recombinations of elements that had been earlier appreciated and stressed.

3. THE INTERWAR HIATUS AND THE RISE OF DEVELOPMENT/ MODERNIZATION THEORY

Despite the fact that some of the works referred to in the preceding section were written in the period between World War I and World War II, that period must be regarded as a barren one from the standpoint of social change theory. The two most notable contributions of the period were those of Kroeber (1944) and Sorokin (1937). Both of these theories had to do with the rise and fall of whole civilizations and both were "emanationist" in the sense that social and cultural change was regarded as the unfolding of possibilities contained in fundamental cultural premises or assumptions. The causes for the relative stagnation of interest in development and change are no doubt complex, but certainly among them are the fact that much of American social science was preoccupied with the short-term crises of economic depression and war and much of European social science was brought to a standstill, if not destroyed by the crises of economic depression, fascism, and war.

In the 1950s the social sciences witnessed a great birth of interest in the subjects of growth, development, and modernization, and much of this interest focused on societies that were referred to as "underdeveloped," "developing," or simply "new." Among economists there was a surge of interest in "growth economics." Sociologists theorized about the distinctive institutional characteristics of modernity. Political scientists expanded their comparative sights and included kinship, tribal arrangements, communities, and other "premodern" political arrangements in their scope of interest. Although development/modernization theory has been characterized as a coherent entity by subsequent critics, it was in fact quite diverse with respect to its identification of what is distinctively modern, what mechanisms make for modernization, and what the obstacles to modernization are.

One variant of modernization theory involved a kind of resuscitation of the *Gemeinschaft-Gesellschaft* distinction (or related distinctions, such as Weber's traditional-modern, Durkheim's mechanical-organic, or Redfield's folk-urban), which was then used to characterize the modernization process. Some (Hoselitz 1960; Levy 1966) made extensive use of Parsons's pattern-variables and regarded the essence of modernization as the displacement of ascriptive standards by achievement standards, particularistic ties by universalistic ones, and diffuse and inclusive personal relationships by more functionally specific ones, and so on. Parsons himself (1971) made some use of these distinctions in his writings on development, but in the end the concept that played the most central role for him was the idea of structural differentiation—between the family and the workplace, between religion and the state, between the polity and the economy—as the hallmark of development (Parsons 1961). Subsequently, Parsons generalized his views of change into a neoevolutionary scheme that regarded evolution as adaptive upgrading through economic growth, structural differentiation, the inclusion of diverse social groups and classes, and the generalization of values (1971).

The modernization literature yielded a kind of composite picture of what is involved in the process: Traditional religious systems tend to lose influence. Often powerful nonreligious ideologies, such as nationalism, arise. Traditional privileges and authority become less important and the basis of the class system shifts to personal achievement and merit. The family ceases to be the main unit of economic production. Extended family and kin groups break into smaller units. Personal choice, not the dictates of parents, becomes the basis for courtship and marriage. In education the literacy rate increases greatly and formal educational institutions develop at all levels. At the same time, the mass media serve as a vast educational resource and information channel. Informal customs and mores decay as new techniques of social control and systems of formal law arise. New forms of political organization (for example, political parties) and more complex systems of administration develop. Some scholars made the theoretical and empirical case that there is such a thing as a "modern man," who is created by institutions such as the factory and the school.

> [The modern man] is an informed participant citizen; he has a marked sense of personal efficacy; he is highly independent and autonomous in his relations to traditional sources of influence, especially when he is making basic decisions about how to conduct his personal affairs; he is ready for new experiences and ideas, that is, he is relatively open-minded and cognitively flexible. (Inkeles and Smith 1974, 290)

Modernization theorists also identified obstacles to the process, mainly in the traditional religious, communal, and kinship forms. Moore, for example, argued that the kinship system in nonindustrial societies "perhaps . . . offers the most important single impediment to individual mobility, not only through the competing claims of kinsmen upon the potential industrial recruit but also through the security offered in established patterns of mutual responsibility" (1951, 24).

One interesting variant of the growth literature of the 1950s was the psychological theory of entrepreneurs. Many observers regarded the entrepreneur as the major driving force of development. McClelland (1961), building on Weber's theory of the Protestant ethic, suggested that the key motivation of entrepreneurs is a need for achievement, which involves an interest in exercising skill in medium-risk situations and a desire for concrete signs of successful performance. This need, moreover, develops in the period of early socialization, when the child is exposed to self-reliance training and high standards of performance. McClelland also argued that the combination of a loving mother with a nondominant father was important in fostering the need for achievement. Although it also relies on child-rearing patterns and motivation, the theory of Hagen (1962) is more complicated than McClelland's. Hagen argued that stable traditional societies generally employ authoritarian child-rearing practices that develop passive noninnovative personality types. When such societies are shaken by external disturbance (such as colonial domination), the first response is a kind of "retreatism" that manifests itself in the family as a decline of the father's status and an enhancement of the mother's status. This in turn "frees" the son from a repressive father in the subsequent generation and releases creative and innovative energies in the economy.

In the 1960s and the 1970s modernization theory was subjected to a vast array of specific and general criticisms. I list only those that have the most direct relevance for the themes of this chapter:

1. Many observers argued that modernization theory is Western-centric and erroneously regards development as a process whereby developing societies will converge toward a common model. Certainly some of the statements and analyses of functionalist theories can be characterized in this way. Lerner, for example, defined modernization simply as "the process of social change whereby less developed societies acquire characteristics common to more developed societies" (1958, 386). The work of Kerr et al. (1960) on industrial relations systems argued that a number of historically distinct patterns were evolving toward a common one, despite the persistence of ideological and political differences among nations. Goode (1963) argued that, despite vast cultural differences in kinship, the modernization process—mainly industrialization and urbanization—pressed heretofore diverse family structures in the direction of the conjugal type and made for a narrowing of national differences in family-related behavior, such as divorce rates.

    Gusfield (1967) was one of the most forceful critics of the modernization perspective. He challenged statements found in the modernization literature that traditional societies are static and unchanging; he pointed to the heterogeneity of different traditional forms. Most important, he argued that the old and the new are not always in conflict. He argued that modern institutions do not simply replace traditional ones; often the two types reinforce each other. He stressed the blends and compromises that different cultures achieve in processes of development. His critique echoes the "historicist" elements of Weber's earlier polemic against classical evolutionary theory. Bendix, also criticizing the implicit evolutionary conceptualizations of modernization as a uniform process, defined modernization as "a type of social change which originated in the industrial revolution of England, 1760–1830, and in the political revolution of France, 1794" ([1964] 1977). Modernization is a historically specific process that contrasts sharply with the experience of "follower" societies who struggle to narrow the gap between themselves and those nations that have already modernized. And Dore, focusing on factory organization and labor relations in Japan, argued that because more advanced technology was available in the case of Japan—among other resources—it could skip, as it were, many of the historical processes pragmatically worked through by Britain in its development of factory organization (Dore 1973). The notion that the developing countries have a range of technology, educational techniques, types of mass communication, etc., potentially at their disposal—and that the developing West did not—is a position reminiscent of the diffusionist critique of classical evolutionary theory, and, similarly, results in a greater stress on the historical diversity of developmental processes.

2. Other observers have argued that modernization theory ignores the political dimension, particularly group conflict. In one respect development/modernization theory can be regarded as a kind of dynamic part of the functionalist perspective, namely, it regarded both traditional societies and modern societies as having more-or-less coherent and consistent cultural and institutional patterns. Insofar as the functionalist perspective in general came in for the criticism that it was either incapable or unwilling to deal with domination, dissensus, and conflict (Coser 1956; Dahrendorf, 1959), that criticism spilled over to development/modernization theory. Applied to modernization, such a criticism appears to have only partial merit. The "political system" approach adopted by Almond and Coleman (1960) focuses on "input functions," such as interest articulation and political communication, and "output functions," such as rule-making, rule application and rule adjudication. This focus connotes a lesser place for domination and coercion than in some other types of political theory. But many theorists who might on general grounds be regarded as functionalists stressed the political dimension of modernization. Eisenstadt (1964), for example, traced "breakdowns in modernization" to the specific failure of

elites to consolidate integrative mechanisms and symbols, and in general he gives a central role to political elites in the developmental process. Hoselitz (1960) drew a fundamental distinction between developmental patterns that were "autonomous," that is, relatively free from governmental intervention, and those that were "induced" by government. And Smelser, in a general essay on the process of modernization, characterized it as a conflictual process: "a three-way tug-of-war among the forces of tradition, the forces of differentiation, and the new forces of integration" (1963). One suspects that the real animus in this critique is not the complaint that the political dimension in general is ignored, but rather that a particular *type* of political situation—the domination of one economic class over others—is understressed, absent, or denied.

3. Yet another group of observers assert that development/modernization theory ignores external factors in social change. Bendix rejected the three evolutionist assumptions that closed systems (1) are either traditional or modern, (2) undergo internal differentiation, and (3) inevitably develop. These assumptions, he argued, are especially inapplicable to newly developing nations:

> If we want to explain the historical breakthrough in Europe, our emphasis will be on the continuity of intra-societal changes. If we wish to include in our account the worldwide repercussions of this breakthrough and hence the differential process of modernization, our emphasis will be on the confluence of intrinsic and extrinsic changes of social structures. ([1964] 1977, 433)

Frank asserted that most studies of development and underdevelopment "fail to take account of the economic and other relations between the metropolis and its economic colonies throughout the history of the worldwide expansion and development of the mercantilist and capitalist system" (1969, 3). The same critique underlies the basic premises of world-system theorists as well.

Although possessing some merit, this line of criticism also seems overdrawn. Hoselitz, the "developmentalist" bête noire of Frank's polemic, systematically incorporated two international dimensions into his analysis of economic growth: whether growth takes place in the context of political expansionism or in an intrinsic way, and whether the country is politically and economically dominant or satellitic. And Rostow, another target of Frank's criticisms, made a fundamental distinction between early and late developing countries:

> As a matter of historical fact a reactive nationalism—reacting against intrusion from more advanced nations—has been a most important

and powerful motive in the transition from traditional to modern societies, at least as important as the profit motive. Men holding effective authority or influence have been willing to uproot traditional societies not, primarily, to make more money but because the traditional society failed—or threatened to fail—to protect them from humiliation by foreigners. (1960, 26–27)

And Parsons, commenting on the postwar economic situation, observed the following:

> World industrialism must affect the problem of political independence for former colonial areas. It is also the primary source both of markets for many of their products and of competition for their own attempts at new lines of production. It can also be a source of technical and managerial help and financial support, and the degree and nature of control which may go with such help is always a complicated and touchy problem. (1960, 117)

Again, one suspects that the true complaint is not that development/ modernization theorists were unaware of the international dimension or that they failed to stress it; the true complaint is that they failed to acknowledge what critics regarded as one *type* of international relationship, namely, the continuing domination of world capitalism over the dependent areas of the world.

4. THE RESURGENCE OF THE INTERNATIONALIST PERSPECTIVE

The positive result of this critique of development/modernization theory was the generation of a number of alternative versions of the process of development and change. One example is Bendix's notions regarding the greater role of states and innovative ruling elites in "follower" societies than in those Western European countries that developed initially ([1964] 1977). Probably the most influential theoretical developments that emerged, however, came from a group of social scientists in Latin America. (A more general observation can be made here: as semi-autonomous academic social-science traditions develop in the Third World countries, one evident result is that international factors will receive heavier stress.) In the 1950s a number of economists associated with the Economic Commission on Latin America, notably Prebisch (1950), generated a perspective based on the primary assumption that the underdevelopment of Latin American countries rested not primarily on internal factors but on the fact that these countries were an integral part of the world economy. Prebisch proposed that the world economy could be regarded as having a "center" and a "periphery." Neoclassical economic analysis suggests that the terms of trade should be more favorable to the periphery because the increased use of technology in the center lowers prices on industrial products in relation to the agricultural products from the developing countries. The reverse has happened, however, and Prebisch thought the reason was that unions in industrialized countries prevented wages from falling and that oligopolies in the center kept prices on industrial products artificially high.

A more general perspective, "dependency theory," grew out of this approach. It is associated with the names of Cardoso, Dos Santos, Frank, and others. Cardoso's definition of dependency is as follows:

> Capitalist accumultion in dependent economies does not complete its cycle. Lacking autonomous technology, as vulgar parlance has it, and compelled therefore to utilize imported technology, dependent capitalism is crippled. . . . It is crippled because it lacks a fully developed capital goods sector. The accumulation, expansion, and self-realization of local capital requires and depends on a dynamic complement outside itself. It must insert itself into the circuit of international capitalism. (1973, 163)

Dependency, then, involves a reliance on outside capital, and the more this reliance is concentrated on one or a few other nations, the greater the vulnerability and dependency of the dependent country. Furthermore, this dependency causes the internal fragmentation of the economy's sectors. The most sophisticated dependency theorists, however, argue that only the grossest information can be gathered by focusing on only the international phenomenon of economic penetration:

> The expansion of capitalism in Bolivia and Venezuela, in Mexico or Peru, in Brazil and Argentina, in spite of having been submitted to the same global dynamic of international capitalism, did not have the same history or consequences. The differences are rooted not only in the diversity of natural resources, nor just in the different periods in which these economies have been incorporated into the international system. . . . Their explanation must also lie in the different moments at which sectors of local classes allied or clashed with foreign interests, organized different forms of state, sustained distinct ideologies, or tried to implement various policies or defined alternative strategies to cope with imperialist challenges in diverse moments of history. (Cardoso and Faletto 1969, xvii)

The dependency perspective marks not only a clear focus on international factors but also a resuscitation of the perspective of economic and political domination found in the works of Marx, Lenin, and Weber. In this sense it contrasts in another way with development/modernization theory, which lays greater stress on institutional and cultural patterning.

Another major international theory of change is "world systems theory," associated with the names of Brunel and Wallerstein. Although this approach also distinguishes between core and periphery, it identifies a semiperiphery between them as well. These formations set the stage for patterns of economic domination and competition. Wallerstein has divided the history of the capitalist economy into three broad phases, each characterized by different patterns of relations among the core, semiperiphery, and periphery, with these relations largely determining the internal economic fates of the nations in each category.

The influence of these internationalist perspectives, cast mainly in a neo-Marxist framework, has increased greatly in the social sciences in the past two decades. In 1980 the Executive Committee of the Research Committee on Economy and Society of the International Sociological Association circulated a questionnaire to all its members asking about their areas of research and perspectives used. About one hundred responses were received from scholars in a large number of nations. The areas of research most commonly mentioned were (1) the relations of social classes or groups to the economy, (2) institutions, the state, and the economy, and (3) the world system. And topics listed under the first two headings frequently referred to the international dimension. When asked, "What theoretical position do you believe is most often used in the study of economy and society?" 90 percent of the respondents responded "Marxist or neo-Marxist" (Makler, Sales, and Smelser 1982).

5. SUMMARY

Although the foregoing glimpse of the geography of social-change theory reveals a great diversity of strands that defy any simple overall characterization, it is possible to identify two cycles that bear some overall similarity to one another. The first cycle (corresponding to classical evolutionary and development/modernization theory) begins with a view of development and change that, with all the noted qualifications, tends to have the following characteristics:

1. A stress on the internal determinants of societal change.
2. A stress on the regularities and uniformities of change.
3. A stress on the convergence of developing societies toward a common model, that of the developed West.
4. A stress on institutional patterning.
5. At least implicit political conservatism.

These theories are then subjected to polemical attack and give way to a new range of emphases that contrast with the former on each count:

1. A stress on the external determinants of societal change.
2. A stress on the diversity of patterns of change.

3. A stress on the divergence and the many paths of development, with a resulting relativism.
4. A stress on economic and political domination.
5. At least implicit political radicalism.

Not all of these ingredients hang together in every subbranch of theory I have referred to. Nor are they connected to one another by a larger logic. They do, however, constitute recurrent themes. Some of the themes are quite general and occur in debates throughout the behavioral and social sciences—the themes of universalism versus relativism and general laws versus historical specificity are examples—but the dimension of internal versus external appears to be especially salient in the study of societal change.

This chapter is not the place for a sociology-of-knowledge analysis of these apparent trends, but a few speculative reflections might be in order. At one level the parade of perspectives can be seen as a partial reflection of historical trends. The colonial consolidation of the last part of the nineteenth century was, in fact, a great step in the internationalization of the world in that a multiplicity of new connections—economic, political, and cultural—were established between the colonizing and the colonized societies. One of the ideological significances of classical evolutionism was that it served as a kind of apologia, a justification of colonial domination. Theorists such as Hobson, Lenin, and Malinowski took note of this situation of international domination and built it into their analyses. Development/modernization theory grew and flourished in the immediate wake of the great decolonization period following World War II, and in one sense perhaps represented a kind of ideological hope held out to—and in many cases, adopted by—the newly independent nations of the world. Of course the hope proved to be a false one. The realities of international production, trade, finance, and politics since World War II have in fact demonstrated that the developmental fate of most countries in Latin America, Africa, and Asia is not entirely in their own hands but is dependent in large part on the strategies of firms, banks, and nations that impinge on their economies and polities. The subsequent surge of internationalist theory reflects these realities and simultaneously represents the disillusionment of those who have in earlier decades embraced the more optimistic development/modernization perspective.

It could well be the case that we will witness similar oscillations of emphasis on the internal and external when it comes to efforts to explain the dynamics of our past. With respect to understanding change in the contemporary world, however, it appears that the international dimension is here to stay and that the proper strategy is to work toward the development of interactive models that (1) pinpoint the precise kinds of international influences that are most salient: production, markets, finance, migration, the media, the threat of war; (2) identify the precise mechanisms by which international influences impact on nations' economies, institutional structures, political processes, and cultures; and (3) examine how these internal changes shape the strategies of leaders in these countries and how these strategies themselves spill over as influences on other nations of the world. We do not have such models of change readily available, in part because of the tendency of proponents of internally and externally based theories to polarize in polemical opposition to one another. The most appropriate agenda for the future, however, is to work toward the development of these kinds of synthetic or integrative models of change. To this end, I conclude by sketching what I regard as the most important dimensions of internal-external penetration and interaction in the contemporary world.

6. CONCLUSION

I focus on four dimensions of internationalization: economic, political, cultural, and what I refer to as the growth of international societal communities. In regarding the contemporary world scene, it seems essential to begin with the economic dimension, largely because it is so conspicuous and so salient. This dimension must be subdivided into several partially separable subdimensions. One subdimension is the increasing internationalization of the world economy through trade: the vicissitudes of national economies that are buffeted by international competition and fluctuating currency rates are the most evident manifestations of the magnitude of this trend. Another facet, closely related but not identical, is the internationalization of production, which refers not only to firms that open up the production of goods and services in many countries in the form of "multinationals" but also to independent firms that manufacture and export parts that are assembled elsewhere into final products. Another subdimension is the increased internationalization of capital—finance and credit—with its own distinctive set of vicissitudes. Finally, much of the migration of persons, both international and within countries, is determined by international economic forces, as opportunities open and close with changing patterns of international employment and unemployment.

The dynamics of change in this economic arena are complex and combine internal and external factors. Some shifts along the subdimensions can—in keeping with the Leninist and contemporary internalist perspectives—be laid at the door of "internal crises" of national systems of capitalism that may result from increasing costs, diminishing opportunities, and class conflict that induce firms to relocate their activities. At the same time, such crises may partially be determined by international influences, as national economies fall victim to the forces of international competition. Once these international forces are in motion, they penetrate individual economies and influence inflation, unemployment, and the general course of economic growth, stagnation, and decline. No economy is invulnerable to these effects, as both the impact of the oil shocks of the 1970s on the developed industrial economies and the impact of the flattening of the oil market on the producing countries— including the Soviet Union—demonstrate. The contemporary debt situation in the world tells the same story. Generated in part by the flow of petrodollars into Western banks and then their channeling to countries like Brazil, Argentina, Mexico, Poland, and Yugoslavia, the great burden of international debt has in one respect brought the debtor countries to their economic knees as they have had to divert much of their national income to debt servicing. At the same time, this debt has generated a precarious situation for the lender banks and countries, who face imminent crisis if defaulting becomes widespread. The result is a kind of mutually dependent standoff, held in place by the uneasy mutual interest that all parties have in avoiding unmanageable financial instability, if not collapse.

If we assume that the contemporary international economy and the various national economies constitute one system, this system is operating according to a semiautonomous logic of its own. Such an observation, however, fails to notice the essential political dimension of that system. In many respects the state is a kind of fragile balance wheel between the international and national economies. Not immediately responsible for fluctuations in import-export ratios and with very limited control over the international fluctuations of currency rates, states—as guarantors of the integrity of the national economy—must meet accumulated obligations either directly or through borrowing. In addition, in the newly industrializing and Third World economies the state is the agency to which falls the task of executing and implementing—or resisting—the strictures imposed by other national governments and international banking agencies, such as the International Monetary Fund. In this role the state has less control over the fate of its economy—and therefore its own political fate—than before.

However, the state has also become a stronger agency. Because it is cognizant of its own vulnerability, the state tends to insert itself into the economic process with greater assertiveness in the interests of its own survival: assertiveness with respect to encouraging the productivity and exporting capacity of its industries, with respect to maintaining monetary stability and low rates of inflation, and with respect to regulating and working out a symbiosis with foreign firms and banks that are established on its own territory.

The state has another delicate balancing act to perform as well. Although national economies have become increasingly internationalized, national politics remain national in character. The result is that the state finds itself, more and more, the arbiter of economic contradictions and tensions and the political conflicts that are fueled by them. National elections and political infighting are conducted as if the most important political issues were domestic because the national state remains the agency that is defined as being responsible for political problems. This constitutes a peculiar squeeze on national states. They must respond to forces that are neither of their own making nor of their own society's making. These international forces work themselves out in various ways. First, as previously mentioned, external political and financial agencies join the domestic political arena as they attempt to influence economic policy; these agencies also enter domestic politics as they are singled out as politically responsible agents. Second, another source of the internationalization of politics is the presence of international political movements—human rights, peace, environmentalist, and others—which often constitute political pressures on domestic governments. Third, the development of systems of international politics in the United Nations and in various regional federations and coalitions involves an interplay among national political interests and international processes.

The third dimension of internationalization is cultural. The most conspicuous elements of this dimension are technology and science and their diffusion. This diffusion occurs by a number of mechanisms, including the internationalization of science in universities, academies, and international science-based associations. Competitive mechanisms also play a role, as firms, militaries, and governments make deliberate efforts to discover and appropriate technology in the interests of augmenting their economic competitiveness and military positions. The effect of technological and scientific diffusion and acquisition, however, depends above all on how effectively it is applied in the institutional context. A second type of cultural diffusion, often out of the hands of national governments, is cultural diffusion through the mass media. This diffusion influences consumer tastes and expectations, popular attitudes, and political understandings and sentiments. Even those countries whose governments resist the infusion of cultural influences regarded as alien have difficulties in doing so; and once a society has opened the door to international exposure through the mass media, it is difficult to shut it again. S. N. Eisenstadt, in the final chapter in this volume, identifies a peculiarly global kind of international cultural diffusion, evident in earlier eras in the international spread of the great religions and cultures but today manifesting itself as a kind of "culture of modernity," that envisions economic development, political participation, cultural pluralism, and other values as cultural ideals. The cumulative force of this diffusion has been profound throughout the world. Each of the cultural influences I have mentioned, however, is shaped by domestic traditions, values, and interests, once again illustrating the interplay between external and internal processes.

For lack of a better term, the final dimension of internationalization might be called the growth of multiple international societal communities. Partly cultural in character, this term refers to the development of normative rules and understandings that emerge in the course of increased international interaction. Perhaps the most important—albeit precarious— focus for this kind of growth is in the arena of international security, involving the nuclear superpowers above all but other countries as well. This term involves the evolution of understandings and symbolic meanings of, for example, what international lines may not be crossed without threatening to precipitate international nuclear destruction, what actions are available to back down in confrontations without losing face, how to interpret both threats and friendly gestures, how to understand when bluffs are bluffs and when they are not, and so on. In the atmosphere of almost permanent international tension in the security arena these normative elements are often lost sight of, but they nonetheless have developed. Similar rules, agreements, and understandings emerge in other settings as well—in diplomatic circles, in the international banking community, among economic competitors, in international scientific and scholarly associations, and in educational exchange programs.

In the recent past scholars have made distinctions such as center versus periphery in national cultural traditions, cosmopolitan versus local in cultural orientations, and "big traditions" versus "little traditions" in cultures, stressing the differences in the polar terms and the ways that each term stands in tension with the other. It may be time to draw a similar distinction between "international" and "national" or "local" because the international dimension seems to have evolved to a position of independent significance in the contemporary world.

I hope that this brief discussion of some of the multiple dimensions of international-national life may contribute to the development of the complex, integrative kinds of models that appear to be called for in order to understand the contemporary world situation. Certainly the discussion about how to understand the contemporary world calls for abandoning the either-or polarization in contemporary scholarship and debate with respect to the relative roles of external and internal factors in the explanation of social change. This kind of polarization is as outdated as many of the older theoretical positions considered in this chapter.

REFERENCES

Almond, Gabriel, and James S. Coleman, eds. 1960. *The politics of the developing areas.* Princeton: Princeton University Press.

Bendix, Reinhard. [1964] 1977. *Nation-building and citizenship.* Berkeley: University of California Press.

Cardoso, Fernando H. 1973. Associated dependent development: Theoretical and practical implications. In *Authoritarian Brazil: Origins, policies and futures,* ed. Alfred Stepan, New Haven: Yale University Press.

Cardoso, Fernando H., and E. Faletto. 1969. *Dependency and development in Latin America.* Berkeley: University of California Press.

Coser, Lewis. 1956. *The functions of social conflict.* Glencoe, Ill.: Free Press.

Dahrendorf, Ralf. 1959. *Class and class conflict in industrial society.* Stanford: Stanford University Press.

Dore, Ronald Philip. 1973. *British factory, Japanese factory: The origins of national diversity in industrial relations.* Berkeley: University of California Press.

Eisenstadt, S. N. 1964. Breakdowns of modernization. *Economic Development and Cultural Change* 12, no. 4:345–69.

Engels, Friedrich. [1884] 1969. *The origin of the family, private property, and the state.* New York: International Publishers.

Frank, Andre Gunder. 1969. *Latin America: Underdevelopment or revolution? Essays on the development of underdevelopment and the immediate enemy.* New York: Monthly Review.

Goode, William J. 1963. *World revolution and family patterns.* New York: Free Press.

Gusfield, Joseph R. 1967. Tradition and modernity: Misplaced polarities in the study of social change. *American Journal of Sociology* 72:351–62.

Hagen, Everett. 1962. *On the theory of social change.* Homewood, Ill.: Dorsey Press.

Hoselitz, Bert F. 1960. *Sociological factors in economic development.* Glencoe, Ill.: Free Press.

Inkeles, Alex, and David H. Smith. 1974. *Becoming modern.* Cambridge: Harvard University Press.

Kerr, Clark, John T. Dunlop, Frederick H. Harbison, and Charles A. Myers. 1960. *Industrialism and industrial man.* Cambridge: Harvard University Press.

Kroeber, Alfred L. 1923. *Anthropology.* New York: Harcourt Brace.

———. 1944. *Configurations of culture growth.* Berkeley: University of California Press.

Lenin, V. I. [1917] 1939. *Imperialism: The highest stage of capitalism.* New York: International Publishers.

Lerner, Daniel. 1958. *The passing of traditional society: Modernizing the Middle East.* Glencoe, Ill.: Free Press.

Levy, Marion J. 1966. *Modernization and the structure of societies: A setting for international affairs.* Princeton: Princeton University Press.

Lowie, Robert H. 1937. *The history of ethnological theory.* New York: Rinehart.

McClelland, David. 1961. *The achieving society.* Princeton: Van Nostrand.

Makler, Harry, Arnaud Sales, and Neil J. Smelser. 1982. Recent trends in theory and methodology in the study of economy and society. In *Sociology: The state of the art*, ed. Tom Bottomore, Stefan Nowak, and Magdalena Sokolowska, 147–72. London: Sage.

Malinowski, Bronislaw. 1945. *The dynamics of culture change: An inquiry into race relations in Africa*. Ed. Phyllis M. Kaberry. New Haven: Yale University Press.

Marx, Karl. 1853a. The future results of British rule in India. *New York Daily Tribune*, 8 Aug. 1853.

———. 1853b. Revolution in China and Europe. *New York Daily Tribune*, 14 June 1853.

———. [1867] 1949. *Capital: A critique of political economy*. Vol. 1. London: George Allen and Unwin.

Moore, Wilbert. 1951. *Industrialization and labor*. New York: Cornell University Press.

Morgan, Lewis Henry. [1877] 1963. *Ancient society: Researches in the lines of human progress from savagery through barbarism to civilization*. Cleveland: World Publishing.

Ogburn, William Fielding. 1922. *Social change: With respect to culture and original nature*. New York: B. S. Huebsch.

Parsons, Talcott. 1960. *Structure and process in modern societies*. Glencoe, Ill.: Free Press.

———. 1961. Some considerations on the theory of social change. *Rural Sociology* 26: 219–39.

———. 1971. *The system of modern societies*. Englewood Cliffs, N.J.: Prentice-Hall.

Prebisch, Paul. 1950. *The economic development of Latin America and its problems*. New York: United Nations, Department of Social and Economic Affairs.

President's Research Committee on Social Trends. 1933. *Recent social trends in the United States*. New York: McGraw-Hill.

Radcliffe-Brown, A. R. 1935. On the concept of function in social science. *American Anthropologist* 37:394–402.

———. 1952. *Structure and function in primitive society*. Glencoe, Ill.: Free Press.

Rostow, W. W. 1960. *The stages of economic growth: A non-communist manifesto*. Cambridge: Cambridge University Press.

Roth, Guenther. 1968. Introduction. In *Economy and society*, by Max Weber, xxvii–cvii. New York: Bedminster Press.

Smelser, Neil J. 1963. Mechanisms of change and adjustment of changes. In *Industrialization and society*, ed. Wilbert E. Moore and Bert F. Hoselitz, 32–55. Glencoe, Ill.: Free Press.

Sorokin, Pitirim. 1937. *Social and cultural dynamics*. 4 vols. New York: American Book Company.

Weber, Max. [1916] 1970. India: The Brahman and the castes. In *From Max Weber*, ed. H. H. Gerth and C. Wright Mills, London: Routledge and Kegan Paul.

———. [1920] 1950. *General economic history*. Trans. Frank Knight. Glencoe, Ill.: Free Press.

Globality, Global Culture, and Images of World Order

Roland Robertson

The general concern of the following discussion is the phenomenon of globality. I propose that the process of globalization—involving, from one perspective, the implosion of the world and, from another perspective, the explosion of societally and civilizationally situated cultures, institutions, and modes of life (Robertson and Chirico 1985)—should be regarded in sociological-theoretical terms as subsuming the classical concern with the transformation of societies, which was analytically centered largely on the processes of industrialization, development, and modernization (Nettl and Robertson 1966).

Previously, I tried to demonstrate that there is an unappreciated global perspective in the work of the classical sociologists and some of their precursors, particularly in the view that the transformation of Western societies has been but a part of a general trend toward globality (Robertson and Chirico 1985). In other words, the passing of premodern society itself involved a strong shift toward globality, which I define as the circumstance in which the entire world is regarded as "a single place." The globalization perspective is not merely an extension of what can (for the sake of convenience and simplicity) be called the "*Gemeinschaft* to *Gesellschaft*" theme. Rather, the phenomenon of the world as a single place may fruitfully be viewed as both an extension of the Great Transformation, as Polanyi (1957) called it, and a subsumption of it. Put another way, the *Gemeinschaft-Gesellschaft* contrast has been relativized diachronically and synchronically by processes of globalization so that rather than speaking of processes of societal change in an objective, directional sense, we are now constrained to think increasingly of the

I am grateful to Gary Abraham and Neil Smelser for their comments on an earlier version of this chapter.

tensions between *Gemeinschaft* and *Gesellschaft* as quotidian images of sociocultural organization anywhere in the contemporary world. More specifically, the *Gemeinschaft-Gesellschaft* theme has itself been globalized: first, with respect to images of how societies should be patterned; second, with respect to how the world-as-a-whole should be structured.[1]

In this chapter I am concerned with two closely related aspects of globality (centered on the perceived facticity of a single world) and globalization (the set of processes that yields a single world). First, I consider the degree to which a direct interest in globality and globalization makes a significant difference to the ways in which sociological theorizing, especially the analysis of large-scale and long-run change, is undertaken. Second, I focus on a specific application of the globalization perspective: images of world order and the potential for social movements developing in terms of these images.

THE GLOBAL CIRCUMSTANCE: PRIOR TREATMENTS

It has become commonplace, almost a cliché, in recent years to speak of "the global village." Certainly the mass media in various parts of the world have used this term (which is, of course, highly problematic from a disciplined sociological vantage point) with increasing frequency and have seemingly subscribed to the McLuhanist claim that it has been wrought largely by technological changes in the media of communication. It is as if the printing press largely promoted *Gesellschaft*, and the satellite dish—and its potential miniaturization—is promoting a global *Gemeinschaft*. Notwithstanding the severe shortcomings of this point of view, not to speak of its self-serving features, the use of the term "global village" is a remarkable indicator of the degree to which a consciousness of the world-as-a-whole has crystallized. Indeed, the explosion of the use of the adjective "global" is an indicator in its own right of the process of globalization.[2] Further evidence of this process can, of course, be found in the readily perceivable and much-noted interlocking of sociocultural phenomena across societal boundaries on a global scale, particularly in economic respects; the rapid expansion and increase in the number of global institutions; the proliferation of global

1. Dumont has made a major attempt to distinguish between Western and Eastern worldviews (what he calls ideologies). In the course of his analysis he relativizes Tönnies's *Gemeinschaft-Gesellschaft* distinction as an intra-Western version of a much more general East-West difference. See Kavolis 1986.

2. A word of warning is necessary here, for quite a lot of "globe talk" does not directly address the world-as-a-whole. "Global" is sometimes used—particularly in the United States—as a synonym for international or comparative. Nevertheless, I believe my general claim to be valid.

events and representative gatherings; the increasing concern with globe-threatening military, chemical, medical, and ecological problems; the considerable expansion of so-called international or global education; the aspirations of the leaders of some contemporary societies— most explicitly and conspicuously, the Japanese—to make those societies "global"; and so on. Also, the legitimacy of societal actions, attributes, and trends has increasingly become an issue that is cast in global terms, and terms such as "global public" and "world citizenry" have become part of contemporary public discourse.

Interest on the part of sociologists in the global circumstance as a definite theme did not crystallize until the 1960s. At that time social scientists mostly situated their concern with the world-as-a-whole within the then-thriving debate about societal modernization, and did so as a revamped version of the original *Gemeinschaft-Gesellschaft* problem (Robertson and Lechner 1985).[3] The thematization by social scientists (as opposed to specialists in international relations) of what later came to be widely (but not unproblematically) called the world-system was thus from the beginning largely centered on the theme of societal-structural change, specifically in reference to the differences between the societies of the "Third World" (itself a concept that had crystallized only a little earlier) and those of the West and/or the Soviet bloc. However, even at that time steps were being taken toward the analysis of culture at the global level. In our rejection of the prevailing conceptions and theories of societal modernization Nettl, Tudor, and I called for an approach that viewed modernization as a process of catching up with or surpassing another society or set of societies with attributes deemed to be, in whole or in part, desirable (Nettl and Robertson 1968; Robertson and Tudor 1968). Employing a mixture of Parsonian action-and-system theory, symbolic-interactionist ideas concerning (societal) identity and (societal) reflexivity, Schutzian ideas about multiple realities, and emerging conceptions of the structure of the system of intersocietal stratification, we attempted to refocus the field of modernization theory. Thus, we opposed to all intents and purposes what poststructuralists and postmodernists now call a "grand narrative" account of the past, present, and future—although that does not mean that the resulting perspective can be described, in the recent meaning of the term, as postmodern (Lyotard 1984). In place of theories that stood more or less directly in line with the nineteenth-century philosophies of history that indicated a definite, progressive movement of societies and civilizations along a particular (mainly Western) path, we offered a view of what, at the time, we contin-

---

3. Much of the relevant literature of that period is discussed, or at least cited, in Nettl and Robertson 1966, Robertson and Tudor 1968, Nettl and Robertson 1968, and Robertson 1968.

ued to call the "international system" as a place in which societies (or, more accurately, influential elites within societies) construct their own identities in tandem with the invocation and construction of ideas concerning the system as a whole. In this perspective societal modernization was not to be pivotally analyzed as an advance in a "progressive," Western direction or even as a move in the direction of either the First or Second worlds. Rather it was to be regarded analytically as indicating a *field of definitions* of the global situation, on the one hand, and self-societal *definitions*, on the other.

Generally speaking, the theory of modernization that we proposed in the 1960s was voluntaristic in the sense that Parsons (1937) had introduced that term. Although acknowledging—indeed emphasizing—that the global intersocietal system possessed its own structural properties and, thus, that societies acted under external-systemic (as well as internal) constraints, we also maintained that there was a strong element of "choice" involved as to the ideal direction or directions of societal change and the form or forms of global involvement. That element was seen to be centered on an emergent global culture, a global culture that demanded that all extant societies adopt an orientation to, if not necessarily an acceptance of, the idea of modernization. Thus, what was taken to be modern—or, more loosely, what was taken to be a worthy direction of societal aspiration—was something that was constructed in the global arena in relation to the constraints on (most) societies to maintain their own identities and senses of continuity in relation to the "international system." It was not just a case of the First or Second worlds presenting images of trajectories of modernization to Third (or Fourth) World societies but rather a much more complex situation of globewide "reality construction," in which intra- and intercivilizational and intra- and intersocietal traditions and circumstances all played important parts.

What placed the study of the global scene very firmly on the social-scientific map was, of course, the publication of Wallerstein's first extended statement on the making and history of what he called the modern world-system and the ensuing elaboration of his standpoint and debates about it (Wallerstein 1974). This chapter cannot be the place for a comprehensive analysis of the Wallersteinian program or its numerous extensions, variations, and rival perspectives.[4] However, what does need to be noted is that it was, as quite a few critics have pointed out, remarkably economistic in its genesis but that in recent years there has been an increasing acknowledgment in Wallersteinian and neo-Wallersteinian circles of the significance of culture (Robertson and Lechner 1985). Wallerstein's

4. Among the numerous and still proliferating discussions, see the following: Robertson and Lechner 1985, Chirot and Hall 1982, Worsley 1984, Markoff 1977, Berger 1986, and Gold 1986.

own program seems to be following the path taken by a number of Marxist theories: it started in an economic-deterministic mode and then, when impediments to the transition to (world) socialism were found to be very formidable, it turned to "the problem of culture" (Robertson 1985; Robertson and Lechner 1985).

More specifically, the world-system has come to be seen by Wallerstein himself as partly guided and sustained by "metaphysical presuppositions" deriving historically from ideas developed during crucially formative periods of Western capitalism (Wallerstein 1983). These presuppositions— amounting to a kind of deep culture of and for the capitalist world system per se—constitute, according to Wallerstein, an obstacle to the transformation of the world-system in a socialist direction. Hence, they need direct analytical (as well as political) treatment. Until the announcement of this view Wallersteinians had, more often than not, addressed the theme of culture by insisting that the variety of national and ethnic cultures produced in the world-system were epiphenomena of the shifting division of international-economic labor.[5] Thus, the idea of a global culture was alien to the Wallersteinian school of thought, not least because it was, and still is, widely assumed by world-system theorists—and many other social scientists—that "culture" must always refer to a commonly held, relatively explicit body of ideas, values, beliefs, and symbols that constitutes a more or less binding consensus. Few would be so foolish as to assert that a global culture exists in this strong sense—with the important exception of those who strongly emphasize the force and significance of the global homogenization of popular culture, styles of consumerism, individual "life-styles," "global information," and so on—but it does not follow from the rejection of such an idea that culture must be regarded as inconsequential and usually epiphenomenal in the global situation. Regardless of the viability of Wallerstein's ideas about the presuppositions of the world-system, it is perfectly reasonable to think of global (or any other) culture as consisting in large part of contested and conflicting images and definitions of the global circumstance.[6]

World-system theorists and researchers have clearly accomplished something of significance in emphasizing the idea that the world is a systemic phenomenon and that much of what has been traditionally ana-

5. What is sometimes called the Stanford school of world-system analysis has ventured much further than others in a cultural direction. See, in particular, Meyer 1980 and Thomas et al. 1987. See also Wuthnow 1980. Separately, the many contributions of Galtung since the early 1960s should be given special emphasis. Of particular relevance in the present context is Galtung 1980, not least because he has linked certain aspects of world-system theory to a discussion of possible forms of the world-as-a-whole.

6. Other more specific layers of world culture are discussed in Nettl and Robertson 1968.

lyzed by social scientists in societal, or more broadly, civilizational terms can and should be relativized and discussed along global-systemic lines. That being granted, the fact remains that major difficulties arise from the Western-centeredness of the history of the Wallersteinian world-system. For this history, the issue of the making of the world-system is, empirically, a version of the problem of the transition from feudalism to capitalism, which was itself a sociological precursor of, inter alia, the status-contract, *Gemeinschaft-Gesellschaft,* mechanical-organic, and segmented-stratified *Problemstellungen.* But a more challenging and sociologically appropriate strategy is to relativize these *Problemstellungen* in such a way as to view the global system in a much more far-reaching perspective, one in which "the world" is not assumed to have been made simply from and out of the West (even though clearly in some respects it has).[7]

GLOBAL CULTURE?

The long detour that Wallerstein took on his way to recognizing the significance of culture in the global system is all the more regrettable when we acknowledge that it was clear even in the 1950s and 1960s that a variety of images of desirable trajectories of societal change was available (Nettl and Robertson 1968). To be sure, there was a sense in which the notion of modernity itself was conceived both in social science and in the everyday world of national and institutional leaders along distinctively Western lines, but even in those decades the more general notion of what may be called societal improvement took different forms (of which "modernization" in the restricted sense was certainly one). By now, as a number of East Asian cases, in particular, clearly show, the term modernization itself has been so generalized in the real world that it carries much less specificity than it did at the time it fell out of favor in many social-scientific circles (largely in response to the Wallersteinian argument that the proper unit of analysis was not the national society but the world-system).[8]

Thus Wallersteinian (and other Marxist or Trotskyist) theories of the world economy and its sociocultural ramifications have—at least until very recently—largely chosen to ignore (or, at least, play down) the idea that not merely are there ideal as well as material interests of great sociocultural significance but that "world images" play a crucial role in framing the directions in which these interrelated sets of interests are pursued. The concept of world images has to be taken very seriously and employed more literally than it was in Max Weber's work. I use the term

7. On this point see Worsley 1984 and Bull and Watson 1984.

8. The recent rapid economic growth of a number of East and Southeast Asian societies has been used to mount harsh critiques of the world-system and other closely related perspectives. See Berger 1986 and Gold 1986.

mainly—as I have already implied—in the sense of images of global order. In a more technical, neo-Kantian sense, I am addressing the issue of how the world is variously, and often conflictually, regarded as possible. Whereas Weber's concept of world images referred to very general orientations to and conceptions of the human condition (particularly, Weber was interested in the relationship between the intramundane and the supramundane aspects of the cosmos), the concept of world images as I employ it here refers mostly and more concretely to conceptions of how the intramundane world is or should be structured. That does not mean, however, that the wider cosmic aspect of the concept of world images is irrelevant.

Weber's work as a whole was, of course, directed largely at issues centered on the crystallization of modern rationalism. His interest in world images was largely dictated by his desire to comprehend the historical circumstances of the rise of rationalism in the Occidental world. A rather different, but not incompatible, orientation to the phenomena that were of central significance to Weber was promoted in one of Parsons's very last essays. In "Religious and Economic Symbolism in the Western World" Parsons (1979) discussed the cultural responses to what, for the sake of brevity, he called the industrial revolution. This topic constituted a very significant turn in Parsonian action theory, but one that has received exceedingly little attention. Parsons argued that the industrial revolution of the late eighteenth century stood diachronically in line with the thematization of the erotic-sexual aspect of human life, which had occurred in the period of early Christianity and the shift from ancient Judaistic particularism to early Christian universalism. In ancient Judaism, he argued, the sexual-erotic dimension of life had been, so to say, hidden by laws and rituals concerning familial relationships and the Deuteronomic distinction between in- and out-group relations (Nelson 1969); however, the early Christian doctrinal obliteration of the in-group/out-group distinction involved a confrontation with the "dangers" of sexuality and eroticism. (This assertion is, almost needless to say, a controversial and fragile one in light of the actual history of Christian attitudes toward the Jews.)

Parsons claimed that the industrial revolution of the late eighteenth century was both a diachronic-functional equivalent and an evolutionary upgrading of the mission to the Gentiles. It constituted another crucial stage in the odyssey of particularism-universalism, involving the "revelation" of the economy as a potentially autonomous realm. The market economy represented at one and the same time a vehicle of universalistic, potentially global social interaction and exchange, on the one hand, and a "dangerous" intrusion on traditional forms of sociality and solidarity, on the other. It was part of Parsons's argument that the general character of modern social theory, ideology, and political culture was largely shaped during the early-nineteenth-century response to the thematization of the economy as a relatively autonomous realm of life.[9] To this argument I add the claim that responses to globality are very likely to frame the character of social theory, doctrine, ideology, and culture in the decades ahead. The meanings ascribed to the "dangers" of the world as a single sociocultural entity (notably, concerns about threats to humanity as a whole, on the one hand, and the massive relativization of identities and traditions, on the other) constitute the crucible in which major ideas of great potential significance are being formed. More than that, responses to globality are potentially the focal point of the social movements of the future. The revelations of the productive forces of sex and the economy have been followed by the baring of the problem of the fate of the human species as a whole (Robertson 1982). However, this does not suggest that these productive forces have diminished in socio-cultural significance. On the contrary, they have now acquired explicitly global significance—as AIDS and current problems of global economic justice clearly demonstrate.

To a small, but not insignificant, degree the perspective I bring to bear on the contemporary world-as-a-whole is in line with certain analytical trends within the general world-system theoretical framework. For example, Jameson—a literary critic and interpreter of culture who at-tunes much of his current work to Wallerstein's ideas—in his plea for "the reinvention, in a new situation, of what Goethe long ago theorized as 'world literature,' " argues that contemporary "cultural structures and attitudes" of relevance to the world culture scene were "in the beginning vital responses to infrastructural realities (economic and geographic, for example)" (Jameson 1968, 68). Such cultural structures and attitudes should, he insists, initially be seen as "attempts to resolve more funda-mental contradictions—attempts which then outlive the situations for which they were devised, and survive, in reified forms as 'cultural pat-terns' " (Jameson 1986, 78). Jameson then goes on to argue that "those patterns themselves become part of the objective situation confronted by later generations, and . . . having once been part of the solution to a dilemma, then become part of the new problem." His argument is not unpersuasive, but at the same time it illustrates some of the problems in the world-system perspective on culture. In one sense Jameson's observa-tions are clearly compatible with the way in which Parsons treated West-ern cultural responses to the onset of the industrial revolution. However, the term "infrastructure" gives the impression of cultural responses be-

9. Parsons's analysis appears in some respects to be continuous with Smelser's extended discussion (1959) of situational responses to structural differentiation in the early English industrial revolution.

ing essentially secondary to material factors. Moreover, Jameson appears to be trying to sustain the view that in a globalized world the major point of reference is still the economic infrastructure rather than globality itself, which—as I have been insisting—transcends, although it still includes, the global economy. Furthermore, in a situation of increasing consciousness of the world-as-a-whole one would expect civilizational conceptions of the entire world that predate the emergence of the infrastructure to be activated. In other words, even though national, regional, and other cultural patterns have undoubtedly been partly formed as responses to the growth of the capitalist world-system, the contemporary concern with the world-as-a-whole recrystallizes, in varying degrees, the historical philosophies and theologies of ancient civilizations concerning the structure and cosmic significance of the world. The critical difference between, for example, traditional Islamic or Chinese conceptions of the world and present ones is that the modern worldviews, unlike the old ones, are being reformulated or upgraded in terms of a very concrete sense of the structure of the entire world in its modern (or postmodern) form.

At this point it is necessary to become more precise about the use of such terms as world-system, global condition, and so on. One of the major limitations of the world-system perspective is its concentration on the relationships between and connections among societies—and, of course, its casting of those relationships and connections in primarily economic terms. Moreover, even were the comprehension of intersocietal relationships to be more broadly conceived, the problem would remain that what Parsons (1971) called the system of modern societies is but one among a number of facets of the global-human circumstance that are clearly part of contemporary consciousness. Therefore, in trying to pinpoint for analytical purposes the very general structure of the global-human condition I suggest (Robertson and Chirico 1985) that in addition to the world-system of societies there are three other major components: societies as such, individuals, and humankind. Together, the system of societies, societies, individuals, and humankind constitute the basic and most general ingredients of what I call the global-human condition, a term that draws attention to both the world in its contemporary concreteness and humanity as a species. Finally, as I noted before, globality refers to the circumstance of extensive awareness of the world-as-a-whole, including the "species" aspect.

The set of major components of the global-human condition that I specify may be used to treat responses to and symbolic constructions of the thematization of globality in the same analytical spirit as Parsons typified responses to the thematization of the economy in the late eighteenth and nineteenth centuries. I depart slightly from Parsons, however, in producing a typology of general images of the contemporary world-as-a-whole (or the global-human condition) rather than the specific social-theoretic and ideological responses that he delineated in respect of the industrial revolution (Parsons's "types" included socialism in its more economistic forms, *Gemeinschaft* romanticism, what I summarize as corporatism, and utilitarian individualism). Moreover, I do not press as hard as Parsons did the idea that each response, when it explicitly rejects the other three, constitutes a form of reductionism or avoidance of complexity in the mode of fundamentalism (cf. Robertson 1983). That is not because of disagreement with Parsons on this interpretive matter but rather because my primary concern is simply to map, describe, and provide a rationale for the very idea of analyzing major general responses to globalization and globality.

IMAGES OF WORLD ORDER AS CULTURAL RESPONSES TO GLOBALITY

First, I present four images of world order in relatively formal terms. Having done this, I then add some empirical flesh.

Global Gemeinschaft 1. This conception of the global circumstance insists that the world should and can be ordered only in the form of a series of relatively closed societal communities. The symmetrical version of this image of world order sees societal communities as relatively equal to each other in terms of the worth of their cultural traditions, their institutions, and the kinds of individuals that inhabit them. The asymmetrical version, however, regards one or a small number of societal communities as necessarily being more important than others. Those who advocate global "relativism" based on the "sacredness" of all indigenous traditions fall into the symmetrical category; those who claim that theirs is "the middle kingdom," "the society of destiny" or "the lead society" fall into the second category. In the late twentieth century, both versions tend to seize on the idea that individuals can only live satisfactory lives in clearly bounded societal communities. However, this idea does not mean that either of these two versions emphasizes individualism or individuality. Rather, they are particularly concerned with the problem of the "homelessness" of individuals in the face of the "dangers" of globalization.

Global Gemeinschaft 2. This image of the world situation maintains that only in terms of a fully globewide community per se can there be global order. Corresponding to the distinction between symmetrical and asymmetrical versions of *Gemeinschaft 1*, there are centralized and decentralized versions of this image of the world as almost literally a "global village." The first version insists that there must be a globewide Durkheimian "conscience collective," and the second version maintains that a global community is possible on a much more pluralistic basis. Both versions of this second type of *Gemeinschaft* stress humankind as the pivotal ingredient of the world-as-a-whole. Thus the dangers of globalization are to be overcome by commitment to the communal unity of the human species.

Global Gesellschaft 1. This variant of the image of the world as a form of *Gesellschaft* involves seeing the global circumstance as a series of open societies, with considerable sociocultural exchange among them. The symmetrical version considers all societies as politically equal and of reciprocally beneficial material and cultural significance; the asymmetrical version entails the view that there must be dominant or hegemonic societies that play strategically significant roles in sustaining the world and, indeed, that these societies are the primary mechanism of world order. In both cases national societies are regarded as necessarily constituting the central feature of the modern global circumstance. Thus the problem of globalization is to be confronted either by extensive societal collaboration or by a hierarchical pattern of intersocietal relationships.

Global Gesellschaft 2. This conception of world order claims that world order can only be obtained on the basis of formal, planned world organization. The centralized version of *Gesellschaft 2* is committed to a strong supranatural polity, but the decentralized form advocates something like a federation at the global level. Both variants take the world system of societies as constituting the major unavoidable dimension of the contemporary global-human condition. Both variants share the view that the only effective way of dealing with the dangers of globalization is by the systematic organization of that process.

In attempting to provide empirical nuance to each of the four major types of orientation to world order, I emphasize that I am particularly interested, given my continuing insistence on the fairly recent emergence of globality as an aspect of contemporary consciousness, in explicitly globe-oriented ideologies, doctrines, and other bodies of knowledge. I define an explicitly globe-oriented perspective as one that espouses as a central aspect of its message a concern with the patterning of the entire world. In so doing, I allow room for perspectives that even though concerned about the phenomenon of globality may actually be militantly opposed to those who urge studying or embracing the globality of contemporary life.

A significant example of what has been sometimes described by its proponents as "antiglobalism" is provided by recent attempts in parts of the American South to limit the exposure of children in public schools to ideas that might involve relativization of American culture and citizenship. What is of particular interest about these occurrences is that they have grown almost directly out of a continuous reference to an older opposition to the alleged dangers of "secular humanism." Antiglobalism thus becomes a symbolic vehicle for generalizing beyond the dangers of intrasocietal secular *Gesellschaft* to the perceived threats from other cultures and the world per se. Initially, the objection was to a "national" secularity that was indifferent to religion and local custom; now the objection, in the face of the relativizing dangers of globalization, is also—perhaps even more—to the contaminating effects of exposure to alien doctrines and philosophies, such as those of Islam. In other words, the shift from the problem of the making of the modern West to the problem of the world-as-a-whole is not simply a shift in the focus of intellectual social theory but of real-world practice (and certainly not only in the West itself).

Thus, antiglobal movements and sociocultural tendencies are to be included conceptually in the family of globe-oriented orientations. Their growth provides just as much evidence of the development of a consciousness of globality as is the more-often studied rise of movements that are concerned in one way or another with organizing what are perceived to be the crucial aspects of the entire world (such as Greenpeace, Friends of the Earth, or the international women's movement) or, indeed, the world in its entirety (as is apparently the case with some religious movements such as the South Korea-centered Unification Church and the Japan-based Soka Gakkai). Moreover, even though antiglobal perspectives are not pivotally concerned with the theme of world order per se, they are surely held to a significant degree in "subliminal thrall" by that which they oppose. They address the problem of the world-as-a-whole negatively but nonetheless their attitude toward the latter tends to imply a conception of how the contemporary global-human circumstance is possible. (Although in the case of some American Christian fundamentalist groups there is evidence that the world-as-a-whole is considered to be impossible—a view that is expressed in apocalyptic symbolism.)

Views of the world-as-a-whole as consisting of a series of relatively closed societal communities (*Gemeinschaft 1*)—with each community conceived of as preciously unique—became evident in the West toward the end of the eighteenth century, notably in the writings of Herder. The symmetrical version of this view has found twentieth-century expression in anthropological relativism and within certain contexts of the apparently worldwide ethnic revival (Smith 1981; Lechner 1984). The asymmetrical version—which insists on the greater worth of one or a small number of societal communities in comparison to others—is much older; the paradigmatic case is the classical Chinese conception of China as the Middle Kingdom at the center of a world that is structured as a series of concentric circles of communal forms of life. Historically, there have also been strong parallel versions of this kind of conception in Islam. In the modern period of mature globality the asymmetrical dispersed *Gemeinschaft* worldview is to be seen in the large number of politicoreligious fundamentalist movements that have arisen around the world. Many of these movements advocate the restoration of their own societal communities to a pristine condition, with the rest of the world being left as a series of closed communities posing no threat to the "best" community. This conception involves a kind of "apartheid" view of the world, although it does not necessarily rest on principles of racial superiority per se.

The idea of the world as being in and of itself a single community (*Gemeinschaft 2*), or at least having the potential for so becoming, has a very long history, having been expressed in such notions as worldwide earthly paradise and the Kingdom of God on earth. In the modern period a number of new religious movements have arisen that advocate, and in fact are taking, concrete steps toward nothing less than the global organization of the entire world. The movement that surely can lay legitimate claim to being the oldest significant globe-oriented organization—namely, the Roman Catholic Church—has recently become a particularly effective globe-oriented actor across most of the world, claiming humanity to be its major concern. Perhaps the most striking of the new religious movements in this regard tend to be of East Asian, particularly Japanese, origin, where the idea of harmonizing different worldviews has a very long history. For the most part such movements may be associated with the centralized version of global *Gemeinschaft* because they often appear to seek a global harmonization of existing worldviews under a theocratic umbrella of "absolute values" (such is the case of the Unification Church). The more decentralized version of the view of the entire world as a single community is to be found in many strands of the contemporary peace movement and in romantic Marxism. In such cases the response to globality is to argue, in effect, that the only way to save the world from extreme complexity and turmoil is to establish a global community that is highly respectful of local tradition and cultural variety. Thus whereas the centralized version of globewide *Gemeinschaft* seeks a "harmonizing theocracy" at the global level, the decentralized version is what might be called "concultural" in its conception of world order (Mazrui 1976). The concultural view character-izes cultural traditions as constituting a set of indigenous variations on the condition and predicaments of humankind. Some of the numerous move-ments centered on theologies of liberation that have arisen in many parts of the world (often through emulation of the most solidly established liberation theology—namely, that of Latin America) appear to subscribe to this perspective on world order.

The image of world order that emphasizes the pivotal significance of national societies (*Gesellschaft 1*) involves in its symmetrical version the idea that we should see the world as a kind of aggregate of all societies. This image is what we might call the small society view of the world, although one finds strands of such thinking in societies that are certainly not small geographically or in terms of their resources (for example, Canada). This orientation seems to constitute a societal parallel to the decentralized version of *Gemeinschaft 1* in that it advocates a kind of global consociationalism in which very different interests are more or less systematically combined so as to realize the interests of the whole. In contrast, as I have suggested, the asymmetrical version of *Gemeinschaft 1* rejects the view of a world order centered on all societies. It stands in the tradition of international *Realpolitik* and needs no further elaboration. It may be added, however, that social movements can and do directly advo-cate this standpoint (quite apart from its advocacy by politicians and rulers in great-power societies). Certain religious and ideological points of view hold that the great-power arrangement of the world is the only thing that prevents cultural contamination. Thus, for example, *Gesell-schaft 1* in its asymmetrical form may be combined with the asymmetrical version of *Gemeinschaft 1,* the former being instrumental in promoting a world of "greater" and "lesser" societal communities.

The *Gesellschaft 2* image of world order conceives of the world primar-ily in its thoroughly systemic nature—or at least advocates that only formal systemicity can, so to say, save the world from the chaos of globality. In its centralized form this image involves a conception of strong world government, an idea that has been most frequently pro-posed during the present century by liberals, on the one hand, and Marxists, on the other. The difference between the two is that the liberals see a potential world government as mainly necessary to prevent global chaos, whereas the Marxists seek to use it to usher in and sustain world socialism (often leaving open the question of whether the world state should wither away in favor of another type of global order). Finally, the decentralized form of the image of the world as *Gesellschaft 2* is best illustrated by the so-called world federalists, although, in ideological terms, the Wallersteinians' view of the present condition of the world also fits here. The major difference between the world federalists and the Wallersteinians is, of course, that whereas the former aspire to overcome the problems of globality by federalizing a disorderly world-system, the latter see the present world-system as ordered but with dynamic contradictions that will eventually transform it to a higher and preferable form of order.

I have attempted to develop some ideas concerning global culture, particularly in the form of cultural responses to globality and globalization. My approach has used the term global culture in a way that, to a considerable extent, parallels the use of the term economic culture as a concept that refers to those aspects of a culture that have a specific bearing on economic action and institutions. Thus global culture refers particularly to culture that has a close bearing on the phenomenon of globality as a "dangerous" phenomenon of world-historical significance. Globality is a virtually unavoidable problem of contemporary life. The general images of world order that I have expounded have a number of further possible applications, including the analysis of the terms in which societies formulate (and display internal conflicts with respect to) their modes of participation in the modern global-human circumstance (Robertson 1987).

REFERENCES

Berger, Peter L. 1986. *The capitalist revolution.* New York: Basic Books.

Bozeman, Adda B. 1971. *The future of law in a multicultural world.* Princeton: Princeton University Press.

Bull, Hedley, and Adam Watson, eds. 1984. *The expansion of international society.* Oxford: Clarendon Press.

Chirot, Daniel, and Thomas D. Hall. 1982. World system theory. *Annual Review of Sociology* 81:81–106.

Galtung, Johan. 1980. *The true worlds: A transnational perspective.* New York: Free Press.

Gold, Thomas P. 1986. *State and society in the Taiwan miracle.* New York: M. E. Sharpe.

Jameson, Fredric. 1986. Third-world literature in the era of multinational capitalism. *Social Text* 15 (Fall):65–88.

Kavolis, Vytautas. 1986. Civilization paradigms in current sociology: Dumont vs. Eisenstadt. *Current Perspectives in Social Theory* 7:125–140.

Lechner, Frank. 1984. Ethnicity and revitalization in the modern world system. *Sociological Focus* 17:243–56.

Lyotard, Jean-François. 1984. *The postmodern condition: A report on knowledge.* Minneapolis: University of Minnesota Press.

Markoff, John. 1977. The world as a social system. *Peasant Studies* 4 (no. 1):2–8.

Mazrui, Ali A. 1976. *A world federation of cultures: An African perspective.* New York: Free Press.

Meyer, John W. 1980. The world polity and the authority of the nation-state. In *Studies of the modern world-system*, ed. Albert Bergesen, 109–38. New York: Academic Press.

Nelson, Benjamin. 1969. *The idea of usury: From tribal brotherhood to universal otherhood*. Chicago: University of Chicago Press.

———. 1981. *On the roads to modernity*, ed. Toby E. Huff. Totowa, N.J.: Rowman and Littlefield.

Nettl, J. P., and Roland Robertson. 1966. Industrialization, development or modernization. *British Journal of Sociology* 17:274–91.

———. 1968. *International systems and the modernization of societies: The formation of national goals and attitudes*. New York: Basic Books.

Parsons, Talcott. 1937. *The structure of social action*. Glencoe, Ill.: Free Press.

———. 1971. *The system of modern societies*. Englewood Cliffs, N.J.: Prentice-Hall.

———. 1979. Religious and economic symbolism in the Western world. *Sociological Inquiry* 49 (nos. 2–3):1–48.

Polanyi, Karl. 1957. *The great transformation*. Boston: Beacon Press.

Robertson, Roland. 1968. Strategic relations between national societies: A sociological analysis. *Journal of Conflict Resolution* 12 (no. 2):16–33.

———. 1982a. Parsons on the evolutionary significance of American religion. *Sociological Analysis* 43:307–26.

———. 1982b. Religion, global complexity, and the human condition. In *Absolute values and the creation of the New World*, 1:185–212. New York: International Cultural Foundation.

———. 1985. The sacred and the world system. In *The sacred in a secular age*, ed. Phillip Hammond, 347–58. Berkeley: University of California Press.

———. 1987. Globalization and societal modernization: A note on Japan and Japanese religion. *Sociological Analysis* 48:35–42.

Robertson, Roland, and JoAnn Chirico. 1985. "Humanity, globalization and worldwide religious resurgence: A theoretical exploration. *Sociological Analysis* 46:219–42.

Robertson, Roland, and Frank Lechner. 1985. Modernization, globalization and the problem of culture in world-systems theory. *Theory, Culture and Society* 2 (no. 3):103–18.

Robertson, Roland, and Andrew Tudor. 1968. The Third World and international stratification: Theoretical considerations and research findings. *Sociology* 2 (no. 2):47–64.

Smelser, Neil J. 1959. *Social change in the industrial revolution*. Chicago: University of Chicago Press.

Smith, Anthony D. 1981. *The ethnic revival*. New York: Cambridge University Press.

Thomas, George E., et al. 1987. *Institutional structure: Constituting state, society, and the individual*. Beverley Hills: Sage.

Wallerstein, Immanuel. 1974. *The modern world-system*. New York: Academic Press.

———. 1983. Crisis: The world-economy, the movements, and the ideologies. In *Crises in the world-system*, ed. Albert Bergesen, 21–36. Beverley Hills: Sage.

Worsley, Peter. 1984. *The three worlds: Culture and development.* London: Weidenfeld and Nicolson.
Wuthnow, Robert. 1980. World order and religious movements. In *Studies of the modern world-system,* ed. Albert Bergesen, 57–76. New York: Academic Press.

A Reappraisal of Theories of Social Change and Modernization

S. N. Eisenstadt

In this chapter I reexamine theories of modernization in the framework of a more general reappraisal of the classical theories of social change, especially the evolutionary and semievolutionary theories. I first reexamine some of the basic assumptions of classical evolutionary theories of change and then proceed to the presentation of a somewhat new approach to the processes of social change—from the point of view of what can be called a "civilizational" perspective. I conclude with a reexamination of theories of modernization from this perspective.

1. THEORIES OF SOCIAL CHANGE

1.1 Some Assumptions of the Classical Evolutionary Perspective

The classical evolutionary perspective in social change was based on several assumptions. First, the classical perspective assumed that structural differentiation is manifest in the development of relatively specialized roles that organize the flow of resources and the consequent social division of labor in all institutional spheres: technological, economic, political, religious, and the like.

Second, the classical approach accepted a relatively closed systemic view of society. It strongly emphasized that the social division of labor is manifest both in different degrees of structural differentiation and in the development of specialized roles and institutional spheres that organize the flow of resources. The classical perspective held that these features explain the basic characteristics and dynamics of any given institutional structure.

Third, this perspective maintained that criteria similar to those already employed in the study of institutional differentiation could be readily applied, without modification, to examinations of the cultural sphere.

Fourth, the classical evolutionary perspective assumed that there is a "natural" tendency toward the parallel development of differentiation in all spheres. Exceptions to this tendency, such as partial or delayed differentiation, were generally treated as unusual or problematic.

The major criticisms of this perspective, as they have developed in the social sciences, are well known and need not be repeated here. Rather, I attempt to point out some new directions for the analysis of social change from the point of view of a more general approach to the study of the construction of social order.

1.2. Elites, Cultural Orientations, and Systems of Control

This approach to the analysis of the construction of the social order and of the major social actors participating in it stresses that any institutional setting is brought into being by a combination of several major components. The first component is the level and distribution of resources among different groups in society, that is, the type of division of labor that is predominant in a given society. The second component is the institutional entrepreneurs or elites that are available—or competing—for the mobilization and structuring of such resources and for the organization and articulation of the interests of major groups generated by the social division of labor. The third component is the nature of the conceptions or, especially, ontological "visions" that inform the activities of these elites and that are derived from the major cultural orientations or codes prevalent in a society.

The institutionalization of these visions provides the arena for both concretizing the charismatic dimension of social order and striving for a meaningful social order. This institutionalization is effected and crystallized by the activities of the major elites. The most important among such elites are, first, the political elites, who deal most directly with the regulation of power in society, second, the articulators of the models of the cultural order whose activities are oriented to the construction of meaning, and third, the articulators of the solidarity of the major groups, who address themselves to the construction of trust.

The structure of these elites is closely related to the basic cultural orientations or "codes" prevalent in a society. In other words, different types of elites are carriers of different types of ontological visions and orientations. These elites tend to exercise different modes of control over the allocation of basic resources in the society in connection with their types of cultural orientation. In this way they combine the structuring of trust, the provision of meaning, and the regulation of power with the division of labor in society, institutionalizing the charismatic dimension of the social order.

Such control is exercised by these elites (or rather by coalitions of elites) primarily through control over access to the major institutional markets (economic, political, cultural, etc.), control over the conversion of the major resources between these markets, and control over the production and distribution of information that is central in the structuring of the cognitive maps of the members of their society, that is, the members' perceptions of the nature of their society in general and of their reference orientations and reference groups in particular.

Different coalitions of elites, together with the modes of control they exercise, shape the major characteristics and boundaries of the social systems that they help to construct, namely, the political system, the economic system, the system of social stratification and class formation, and the overall macrosocietal system. The differing modes of control shape the power aspects of the institutional structures in different societies. Especially important among these structures are the structure of authority, the conception of justice, and of political struggles, the principles of social hierarchy, and the definition of the scope of membership of different communities.

However, the concretization of these tendencies takes place in different political-ecological settings. Two aspects of such settings are of special importance. The first aspect, heavily stressed in recent research, is the importance of international political and economic systems. The places of societies within these systems and the different types of relations of hegemony and dependency are issues of particular importance. The second aspect is the recognition of the great variety of political-ecological settings of societies, including differences between small and large societies, their respective dependence on internal or external markets, and the like. Both of these aspects greatly affect the ways in which institutional contours and dynamics tend to develop.

The approaches developed here have several implications for the analysis of the systemic qualities of social life.

1. The construction of the boundaries of collectivities and social and, above all, political systems is a basic component or aspect of human social life.
2. Such systems and boundaries do not exist—as has often been assumed in sociological, anthropological, and historical analysis—as natural closed systems. Rather they are continuously constructed, open, and very fragile.

3. No human population is confined within any single such system. Rather human populations exist in a multiplicity of only partly coalescing organizations, collectivities, and systems.
4. Such systems—and the division of labor that they entail and that is not naturally given—are constructed by special social actors and carriers, especially by carriers of different ontological visions. In the process of such construction, ideological, power, and material components are always closely interwoven.
5. Such construction of boundaries denotes the delineation of the definite relations of the various collectivities or systems with their respective environments. However, such environments are not given in "nature"; they are themselves constructed by social actors through the construction of the boundaries of social systems.
6. Of central importance in the construction and maintenance of such systems are different integrative mechanisms that acquire an autonomy of their own. The assurance of the working of these mechanisms is of crucial importance in the maintenance and change of societies or civilizations.
7. Such integrative mechanisms become more important and autonomous the more complex social and political systems and civilizational frameworks become.
8. Such complexity is manifest not only in the different levels of structural differentiation and the division of labor but also in other dimensions, such as the degree of overlap or coalescence or the degree of difference among different organizations and collectivities. These dimensions, in turn, are influenced by different ideological and power elements.

Thus the process of the construction of collectivities, social systems, and civilizational frameworks is a process of continuous struggle in which ideological, material, and power elements are continuously interwoven. These processes are structured, articulated, and carried by different social actors. The boundaries of these systems and frameworks are defined by different coalitions of such actors.

Several types of social actors or carriers have to be distinguished. First, there are those who structure the division of labor in a society, that is, its economic differentiation and ecological setup. Second, there are carriers who articulate ideologies and political control. Finally, there are carriers who are extremely important in the study of the construction of boundaries of collectivities, namely the carriers of solidarity for different ascriptive groups.

Among these different carriers there develops a very complex interaction that goes beyond what has been assumed in sociological, anthropological, and historical analysis in general and in the literature that deals with collapse in particular.

1.3. Protest, Conflict, and Change
Thus different coalitions of elites construct the boundaries of social systems, collectivities, and organizations. Yet no such construction can be continuously stable. The crystallization and reproduction of any social order, of any collectivity, organization, political system, or civilizational framework is shaped by the different forces and factors analyzed in the preceding section and generates processes of conflict, change, and possible transformation.

Conflict is inherent in any setting of social interaction for two basic reasons. The first reason is the plurality of actors in any such setting. The second reason is the multiplicity of the principles inherent in the institutionalization of any such setting—the multiplicity of institutional principles and of cultural orientations—and the power struggles and conflicts among different groups and movements that any such institutionalization entails.

Any setting of social interaction, but particularly the macrosocietal order, involves a plurality of actors—elites, movements, and groups—with different levels of control over natural and social resources. These elites continuously struggle over the control, ownership, and the possibility of using such resources, generating ubiquitous conflicts on all levels of social interaction.

The ubiquity of conflicts in any setting of social interaction is intensified by the interweaving of the plurality of actors with the basic characteristics of the social division of labor and the establishment of institutional principles. Such specification entails conflicting principles, premises, and prerequisites, each of which is carried by a different social actor who may also carry different cultural orientations. Different actors may stress the centrality of their respective spheres and develop their own autonomous dynamics at the expense of others, thus generating different types of systemic contradictions.

The processes of institutionalization of any social order entail a certain heterogeneity and pluralism. Such heterogeneity is above all rooted in the multiplicity of actors and the cultural orientations inherent in any such institutionalization and in the incipient tendencies toward the development of alternative ontological visions mentioned above.

Accordingly, whatever the success of the attempts of any coalition of elites to establish and legitimize common norms, these norms are probably never fully accepted by all those participating in a given order. Most groups tend to exhibit some autonomy and differences in their attitudes toward these norms and in their willingness or ability to provide the resources demanded by the given institutional system. Some groups may be greatly opposed to the very premises of the institutionalization of a given system. Others may share its values and symbols only to a very small extent and accept these norms only as a necessary evil and as binding on them only in a very limited sense. Still others may share these values and symbols and accept the norms to a greater degree but may look on themselves as the more truthful depositaries of these same values. They may oppose the concrete levels at which the symbols are institutionalized by the elite in power and may attempt to interpret them in different ways. They may not accept the models of cultural and social order that they think are upheld by the "center" as the legitimator of the existing distribution of power and resources, and they may uphold cultural orientations different from or counter to those upheld by the center. Other groups may develop new interpretations of existing models.

In any social order, then, there is always a strong element of dissension about the distribution of power and values. Hence, as we have seen, any institutional system is never fully homogeneous in the sense of being fully accepted or accepted to the same degree by all those participating in it.

Even if for very long periods of time a great majority of the members of a given society may identify to some degree with the values and the norms of the given system and be willing to provide it with the resources it needs, other tendencies develop in connection with intergroup conflicts, demographic changes, and the development of heterodox ontological visions and these changes may give rise to changes in the initial attitudes of any given group to the basic premises of the institutional system.

Thus "antisystems" may develop within any society. Although the antisystems often remain latent for long periods of time, they may also constitute, under propitious conditions, important foci of systemic change. The existence of such potential antisystems is evident in the existence in all societies of themes and orientations of protest. These social movements and heterodoxies are often led by different secondary elites. Such latent antisystems may be activated and transformed into processes of change by several processes connected with the continuity and maintenance, or the reproduction, of different settings of social interaction in general and the macrosocietal order in particular. Such processes include, first, shifts in the relative power positions and aspirations of different categories and groups of people, second, the activation in members of the new generation, particularly in young members of the upper classes and elites, of the potential rebelliousness and antinomian orientations inherent in any process of socialization, and third, several sociomorphological or sociodemographic processes through which the biological reproduction of the population is connected with the social reproduction of settings of social interaction, and fourth, the interaction between such settings and their natural and intersocietal environments, such as movements of population, conquest, and the like. The crystallization of these potentialities of change usually takes place through the activities of secondary elites, who attempt to mobilize various groups and resources in order to change some aspects of the social order as shaped by the ruling coalition of elites.

The possibility of the failure of integrative and regulative mechanisms is inherent in any society. Every civilization and every type of political and economic system constructs some specific systemic boundaries within which it operates. But the very construction of such civilizations and social systems also generates within them various conflicts and contradictions that *may* lead to change, transformation, or decline, that is, to different modes of restructuring their boundaries.

Although these potentialities of conflict and change are inherent in all human societies, their concrete development, their intensity, and the concrete directions of change and transformation they engender differ greatly among different societies and civilizations. Societies vary in their specific constellation of the specific forces analyzed here, that is, different constellations of cultural orientations, elites, patterns of the social division of labor, and political-ecological settings and processes.

My approach makes four assumptions. First, at all levels and in all types of technological and economic development and structural differentiation, the interaction between various aspects of the social division of labor and the activities of the major elites generates the different patterns and the different dynamics of centers and institutional formations. Second, at any given level or in any given type of differentiation or social division of labor, a very wide variety of such patterns may have developed in different circumstances. Third, the differences in such dynamics are principally shaped by the crystallization of different coalitions of elites. And fourth, some aspects of these dynamics may be relatively similar (even if they can never be exactly the same) across the different levels and types of the social division of labor and social differentiation.

1.4. The Perspective of International Systems in the Study of Social Change
A crucial component of my approach is the importance of international systems. Such an approach, however, entails a reappraisal of the initial literature on this subject. In this reappraisal I criticize this literature's assumptions that the modern capitalist world system is the most important single determinant of the dynamics of all contemporary international systems, that the dynamics of the modern capitalist world system epitomize the dynamics of all contemporary international systems, and

that this system is the embodiment of a full-fledged international system. The reappraisal also criticizes the literature on international systems for its tendency to reify the (capitalist) international system. This reification is often made in terms similar to those allegedly employed by the structural-functional school in its analyses of social systems, which has been the butt of many of the criticisms of the scholars who have stressed the new international perspective.

The international systems approach has not recognized (1) that any single dominant, hegemonic international system, such as the Roman Empire, exists in close ecological relations with other systems or political units; (2) that within the confines of any seemingly single international framework, there may in fact develop several different international systems—political, economic, cultural, etc.—each with some autonomy of its own; and (3) that the interrelations among these systems are of crucial importance for the understanding of other dynamics.

Also, this approach, because of its emphasis on the international system and its neglect of the internal structure of both the hegemonic and the dependent units, has been unable to analyze fully the different types of impact of the various hegemonic centers, the different responses of potentially dependent units to the impact of the hegemonic center, and the shifts of power in different international systems or the possibilities of their internal transformation.

2. A REAPPRAISAL OF THEORIES OF MODERNIZATION

2.1. The Development of the Problem in Modern Social Analysis

The problem of the distinctive characteristics of modern societies in general, and of the first such society—Western Europe—in particular, and of the differences between modern and other societies has constituted a basic concern of modern social thought from its very beginning in the eighteenth and nineteenth centuries. In the nineteenth and early twentieth centuries observers emphasized the uniqueness of modern Western society in comparison with other societies, but even then the exact nature of this uniqueness constituted a rather difficult problem.

To the evolutionists this uniqueness seemed to lie in the fact that modern European societies were the apogee of the evolutionary potential of humanity, an apogee that had not been reached elsewhere. For Marx European society was the only society in which capitalism developed. Although he sometimes could be interpreted as believing that all societies would go through the same basic stages of evolution, his concern with the Asiatic mode of production shows that he was aware of the distinctiveness of Western civilization,—the only one that had generated a capitalist system and the one from which this system was spreading throughout the world.

Perhaps the most articulate formulation of the uniqueness of Western civilization can be found in the work of Max Weber. At the same time, however, Weber's work contains some of the more problematic aspects of this approach, especially when it is applied to the study of the spread of modernization beyond Europe. Weber's basic *Problemstellung* was to explain the specificity and uniqueness of European modernity, to explain why the "radical" tendency to rationalize the world developed in the West and not in other civilizations. Weber saw this specificity in the tendency toward the overall rationalization of social life. Major manifestations of this tendency occurred in all spheres of social life: in the emergence of capitalist civilization, in the bureaucratization of different forms of social life, in the secularization of the world view, and in the development of modern science and the so-called scientific world view, which bears within itself the radical tendency toward *Entzauberung,* the disenchantment of the world. He saw the roots of all these processes in the potentially rationalizing tendencies of the Protestant religious orientations.

In order to understand the specific transformative potentialities of these orientations, Weber compared Protestantism with other world religions. He attempted to combine the analysis of world religions and the analysis of the internal dynamics of their associated civilizations, especially the tendencies toward rationalization inherent in them. He then compared these dynamics with those that had taken place in the West. He stressed (and this is indeed one of his great contributions) that the non-Western modes of rationalization, together with their related institutional systems, differed greatly from the Western mode. Thus he recognized, at least implicitly, that each mode of religious rationalization develops its own pattern of dynamics.

However, because of his comparative starting point and his major concern with the uniqueness of the West, Weber did not fully explicate these implicit comparative orientations. He tended to minimize the internal dynamics of these civilizations and the full explication of his implicit recognition of such specific dynamics, and instead to stress in different ways the "traditional", seemingly nondynamic aspects of these civilizations. On the one hand, Weber emphasized the uniqueness of the West and its role, as it were, as the model for the world; on the other hand, he recognized the specificity of the dynamics of other civilizations. This contradiction, although not fully visible in Weber's or Marx's own times when the spread of capitalism and modernization beyond Europe and the West were only in the incipient stages, became much more visible in the later stages of the development of modernization studies after the Second World War.

2.2 Studies of Modernization after the Second World War

In the first stages of the burgeoning of modernization studies after the Second World War, a burgeoning that signaled the revival and fuller systematic development of macrosociological and comparative historical studies, the contradiction between the uniqueness of the West and the specificity of other civilizations became perhaps even more dimmed than in Marx's or Weber's original works. This development occurred because these studies of modernization and development involved a very far-reaching shift in their basic orientations compared with earlier "classical" studies. Instead of stressing the specificity of European civilization and European modernity, these studies assumed that the development of modernity constituted the apogee of the evolutionary potential of mankind and that the kernels of this process are in principle to be found in most human societies. Hence they asked questions about which conditions facilitate and which conditions impede the development of such modernization in all human societies. At the same time, however, they took for granted that the European (and perhaps also the American) experience constitutes the major paradigm of such a modern society and civilization. One of the most important offshoots of these studies was that of the convergence of industrial societies, perhaps best illustrated in the work of Clark Kerr.

In these works observers attempted to combine studies of micro settings and various social processes—communication, urbanization, value-transformation, and the like—with a broader macrosocietal framework. The first studies of modernization and development, and many later ones that continued in this vein, evaluated societies by various indices of modernity, development, and modernization. They then tried to determine either the extent to which the societies studied approximated the model or models of modern industrial society or the factors that impeded their advance in terms of these indices. The possibility that a modern social order might develop from within various societies was recognized and explored.

Although with the passing of time there developed a growing recognition of the possible diversity of transitional societies, observers still assumed that such diversity would disappear in the final stage of modernity. This assumption was evident in the theory of the convergence of industrial societies. To quote Goldthorpe:

> The diversity within the industrializing process which he [Kerr] emphasizes turns out to be that evident in the relatively early stages—in Rostovian language, those of the "break with traditionalism," "take-off," and the "drive to maturity." And when the question arises of the "road ahead"— for already advanced, as well as developing societies—Kerr's view of the logic of industrialism is in fact such as to force him, willy-nilly, away from a

multilinear and towards a unilinear perspective; or, to be rather more
precise, to force him to see hitherto clearly different processes of industrialization as becoming progressively similar in their socio-cultural correlates.
As industrialism advances and becomes increasingly a world-wide phenomenon then, Kerr argues, the range of viable institutional structures
and of a viable system of value and belief is necessarily reduced. All societies, whatever the path by which they entered the industrial world, will
tend to approximate, even if asymptomatically, the pure industrial form.
(Goldthorpe 1971, 263)

Behind these theories there loomed a conviction of the inevitability of
progress toward modernity—be it political, industrial, or cultural—and
toward the development of a universal modern civilization.

The ideological and institutional developments in the contemporary
world, however, have not upheld this vision. The fact that great institutional variability exists among different modern and modernizing
societies—not only among the transitional but also among the more
developed and even the highly industrialized societies—became more
and more apparent. The growing recognition that great symbolic and
institutional variability and different modes of ideological and institutional dynamics attend the spread of modern civilization gave rise to a
search for a systematic explanation. Two major approaches have developed in response to the disintegration of the initial model of modernization. The first approach stresses the importance of the traditions of
different societies. The second approach referred to above stresses the
dynamics of the international, especially the capitalist, system as the
major factor explaining the variability and dynamics of different modern or modernizing societies.

These approaches have indeed pointed to very important factors that
influence the dynamics of modern or modernizing societies. Yet they
have also encountered many difficulties in their attempts to explain
systematically the great variability of the dynamics of these new modern
civilizations, the concrete patterns of change that have been taking place
in different traditional societies, and the relations of these patterns to
their respective historical experiences and to the new situations created
by the spread of modernity.

*2.3. New Indications—Modernity as a New Civilization and its Differential
Expansion*

Out of these various controversies emerge some indications of a possible
new perspective for the understanding of the contemporary world. This
perspective is based on a particular combination of elements from the
classical paradigms of modernization, from Marx (especially his analysis

of the Asian mode of production), from Gramsci, but, above all, from Weber, especially from his powerful insights about the internal dynamics of different civilizations. This perspective recognizes, on the one hand, the uniqueness of the civilization of modernity and its component of economic development and, on the other hand, the great variability of the symbolic, ideological, and institutional responses to it and the variability of the ways in which different civilizations and societies interpret different symbolic premises of modernity and different modern institutional patterns and dynamics.

This perspective entails a far-reaching reformulation of the vision of modernization and modern civilization. It does not view the process of modernization as the ultimate end point of the evolution of all known societies. It does not assume that the process of modernization brings out the evolutionary potential common to all societies. And it does not assume that the European experience is the most important and succinct manifestation and paradigm of the modernization process. Rather it considers that modernization or modernity is one specific type of civilization that originated in Europe and spread throughout the world, encompassing—especially after the Second World War—almost all of it.

The crystallization of this new type of civilization was not unlike the spread of the great religions or the great imperial expansions in past times. But because the expansion of this civilization almost always combined economic, political, and ideological aspects and forces, its impact on the societies to which it spread was much more intensive than in these other historical cases.

This perspective also entails the recognition that when historical civilizations expand, they challenge the symbolic and institutional premises of the societies that are incorporated into them. This challenge calls for responses from within these societies, which has the effect of opening up new options and possibilities. A great variety of modern or modernizing societies have developed out of these responses. They share many common characteristics but also evince great differences among themselves. These differences crystallized out of the selective incorporation—hence also the transformation—of the major symbolic premises and institutional formations of the original Western civilization as well as of their own civilizations.

This perspective necessitates the analysis of the basic characteristics and premises of this new, modern civilization, that is, the basic premises of European and Western civilization. The most salient of these premises, from the point of view of my concern, has been, first of all, the "revolutionary" origins of its visions and orientations. The revolutionary orientations that were at the root of most breakthroughs to modernity

have been oriented toward a far-reaching transformation of the nature
and content of the centers of the social and cultural orders, the rules of
participation in them and access to them, and the relations between these
centers and the periphery. For these centers the major transformation
that occurred concomitantly with modernity was the growing secularization of the centers, the rejection of the "givenness" of the centers' traditional contents and symbols, and the spread of the assumption that these
contents and symbols can indeed be reexamined. These changes were
closely connected with the growing autonomy of the political, cultural,
and societal centers and above all with the changes in the relations between these centers and the periphery. They were also linked to the
growing impingement of the periphery on the center, the periphery's
increased access to the center, and the permeation of the periphery by
the center, all of which often culminated in the obliteration of the differences between center and periphery, and made membership in the collectivity tantamount to participation in the center.

   These processes were also closely related to changes in the basic orientations toward tradition and the bases of the legitimation of authority.
The sanctity and givenness of the past as the major symbolic regulator of
social, political, and cultural change and innovation gave way to the
acceptance of innovation and an orientation to the future as the basic
cultural dimensions.

   Such changes were of course very closely connected in Europe with the
assumption that the human and natural environments can be directed,
and even mastered, by the conscious effort of man and society. Indeed, the
central premise of European modernity was the possibility of the active
transformation of crucial aspects of social, cultural, and natural orders by
conscious human activity and participation. The fullest, although not the
only, expression of these premises could be seen in the transformations
and repercussions of the Protestant ethic in the economic, scientific, and
political spheres and later in the impact these transformations had on the
Enlightenment and the industrial revolution. Accordingly, the special
characteristics of European modernity were initially focused on attempts
to form a "rational" culture, an efficient economy, a civil (class) society, and
nation-states where these rational tendencies could become fully articulated and within which major social actors, leaders, and influences could
create a social and political order based on freedom.

   The new civilization of modernity, which emerged from this background, was based ideologically and politically on the assumption of equality and the growing participation of the citizens in the processes of the
center. These trends were most clearly evident in the establishment of
universal citizenship and suffrage and some semblance of a "participant"
political and social order, which gave rise to ideologies of participation.

Such goals were aimed at the establishment of a social and cultural order characterized by a high degree of congruence between the cultural and the political identities of the territorial population, a high level of symbolic and affective commitment to the centers, a close relationship between these centers and the more primordial dimensions of human existence, and a marked emphasis on common, politically defined, collective goals for all members of the national or class community.

In many ways these characteristics of the European nation-state were derived or transmitted from several parts of their premodern sociopolitical traditions: from their imperial traditions and from their city-state and feudal traditions. They combined the strong activist orientation of the city-state, the broad conception that the political order was actively related to the cosmic and cultural orders of many imperial traditions and the traditions of the great religions, and the pluralistic elements of the feudal traditions. In the European (especially Western European) traditions these various orientations were rooted in a social structure that was characterized by a relatively high degree of commitment by various groups and strata to the cultural and political orders and their centers and a high degree of autonomy in their access to these orders and their respective centers.

The ideology of economic development, which became an important component of this civilization, developed out of the combination of the strong sanctification, under the impact of Protestantism, of economic activity as an arena of salvation, the conception of human mastery of the human and nonhuman environments, and the development of science and technology. This emphasis on technological and economic development became one of the major premises of European civilization.

These ideological or symbolic developments in Europe were very closely connected with the processes of economic development, which was evident first in commercial and later in industrial expansion, and with the unprecedented growth of technology and economic expansion. These trends culminated in the first self-sustained industrial system, that of industrial capitalism.

The structural-economic and the more symbolic aspects of development and modernity were very closely connected. Yet even in Europe, a single, one-to-one relationship between them did not exist. They developed to some degree independently of one another, but they always constituted continuous interrelated challenges to the societies in which they developed and on which they impinged.

2.4. The Construction of Multiple Modern Civilizations

The new civilization that developed in Europe later spread throughout the world, creating a series of international systems. Each system was

based on some of the premises of European civilization, but at the same
time each system had its own internal process of change. The expansion
of European civilization resulted in a tendency toward the development
of universal, worldwide institutional and symbolic frameworks. Such
frameworks are unique in the history of mankind. The expansion of
Europe also resulted in not one but several worldwide systems developing. Although these different systems originated in the same place—in
Western Europe—and were closely interrelated, the centers of power
and influence within each system were not identical. Each developed a
dynamic of its own and each often reacted to the others. Most important,
within the international ideological and cultural systems, very strong
reactions developed against the problems generated by the international
economic system. These reactions were most evident in a variety of national and social revolutionary ideologies.

The spread of the various modern ideologies and premises of European civilization throughout the world has been accompanied by far-
reaching structural and organizational changes, especially in the economic and political fields. This diffusion took place through a series of
social, political, and cultural movements that, unlike movements of
change and rebellion in many other historical situations, tended to combine protest with strong tendencies toward institution-building and
center-formation. As a result of this combination, it has been difficult to
isolate the different international systems from one another and to maintain any one of them in a continuous equilibrium. The interrelations
among systems are never static or unchanging in any given international
setting. Indeed, the dynamics of such settings give rise to continuous
changes in the interrelations among the different systems and the forces
created by them, thus generating various processes of change in these
systems.

At this point it is important to recognize the nature of the historical
process by which modernity spread beyond Europe and how it differs
from the development of modernity in Europe. Within Western Europe,
modernity, despite great differences among different societies, largely
developed indigenously through the fruition of the internal transformative potentials of some of its groups and through a continuous interaction among these groups. In contrast, the spread of modernity beyond
Europe was much more in the nature of the impingement of the external
Europe on traditional societies and civilizations. Hence the premises of
Western European societies constituted the major challenge to which
different responses developed. Needless to say, within the various Asian,
African, and Latin American civilizations different modes of response
developed.

2.5. Some New Indications: Problems and Possibilities

The continuous expansion of international systems and movements gives rise to the incorporation of societies and civilizations that do not share either the basic symbolic premises of this new civilization or most of its specific institutional contours. Such an expansion also, of course, undermines the symbolic and institutional premises of these non-Western societies, opens up new options for various groups within them, and generates within them far-reaching processes of change, responses to these changes, and the concomitant crystallization of new symbolic and institutional formations.

These responses are shaped by the continuous interaction among several basic factors. First, the patterns of response are affected by the "point of entry" of any society into the new international systems and the specific aspects of its institutional structure that are undermined by this entry, the options that this entry opens, and the continuous development and changes of these processes. Second, the patterns of responses are influenced by the modes of technology and economic formations existing in these societies. Third, the responses are shaped by the basic premises of the civilizations and societies on which they impinge, that is, by the basic perceptions of the relationship between the cosmic and the social orders, the social and cultural orders, and hierarchy and equality that are prevalent in them. They are also shaped by the structure of the predominant elites that are the carriers and articulators of these perceptions and visions and the modes of control that these elites exercise. Fourth, the responses are shaped by the tradition of responses to the historical situations of change that have developed in most of these civilizations. In the "great" or "axial age" civilizations, particular experiences or traditions of external and internal changes, and of responses to these changes, have crystallized.

Here it might be fruitful to follow Weber's emphasis on the great importance of heterodoxies in the dynamics of different civilizations. Such heterodoxies are of course found in Europe and Weber concentrated on the split between Catholicism and Protestantism and especially on the innovative and transformative potentialities that developed.

Heterodox groups and movements vary according to the cultural orientations predominant within them, the structure and autonomy of the religious institutions and organizations prevalent in their respective societies, and their internal cohesion and relations to broader strata of the society. The relationship of these aspects of the different heterodoxies to the respective orthodoxies of their civilizations greatly influence the direction and the transformative capacities of different civilizations, their responses to change, and their innovative directives. Such was also the case with respect to the development of modernity in Europe. The different innovative potentials that are carried and articulated by different primary and secondary elite groups in different orthodoxies and heterodoxies within these civilizations are not only of one kind. They are always varied and heterogeneous and often move in different directions. This variety indicates that the different transformative potentials of any civilization may move in different directions, depending on concrete historical situations that facilitate or favor some lines of development and not others.

The continuous interaction and feedback among all these processes—the basic premises of the civilizations and societies on which the new modern international systems impinge; the points of entry of these societies into these international systems; the types and modes of technology and economy prevalent in these civilizations; the tradition of response to situations of change; and the traditions of heterodoxy, rebellion, and innovation that have developed in the history of these civilizations has generated the varying institutional and symbolic contours of different modern and modernizing societies, their dynamics, and the different patterns of economic development within them. Out of these processes crystallize, in different societies and different modes of incorporation and reinterpretation of the premises of modernity, the different symbolic reactions to modernity. And from these processes develop the different modern institutional patterns and dynamics, or conversely, the different modes of reinterpretation of the premises and historical traditions of these civilizations. These different symbolic and institutional constellations develop with respect to the interpretation of the basic symbolic conceptions and premises of the different modern civilizations. They develop according to the ways in which these basic symbolic premises of modernity are selected and reinterpreted in relation to the new "modern" traditions, according to these societies' conceptions of themselves and their past, and according to their new symbols and collective identity and their negative or positive attitudes toward modernity in general and to the West in particular. In other words, within different modern societies there develop different cultural meanings and programs of modernity.

Such processes of reinterpretation also apply to the basic conception of economic development. Although the emphasis on economic and technological development has become part of each modern or modernizing society, they differ greatly with respect to the meaning of such development in the context of their overall cultural and social premises. Above all, they vary in the degree to which the emphasis on economic development is connected with an emphasis on the mastery of the environment rather than adaptation to it, in the relative importance of economic goals in the panorama of human goals, and in the conceptions of the social order. They vary in having productive or distributive economic orientations, in their type of political regime (authoritarian, pluralist, or totalitarian), in their major modes of political protest and participation, and in their conceptions of authority, hierarchy, and equality.

Similarly, the crystallization of different constellations has been continuously taking place, in close relation to those on the symbolic level, with respect to the different modes of modern organizational and institutional levels. Although such processes as urbanization, industrialization, and the spread of modern communications are common to all these societies, the concrete institutional answers to these problems tend to vary greatly. This variation is closely related, of course, to the basic conceptions of social and political order that have developed within each society.

As in all cases of historical change, the crucial element in the process of the crystallization of new symbolic and institutional formations is old and new elites, that is, the leadership groups on different levels of the social structure in continuous interaction with broad social sectors, the visions they carry, and the various coalitions among them, including coalitions with different external forces in the new international systems. These groups are of crucial importance in shaping the different responses to the continuous challenges of modernization. As in the case of the different heterodoxies analyzed above, these groups are not uniform. They are indeed quite variable, and even the new elites that have developed are much more influenced by the various traditions of response to change and the heterodoxies and innovation existing in any society than has often been assumed.

The systematic comparative exploration of all of these processes is still very much before us, but it constitutes a very important—even if very difficult and arduous—part of the agenda on the comparative sociological and historical research of modernization, modern civilizations, and the contemporary world.

REFERENCE

Goldthorpe, John H. 1971. Theories of industrial society: Reflections on the recrudescence of historicism and the future of futurology. *Archives Européennes de Sociologie* 12:263–88.

NAME INDEX

SUBJECT INDEX

Compositor:	Huron Valley Graphics
Text:	10/12 Baskerville
Display:	Baskerville
Printer:	Maple-Vail
Binder:	Maple-Vail

DATE DUE

OCT 2 4 2001			
GAYLORD			PRINTED IN U.S.A.